TIME AND SACRIFICE
IN THE AZTEC COSMOS

TIME AND SACRIFICE IN THE AZTEC COSMOS

Kay Almere Read

INDIANA UNIVERSITY PRESS
Bloomington and Indianapolis

This book is a publication of

Indiana University Press
601 North Morton Street
Bloomington, Indiana 47404-3797 USA

www.indiana.edu/~iupress

Telephone orders   800-842-6796
Fax orders   812-855-7931
Orders by e-mail   iuporder@indiana.edu

The paper used in this publication meets
the minimum requirements of American
National Standard for Information
Sciences—Permanence of Paper for
Printed Library Materials, ANSI Z39.48-
1984.

Manufactured in the United States of America

Library of Congress Cataloging-in-Publication Data

Read, Kay Almere, date
Time and sacrifice in the Aztec cosmos /
Kay Almere Read.
      p.   cm. — (Religion in North America)
Includes bibliographical references and index.
ISBN 0-253-33400-4 (cloth : alk. paper)
1. Aztecs—Religion. 2. Sacrifice—Mexico.
3. Human sacrifice—Mexico. 4. Aztec calendar.
5. Time—Religious aspects.   I. Title.
II. Series.
F1219.76.R45R43   1998
299'.78452—dc21   97-45753

1 2   3   4   5   03   02   01   00   99   98

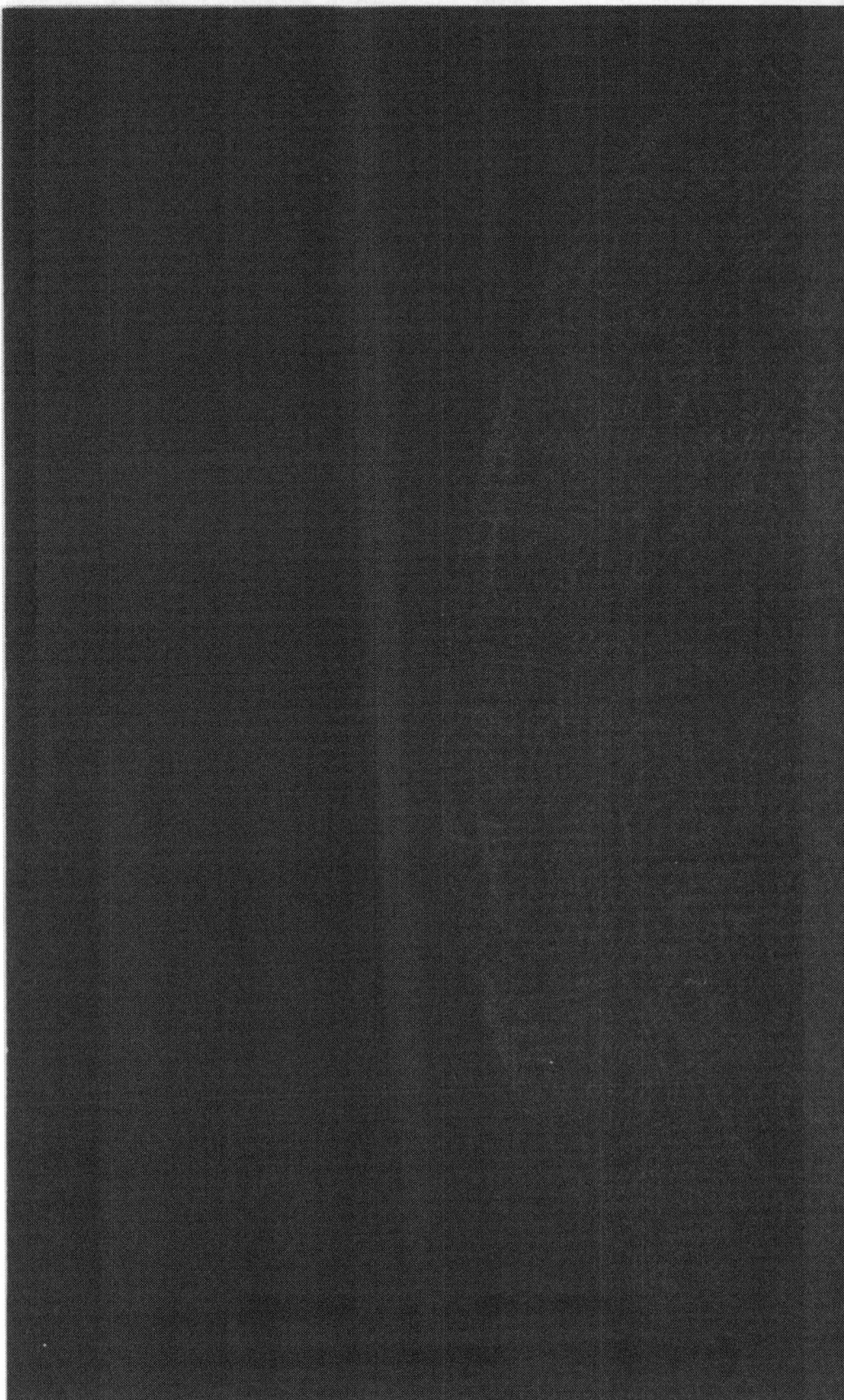

CONTENTS

Foreword by Catherine L. Albanese and Stephen J. Stein xiii
Preface xvii
A Note on Terminology xxiii

1
INTRODUCTION 1
2-Reed: A Sacrificial Beginning

Part 1 *Binding Reeds: Paradigms of Temporal Transformations*

2
TIMING SHAPES 47

3
SHAPING TIME 89

4
TIMING AND SHAPING PEOPLE 109

Part 2 *Burning Hearts: Processes of Sacrificial Transformations*

5
123 THE COSMIC MEAL

6
156 BURNING AND BINDING FIRES

7
189 EPILOGUE
2-Reed: A Sacrificial *Completion*

Appendix 1: Glossary of Mexica Names and Terms   *199*
Appendix 2: Calendrical Workings   *211*
Notes   *237*
Bibliography   *283*
Index   *303*

FIGURES

1. The 2-Reed plaque   1
2. The Templo Mayor, from the *Codex Telleriano Remensis*   10
3a and 3b. Drawings of a hand   19–20
4. *Trecena* 8, from the *Codex Borbonicus*   21
5. Various 2-Reed glyphs   22
6. Frontispiece of the *Codex Mendoza*   23
7a and 7b. Mayan and Toltec-like glyphs showing time being borne by tumplines   89–90
8. Various pre-Conquest and post-Conquest drawings of porters bearing burdens   91
9. The depiction of the fifty-two-year cycle, from the *Codex Aubin*   93
10. The calendar wheel from Fray Bernardino de Sahagún's *Códice Matritenses*   97
11. The New Fire Ceremony, occurring in the month of Panquetzaliztli   102
12. The Sun Stone   131
13. Relief of a descending earth monster   140
14. The frontispiece to the *Codex Fejérváry-Mayer*, folio 1   212
15. The day-signs and night lords   215
16. The first two thirteen-year rounds of the fifty-two-year cycle as depicted in the *Codex Borbonicus*, folio 21   217
17. The second two thirteen-year rounds of the fifty-two-year cycle as depicted in the *Codex Borbonicus*, folio 22   218
18. Graph of the *tonalpohualli* coordinated with the *xiuhmolpilli*   228
19. Graph of the year 1-Rabbit   230
20. Graph of the year 2-Reed   232

TABLES

1. Days and dot numbers of a *trecena* round   220
2. Days, dot numbers, and night lords of a *trecena* round   221
3. *Trecenas* 8 and 9 of the *tonalpohualli* round   222
4. The fifty-two-year cycle of the *xiuhmolpilli* round   225
5. The count of the five suns   233

FOREWORD

In 1984, when we began the Religion in North America series, we consciously chose that title for our enterprise to signal our intent to publish works on religion that reached beyond the political boundaries of the United States. We understood North America as geographers did; and so we looked south as well as north, toward Mexico and Guatemala as well as toward Canada and the Arctic regions. Our vision, hence, was large; but our reality—governed by submissions to the series—was smaller. With this new volume, though, we begin to make good on the larger vision.

Kay Read's *Time and Sacrifice in the Aztec Cosmos* explores major concepts in the religious life of the Mexica-Tenochca—better known to us as the Aztecs—in what is now the central part of the state of Mexico. Read's Mesoamerican focus is achieved through an interdisciplinary method that combines a revisionist approach to Eliadean history of religions with art historical and general historical scholarship. And handily, the scholar turns artist as Read illustrates her own text with a series of line drawings and graphics that lend pictorial precision to her argument.

Dominating a study that develops its central insights concentrically is the so-called 2-reed plaque discovered in the archaeological remains of the great Templo Mayor in Mexico City. The plaque is a calendric device that announces the "birth" of a new year and era—in fact, a new fifty-two-year solar cycle—among the Mexica. So its concern is clearly with conceptions of time. What the plaque does, however, is to present its ideas about time in a pictorial representation that also tells a great deal about the connections that Mexica culture made between time and ritual sacrifice. Thus, as a book-length essay meditation on the meaning of the 2-reed plaque and what it tells about Mexica religion, Kay Read's work exploits material culture with consistency and success. To say this another way, Read literally reconstructs a theology out of its visual remains.

The narrative that results moves well beyond material culture in order to explicate it. Read's work is, indeed, ambitious and rigorous in its employment of contemporary (to the period) Spanish sources, present-day native writings, and, then, late-twentieth-century interpretive studies. Putting all of this together, her book argues the interconnectedness, for the Mexica, of religious concepts of time and space, challenging conventional academic dichotomies, commonly employed in the history of religions, that separate them. She also argues a thesis regarding the theological meaning of calendric rites of human sacrifice that must be seen overall as an apology for the Mexica, a defense of the seeming violence and brutality of their ritual life.

Indeed, her elegant study builds through small clues to a convincing case for what Mexica sacrifice meant religiously and for how it came to be that human sacrifice of staggering proportions could be accepted, apparently matter-of-factly, by the Mexica people. The upshot of all this is that Read argues for a Mexica cosmos that is moderate in spite of its violence and for a Mexica ritual of killing that is culturally controlled and morally necessary. In order to advance this view—with an argument that is formidable in its richness and sophistication—Read invokes categories of the ordinariness of the sacred. And she persuades in a critical perspective that is subtly feminist, seeing among the Mexica the reality of a spirituality that was ultimately domestic and among scholars the need for a methodology that is interactive and relational.

The specific way that Read teases all of this out is through her understanding of "deformative transformation"—basic, she says, to Mexica religion and worldview. The idea is encapsulated in the myth of the birth of the Fifth Sun, which Read elaborates, and it is worked out by the Mexica in a series of spatio-temporal equations. Time *equals* space for the Mexica, Read tells us again and again. If so, then, as she insists, "the shapes that occupy space must embody time as an inherent characteristic." The logic and mythologic of that view mean, in effect, that shapes change and transform. Still more, change and transformation preoccupied Mexica culture to such an extent that it developed an intricate and complex calendric system that embodied its theology and cosmology. To her credit, Read grapples with its numerous convolutions and illuminates its symmetries and subtleties in ways that go well beyond surface readings.

What underlies the merciless precision of the calendar with its mathematical version of rationality, however, is a more organic tale of death and continued life. In the sacrificially transformative cosmos of the Mexica, the killing and eating of human beings fed the sun, gods, and other power-filled beings, providing energy for human life and balancing it in its cosmic "house." Sacrifice, Read says, was "the systematized manipulation of various life-giving powers via their feeding." Thus, Read's reading of Mexica food philosophy—if we may call it that—makes nutrition a major analogical trope for Mexica understanding of the cosmos and the place of humans within it. Just as the processes of preparation, eating, and digestion change food from one substance to another, so humans and the world in which they find themselves can expect change—from raw to cooked, from ripe to rotten, and from old form to new. There is a logic, then, in Mexica participation in the sacrificial New Fire rites, a logic rooted not in the extraordinary and abstract but in the ordinary and experiential realities of daily life. Read's domestic orientation is notable in arguing the point.

The Mexica religious universe that emerges from Read's treatment on the one hand challenges Eliadean axioms that mythic origin times are static and fixed with evidence of a fluid and ever-shifting Mexica cosmos. For her, the figure of the spiral becomes shorthand for a Mexica spirituality in which the beginning never stays in the same place and time. Still more, even as Mircea Eliade's work has separated sacred and profane worlds, Read offers concrete evidence that the Mexica fused them. On the other hand, arguing for a domestic theology among the Mexica means that, like Eliade, Read minimizes political considerations in her exploration of her topic. Readings of political terror and hegemonic imperative receive short shrift here, left for the work of other interpreters.

The book that results, therefore, in some sense moves away from "fashionable" themes about social and political power in current postmodern and critical scholarship. But it does so to introduce a new critical discourse of its own. In so doing, Kay Read has begun a conversation that is new not only to the Religion in North America series but to Mesoamerican religious studies scholarship as well. We hope the conversation continues.

Catherine L. Albanese
Stephen J. Stein
Series Editors

PREFACE

The Mexica-Tenochca (known by many as the Aztecs)[1] were the people who held hegemony in Mesoamerica at the moment of Hernán Cortés's march into Mexico (1519). It is their name that Mexico bears today. People often forget that pre-Conquest Mesoamerica (or Middle America) was also rightfully part of native North America (something still true today). With the current, rather self-interested romanticism over an imagined loss of gentle indigenous spirituality north of the Rio Grande, the violence of Mesoamerican human sacrifice may seem too harsh to acknowledge as belonging to the same native history. Yet it did, and nor was all native sacrificial violence due to Mesoamerican influence.[2]

How scholars have divided up the Americas has contributed to this exclusion of Mesoamerica from North America's native history. Boundary divisions can be slippery, resisting tight definitions. In 1952, Paul Kirchhoff made an impressive effort to bring some order to the matter, especially with respect to Mesoamerica's place in the continent. He noted that it was traditional to divide the Americas in two ways: in three divisions among north, central, and south; or in two between the north and south. This series on religions of North America takes the latter approach for good reason.

Kirchhoff placed Mesoamerica's boundaries at the moment of Cortés's entrance in the north along a line drawn from present-day northern Sinaloa through an area north of Mexico City to northern Veracruz, and in the south along a line running through the middle of Nicaragua.[3] Forty-five years later, the accepted boundaries have remained quite close to these.[4] Kirchhoff formulated these divisions by examining a number of linguistic and cultural traits that, at the same time they established workable borders, pointed out those borders' problems.

One problem is particularly instructive to this series. Historically, Mesoamerica's northern border has never remained stable either linguistically or culturally, indicating the reasons a tripartite division of the Americas does not quite work. This was due to a great deal of mobility and insecurity, which was characterized by alternate periods of expansion northward and retraction to the south (ibid., 6). Indeed much is comparable between Mesoamericans and peoples to the north. Native traditions of both the southwestern and southeastern United States share a great deal with those of Mesoamerica. Kirchhoff also pointed out that, due to diffusion, some cultural traits are shared by even the Pawnee, who lived on the great plains in the United States. The Pawnee practiced a rite of human sacrifice that closely resembles a Mesoamerican ritual (Hall 1984). Moreover, a number of scholars accept at least a Mesoamerica-like tint to some of the cultural traits of the Mississippian cultures found at places such as Cahokia in southern Illinois and Spiro in Oklahoma.[5] Sacrificial burials have been uncovered at Cahokia, one at least was quite extensive (Fowler 1989, 144–50; 1991). Although the nature of the various moments of contact are not yet fully understood, it is clear that ancient Mesoamericans throughout their history intermeshed with their northern neighbors in the most complex ways, some of which apparently included sacrifice.

In this book I consider the temporal and sacrificial concepts of what may be the most popularly known Mesoamericans, the Aztecs, here known as the Mexica-Tenochca or Mexica. An introduction to the Mexica-Tenochca is followed by a discussion of a few theoretical issues pertinent to why time and sacrifice must be understood as a single concept. Central to this discussion is the thesis that any of the many Western concepts based on a sacred and profane dichotomy (or no change versus change) must be abandoned if Mexica worldviews are to be understood, for the Mexica made no such division. Rather they lived in what I have dubbed a biologically historical world. Five Western dichotomies related to the sacred and profane are considered. The book then is divided into two parts, each based on two images, which depict a major sacrificial rite performed prior to Cortés's coming. The first image, binding fifty-two reeds, conveys the first three messages concerning time. The second image, a fire drill[6] sparking a sacrificial fire, sends the last two messages concerning sacrifice.

In Part I, I discuss the first image, the binding of fifty-two reeds, which stood for the ritual occurring at the end of a fifty-two-year solar cycle, the Binding-of-the-Years ceremony. This image's first message was fundamental: *temporal transformation.* For the Mexica, all things constantly changed because everything moved with the powers of life. Its second message said that all things must be timed. The biologically historical Mexica made no distinction between physical spaces and their temporal motions; space equaled time because one could not occur without the other. People, plants, and even cities, therefore, embodied particular time spans. The image's third message suggested that, if space equaled time, then time had to equal space; the calendar must have a shape as well as a motion. As will be seen, because the calendar had both linear and cyclical motions, it spun time into calendrically interlocked spirals that moved forward as they moved around.

In Part II, I discuss the second image, a fire drill sparking a sacrificial fire. This image stood for the same ceremony not just because fifty-two reeds were bound at that time but also because a new fire was begun that gave birth to the next new sun, hence the ritual's second name, the New Fire ceremony. This image's first message presents a second fundamental concept: *sacrificial transformation*. The Mexica cosmos is filled with living entities who must eat other entities if they are not to die before their time spans are completed. Through controlled acts of sacrificial feeding, the inevitable, transformational motion of this cosmos was ordered. Moreover, sacrifice was a morally significant yet very ordinary act. The mundaneness of this eating cosmos fueled participation in sacrificial rituals, for sacrifice was founded upon everyday experiences telling people that if all must eat, then all must be eaten someday. Because eating provides the energy living beings need to move and because sacrifice involves eating, sacrificial rituals could make sense of, even control, the motion of consumption.

A note of caution may be in order before proceeding. This book was researched from positions that may be different from those of the audience for whom it now is written. The research included sources on not only the Mexica-Tenochca and other native North Americans (historical and contemporary); it also explored theoretical works of anthropologists, art historians, philosophers, feminists, ethicists, cognitive scientists, theologians, and scholarly works on cultural areas outside of North America. This large range of resources helped me define my approach and provided alternative paradigms that allowed me "to think with" the Mesoamerican sources in helpful ways. Hence, the book may be useful to people with widely differing interests in the Mexica-Tenochca, time, or sacrifice. It is written, however, specifically for people trained in Religious Studies but not familiar with the Mexica-Tenochca.

This means that different readers may find different areas overly simple or overly complex. Art historians and archaeologists may find my discussion of iconology a bit obvious; they should understand that, for many people in Religious Studies, this is a new area of interest that has been underexplored due to the field's traditional, almost exclusive emphasis on written texts. Religious Studies people may find the discussions of calendrics and linguistics a bit tedious at times, even though I have tried to minimize them; they should understand that, from a Mesoamericanist point of view, these discussions often are necessary to demonstrate adequate support. Mesoamericanists may find the philosophic discussions of religious and ethical issues a bit boring or even strange; they should remember that, no matter how self-evident, esoteric, or weird those discussions may seem, to those of us trained in Religious Studies, these topics may be multilayered, pertinent, and within the bounds of familiar debates. To help the reader unfamiliar with the Mexica terms, a glossary has been included (Appendix 1); to help those who may hanker for further details on calendrics, a second appendix also has been included (Appendix 2). I apologize to those who read Nahuatl; the translations of my primary texts that I had hoped to include were eliminated because otherwise no one could have afforded the book.

The long journey toward the book's completion began in 1979 at the University of Colorado. It was then that I rashly decided to abandon a career as a fiberist and studio art teacher to go back to school in Religious Studies. Little did I know what I was getting into. This project has since seen three university degrees and a decade of employment; needless to say, it is no longer what it began as or progressed to along the way. This finally final version of *Time and Sacrifice in the Aztec Cosmos* resembles my first undergraduate encounter with human sacrifice, in which the blood, guts, and gore shocked me into long-term fascination. I have since seen similar reactions (although thankfully shorter-term) in my neophyte students; fortunately my own fascination has grown well beyond sacrifice's shock value. The book has a somewhat closer resemblance to my dissertation for the Ph.D. (University of Chicago, 1991). But like the children's game of telephone, this final result is only remotely like those earlier whispered expressions.

Many people have assisted along the way. At the University of Colorado, Davíd Carrasco, Sam Gill, and Frederick Denny played particularly memorable roles. At the University of Chicago, Don Rice and Ray Folgelson offered much encouragement and good learning during my early years. The members of my dissertation committee also offered much: my advisor, Frank Reynolds, Wendy Doniger O'Flaherty, Richard Townsend (Art Institute of Chicago), and Alfredo López Austin (Universidad Nacional Autónoma de México). While all four members generously gave of their time, fosterage, and their own particular brands of perceptive advice, López Austin was especially influential and much of what I did there and continue to do was and is founded on his work.

The reader responses from Indiana University Press helped point the way for radically remolding the original project into the present; Catherine Albanese in particular helped shape its final form. Dennis McCann and Frank Reynolds patiently read the complete manuscript and offered truly valuable suggestions, pointed out some really bad mistakes, sent me to key resources, and prodded me on difficult issues. Frequent discussions with my colleagues at DePaul University helped me to clarify my ideas. Special thanks go to Frida Furman, Jack Leahy, Doug Howland, and Anna Peterson, who read and commented on large sections. Jane Rosenthal has been my partner in doing all the Nahuatl translations. Barbara Hofmaier helped pull me out of the doldrums with her interest and excellent editing skills; Dot Jewell, working beyond the call of duty, energetically edited the dissertation. Other people have given me room, board, and companionship while I did research in Mexico. Among these are Mariana Yampolsky (my home away from home), Debby Nagao, Wendy Schoenfeld, and Xavier Noguez. Doris Heyden (my other home away from home) opened her house and library to me and was always ready to listen. Anthony Aveni and Karin Dakin (who both read portions of the dissertation), Lawrence Sullivan, Emily Umberger, Wayne Ruwet, and Michael Steiber all assisted with research in one way or another. Joe Hallman offered useful advice, and over beers at Jimmy's, Carol Anderson commented on many parts of this project. Ian Evison gave (and continues to give) numerous good insights, very practical advice, and much needed encouragement during our on-going Friday morning breakfast discussions.

When an academic is also a mother, a circle of people intimately involved with her often find themselves (sometimes to their own surprise) sharing in her work. During the course of writing this book (which seemed to take on an eternal life of its own), my children somehow managed to grow up, move on to college, find gainful employment, and marry; two of their grandparents and an uncle passed away; and I graduated, became employed, and moved into associate professorhood. The result is that an awful lot of familial members need to be acknowledged and remembered. My husband, Ned Read, assisted with the mathematics involved in the calendrical work and continued to give support and encouragement during the years of turning it into the product it finally became. During the dissertation phase, my eldest son, Nils Gonzalez, gave his support under difficult circumstances; my middle son, Jason Gonzalez, taught me to use the computer and helped correct that massive work; and my youngest, Ian Read, drew some of the tracings for the illustrations. When they were still young, Nils and Jason spent a month each summer with their father, Duncan Gonzalez, uncle and aunt Erik and Marti Gonzalez, and grandparents Theodor and Edith Parthenais, creating free time for me to work. My mother, Matilda Schwalbach, opened her home in Wisconsin's North Woods to all three boys when their parents were not available. Finally, this project is written with the memory of three people: my mother-in-law, Helen Read, my brother James B. Schwalbach, and my father, James A. Schwalbach. Helen both watched the boys when they were little and provided the whole family with a comfortable escape from whatever stresses were barking at the door. My brother Jim and his wife, McKay, also watched the boys, making travel possible. All these people were sorely needed, especially when there were children to be watched. And we miss those who are gone. The book is dedicated especially, however, to my father, for it was he who first taught me about the arts, history, human creativity, and the imagination. The drawings were done because he wanted them.

A NOTE ON TERMINOLOGY

The use of the word *Aztec* appears in the title of this book more for purposes of easy recognition than accuracy. In all probability, the people who lived in the great city of Tenochtitlan were no longer calling themselves Aztecs when the sixteenth-century Spaniards forcefully and audaciously turned their urban center into Mexico City. Nineteenth-century scholars are the ones we can blame for popularizing the word *Aztec*. The sixteenth-century inhabitants of Tenochtitlan more than likely called themselves *Mexica* or *Mexica-Tenochca*. For the sake of accuracy and out of deference to those original inhabitants of Tenochtitlan–Mexico City, I will use these two names throughout the rest of the book instead of Aztec.

K.A.R.

TIME AND SACRIFICE
IN THE AZTEC COSMOS

INTRODUCTION

2-Reed: A Sacrificial Beginning

Talking with a Plaque

On a wall of one of Mexico City's museums, a small but elegant stone plaque hangs dramatically lighted inside a sleek Plexiglas box (figure 1). Its surface is carved with imagery which, while pleasing in design, may seem curious to the uninitiated because the images are not immediately recognizable. This frieze, although partly broken, is carved skillfully out

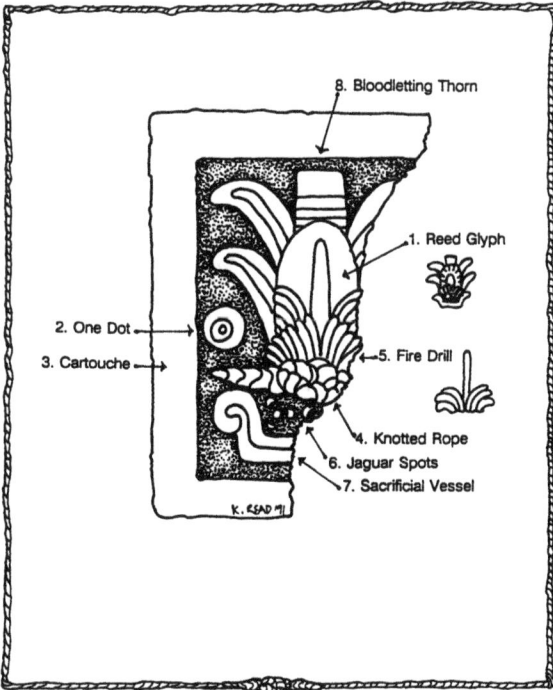

FIGURE 1.
2-Reed plaque.
Museo del Templo Mayor, Mexico City.

of the same plain gray stone of most pre-Conquest Mexican sculpture. Framed by an unadorned cartouche, or outer border, the central figure forms a plantlike shape with "leaves" branching to each side of its innermost leafy shape. To the left of this plant is a double ring protruding like a dot against the recessed background. Looking more closely, one may recognize at least one image lying beneath the plant, a length of spun rope that has been knotted in the middle in a complicated manner. Beneath this rope are two flowerlike depictions encased by a coiled border, which repeat the right angle of the cartouche's lower left corner.

After admiring the clean lines and pleasant design of this apparently simple and unimposing plaque, one not familiar with its "language" could say, "Isn't that beautiful!" and then move to the next display. But that would be unfortunate, not to mention wholly inappropriate, for the depictions carved on this stone's surface, while beautiful in their elegant simplicity, indicate to those who do know the language a somewhat messy and highly complex system of interlocking images, interrelated significations, and polyvalent metaphors. These metaphors founded pre-Conquest Mexica (or Aztec) conceptions of time and sacrifice, a system which to many may seem more terrifying than beautiful. So what is this little plaque about?

The museum in which it quietly hangs is dedicated to the Templo Mayor (Great Temple), the single most important Mexica temple. This huge, grandiose, and imposing pyramid settled itself in the heart of Tenochtitlan, the Mexica's capital city. It centered their most potent, most vital ritual district, which now lies beneath the central area of present-day Mexico City. The small plaque probably dates to the mid-fifteenth century (almost seventy-five years before Hernán Cortés entered Mexico) and was unearthed from this Great Temple's remains during excavations that began in 1979.[1] Because this unimposing, even ordinary plaque can both tell us about Mexica concepts of time and sacrifice and raise issues about how we may come to understand both them and ourselves, it will serve as a window into the Mexica world and our own. This bit of gray stone will constitute the beginning place for a dialogue between peoples of two different centuries and geographical locations. And, as Mexica cosmological notions themselves demand, we will use this plaque not just as a window between two worlds, but also as a spindle by which those disparate times and places may be spun together.

But how does one interpret the imagery carved on its surface when its fifteenth-century sculptor is long gone and no Mexica survive to tell about it? There is one quite deceptively simple way: if one can no longer enter into a direct conversation with the sculptor, one can enter into a kind of indirect conversation with him through his plaque. In order to do so, one need only recognize that, although only the plaque remains today, nevertheless, "someone is saying something about something to someone else."[2]

The plaque may be new to modern eyes, but its visual messages are old and, at one time, were central to Mexica culture; similar messages have been continually presented by other Mexica sculptures, pictures, and buildings to different people across a span of about five hundred years, from the Spanish Conquest to the present. During this time, the conversation has constantly changed as each participant took it up, examined it, reconstructed it, and then re-presented it to other conversationalists. Some of these participants will be particularly highlighted here: of course, (1) the Mexica sculptor and his ruler (the "someones" who were doing the talking), and (2) the inhabitants of Tenochtitlan (the "someone elses" to whom they were talking). But these are not all, for other important post-Conquest "someone elses" also hear about or listen in on the Mexica conversation without speaking directly to either the sculptor or his ruler. These people will include the sixteenth-century Spanish, indigenous folk living today, and contemporary scholars.

The various messages of this conversation will be explored through the lenses of three levels of visual communication: (1) a level of demarcation (the "saying," which forms and controls the images); (2) an iconographic level (the "something," which concerns itself with particular images' significations); and (3) an iconological level (the "about something," which explores the complex logic of its images and their many levels of meaning). By taking each of these in turn, one can learn much about the plaque and its makers, audiences, and messages.

Many Speaking Seers: Mexica, Spanish, and Indigenous

One cannot come to know the Mexica without also knowing the Spanish, for without the Mexica's conquerors, today's seers would understand a lot less about the various Mexica seers responsible for the original plaque. The sixteenth-century Spanish destroyed much, but they also collected, rewrote, redrew, and preserved the bulk of the resources used currently by scholars to understand what went on in pre-Conquest times. Without those early efforts at preservation, little would be known today. These two earliest groups of seers, the Mexica and Spanish, are considered in this section along with their current heirs, indigenous peoples living today in Mesoamerica; a second current group of seers, contemporary scholars, is considered later.

A Mexica Sculptor and His Ruler

The artist who carved this plaque was a man (all Mexica sculptors were male) who probably was born in the earlier half of the fifteenth century. The style of the plaque suggests he came from a family of sculptors dwelling in a city in the Mexican Highlands close to Tenochtitlan, perhaps even in the capital itself. Mesoamerica was then populated by a number of groups living in cities all over the geographic area, each quite distinctive.[3] The sculptor's home of Tenochtitlan would have been viewed as a self-contained cosmic center, an urban nexus for its inhabitants' own distinctive sense of reality. His city, like every city in Mesoamerica, would have been linked directly with its particular geographic and celestial topography; with its own mountains, hills, and ravines; and with the distinctive motions of its own heavenly objects that served to mark topographical and spiritual boundaries.

As an adult, the plaque's sculptor may have lived in Tenochtitlan, the capital of the extensive Mesoamerican domain over which the Mexica held hegemony when Cortés arrived. The sculptor surely spoke Nahuatl, a tongue still heard in Central Mexico today. As in all of Native America now, the huge diversity and wide range of indigenous languages created complex and often confusing situations in pre-Conquest Mesoamerica, for rarely could people speaking different languages fully understand one another (even dialects of a single language could be so different as to be unintelligible). Nahuatl was the language spoken in Tenochtitlan and its surrounding environs. And, because of Mexica hegemony, by the time of the Conquest, Nahuatl had become a kind of lingua franca that helped resolve the communication problems. The sculptor probably was not called an Aztec, however, for it was nineteenth-century scholars who latched on to that name, using it to refer loosely to almost any indigenous group living in Mesoamerica at the time, no matter where they were located or what they spoke. To gain a bit more precision, I use the term *Mexica-Tenochca* or simply *Mexica* to refer to the particular inhabitants of Tenochtitlan and its associated genealogical lineages.[4] *Nahua* will refer to all related Nahuatl-speaking peoples who inhabited Central Mexico in the post-Classic period (1200–1521 c.e.) just preceding Spanish rule.

The Templo Mayor, in which this particular Nahua sculptor's plaque was buried, was rebuilt by every new Mexica ruler after his election to show his might, power, and generosity. Each young ruler constructed a new and larger layer over the old ruler's pyramid, causing the Great Temple to grow even greater. The plaque had been thrown into the ground as filler between two of these layers. This distinctive placement dates it to before 1502 and most likely to the reign of the ruler Chief Speaker (Tlatoani)[5] Motecuhzuma the Elder, one of the greatest Mexica rulers. He or someone in his court acting for him most likely commissioned the sculptor to carve it.

The Inhabitants of Tenochtitlan

Most consider the Mexica relative latecomers to the richly textured cultural environment of Mesoamerica and its Mexican Highlands, although their historical origins are somewhat obscure. Mesoamerican civilization has an extremely long and variegated history with many peoples contributing to its development. Before the Mexica-Tenochca of Tenochtitlan, three great urban civilizations claimed especially wide-ranging influence throughout vast reaches of the area: the Olmec, the Classic Maya, and the Teotihuacaners. The Olmec (ca. 1500–100 B.C.E.) centered their cities near the Gulf coast in what is now Veracruz and Tabasco. The Classic Maya (ca. 250–850 or 900 C.E.) lived in numerous urban centers in the Yucatan, southern Mexico, Belize, Guatemala, Honduras, Nicaragua, and El Salvador. And the Teotihuacaners (ca. 200 B.C.E.–650 or 750 C.E.) centered themselves in the Valley of Mexico within the confines of a single, highly concentrated urban area going by the same name. From there Teotihuacaners extended their influence further than any group that came before or after, including the Mexica. The remains of this largest and most powerful of all Mesoamerican metropolises rest just northeast of Mexico City.[6] Today they are called simply the Pyramids (las Pirámides).

The Mexica-Tenochca (ca. 1350–1521) first entered the Valley of Mexico some six or seven centuries after Teotihuacan's decline and disappearance. They were the final great power to influence Mesoamerica before the Spanish. Their own historians recount[7] that they were the last of seven small groups to enter this attractive and advantageous setting in the Mexican Highlands. The lush Valley of Mexico contained a huge basin called Lake Texcoco and offered rich possibilities for agriculture and hunting (Adams 1991, 367–69), not to mention good sources for the highly prized obsidian used for weaponry and a host of other items. Before the Mexica arrived, the six other groups already had established themselves and built successful urban centers.

Emerging from the same place as the others, The Place of Seven Caves (Chicomoztoc), the Mexica wandered in as crude and rude hunter-warriors. At first, they visited many of the Mexican Highland's landmarks and urban centers both past and present, including Teotihuacan, by then in ruins and quite deserted. During these travels, or so their stories tell us, they acquired agriculture and a sedentary way of life. The year 1372 is one of the possible founding dates given for their capital, Tenochtitlan.[8] By the fifteenth century, when the sculptor and his ruler lived there, the city had become a huge, complex urban center concentrated on a densely packed island floating in the southern end of Lake Texcoco. After the Spanish Conquest, the lake was filled in almost completely; Mexico City now covers the lower half of the valley. Its spiritual and secular center was placed carefully on the very same spot where Tenochtitlan's great ritual center once lay. Now Mexico City's centuries-old National Cathedral and Palacio lie cheek to jowl with the Mexica Zócalo, the Templo Mayor's ancient remains and its brand-new modern museum.

The environment of the Mexican Highlands, then as now, was that of a high and dry mountain park. It had an elevation of over 7,200 feet, or approximately 2,200 meters (Adams 1991, 367), and a biseasonal, semi-arid climate. Five months of the year (June to October) constituted a rainy season, while seven (November to May) were dry. June, July, and early August brought the best rains for agriculture: almost daily, usually gentle afternoon showers. In late August, September, and October, there were thunderstorms accompanied by high winds, the residue of the hurricane season in the coastal areas. March, April, and May were driest, characterized by frontals which could bring dust storms. Droughts were a fairly regular problem, and the high elevation ensured an inherent skittishness in the weather. Surprise frosts in late spring and early fall were common (Vivó Escoto 1964). Successful agriculture in the region—the latitude of the Sahara Desert and the elevation of mountainous areas in Colorado and Wyoming—was a tremendous challenge.

The geography of the Valley of Mexico itself made agriculture even more challenging. Surrounded by high mountain peaks, the valley was largely taken up by a huge basin in which much of the water was saline and not suitable for crops. Irrigation and terracing, therefore, were employed on the surrounding hilly areas, drawing from mountain runoff. In the fifteenth century, part of the basin was also diked off in order to isolate the lower end, which was fed with fresh spring water. Here, the

Mexica used a reverse irrigation method called a *chinampa* system, which they had borrowed from their ancient Mesoamerican ancestors.[9] In this highly efficient system, large strips of land were created by dredging up the rich soil from the bottom of the lake. Seven crops per year could be rotated through these areas, conditions permitting. The Mexica also multicropped: they planted several different species simultaneously, thereby maximizing production and minimizing risk of complete crop failure in poor years (Ortiz de Montellano 1990, 94–97). Even so, given the problems of climate and topography and the fact that by the sixteenth century the Valley of Mexico had reached a population of 1,200,000 with estimates for the island city of Tenochtitlan as high as 300,000 (ibid., 106), adequate agricultural production constituted a serious concern.

The diet of the sculptor and his neighbors, while not exclusively vegetarian, was heavy in plant sources. One factor was the lack of pastoral animals. Unlike some other societies that developed husbandry of cattle or sheep, the fauna available to Mesoamericans did not lend themselves to such agricultural practices. Although they domesticated dogs, turkeys, various birds, and fish, they did not replace hunting with herding. The lack of pastoral animals was not a problem, however, for the Mesoamerican diet was quite adequate (Ortiz de Montellano 1990, 1978).[10] It was largely vegetarian, consisting of a triad of corn, beans, and squash, supplemented by chilies and tomatoes. Amaranth, a plant high in protein, often supplemented corn, even substituting for it at times. And chia provided another source for protein. An algae called *tecuitlatl* (*Spirulina geitlerii*) was eaten with corn or in a sauce of chilies and tomatoes; it is 70 percent protein with an essential amino acid assortment very similar to that of egg. This vegetarian diet was supplemented further by hunting deer, rabbit, birds, rattlesnakes, mice, iguanas, armadillos, frogs, salamanders, various insects, and fish. As Bernard Ortiz de Montellano said: "The Aztecs ate practically every living thing that walked, swam, flew, or crawled" (ibid., 1990, 115).[11] If normal conditions prevailed, the sculptor ate well, thanks to a combination of efficient agricultural methods that compensated for the skittish weather patterns and a multifaceted and creative exploitation of edible natural resources.

The citizens of Tenochtitlan who were meant to see Motecuhzuma's plaque would have come from the city itself as well as from many other urban centers and villages, for Tenochtitlan was a bustling, sophisticated, cosmopolitan center with a diverse population. Its huge marketplace operated in Tlatelolco, a town annexed to Tenochtitlan's northern side in the late fifteenth century. Here men and women hawked goods from all over Mesoamerica, the result of brisk businesses operated by families who concentrated on trade. The Mexica government also contracted for many goods and extracted many more through taxation that came in the form of tribute.

The city itself was apportioned into quarters. Two main, intersecting roads divided it into four main sectors called *calpullies*. Each sector was associated with a distinctive "kinline" that also functioned as a social unit. Linked by either physical, genetic ties or by bonds of friendship, each of the four *calpullies* traced its kinship to a particular patron deity (*calpulteotl*) who gave the people their mythical genetic heritage. *Calpullies* owned land that was distributed among their families and were distinctive economic, political, juridical, and military entities.[12]

The sculptor and his family, like all Mesoamericans, lived in a world in which everything was alive. All lived and moved because all were imbued with many kinds of powers.[13] Trees, rocks, mountains, animals, people, ancestors, even sculptures and buildings were living entities and carried within their bodies specific powers which the sculptor could tap into if needed or avoid as the case might be. As will be seen, many levels of interrelated powers were defined by one's stature as a specific god, a particular kind of human, or some other distinctive being. The powers held by these diverse living beings made things happen, made things move. For better or for worse, they made things work and function. Moreover, these embodied powers traveled through the cosmos in a motion that was never-ending.

The Mexica's own particular cosmos was called 4-Movement (4-Ollin), named for its expected demise in earthquakes and (perhaps) for the constant motion of the powerful beings that coursed through its multitudinous pathways. It was a cosmos divided in half in which forces of growth and decay constantly moved.[14] The upper half was imaged as a warm, dry house. Its floor was the earth's surface, punctuated by tall mountains and ringed by the oceans stretching out to great walls at its edges, rather like the Valley of Mexico itself, which was surrounded by mountains one descended to reach the Gulf of Mexico on the east or the Pacific on the west. The walls at the oceans' edges were made of water, and four huge trees reaching to the sky supported them—one each in the east, north, west, and south. The center pole of this cosmic house was also a giant tree. Below the earth's surface was the underworld, Mictlan, a dank, rotting, and decaying place filled with seeds, insects, excrement, and bones. It was there that the lords of death lived: Mictlanteuctli; his woman, Mictlancihuatl; and the Micteca, or people of the land of the dead.

These worlds were two sides of the same coin. Mountains, plants, and people dwelled on the earth's surface. Rocks, roots, and bones lived below. The upper was dry and warm, the lower wet and cold. One was the world of growth, where mountains, plants, and people lived in their craggy bodies, foliage, and flesh; the other of decay, where things rotted away, reduced to rocks, caves, tunnels, dirt, mulch, skulls, and teeth. In spite of their oppositional natures, these worlds were inseparable. Like twins joined at the chest, they shared the same fiery turquoise heart located in the exact middle at the base of the central cosmic tree.

Tenochtitlan lay at the midpoint of this power-laden world, repeating the cosmos's quarters with its four *calpullies*. Its spacious ritual district rested exactly where the two roads of the city crossed, helping to control the powers governing the Mexica cosmos. Within the district's snake-shaped walls stood the houses of the famed eagle and jaguar warriors, the skull rack holding the heads of sacrificial offerings, a court for the sacred ballgame, the priests school (*calmecac*), temples of various deities, and the *coacalco*, the house that held captive the patron deities of defeated cities. In the center of this ritual district's eastern side sat the Templo Mayor.

The Great Temple rose tall above all else. It held absolute dominion over the power-filled ritual center (figure 2). It forced its awesome presence on Tenochtitlan's inhabitants, its image demanding their attention, calculating its strength by the powerful cosmic patterns embodied in its structures. Two staircases climbed up its western face, each leading to one of two small temples on its summit. The northern temple housed a most ancient Mesoamerican power, a god of mountains, rain, and agriculture called Tlaloc by the Mexica. The southern was the house of Huitzilopochtli, the special patron deity of the Mexica-Tenochca, their ultimate ancestor and source of strength in war. Because of these ancestral links, extending from families to the god of their *calpulli* and on to the patron god of the Mexica themselves, one could say that the state, as the largest social unit, was the center of the sculptor's communal, familial, and personal life. Whatever the sculptor gave to his state by means of his personal powers, he also gave to his family, for if the state could gain enough powers to ensure a smoothly running cosmos, the city, his *calpulli*, and his family all benefitted.

A potent calendrical system shaped this power-filled cosmos in which

FIGURE 2.
The Templo Mayor, drawn from the
Codex Telleriano Remensis, folio 39r.

the sculptor lived. For, like all Mesoamerican cosmoses old and new, the
Mexica cosmic space was formed by the motion of time. The particular
calendar used by the Mexica-Tenochca echoed fundamental aspects of
basic Mesoamerican calendrics, which are extraordinarily ancient and
have permeated all aspects of life for centuries, continuing even today.

People before the Olmecs developed at least the rudiments of counting time, and many others perfected complicated variations after that. The import of calendrics for Mesoamerican culture cannot be overstated.

The calendrical system ruled much of daily life. One did almost nothing important without first figuring out its calendrical meaning; the system calculated every ritual, great and minor, in which the sculptor might participate. The calendar controlled the boundaries of life itself, for all the diverse living beings of the cosmos lived for particular periods of time, time spans that could be counted calendrically. Even the earthquakes that would end the Mexica cosmos would not come until 4-Movement's life was over, when 4-Movement's calendrically calculated time span had ended.

Conjunctions of calendrical moments made things happen. For example, after fifty-two solar years, two of many calendrical cycles—a 365-day solar count and a 260-day divinatory count (a calendar used for divination)—ended on the same day in a year called 2-Reed. The current sun's lifespan was now complete; its death had arrived. Therefore, a major rite called the New Fire or Binding-of-the-Years ceremony was held to give birth to a new sun, starting up a new fifty-two-year spiral. And 676 fifty-two-year solar lives brought the end of the Mexica cosmic age, the moment of 4-Movement's death. Even human history was calculated according to the same complicated calendrical system. The stories relating the past history of the Mexica were calendrically shaped, and all major events occurred according to mathematically significant dates, when potent calendrical counts all converged. The Mexica and their close neighbors, the Tlatelolcans, both founded their towns in years bearing the name house. Fire was created, the Mexica cosmos shaped, and new suns given birth on years called Reed. History was written and rewritten so that historical events would occur on mathematically significant dates.

In the sculptor's cosmos, moreover, time and space were one; they were not separate. The Templo Mayor wove temporal and spatial images into a single cloth so tightly there existed no distinction between them. Its northern side housed the rain god, Tlaloc, echoing the motions of the sun in the seasonally wet summer (the time of agriculture), for at that time the sun was in the northern half of the sky. Its southern side housed the war god, Huitzilopochtli, echoing the sun in the seasonally dry winter (the time for war and conquest); in the winter, the sun moved in the southern half of the sky. Externally, the pyramid's stone-dry image spoke of things of the upper world and the temple-houses of gods. But internally it spoke of things of the underworld. Hidden inside its dark, wet innards (where no one could go) sat the layers of past rulers' time span, like so many nested boxes, for when a ruler died, the next one built his pyramid over the old one. And with each important calendrical conjunction, event, and construction, the Mexica buried within the pyramid's guts the cremated remains of especially revered elite personages, offerings upon offerings of hundreds of sacrificed animals, objects from the oceans and mountains, vases given to Tlaloc, beads, things carved of obsidian and jade, and even a few human bones. Just as the upper and lower worlds of the Mexica cosmos spoke of growth and decay moving together, so too the visible external image of the Templo Mayor spoke of the moving seasons that governed growth on earth's surface, while its invisible inner image spoke of decaying bodies and the count of past lives. As will be seen, these buried bodies and past lives helped maintain growth on the earth's surface. But all this was transformed into new shapes when the Spanish arrived.

The Sixteenth-Century Spanish

Dominican, Franciscan, and Augustinian mendicants as well as the requisite governmental authorities, opportunists, explorers, and adventurers arrived closely on the heels of the conquistadors. Later, echoing developments and tensions in Europe, the Inquisition's arm reached to New Spain, and the secular clergy and Jesuits also appeared. The latter administered to a growing Creole population. By the second half of the century, not only had people of Spanish blood been born in New Spain, but Indian and Spanish people had intermarried, and Black and Jewish people had joined the mix. New Spain had become an interracial and interethnic reality with all the disagreements and tensions that come with such diversity. One thing needs to be noted from these simple facts: the "Spanish" (whatever that meant by midcentury) might agree that they held a variety of relationships with Spain but not always on what they saw or heard in the New World.[15] And it is these diverse settlers of New Spain who are responsible for much of what is known about the Mexica.

On the one hand, in the process of conquest and colonization, Spanish settlers destroyed vast quantities of written and archaeological materials. No clearly pre-Conquest text written by the Mexica themselves survived the Conquest. A number of texts from other cities escaped this fate, but all Mexica codices were burned.[16] The colonists also razed to the ground buildings situated in the temple district of Tenochtitlan, using their stones to build Mexico City; the National Cathedral and Palacio stand on that site today thanks to Mexica stone masons. In 1978, the remains of the Templo Mayor were discovered buried beneath apartment buildings, offices, and stores just behind the cathedral and one short block away from the Palacio.[17]

On the other hand, zeal to missionize the Mexica effectively and to satisfy European curiosity for information on the New World also led the colonists to amass numerous collections telling about pre-Conquest times. They ranged from a medieval encyclopedia on Nahua life and religion (*Florentine Codex*, FC) and a history of the Mexica (*Historia de las Indias de Nueva España e islas de la tierra firme*, HI 1984 or 1994)—both intended to promote more effective conversion and educate a European audience—to a copy of a sixteenth-century indigenous history in Nahuatl, collected by a Mexican historian fascinated with the pre-history of his country ("The Legend of the Suns" in the *Codex Chimalpopoca*, CC). These many documents constitute a rich source of information on indigenous life and history, although the conditions of their collection present considerable challenges.

First, adequate information is often missing. "The Legend of the Suns" (*Leyenda de los Soles*) (CC), for example, is a particularly fine example of a Mexica-related history. Using the pre-Conquest calendar, it dates each event with a specific solar year, listing all the intervening years in sequence. Moreover, its value is increased because it tells its tales in Nahuatl, something that helps the text retain an authenticity lost in those preserved only in Spanish. The "Legend" itself states that the story is being told on 22 May 1558, yet so little else is known about the circumstances of its collection that little can be said about its provenience. It is part of the *Codex Chimalpopoca*, a codex containing two histories, the "Legend" and the "Annals of Cuauhtitlan," which belonged to a neighboring city of Tenochtitlan. A single scribe's hand signals that these two histories were copied from two earlier documents. The handwriting of the famous seventeenth-century historian Fernando de Alva Ixtlilxochitl may appear in parts. He claimed Nahua blood from the region near Cuauhtitlan; it is possible, then, that he was the collector (Wauchope, 15:333, 337). To complicate matters more, the original manuscript seems to have been lost in a plane crash in 1949, and only a photographed edition published in 1945 remains.[18] This sketchy history of collection and preservation makes the document's pre-history even more uncertain. Although the stories of the "Legend" belonged to Nahua speakers, the speakers are hard to identify. The document ends with a list of Mexica rulers, yet other elements suggest it is heir to other Nahua-speaking groups as well.[19]

Second, the colonists didn't always get things right, often insisting on seeing the Mexica through their own sixteenth-century European lenses. For example, the Dominican lay brother Pedro de los Ríos helped produce and annotate the *Codex Telleriano Remensis* (facsimile, 1899), a reproduction of three different pictorial calendrical texts. Although the primary artist in this text was a skilled native, he nevertheless eliminated many of the rich details, really only pictorially summarizing what was probably in the earlier, lost manuscripts. He even drew the Templo Mayor backward in this reproduction (figure 2), reversing its northern and southern sides. In his efforts to comprehend what he was encountering in this strange new world, Ríos frequently drew false parallels between pre-Conquest visions and his own. A picture of a weeping female deity becomes Eve who has fallen, the figure near her becomes Adam (*Codex Telleriano Remensis*, facsimile 1899, fols. 10v and 11r). Likewise, the annotator of the *Códice Vaticano Latino* (reproduction, 1964, fols. 1–3)—a copy of Ríos's copy (Quiñones Keber, 1995, 129–30)—describes Mexica cosmological space as a Dante-like, multilayered medieval cosmos, complete with the Creator and First Cause. In this description, the author mistranslates the Lord of Twoness (Ometeule) as the "Lord of Triple Dignity."

One crucial resource is the *Florentine Codex: A General History of the Things of New Spain* (FC), a medieval-like encyclopedia on the Nahua and related groups produced in the sixteenth century under the direction of the Franciscan cleric Fray Bernardino de Sahagún.[20] Collected in three languages, Latin, Spanish, and Nahuatl, this text is invaluable for its breadth of information and, like "The Legend of the Suns," its highly prized Nahuatl texts. But unlike the texts of the "Legend," the texts of the *Florentine* often are in the most elegant and cultured styles, offering up beautiful prose and poetry. Some caution, however, is needed with this wonderful work, even though its author, Sahagún, was by far one of the most intelligent and sympathetic sixteenth-century collectors. His work should not be viewed as comparable to a modern-day ethnography, for its objectives were very different. Sahagún's primary aim was evangelization, and his work, like Ríos's, was shaped by his cosmological orientations.

Sahagún presumed, for example, that a pantheon of discrete deities existed which could be identified by merely asking questions about each god's title, attributes, characteristics, and abilities, questions that were quite incompatible with the concept of multiple animistic powers inherent in all things in the Mexica cosmos (López Austin 1974; 1988b, 185–236). In some sections of his encyclopedia, he describes the being Quetzalcoatl as though he is an almost human personality with a distinctive identity (FC, bk. 1, pt. 2, chp. 21:69; bk. 3, pt. 4, chp. 3–14:13–38). Yet when one consults other sources, or even other sections of the *Florentine* itself, Quetzalcoatl's identity becomes very confusing. At one moment he takes on the characteristics of Ehecatl, the wind being, at another, those of Topiltzin, a humanlike Toltec priest (someone from Tula).[21] At one time, he might be sporting feathers and snake scales; at another, a feathered serpent (with no allusion to either winds or priests) might display a human head emerging from between its fangs. Mexica deities had split personalities, multiple identities they could take off and put on, combine and recombine like so many articles of clothing, all depending on the powers required for the moment. Sahagún's category of deity constrained his and possibly our understanding. This all-too-frequent situation of radical differences between the Spanish collectors and their Mexica informants presents a special problem for the twentieth-century scholar. If Sahagún's own cosmic visions are not accounted for, present-day seers may continue to re-present the Mexica as though they shared his sixteenth-century Spanish views.

Present Peoples with Pre-Conquest Ties

In spite of the Conquest and its enormous destruction, many peoples continue to live today in ways that can be directly related to the ways of their pre-Conquest ancestors. Anthropologist Rossana Lok notes that "the vitality of Mexico's precolumbian cultures did not vanish together with its spiritual leaders and elite at the time of the Conquest" (Lok 1987, 211). She suggests that every member of a culture is a carrier of at least a part of cultural meaning. The destruction of an elite class does not necessarily destroy cultural meaning, for cultural meaning will be carried on in other ways by other people. Lok argues that meaning may be found as much in ordinary structures of human existence, such as people's houses and firepits, as in the artifacts and texts of religious specialists such as priests, healers, or diviners.

Many present-day Mesoamericans continue living in ways that give clues about how the ancient sculptor and his neighbors probably lived. Although the elite calendars governing high state functions no longer are used, the 260-day divinatory calendar, often called the "count of the days," remains fundamental to Mesoamerican existence and continues to flourish today (B. Tedlock 1982). Marriages, births, and business deals are still determined by its mathematically shaped conjunctions. And even in a Christian world, today's Mesoamerican underworld still is a wet, dark realm of the dead, the antithesis of the earth's dry surface where people dwell (Tax, forthcoming). Houses are still constructed on cosmological patterns recalling pre-Conquest traditions (Lok 1987), and myths are still told which have pre-Conquest antecedents (D. Tedlock 1985). To ignore these contemporary corollaries would mean missing some extraordinary resources which can help scholars today richly imagine how life might have been back then. When one takes into consideration these various conversants old and new, the plaque's visual messages become easier to decipher. But an understanding of the participants alone cannot explain fully the plaque's messages; for that, one must account for the visual nature of those messages.

Many Visible Messages: Three Levels of Expressive Imagery

Useful similarities exist between visual and verbal modes of communication, and these aid one's understanding of the plaque immensely; however, one should never forget the differences. Throughout the book, I use terms such as "language" and "conversation" to describe the plaque's communicative capacities. Images "speak" and "talk," which makes it possible to "read" these visual "texts." By so doing, I note the similarities between verbal and visual forms of expression; I refer to the ability this plaque and other objects have to communicate clear messages to their audiences, as clear as any spoken or written words might convey.

Similarities are easy to find. Both verbal and visual texts are created by people who live in specific cultural and historical contexts. Both make sense of people's existentially lived realities, and both help reorder people's multiple understandings of those realities when change occurs. They interact, playing together in complex forms of human communication, something at which the Mexica were masters. Visual communication, like verbal communication, is discourse—a human capacity to systematically order, reorder, and communicate those orders to others.

The fact that words and images are each a form of discourse is important for both general principles of interpretation and historical reasons based in the particular Mesoamerican context. With only written (or even oral) texts, it is impossible for a scholar to get a full view of human experience. Margaret Miles noted that doing so makes discourse a self-referential activity because it excludes alternatives to the "world of words." Furthermore, it elevates verbal skills in a way that gives an absolute advantage to those with linguistic training and talents, thereby excluding both "all people some of the time, and some of the people all of the time" (1985, xi).

Moreover, images are as true as words in the Mesoamerican context. There, verbal skills may not be the single or even primary mode of expression. First, because the Conquest assured that all verbal resources would be sifted and categorized according to Spanish concerns, the conquerors effectively accomplished their conquest not just by mere force but also by the control of communication. As soon as the sword had won, the conquerors stepped in as the primary interpreters for the conquered; this meant that no matter how sympathetic they may have been (and many were), the conquered eventually lost their own unique voice and became like their conquerors.[22] The import of this for today's scholarship is enormous, for, because of the intense interaction of the Spanish with post-Conquest Nahua and other texts in indigenous languages, the only truly primary resources for pre-Columbian religions are visual texts such as the plaque and other archaeological remains. These texts have been touched least by the Spanish.

Second, pre-Columbians subtly wove together nonverbal forms of discourse with verbal ones. Sculpture, painting, weaving, mask making, and ritual performances—occurring in human-constructed environments carefully coordinated with specific topographical locations—were integrated with music making, chanting, poetry, storytelling and philosophic inquiry in daily, unmarked as well as unusually marked social experiences. The Mexica-Tenochca utilized the full gamut of human cognitive abilities for communication, and honored not only those with strong language skills but also those with visual, musical, and kinesthetic skills. Ignoring this richness would be a major failure of understanding, for the plaque presented its various intended messages by showing and being seen.

Significant differences between verbal and visual forms of communication, however, also exist. Language itself can obscure the incongruities between how the plaque "looks" and how one might describe those "looks." Often, no words exist to describe the purely visual ways in which images communicate, and one is forced to adapt terms meant for verbal communication. Sculptures, after all, don't really speak or talk. This simple fact suggests the extreme emphasis our culture places on words and the degree to which it underplays images. After all, as the biblical John said, "In the beginning there was the word" (not the "image"), yet following passages paint vivid verbal pictures of Jesus' life. When words marking visual expression are lacking, the power of imagery can be masked, working a different kind of effect. But such verbal masking makes images no less potent, no less precise vehicles of effective communication.

Nor does this masquerade require that images communicate in the same way that words do. With sculptures and painting, one is in the realm not of sound but of imagery. One must learn to "read" that which appears only before one's eyes and not in one's ears. An object's visual countenance is, in some ways, very unlike the sounds associated with the black words printed on this white page, although a comparison comes a little closer if someone read these words aloud. For then, not just the printed words would give meaning but also how one said them. How the sculptor depicted and shaped the imagery of his plaque (as a speaker speaks and develops her words) is just as important as the signification of each of those images (like the words on this page and what they stand for). Therefore, skillful seers do not interpret an object by simply cataloging all its visual parts as though they were words meant for combination into meaningful sentences; they do more than mark each image's signification. Skillful seers also mark such things as its colors, lines, shapes, textures, and composition just as skillful listeners hear things such as a speaker's tone of voice, volume, accent, rhythm of speech, and placement of emphasis.[23]

The Level of Demarcation

The first serious step in reading the plaque is to note how its messages are visually presented; learning what the images are saying requires this.[24] Even to the uninitiated, a little of the plaque's message is understandable. The rope looks like a rope. It is precisely carved with clean, sharp edges so that even the twist of its cords can be seen clearly and its knot can be identified. But further research is required to do more than simply identify the rope as a rope, research that includes observing carefully how the marks themselves were made, their style and manner of execution; in short, the conscious decisions the sculptor made during the plaque's creation. An analysis of the plaque's style of demarcation—those expressly visual factors of its creation—is as important to interpreting its message as an analysis of the signification and metaphoric messages of its glyphs, shapes, and pictures. How the rope is carved lends as much to the potency of its message as the simple fact that it is a rope. And the carving is as determined by who made it and who will see it as is the fact that a rope was deemed important to the subject matter.

Marking, as much as speaking, is a culturally defined act. All marking, whether it be expressly visual or referential, is both contextually based and a matter of choice because all discourse, visual or otherwise, is necessarily communal. All artists choose from a range of visual possibilities, a range constrained by both the subject matter and the particular style demanded by their cultural context. To analyze those constraints, one must "learn to see" the subject in a way similar to how the artist learned to see it in the first place.

An artist, for example, never simply copies optical reality.[25] Drawing a hand isn't merely copying a hand. One looks for such things as edges, masses, shapes and forms, shadows, colors, and textures as well as the contoured lines that divide them from the surrounding space, even if some forms do not have a sharply defined edge (such as the rounded forms of the fingers in figure 3a). If one chooses mass instead, one may use a textural pattern of lines formed together to show this mass or perhaps shades of light and dark to give the illusion of the three-dimensional shape being drawn on the flat surface of the paper (figure 3b).

A picture never looks exactly like the object being drawn; it is a series of illusory devices intended to trick viewers into thinking reality sits before them. These devices have been adapted to the medium chosen by

FIGURE 3A.
Contour line drawing of a hand.

FIGURE 3B.
The same hand in lights and darks. Mass is also emphasized.

the artist during the process of drawing in order to allude to an object of nature in a way that embodies a culturally influenced style. Because the artist chooses the various illusory devices available to her after "forgetting" what it is she is drawing in order to analyze it, it can be said that the artist doesn't merely describe that hand but that she *re-presents* it, for there is freedom in the choices made. This is not a total freedom, however, for the artist is controlled by the demands of the object itself, by the restrictions of the medium she has chosen to use for communication, and by her own culturally determined expectations. Her choices, therefore, reflect only a limited range of possibilities.

The plaque's sculptor chose to handle line and edge to re-present the rope, for example. The carved, contoured edges of the rope signify the rounded edges of a real rope without copying it exactly. The carving itself, formed from a series of marks referring to some (though not all) of the elements of optical reality is, then, an optically inexact signifier for the object in nature while at the same time a relatively exact signifier for cultural messages. This means that this first level of demarcation may be compared roughly to the morpho-phonemic level of linguistic translations. In the latter, one focuses on particular sounds to represent certain culturally determined units of reference. Here, visual elements serve a somewhat similar purpose to that of sounds, although by very different means.

The sculptor's crisp, clean style can be found, for example, in the earliest Mexica-Tenochca calendar, the *Codex Borbonicus* (figure 4).[26] Later calendars, drawn under increasing Spanish influence, lose the controlled precision of line inherent in the earlier works. The rope is nearly unrecognizable in the *Codex Aubin's* depiction (figure 5, A), and the rope in the *Codex Mendoza* (figure 6) is a childish caricature when com-

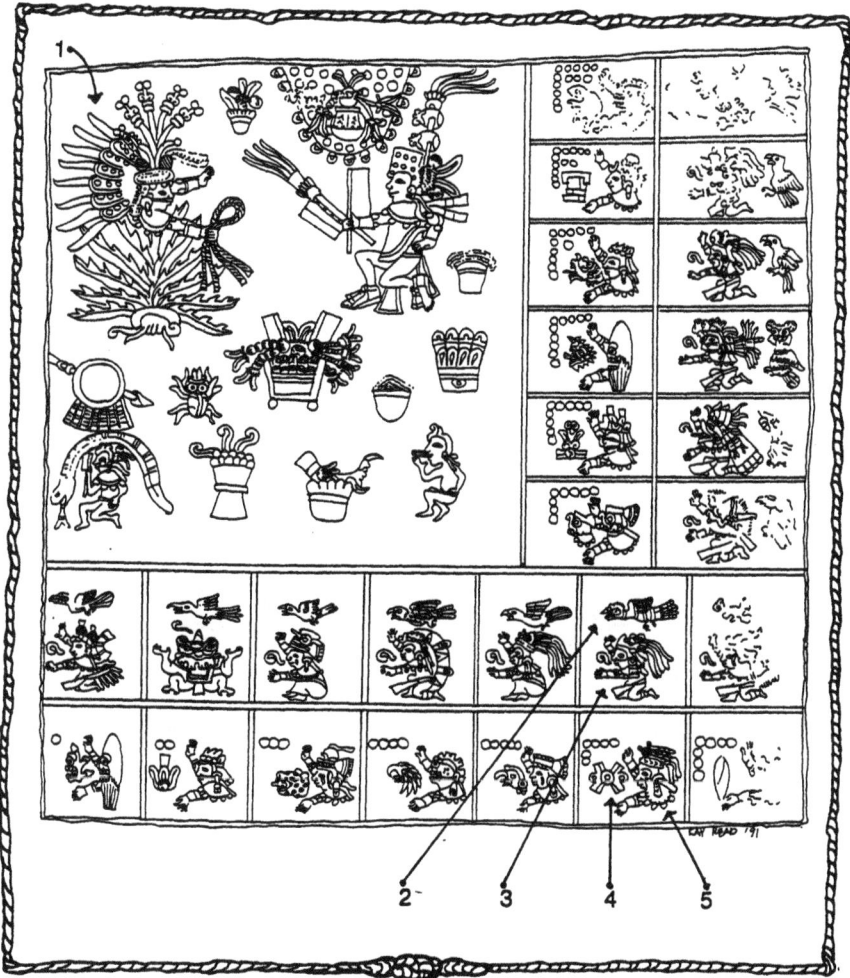

FIGURE 4.
Trecena 8, drawn from the
Codex Borbonicus.

1. Deity governing the thirteen-day week
2. Birds governing each day
3. Day lords
4. Day signs numbered with dots
5. Night lords

pared to the one depicted in the plaque. The execution of the plaque's rope, while stylized, still is precisely linked in some way to optical reality. Later examples done under Spanish supervision and for Spanish consumption usually have begun to lose both this optical link and earlier rendering skills.

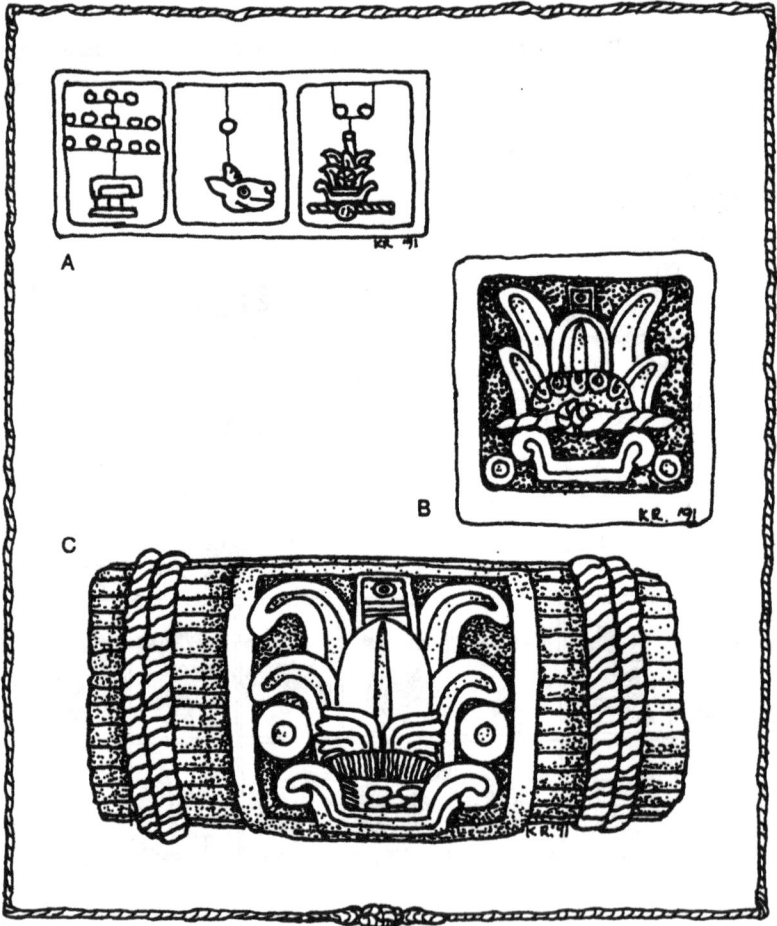

FIGURE 5.
Various 2-Reed glyphs: (A) section of a year count depicting the year 2-Reed, drawn from the *Codex Aubin*, 17; (B) 2-Reed glyph carved on the front of the Teocalli Stone of Sacred Warfare, *Museo Nacional de Antropología, Mexico City;* (C) carved stone bundle of reeds tied with a rope and displaying a 2-Reed glyph on its front, *Museo Nacional de Antropología, Mexico City.*

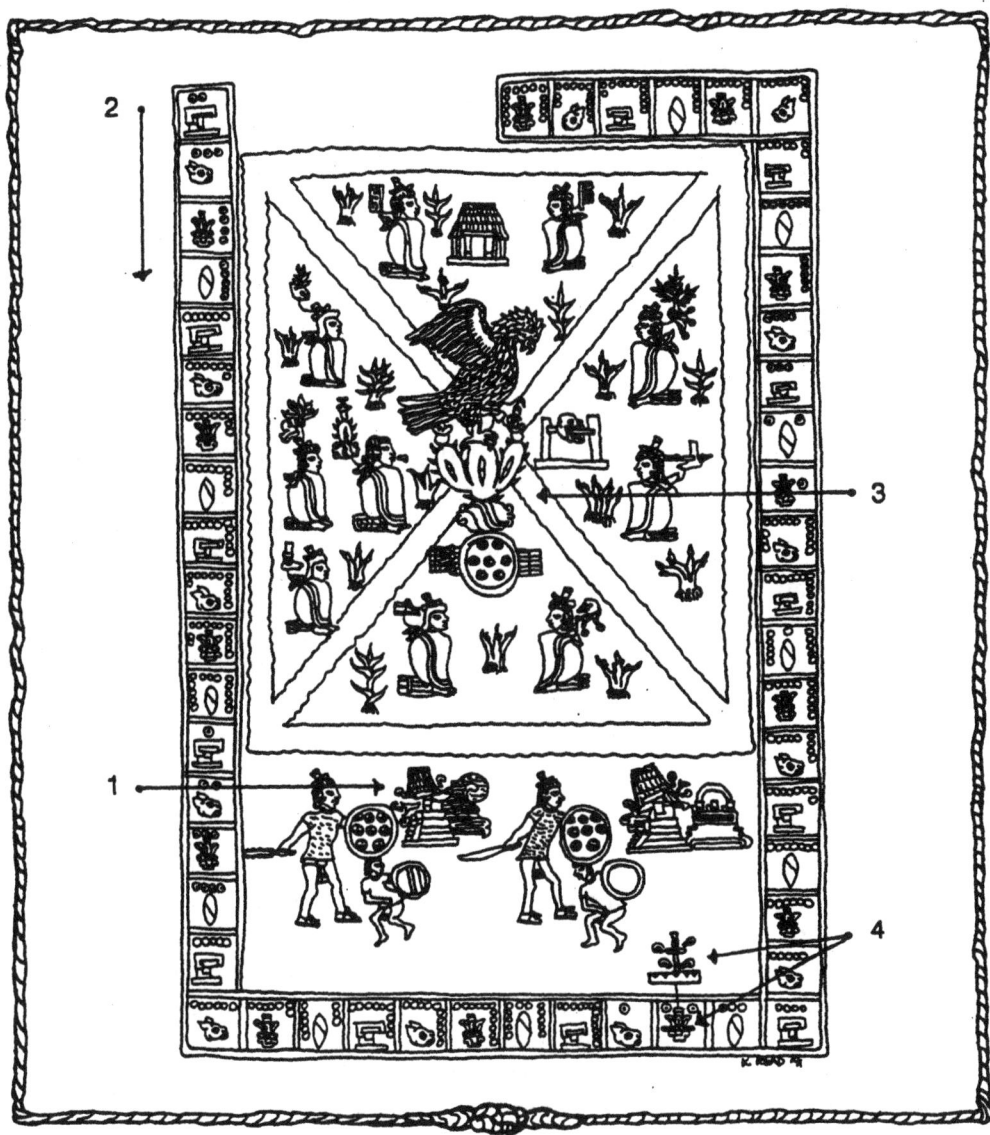

FIGURE 6.
Frontispiece of the *Codex Mendoza*, folio 2.

1. Place glyph for Colhuacan. Represents the
conquest of the city and burning of the temple.
2. Solar-year count
3. Glyph for the founding of Tenochtitlan with
Tenochtitlan's shield beneath
4. 2-Reed glyph and fire drill

The plaque conveyed cosmological messages that were crucial before the Conquest. Under colonial rule, these messages lost their importance, and efforts at precision were spent elsewhere. From the Conquest on, these texts took on a different purpose shaped by the colonists: to communicate the Indians' childlike nature and often perverse habits to their Spanish superiors and saviors.[27] This stylistic shift toward less precise renderings may have something to do with the artists the Spanish employed. The skill of these artists was not as central a criterion as it had been for the Mexica ruler, possibly because many artists had died from the ravages of colonial practices or perhaps simply because Mexica cosmological subtleties were not of interest to a European audience and, therefore, did not require skillful rendering. There is something important to learn from this. A crisp and skillfully contoured edge conveyed precise cosmological messages to a pre-Conquest Nahua audience who cared deeply about their import (even though we may not yet know the import of all this care); an imprecise and unskillful edge conveyed the childish nature of the conquered and the inferiority of their cosmos to a very different audience, their Spanish conquerors. Moreover, such messages were carried most effectively by purely visual markers that bore no relationship to either sound or speech.

The Iconographic Level

Visual forms of communication also are linked with speech. Images do not always stand divorced from other forms of expression but join with sound directly and indirectly. Such links communicate a second level of intended messages, which deepen and expand upon those sent by visual means. The pre-Conquest sculptor presents a sharp, linear quality closely linked to optical reality; such clarity, along with the plaque's symmetrical format and geometric composition, qualifies this work as writing or the linking of speech and image. Image and sound, after all, are often joined in discourse in many ways: nouns (as visually imagined objects), adjectives (visually describing such objects), verbs (objects depicted in action), metaphors (which rely on imagery), phonetic writing (abstracted visual marks encoding certain sounds), glyphs (conventionalized signs standing for spoken messages), rebuses (pictures standing for the phonetic sounds related to words), ideographs (conventionalized signs representing spoken ideas), and pictographs (less conventionalized pictures representing spoken ideas) are but a few examples. The play between sound and image in speech and writing is both multifaceted and necessary to discourse, for people encode and communicate the world through their eyes as well as their ears and mouths.

Writing in Mesoamerica used a variety of iconic devices to link speech with image. It was often pictographic. Glyphs and ideographs were common, however, and rebuses were used to incorporate phonetic elements.[28] Because of (a) their careful use of formal, compositional elements such as symmetry, (b) the precise handling of line and edge, (c) the emphasis on noun elements over verb-like ones, (d) the combination and recombination of fixed and conventionalized visual elements intended to be linked with speech, and (e) the link of some glyphs with phonemic elements in rebuslike structures, Mexica iconic texts such as the plaque may be considered to constitute a form of writing. The rope, for example, is like a noun, adjectivally qualified by the marks which indicate spinning and knotting. This image means "spun and knotted rope."

But not all of the images are as easily identified as the rope. For example, the plaque seems to be dominated by something that looks like a plant, although this is not at all certain. It may not be a plant or, if it is, the variety is unclear. The significance of the rest of the marks is even less transparent. Clearly, further information is called for. The next trick, then, is to begin the research that will lead to a translation of what the rope, this "plant," and the other carefully constructed and arranged images are saying, a task that will be continued throughout this book.

One begins the iconographic level of translation by attempting to identify as many of the images on the plaque as possible. To do this, one must search the sources available to contemporary scholars. Some of the images can be identified very quickly.[29] Eight visual images constitute the plaque's text (figure 1). Number 1, the central plantlike structure, is indeed a stylized depiction of a plant, a *reed* (*acatl*). From number 2, *one dot*, one learns that this is a day-sign because dots were used to indicate dates. And because of number 3, the *cartouche*, one learns that this date is one of the four year signs used in the Mexica calendrical system. Cartouches indicate solar years. Solar years were named by four glyphs: reed (*acatl*), knife (*tecpatl*), house (*calli*), and rabbit (*tochtli*). These four were each numbered from 1 to 13 and rotated in a sequence: 1-Reed, 2-Knife, 3-House, 4-Rabbit, 5-Reed, 6-Knife, 7-House, and so on. The single dot to the left of the reed may signify, then, that this sign is the year called 1-Reed as opposed to, say, 4-Reed (which would have had four dots arranged around the reed plant) or 13-Reed (which would have had thirteen). One knows these things because numerous post-Conquest sources explain the meaning of Mesoamerican calendrical signs and their function within the complicated calendrical system (figure 5).[30] For even though the Spanish didn't always get things right, neither did they always get things wrong.

But number 4, the *knotted rope*, suggests that "1-Reed" may be the wrong interpretation, for such ropes signified the Mexica ceremony called the Binding-of-the-Years or the New Fire ceremony, which took place not in the year 1-Reed but in 2-Reed. The rope found in the *Codex Aubin*, for example, is also situated beneath a 2-Reed sign as is a similar rope on the Teocalli stone (figure 5, A and B). The knotted rope is a fitting image to signify the Binding of the Years, the ritual that was celebrated when, after fifty-two solar years, the divinatory and solar calendars ended on the same day. It was on this date that fifty-two reeds, like the fifty-two years that had just been completed, were gathered into a bundle and bound together with two knotted ropes. Stone sculptures of these bundles often bear the 2-Reed date itself (figure 5, C).[31] One must assume, then, that a second dot, indicating the year 2-Reed rather than 1-Reed, was carved on the piece missing from this plaque.

Given this clue, if one looks very closely, one can make out number 5, the shape of a *fire drill*[32] cleverly worked into the middle of the central plant design. At the climax of the New Fire (or Binding-of-the-Years) ritual, this tool was used to spark a fire in the chest cavity of a human sacrificial offering whose heart had just been given to the cosmos to eat. This fire was the first fire of the next fifty-two-solar-year round, and if it could not be started, it was feared that a new sun would not rise and that time, as the Mexica knew it, would end. Thus, every fifty-two solar years, time was begun with a sacrifice and the making of fire. The Fifth Age itself, the age of the Mexica, was first begun with a similar sacrifice of two gods in a fire called the God Oven.[33] The Binding-of-the-Years ceremony often was indicated by a picture of a fire drill similar to the image found here in the center of the plaque. One can be seen, for example, depicted on the frontispiece of the *Codex Mendoza* (figure 6.4). And at the archaeological site of Xochicalco, there appears a glyph that has been identified as a fire drill and is very similar to the one displayed here.[34]

Number 6, the flowerlike shapes encased in the coiled motif at the bottom of the plaque, depict *jaguar spots* and may be a shorthand reference to the god Tezcatlipoca.[35] This would make sense on a plaque referring to the Binding-of-the-Years ceremony as a rite in which fire is created along with time. Tezcatlipoca not only was a major deity identified with Huitzilopochtli (the patron god of the Mexica) and, therefore, with the cosmic sun or age (Tonatiuh) of the Mexica, but also was associated with the first creation of fire itself (CC 1992a, 144; 1992b, fols. 75:45–76:18, 88). Number 7, the *coiled motif* beneath the jaguar spots, may depict a stylized vessel intended for catching sacrificial blood.[36] And, number 8, the striped square shape protruding from the top of the reed may be the top of a *sacrificial bloodletting thorn*.[37] Such thorns were often shown with stripes similar to these. Because most of the thorn is hidden from view and because such thorns are usually more tapered than this, it is difficult to be sure just what this element is. It is suggestive, however, for sacrificial bloodletting was one of the activities that took place in this rite.

Now that a bit more is known about this plaque, it can be named and at least a little can be said about it. It is a plaque depicting the glyph for the calendrical solar year dated 2-Reed and refers to a rite called both the Binding-of-the-Years and the New Fire Ceremony. Given that this plaque is dated archaeologically to before 1502, it must have been made for the New Fire ceremony that occurred in 1455 during the reign of Motecuhzuma the Elder. Mexica year dates can be correlated with our Julian calendar, allowing one to count backward from the last binding, which occurred in 1507.[38] This, however, is but a superficial translation, for some extraordinary things can still be said about this very ordinary plaque. Its complex and interwoven messages describe the creation and regulation of time and the role of sacrifice in those tasks, messages presented by the iconological level of communication.

The Iconological Level[39]

Visual signs when joined often send far more complicated messages about their shared iconic "logic." Visual spacing and grouping are, for example, crucial for translation because they mark individual images' relationships with each other. In the plaque, the shape of the reed plant along with the rope is seen as a unit distinct from the dot and the lower jaguar and vessel motifs. One's attention is focused on the reed and specifically on the fire drill because of its position in the very middle of the design. Because of this central location and its subtle incorporation into the shape of the reed itself, the fire drill quietly reminds the viewer of the most important feature of the New Fire ceremony, the sparking of the new fire itself. The rope, in a prominent position just below the reed, points to the importance of the binding of time signified by the products of the plant, reeds which stand, in turn, for the years themselves. When the nounlike reeds are visually grouped with the verblike fire drill, the whole image becomes a complex metaphor pointing to a particular calendrical date and ceremony, and as will be seen, to deeply philosophical and cosmological concepts about time and sacrifice.

In fact, this lowly little date plaque uses two images to send five key messages about time and sacrifice. The first image, binding fifty-two reeds, conveys the first three messages, which concern time. The second image, a fire drill sparking a sacrificial fire, sends the last two messages, which concern sacrifice.

In Part I of this book I discuss the first image, the binding of fifty-two reeds, which stood for the ritual occurring at the end of a fifty-two-year solar cycle, the Binding-of-the-Years ceremony. The image's first message was fundamental to Mexica thought and cosmological realities: *temporal transformation*. For the Mexica, all things constantly changed because everything moved with the powers of life. Its second message said that all things must be timed. The Mexica-Tenochca made no distinction between physical spaces and their temporal motions. Space equaled time because one could not occur without the other; time and transformation could not even be noted or counted without physical beings' transformative motions to note or count. At the Templo Mayor, the sun's motions determined the temple's shape and location, while the temple's space marked the motions of that seasonal shaping. Moreover, people, plants, even cities and ages embodied not only time but also particular time spans. For if time is an inherent part of every being's nature, every being must have a lifetime that begins and ends according to its appropriate measure. The Templo Mayor therefore grew with each ruler's life and death. The image's third message suggested that, if space equaled time, then time had to equal space. Space must shape time in concrete ways; the calendar must have form as well as motion. As will be seen, because the calendar had both linear and cyclical motions, it spun time into calendrically interlocked spirals that moved forward as they moved around.

In Part II of this book I discuss the second image, a fire drill sparking a sacrificial fire. This image stood for the same ceremony not just because fifty-two reeds were bound at that time but also because a new fire was begun that gave birth to the next new sun, hence the ritual's second name, the New Fire ceremony. This image's first message presents a second fundamental concept: *sacrificial transformation*. The Mexica cosmos is filled with living entities who must eat other entities if they are not to die before their time spans are completed. Through controlled acts of sacrificial feeding, the inevitable, transformational motion of this cosmos was ordered. Moreover, sacrifice was a morally significant yet very ordinary act. The mundaneness of this eating cosmos fueled participation in sacrificial rituals, for sacrifice was founded upon everyday experiences telling people that if all must eat, then all must be eaten someday. Because eating provided the energy living beings needed to move and because sacrifice involves eating, sacrificial rituals could make sense of, even control, the motion of consumption. Each of these messages concerning temporal and sacrificial transformations is examined in the chapters that follow. But first, those last participants in the conversation with the plaque, contemporary scholars, still need consideration.

Contemporary Scholars: Sacredly Profane Analogies

Scholarship both old and new is shaped and reshaped by the particular analogies that form scholars' visions. Contemporary investigators must take into account the various Spanish interests coloring the texts and drawings that flow out of those ancient pens. And like sixteenth-century Spanish scholarship, contemporary scholarship also flows out of pens, albeit from ballpoints or felt tips instead of crows' quills. And along with the new pens, scholars now use eyeglasses more often than magnifying glasses to inspect the resources and focus their work before drawing. Because their foci and tools have changed, so too the visions they see and draw. The charts scholars now create to map their travels into foreign lands are quite different from those of the friars Sahagún or Durán.

Of course the vistas have changed a bit as well, and new discoveries require new charts. After being lost for almost five centuries, the Templo Mayor has reappeared only recently. This stunning archaeological find is a new resource that demands new ways of depicting the ancient Mexica. But even though the Templo Mayor's new vistas create new questions and demands, visions have been transformed primarily because the scholarly analogies and metaphors that chart the Mexica landscape have been transformed. Scholars are looking at new resources, but they are also looking at the old resources in new ways.

The analogical or metaphorical thinking that informs scholarship is basic to all understanding. Many have noted the importance of visual and verbal metaphors for making sense of the world.[40] Analogies provide charts that help guide us over strange territory.[41] They offer possibilities, passageways that may lead us to understanding. Analogical interpretation negotiates between the passage well traveled and the one not yet tried, between what we think we know and what we have yet to discover or create. Without analogies, we are unable to understand anything at all; we have no idea which passages may prove most useful.

Jonathan Z. Smith (1982, 22–23) once noted that comparisons were a way to overcome strangeness, for an experience of déjà vu returns apparently unique datums back to our home territory. Hence comparison is a kind of "magic" that draws on sympathies across the ether of existence, making odd worlds sensible. One can say then that, because interpretation requires comparative thinking, understanding is a matter of combining the familiar and the strange in order to create the analogies that give structure to weirdness. But creative understanding involves the reverse as well, for any good interpretation accepts the differences, allowing them to startle us out of our comfortable sensibilities, reminding us that there still are things to learn. Smith points out the easily forgotten obvious, that all comparison is based on similarity and not identity; therefore, it involves the very difficult task of explaining why two different things should be the same (ibid., 35). In this sense, comparative interpretation should make both the "familiar strange and the strange familiar" (Read 1987a).

This tension between the familiar and the strange, moreover, is an ever-shifting process. Understanding, like the Mexica cosmos, always is transforming, spiraling from the sculptor to his audience and on to Spanish interlopers, indigenous heirs, contemporary scholars, and beyond. With each turn, new vistas appear that require new charts, which guide the traveler toward yet more vistas. The old analogical maps must be added to, combined with others, partly destroyed, and perhaps even abandoned in order to make new ones. Understanding is never a static entity; it is a never-ending process.

Interpretation, then, is made difficult not because, as J. Z. Smith has said, no Archimedean point exists upon which to stand (1978, 288), but because the points keep shifting as time passes. Understanding is rather like a traveler laboring up the side of a mountain only to see many more peaks to climb once she reaches the top. Or it is as if she sees old views in new ways because she has approached them from new directions; or she discovers that the hitherto solid mountain is really sand and she now must navigate by the stars because terra firma does not stay firm. It makes sense, then, to consider some of the charts people might draw while exploring this strange new Mexica territory, the various metaphoric visions and analogies folks might invent to transform their understanding. Smith is right when he remarks that "'map is not a territory'—but map is all we possess" (ibid., 309). I would add that ours is not so much a problem of "map" as of "mapping."

Our analogical maps may need serious (and ongoing) adjustment for two reasons: one a matter of power, the other of creativity. First, we see the territory according to our own eyeglasses, not necessarily someone else's, and we chart other people's territories using our own pens, not necessarily others'. Likewise, not to recognize the power of our own voice in a conversation is to ignore the power it has to outshout, represent, and even deny the voices of others. It is impossible for anyone to set aside easily those things held near and dear, those little and large prejudices that color understanding of peoples different from oneself, those "true" things we simply take for granted and don't bother to mark as special. At the very least, if we do not make those things conscious, marking them in some way—laying out our current map instead of hiding it in our head—we run the risk of assuming that the stranger shares our own views, is concerned about our own concerns, and should live up to our own expectations because those views somehow pen the boundaries around reality. This is the way, after all, that all scholars (like the sixteenth-century colonial Spanish) affirm their own reality and define it for those they study, how they chart existence both for themselves and for others.

For example, it may be somewhat disquieting for many today to think of apparently wildly violent human sacrifice as a moral act and, even more disturbing, as a normal form of human behavior. The feeling of horror that often accompanies initial encounters with the Mexica-Tenochca can hinder our understanding of them if our horror is motivated by a fear that understanding will somehow make the practice of human sacrifice acceptable. Often, social scientific approaches to other cultures have sought to make otherwise foreign cultural differences more comprehensible to Western sensibilities by placing seemingly strange cultural practices into the foreigner's own historical contexts, thereby making them seem more familiar, more normal. The implication of such approaches sometimes has been that, if such practices as human sacrifice are part of normal human behavior, then they must be considered acceptable. But understanding different and diverse orientations to world "normalities" does not necessarily make them all equally right everywhere. We need not view human sacrifice as acceptable human behavior in our own culture to be able to understand how it might be both acceptable and normal in another.[42]

Second, we deny ourselves the chance to learn something new if we never allow other charts of reality to challenge our own, no matter how scary that may be. If we instead allow the Mexica their own integrity (in spite of all the violence), we are freed to grasp potentially new and fascinating ideas, new ways of mapping. We need not condone violence to do this (I most certainly do not), for not all of the Mexica's ideas need be linked to physical violence. Our initial horror at the practice of human sacrifice may even help if understanding its normality in the Mexica world causes us to question the violence in our own and to ponder how that violence came to be either condoned or considered a normal and familiar part of experience. If that happens, we then might learn something useful about our own ethical and emotional limitations by understanding this seemingly foreign violence and our own horror of it. The only way to turn prejudices and fears such as these into learning experiences is to make them conscious and to examine them by allowing the stranger's voice to challenge them. Entering into the Mexica world is also an invitation to rethink our own.

The Sacred and Profane: Past Western Analogies

Although not necessarily having to do with physical violence, dichotomous thinking is one analogical map that needs major adjustments when one enters Mexica territory.[43] Dichotomous thinking offers only two options, thereby excluding a host of other possibilities. Something is either this or that, white or black, true or false; it is never gray, multicolored, ambiguous, or something else entirely. After all, one is rarely presented with only two paths to follow because there is always more to understanding than two paths alone can provide. Those paths going straight up the mountainside may be better for getting quickly to the top, a path with switchbacks may get one there more slowly but in better health and with less environmental damage, while yet another path offers satisfying views along the way. Knowledge need not be conceived only either as hierarchically arranged (with one chart more correct than all others) or as totally egalitarian (with all charts equally correct). Never is one passageway always better than all others; nor are all passages equally correct under all conditions. Knowledge shifts too much for the first and charts too many true but different territories for the second. Instead, reaching an understanding of Mexica time and sacrifice requires choosing analogies that seem to work well given the present territory as one knows it.

One dichotomous analogical map that needs rethinking is the assumption that humans divide their cosmic realities between the sacred and the profane. Although this Western paradigm has had a remarkably durable and deep effect on a wide range of scholarly travels, this powerful cosmic paradigm both ignores alternative analogies that seem more in line with Mexica concepts of transformation and produces a series of misleading dichotomies. Before the journey into Mexica time and sacrifice can begin, these old analogical maps founded on the sacred and the profane must be altered or replaced with new ones. Otherwise, ancient roads and byways hidden within the mists of our minds may give us an unwarranted sense of déjà vu; they may lead us not into new and strange lands but into old and familiar passages that, in the end, return home.

The sacred and profane dichotomy assumes that the potency of extraordinary experiences shapes people's sense of sacrality and their religious lives. These experiences often mark the sacred itself as something truly out of the ordinary. There is a long history of both anthropological and other approaches, which describe such sacred realities, ranging from Emile Durkheim's sacred objects as those things "set apart and forbidden" (1915, reprint 1965, 60) to Rudolf Otto's "non-ordinary," "synteretic," "awe-filled" yet "fascinating" numinous (1923, reprint 1979), and Gerardus van der Leeuw's extraordinary power of the sacred, a power that sits well beyond limited human capacities either to control or to understand (1933, reprint 1967). In these scholars' worlds, the sacred is never mundane, for it is essentially untouched by all that. Although humans live only in the ordinary and everyday world of the profane, however, occasionally the two realms are bridged, thereby allowing people momentarily to know and accept the power of the extraordinary. Since this cosmological division is at least as old as Plato, I focus here on only a few of this century's authors who form one scholarly "genealogical line" within the field of religious studies.

Working from this idea of the extraordinary nature of the sacred and within the tradition of Otto and van der Leeuw, historian of religions Mircea Eliade created a number of brilliant proposals for how the sacred and profane realms might be bridged temporarily (1954, 1958). At special moments and critical locations, the sacred erupts into the ordinary, profane world, paradoxically joining that which normally cannot be joined. During these events one is returned momentarily to the eternal primordium, that first time when all reality was created, thereby briefly "killing" temporal history. For Eliade, cultures mark those places in which such hierophanous events occur as the axis mundis or the stabilizing cosmic centers of their worlds. The Templo Mayor would be such a center in Eliade's eyes. People experience these world-ordering hierophanies through their own human imaginative capacities. Imagination allows people to abolish the historical, ordinary moments in order to "reintegrate the auroral moment when man [and woman] saw the world 'for the first time'" (1969, 88; 1985). Imagination bridges that which otherwise cannot be bridged.

Eliade's work has been enormously influential, prompting many creative responses and spawning numerous followers. Responding directly to Eliade, philosopher of religion Paul Ricoeur proposed another means for bridging the ordinary and extraordinary realms of the profane and sacred (1985). For Ricoeur, history itself is the link. Symbolic imagination is the route to the sacred, for it is through symbols that communication with the sacred is made possible; through symbols, one may imagine the possibilities of an infinite reality (1960, 1976). Because symbols are historically bound, history becomes central to locating the sacred. Following Ricoeur, one would judge the Templo Mayor a key symbol located in the ordinariness of a finite historical moment, linking the Mexica with their extraordinarily infinite sacred realities.

Largely following Eliade, historian of religions and Mesoamericanist David Carrasco has spun Eliadian (and rather Ricoeurian) approaches for interpreting Mexica cosmic realities. For Carrasco, the Templo Mayor was the center, the axis mundi of the Mexica cosmos, and the primary theater for sacrificial actions. Sacrificial rituals were the extraordinarily creative acts that revitalized the Mexica's mythic and primordial past, tracing back to the fabled, ancestral Toltecs. The instabilities of the historic present were temporarily abolished, and a stable hegemonic ideal of the Mexica was promoted through these rituals (1981, 1982). Via the still contested psychological phenomenon of synesthesia[44] (a rather Ottolike nonrational notion of synteresis), Carrasco suggests that sacrificial rituals imaginatively transformed current situations by joining an underlying cosmic unity to the changing realities of the present. Shifting extraordinary "local knowledges" of Tenochtitlan as they were embodied at the Templo Mayor were thus created to control the ordinary, historic present. These local knowledges themselves, however, were adaptive variations on a larger, stable, and even more extraordinary cosmic truth (1991).[45]

These authors, both current and past—anthropologists, theologians, philosophers, and historians of religions alike—assume two things: (1) that the sacred is an extraordinary, ultimate, and essentially eternal reality that is relative to but beyond the ordinary, changing, historic present; and (2) that religious knowledge and acceptance of the sacred, therefore, must also somehow be extraordinary and beyond normal human experience, temporarily linking people with some ultimate truth that defines but overreaches their mundane existence. The extraordinary takes people out of the ordinary, thereby founding their religious lives.

If we follow Durkheim, the sacred is created by people and given a transcendent, eternal authority in order to validate the ordinary. This humanly manufactured sacred creates the social unity necessary to a harmonious life whose true base is historical. If we belong to the above scholarly genealogy, however, the sacred validates the ordinary precisely because people did not create it. Whether people unite their profane society using the transcendent sacred to authorize that unity, whether their rituals and imaginative experiences belong to the a priori numinous quality of the sacred, or whether synesthesia momentarily unifies divided worlds, what a person does at the Templo Mayor in a sacrificial rite is external to and beyond the radically differentiated flow of everyday life.

But such divisions between the eternally spiritual sacred and the historically concrete profane create a dualism that denies two things important to the Mexica cosmos. For the Mexica, the sacred realm (1) is the *same* as the profane realm of human existence; and (2) itself involves *change* and *transformation* and therefore cannot be described as eternally timeless. We must abandon the chart that draws the sacred in contradistinction to the profane in order to understand the Mexica world. Instead, we need to consider an alternative analogical map that challenges a number of other dichotomous patterns of thinking.

The Biologically Historical: Physically Transformative Analogies for Mexica Worlds

Biology and a related sense of history seem to provide better places to look for analogies. Mexica stories, myths, and poetry speak not so much of a realm beyond the here and now, of some eternal reality that transcends the historically shifting everyday, but more of life as we know it, of life in all its physical ordinariness, life with all its fluctuations, switches, apparent repetitions, and the common necessities that result from the ebb and flow of existence on earth's surface. Transformative change is a biological process, inextricably embedded in all living matter, which for the Mexica included everything from humans to the mountains on which they walked.

One form of this biological analogy appears based in a kind of Mexica "genetics." Although this genetics is distinctly Mexica, it may be understood better if one thinks of some basic human experiences; a sense of déjà vu might indeed help here. Within the lifetime of every individual, enormous changes take place. I was born as a baby, have changed greatly in form, am growing old, and will die—this in spite of all the food I eat, food that comes from the unavoidable killing of other life forms. In the end, all rots and disappears except for my bones, and even those disappear given time.

Questions about change easily arise from these simple but intensely familiar experiences, questions whose answers may not be as immediately recognizable as the experiences themselves. Am I the same person at death as I was at birth? If I change so much, why should anything else stay the same? Moreover, I am not alone in these processes of change, for the experiences have been shared by my ancestors. My mother, father, grandmothers, grandfathers—the people from whose bodies I emerged—all were subject to the same processes of birth, change, consumption, decay, and death. As they rot and disappear, I am born from them and give birth to others, only to rot and disappear in turn. What do I make of these continuous patterns of change, these apparently everlasting processes of creation and destruction?

First, the Mexica seemed to answer these questions in two often related ways, one physically sexual and ancestral, the other physically destructive and corruptive. Both appear "genetic" because in both change is generative. Whether birthing or rotting, engendering or demolishing, one stage creates the next. The first answer draws on images of sexuality and its result, ancestry, to describe transformative change. Things are created sexually and therefore stand as heirs to one another. The second, destruction and corruption, draws on images of eating, decay, and death. Change occurs because things eat and destroy each other in order to live and grow, decay as they age, and eventually die (in spite of all the eating) only to rot some more. Eating destroys one thing but causes another to grow; this leads to aging and death, which results in rottenness. And rotting things become the fertilizer that feeds growth in new things.

In both sexuality and destruction, change is never instantly total but occurs generatively in ancestral stages over time. New things grow so that they become like, but not exactly like their ancestors, just as a child (born from a sexual act) becomes like, but not exactly like her parents. Development continues as ancestors and heirs alike age, die, and rot. This is a very natural metaphor. Seeds rot in the ground to give birth to new plants. We can see the memories of former selves in elderly faces as the flesh wrinkles and wastes away. Even the dead decay slowly before disappearing into the surrounding ground, nourishing the plants that rise from their disintegrating bones. The sexual passing on of ancestral traits and the inevitable corruption of all genetically related living matter continually alters the faces of existence bit by bit.

As will be seen, the Mexica sun appearing every fifty-two years when the new fire was lit was not the old sun reborn again; that sun had died and now lay rotting in the underworld. Instead, it was a brand-new baby sun born from an ancestral sacrificial offering; it was given life and nourished by that offering's burnt body and was itself doomed to decay and die in fifty-two more years. The destruction of the old sun created each new one. And this new baby sun would be like, but not quite like the ancestral sun that preceded it. With genetic and corruptive change alike, no creation ever emerged from nothing; always some physical thing was changed, transformed, and ultimately destroyed so that something else could live. No living thing existed without eating and eventually being eaten. After all, biologically, growth and decay do not subsist on nothing. For the Mexica, physical birth, hunger, corruption, and death were simple facts of life.

Second, these biological transformations take place in history. Temporal change occurs as it always has, in the events of the ordinary physical world. And history, as a form of time, occurs there too. As will be seen, there is no Mexica eternal time before human historical time begins (as there is in Genesis's Eden). The Mexica age, 4-Movement (4-Ollin), was the fifth in a series of ages; time already existed before the Fifth Age came to be, just as it existed before the First Age. 4-Movement was produced by the sacrifice of the Fourth Age, and housed many diverse beings who interacted with each other. History tells the tales of these biological organisms who live, move, and die. It relates their many stories about transformation, about how gods changed into the sun, moon, new ages, and new beings; they tell who gave birth to whom, who ate whom, and how all will die and rot, only to be eaten by something else. Never, in all these physically shaped histories, does a being create something out of nothing, and never does one act alone. For the Mexica, transformation was biologically natural, historical, and communal.

The Sacred and Profane Revisited: Western Analogies to Abandon

If we replace the sacred and the profane with biologically historical analogies, we are led into completely new territory that can and should transform our old maps for understanding. Throughout this book, a number of common Western ideas will be challenged by Mexica thinking, forcing me to find English words that may not fully express these new ideas. Because the old Western ideas behind their English expressions often are so common (one might say even ordinary) that they may go unexamined, I will flag these "re-presented" words with quotation marks the first time they appear and with italics thereafter to remind the reader of their new and altered intent. One particular Western map will receive special attention because of its importance to Mexica cosmology. The sacred in contradistinction to the profane sets up a number of related dichotomous analogies that do not cohere with metaphors based on biological germination, corruption, and their historical transformation. Five analogies in particular may prove misleading. Although each of these will be expanded in the chapters that follow, it may be helpful to mention them here.

First, if the sacred is the profane, then both humans and gods are sacred. Mexica gods and humans occupy the same cosmos, along with a host of other beings, all of whom are endowed with distinctive sacred powers. This makes every profane thing sacred, for everything has power. And while the gods may hold powers not shared by all humans, they do not hold complete power over humans, and neither do any humans hold complete power over anyone else. Rulers like Motecuhzuma the Elder have special powers that allow them to carry out their royal duties; if handled correctly these powers allow a ruler to overcome potent cosmic forces, including some godly ones. But at the same time, these powers are limited to certain actions performed at certain times and cannot be used to extend a ruler's hegemony indefinitely (Read 1994a). Therefore, Mexica gods do not control the fate of humans as might an Old Testament god; all Mexica humans do much to control their own fates. Nor are there people like rulers who are totally in control.

Second, if gods are not completely different from humans because they are simply one of many kinds of beings occupying the cosmos, neither are other natural objects so different from humans or gods. Some humans look rather godlike, as do some animals, mountains, lakes, and trees. And some gods, animals, mountains, lakes, and trees look rather humanlike. Because they are related by their distinctive and limited powers, these many and various beings form a social web of communities based on their relative differences. A spring has the power to flow when, where, and for whom it wants; a ruler has to account for the spring's desires before successfully diverting its water to his city (ibid., 47, 52–

53, 56). History, then, does not apply only to humans. Rather, all the beings of these cosmic communities are in history together; they share stories about the interaction of their powers.

Third, if the sacred is the profane, there can be no eternal time before historical time. No pure being existed outside the physically historical world. Time is physically concrete, not a disembodied, abstract process, a mere idea. Even ideas cannot exist in any disembodied state; the Mexica never knew Plato.

Fourth, if all is embodied (including time), then life's many bodies must constantly change. Old forms must continually die to create new forms. Therefore, life is not opposed to death. In the Mexica world, life existed *because* of death. Without the death of old bodies, the corruption and destruction of previous forms, new bodies could not be born. Both sexuality and death create ancestral heirs.

Fifth, because no sacred eternal world exists beyond the physical profane world, all morality, all good and bad must be embodied in the physical. Good, then, is not opposed to evil, especially any idea of nonmaterial spiritual goodness versus physically embodied evil. Because there is no option beyond the physical, the world as one knows it embodies both. All things are both good and bad. The beings of this cosmos include within their bodies both desirable and undesirable possibilities, both joy and pain, just as they embody both life and death.

The Sacred and Profane Sacrificed: The Power of the Ordinary for Both Worlds

Abandoning inadequate maps opens us to new vistas, new possibilities, things from which we may learn. The Western cosmic dichotomy of the sacred and profane is challenged on some root levels by Mexica territory, a challenge that may ask the traveler to remap her own existence at a deep level. For example, if ideas cannot exist in any disembodied state, then all ideas must be embodied within particular contexts and remain subject to transformation. If the sacred equals the profane, if the spirit is the *same* as the body, then the mind, reason, and logic are not separate from the mundane, material world. Form equals its content, which continually changes with its physical form. The Mexica knew their cosmos through its physically living objects; concrete things like architecture, paintings, sculpture, costumes, dance, and song described its momentary realities via potent images of sex, birth, eating, growing, aging, dying, and rotting. These images or embodied ideas transformed because they embodied distinct powers. No grand reason, no great rationality existed beyond their physical histories.

A few readers may find these suggestions lacking in coherency as defined by Western dualist theories on epistemology, which distinguish reason from matter and conception from perception. I, however (along with Mark Johnson [1987, 1993] and apparently in line with the Mexica), see reason and knowledge as thoroughly embedded in changing, material things; knowing is more a matter of making analogical and metaphorical maps than the classical Western view paints them. Allowing an interplay among physical, social, and cosmological realities, people order their worlds by conveniently creating frames for particular circumstances, telling stories, synthesizing images, and continually shifting their positions and metaphorical maps with changing realities. If we follow this view of epistemology—one that is well documented by cognitive studies (Johnson 1987, 1993; Lakoff 1987)—we are not limited to any one approach to interpretation. This is good, for no single view can ever hope to describe adequately any situation as complex as that of Mexica-Tenochca time and sacrifice. For the Mexica also created frames, told stories, synthesized images, and shifted all those around when new charts were needed.

Such historically based ideas are not unheard of in the West, for some contemporary scholars hold nondualist, transformative epistemological visions as well. Theologian Lynda Sexson (1992) suggests that all one's knowledge and understanding of anything true or real are inextricably bound with the ordinary things of one's life.[46] Birth, death, creation, love, pain—all truths are embodied in objects such as old postcards from an aunt, one's dreams, dry cow bones a child finds to play with, rosary beads gotten at a first communion, and the dishes belonging to a spouse who has passed away. Likewise for the Mexica, sacrality rests in things like corn tortillas, the motions of celestial objects, rocks, trees, mountains, human hearts and livers, and salamanders living in swampy basins.

In keeping with Johnson and Sexson, I suggest that the Mexica need to be understood through eyeglasses very different from those used by Eliade or Ricoeur. The cosmic charts belonging to those scholars depict change as historically bound, mere shadows of or variations on some extraordinary, primordial, symbolic, or ultimately true "theme."[47] But if one can know only through changing realities, then one may believe that reality itself is changing, that the themes of reality also change, no matter how paradigmatic they may be for particular moments in one's life.

The broad differences between the visions of change (and by inference their interpretations of the Mexica) belonging to the line of religious scholars discussed above and my own can be described as between a string of beads in which the beads periodically change as they are added but the string stays the same (theirs), and a spiraling thread in which new threads and knots are continuously being dropped and added (mine). Theirs is like the rather unnatural genetics of cloning, where an organism is a historically molded variation of the same, never-changing genetic code. Mine is like natural genetics where stock may change radically over time and no offspring ever looks exactly like its ancestors, something compatible with the biologically minded Mexica. In the first, a single melody is varied but never so much as to lose its original integrity, a vision of change that gives continuity a static sense of unity. In the first, as well, only a single tune may be varied; there is a unity to continuity. In the second, many tunes are played simultaneously, varied over time. They connect and disconnect to construct ever-developing patterns, like genes linking and not linking to give birth to new children whose traits are like, but not like, those of their ancestors. Here, the presumption of change (either slow or rapid) exists at even the most fundamental levels, something I believe is inherent in Mexica calendrics.

In theirs, change is limited to periodic, surface novelty. In mine, a creativity occurs at all levels, something I find expressed in the Mexica's all-pervasive metaphor of sacrifice. In theirs, change is given authority by a structural stability that stimulates creativity. In mine, change itself is the fundamental, authoritative, creative structure, something coherent with the emphasis on transformation that many Mesoamericanists now recognize as basic to that culture. Theirs contrasts the ordinary and the historically timed with the extraordinary and the eternally timeless, while mine describes reality in a *completely different* way by using a biological metaphor that stresses the motion of constant transformation; it makes ordinary, profane worlds the arena for divine action; the everyday *is* sacred.

If we envision everyday experiences of the changing world as foundational to all experiences (both ordinary and not so ordinary), as intertwined with the knowing of *all* reality, a dichotomy that makes the profane qualitatively different from the sacred is not useful. It becomes a mistake to look to only the grand rituals for the foundations of sacrifice, to ignore what went on in the house, the market, and the field. We must reorder our maps in three ways not allowed by dichotomous thinking. First, we must view human experience and knowing as shaped by normal imaginative capacities. These capacities allow us to continually (not simply periodically) interact and experiment with changing realities both large and small. Second, we must recognize that if human existence is molded by ever-changing, multiple realities embedded in the ordinary experiences of the historical world, then ultimate truths also can be viewed as both ever-changing and embedded in the mundane. Nothing can exist totally outside of the ordinary because everything is somehow intertwined with it. Heaven and hell do not exist, only ever-changing skies above our heads and the rocky, sometimes slippery mountains on which we trudge. And third, if the ordinary is spun together with everything, it must be extraordinary. The skies, the mountain, the path, ourselves, and even our ordinary little maps are all sacred. As will be seen, the Mexica sacrificial world rested in quotidian experiences; sacrifice's power was the shifting of the everyday.

Differences between the above scholarly genealogy and my own thinking, in both how we approach our studies and how we understand the Mexica, may be described not as variations on a shared theme of change but as changes on the core theme itself. We are similar in that we all are concerned with the nature of religious imagination, how knowledge is mapped, and how the reality of change itself may be explained—indeed my scholarly world, at least in part, has been given birth by theirs. But at base, my approach is fundamentally different from theirs and sometimes even opposed.

The profane can be seen as sacred for a Western scholar if she entertains the possibility. We too might see the primordium as ever changing and ever present, a creative and experientially real paradox in which the only unchanging reality is change itself. For example, the unifying capabilities of synesthesia can be contested, for the input from one sense can vie with or even cancel out another. What we hear, smell, or feel can distract us at any given moment from what we see.[48] This makes the process of analogically mapping foreign territory no simple thing, yet it is all we've got to shape our shifting knowledge of reality. It appears that we cannot know anything without the alterations of history any more than the Mexica can. Confronting what the Mexica seem to be saying can help us to take a second look at our own world, to reshape our previous perceptions into new ones, "sacrificially" transforming our old dualistic charts into new and potentially more complex and (I think) more interesting paths to follow.

With the present conversation outlined and its several conversants briefly described, it is time to turn our visions backward from the present, backward from the date 2-Reed, from the year 1455, back toward the beginning of the age whose years that ceremony bound together. It is time to consider fully how and why reeds were bound, what it meant to live in a cosmos where time and space were spun into one single entity and set in motion in a place where things constantly and systematically transformed themselves, and what all that meant for people.

PART 1

BINDING REEDS

Paradigms of Temporal Transformations

Binding the Years

1. One always would go to find it at that time on top [of the mountain], when our years were bound for us. 2. One would come to the [year] 2-Reed. 3. That is to say, indeed one then arrives [when] fifty-two years are completed. 4. Indeed then, [the years] pile up; they join together; they meet each other. 5. [The sun] circled around the four directions for thirteen years [each] as they were named. 6. Thus it is said [that] then they were bound. 7. They were bound for us. 8. Once again they took hold of the years for the first time. 9. In this way, it was indicated when the years were going to sprout. 10. All people took hold of them. 11. Thus once again, immediately there, they begin yet another fifty-two years. 12. Like so 104 years will arrive. 13. It is called one whole old one when two times they circle around, when two times they meet each other at the Binding of the Years place. (FC, bk. 7, pt. 8, fols. 242v–243r, chap. 9:25)

TIMING SHAPES

The fire drill, sparking its little flame in the center of the 2-Reed plaque (figure 1.5), recalls an event that came before all other years named 2-Reed, an event coming before all previous New Fire ceremonies. It recalls that mythic moment in which fire was sparked for the first time in the Fifth Sun at a place called Teotihuacan. This was an event of great magnitude, the making of a whole new age out of a god-built fire. The production of this fire and the sacrifices that took place in it created the Fifth Sun, the age belonging to the Nahua. And all the fires which followed it every fifty-two years thereafter continued that age by extending its life with new rounds of solar years. This cosmically significant event grew out of a sense of the unity of space and time.

The fact that space equaled time created the transformative process out of which all was born and into which all died: ages, food, people, cities, and gods. This fact of spatio-temporal unity and its metaphors for transformation are the topics of this chapter. First, the sixteenth-century Mexica story telling about a transformational culinary moment in which the Fifth Sun was born will be explored because this myth's rich repository of metaphors illustrates the biologically historical nature of Mexica "space-time." This story tells its listeners that the Fifth Sun was born at the ancient city of Teotihuacan (ca. 200 B.C.E.–650 or 750 C.E.). That great urban and cosmological center provided a highly influential paradigm after which many other Mesoamerican cities modeled themselves, including the Mexica's own Tenochtitlan (ca. 1325–1521). Second, therefore, Teotihuacan will be examined for its architectural melding of terrestrial and celestial motions equating time and space. Third, a look at nine chronologically arranged myths, beginning with the four previous ages and ending with the Fifth Sun's future demise, will further reveal the richness of the Mexica conceptions. Finally, these stories and storied cities will be used to give depth to the Mexica fundamental logic of transformation. For *space-time* transformed the Mexica world, structuring and restructuring everything from people to cities.

Birth Story: The Birth of the Fifth Sun

The story telling how the Fifth Sun was born can be found in Sahagún's *Florentine Codex* and in "The Legend of the Suns," (FC, bk.7, pt. 8, chap. 2:3–9, app. 42–58; CC 1992a, 147–49 or 1992b, fols. 77:27–78:23, 90). Although both were preserved in their original Nahuatl, Sahagún's version is particularly exciting, skillfully presented and rich in details; it hints at a traditional storytelling style that now is largely lost.[1] Prior to the Conquest, Nahua oratory and narrative skills were highly developed. Because the orations were inherently religious, however, the Spanish moved to stamp them out. Yet people such as Sahagún and others recorded a variety of Nahua orations by using the Roman alphabet and sixteenth-century orthographic conventions.

While it is fortunate that much was saved in this manner, these conditions of collection also pose problems for scholars today,[2] not the least of which is the nearly total loss of the tradition's ritualistic and oral elements. Understanding the scripted version of this once orally transmitted story is a bit like trying to understand an opera without the music, the singers, the staging, or the audience. All that is left is the written words of the libretto. Only one's imagination can flesh out the experience that once was.[3]

Picture, then, a man surrounded by a group of people including, quite possibly, a number of children. He may be holding a painted manuscript folded like an accordion.[4] With each new development in the plot, a new picture is pointed out. Or, in the case of the story of the Fifth Sun, he may be accompanied by the rhythmic beating of drums, bells, and rattles as he sings the well-practiced phrases, pounding out the strong rhythm with his own dancing feet. Surely he would have embellished his presentation with his own personal style, tailoring his performance to this particular audience. One can imagine this songster captivating his listeners by dexterously manipulating Nahuatl's rhythms; drawing them into the story by switching to the present tense when the action gets exciting; and artfully painting verbal pictures for them, metaphors describing each scene, giving it depth and meaning. Although the event is gone, many of the images remain, like puzzling little arrows pointing to deeply buried messages, like small clues hinting at rich philosophical treasures.

Vivid mental pictures constituted the very heart of Mexica-Tenochca religious life. Analyzing the logic of these forms helps us reconstruct important temporal and sacrificial concepts, so we will revisit key myths along with the 2-Reed plaque.[5] But first, the story about how the Fifth Sun or Age[6] was born must be told.[7]

The Birth of the Fifth Sun[8]

I.

Here it is, the story in which it is told how the	1
little rabbit is stretched out on	
the Moon's face.	
The Moon, it is said, was played with like so:	
Like so they whipped his face,	5
Like so they beat his face,	
Like so they wrecked his face,	
Like so they killed his face,	
The gods did all this.	
When later he came out, he was spread out flat.[9]	10

II.

It is said that:	1
When it was still the dark-place time,[10]	
When there was not yet warmth,	
When there was not yet day,	
They met together,	5
They all consulted together,	
The gods did all this at Teotihuacan.[11]	
They said it, they took counsel:[12]	
"Please come here, oh Gods!	
Who will carry it?[13]	10
Who will bear it:	
The warming,	
The dawning?"[14]	
And then, like so:	
He says it,	15
He steps forth,[15]	
He makes it clear,	
Tecuiçiztecatl did all this.	
He said it: "Oh Gods! Indeed I, I will be the one!"[16]	
Yet a second time, the gods said it:	20
"Who will be another one?"	

Like so, then,
    They, altogether, look at each other,
    They look closely at each other.
    They take counsel with each other.   25
"How will this thing be there?
How will we do it then?"[17]

No one was daring.
No other would step forth there.
    All men were frightened.   30
    They were turning tail.[18]
And still, not even one man would present himself there.

There, in the company of all,
    Nanahuatzin was listening to   35
        what was being said.
Like so, the gods called to him there.
    They took counsel.
    "You! You will be it, Nanahuatzin!"

Quickly he responded to their rallying cry.   40
    He accepted it with pleasure.
He said to them:
    "Indeed, this is good, Oh Gods!
    You have done me a great favor!"

III.

Like so, then,   1
They set forth,
    Preparing themselves to celebrate the rituals.[19]
They fasted for four days,
The two of them together,   5
    Tecuiçiztecatl [and Nanahuatzin].

Also then,
    The fire was set in order,
    Burning there in the fire pit,
They call that fire pit[20] the "God Oven."   10

And he, Tecuiçiztecatl,
He was preparing himself with very precious things:
    His ritual branches were of quetzal feathers,[21]
    His grass heart was woven of gold,[22]
    His spine was of greenstone,   15
Likewise,

The bloodletting,
Blood-covering instrument was of coral,[23]
And, his incense was copal, a very fine copal.
As for Nanahuatzin, 20
His ritual branches were made only of
 green grass and green reeds,
Tied in three bundles,
 Bound bundles of nine each, three in all.
And his grass ball was woven only of pine needles,[24] 25
And his bloodletting spine was only a maguey thorn.
 He was bloodying them well with his own blood.
And his incense consisted of only scabs[25]
 that he was twisting off.[26]

For those two, 30
For each one,
 Their mountain was made.
There, where for four nights,
 They had been ritually celebrating,
It is said that now there are pyramid-mountains: 35
 His pyramid, the Sun's;
 His pyramid, the Moon's.

When they had completed
 four nights of ritual celebration,
They hurled them down, 40
They dashed them down,
Their ritual branches,
 Everything with which they had celebrated.

This was done: 45
 When it was their lifting up.[27]
 When it was just getting dark.
 They would serve as slaves,
 They would create gods.

And when midnight arrives, 50
 They arrange them,[28]
 They adorn them,
 They prepare them.

To Tecuiçiztecatl, they gave
 His tall, round egret headdress and his vest. 55
But to Nanahuatzin, they gave only paper.
Like so:
 They braided his hair,
 They bound his head with its name,[29]

His paper hair,   60
His paper robes and
His paper loincloth.

And, when midnight arrived,
All the gods made a procession around the fire pit,
   They spread out around it.[30]   65
   They praised it as the "God Oven."[31]
   The fire burned there for four days.

The gods lined up on both sides.
   And Nanahuatzin and Tecuiçiztecatl
      were placed in the middle.[32]   70
They stood up very straight.
These two together were called,
   Nanahuatzin and Tecuiçiztecatl.
They faced each other.[33]
They stood facing each other,   75
   At the fire pit.

IV.

Then the gods spoke.   1
They shouted at Tecuiçiztecatl:
   "Oh do it, Tecuiçiztecatl!
   Fall down!
   Hurl yourself into the fire!"[34]

Like so, then,   5
   He is now going!
   He will throw himself into the fire!

The fire became a heated thing,
   A thing not to be faced.
   A thing not to be tolerated.   10
   A thing not to be suffered.
The fireplace was burning well.
   The fire was going well.
   The fire was in good order.
Because of this, he was growing frightened.   15
He stops!
He retreats!
He turns back!
   Once again he goes, but:
He struggles!   20
He tries his hardest to throw
   himself into the fire!

But he dares not to approach that heat!
He retreats!
He turns tail!   25
He cannot do it!
   Four times, four times.
   He tries to do it.
But it was not possible to throw
   himself into the fire.   30
Nevertheless, he persisted four times.
   And he drew back four times.

Like so, then, they called to Nanahuatzin there.
The gods called to him:
   "You!   35
   Quickly, you!
   O Nanahuatzin, on with it!"
Nanahuatzin was the only one who dared.
   He completed it.
   His heart strengthened him.[35]   40
He closed his eyes, but not because he was afraid.
   He did not stop.
   He did not turn back.
   He did not retreat.
He simply threw himself down.   45
He hurled himself into the fire.
   Like so it goes well!

Like so, then, he burns.
   He blossoms.[36]
   His flesh sizzles.[37]   50
And when Tecuiçiztecatl saw him burning,
He hurled himself after him.
   And they say,
   It is said that,
Then an eagle also rose out of   55
   the fire after them.
   He threw himself into the fire.
   He hurled himself into the fire.
The eagle is arranged well
   everywhere because of this.   60
   His feathers are darkened.
   They are smoky.
But the jaguar was last.
Then the fire was no longer very well arranged.
   He fell.   65
Like so,

He was barely burned,
He was burned just a little,
He burned here and there.[38]
The jaguar was not arranged completely.   70
Because of this:
    He was painted.
    He was sprinkled with black soot.
    He was spattered with black soot.

It is said that because of those things:[39]   75
    The traditional words spread out there,
    They were considered there.
In this way,
    He who was brave was named.
    "Eagle-Jaguar" was his name.   80
    That one, the eagle, came first.
It is said,
They say that:
    This is because he went first into the fire.
But the jaguar is only last.   85
    Therefore they say it [as one word]:
        "Eagle-Jaguar."
Because of these things, the jaguar fell into the fireplace afterward.

V.

    When, in this way,   1
The two had both thrown themselves in the fire,
    When they had burned,
Then the gods sat waiting to learn
    from where Nanahuatzin would emerge.   5
He was the first to fall into the fire,
    So he would be the first to shine,
Like so, he would light up first.
For a long time they stretched out there,[40]
    They sat waiting.   10
    The gods stretched out there.

Then, like so, it begins.
    Everywhere it becomes red,
    Everywhere was surrounded,
    The lighting of dawn,   15
    The reddening of dawn.[41]
Hence, it is said that the gods knelt down.
Like so, they will wait
    For the place from which the sun will emerge.
It was done.   20

They would look for it everywhere.
They keep on turning around.
Nowhere were they well united.
    Their traditional words,
    Their oration: 25
Nothing which they said was good.

Some thought he would emerge
    from The Place of the Dead.
    They spread themselves out to look there.
Some thought The Place of Women,   30
Some thought The Place of Thorns,[42]
    They expected this because
    Dawn's reddening encircled everything.

And some did well,
They spread out to look for him   35
    at The Place of Light.[43]
They said it:
    "Already he is way over there,
    Already he is there,[44]
    The sun will be emerging!"   40

Their words were very true,
Those words belonging to
    Those who waited there,
    Those who pointed there.
They say that the gods waiting there were: 45
    Quetzalcoatl,
    A second one was named Ehecatl,
    Along with Our Lord, or Lord Anahuatl,[45]
    Along with the Red Tezcatlipoca,
    And those who were called   50
    the innumerable Mimixcoa,
Along with four women:
    Tiacapan, Teicu, Tlacoyehua, and Xocoyotl.

And when the sun was emerging,
    he was spreading like red dye[46]   55
He was spreading in an undulating way.[47]
    He could not be faced.
    He dazzled a great deal.
    He shines a lot,
    He shimmers.   60
His shimmering rays were coming from everywhere.
    He arose.
His warm rays entered everywhere.

And afterward,
Tecuiçiztecatl came to emerge   65
    from The Place of Light.
He could only follow him,
He came to be spread out like the sun.
    As they fell into the fireplace,
So too did they come out.   70
In this way, they followed each other.

VI.

They say that the gods talk over many things.   1
They discuss and discuss it.
    Their appearance was just alike.[48]
Thus they were shining when seen by the gods.
    Just alike was their appearance.   5

Then once again it was discussed over and over.
[The gods] said: "How will these two be, Oh Gods?
    Will both of them follow the same road?[49]
    Will both of them shine in the same way?"
And the gods all gave their opinion.   10
They said it:
    "Like so it will be, this thing.
    Like so it will be done."

Then like so, a person fled from the gods.
Like so, he beat Tecuiçiztecatl in the face   15
    with a rabbit.
Thus, they wrecked his face.[50]
Thus, they killed his face.
    In this way now,
    Like so, he appears.   20

Right then, like this:
When they were both spread out,
    It was still not possible for them to move.
    They still did not follow their paths.
They were only spread out.   25
They were only spread out on the edge.[51]

Like so, once again, the gods say it:
    "How will we live?
    The sun does not move.
Will we live a life mixed up with the commoners?[52]   30
This one, the sun:
    May he go on.

    May he be revived.[53]
    May we all die!"
Then, like so, that one, Ehecatl, did his work.[54]   35
Right away he kills the gods.
But they say that Xolotl did not want to die.
He tells the gods: "Let me not die, O Gods!"
For this reason,
    He was crying a great deal.   40
    His eyes were very swollen.
    His eyelids were very swollen.

Right then Death quickly comes forward.
Xolotl fled to the field of young corn,
    diving into it.   45
There he transformed himself into something else.
He turned himself into
    the young maize with two stalks.
This is called "Xolotl of the Field."[55]

But he was seen there in the field of young corn.   50
Once again, Death quickly comes forward,
    Again he entered the maguey field.
Like so he turned himself into the double maguey.
Its name is "Maguey Xolotl."

Right away once again, he was seen.   55
    Again he entered the water place.
    He turned himself into the "Water-Xolotl."[56]
Right away, there they went to seize him.
In this way, they killed him.

VII.

And they say that, even though all the gods died,   1
    In truth, still he did not move.
[It was] not possible for the Sun, Tonatiuh,
    To follow his path.

In this way,   5
    Ehecatl did his work.
    Ehecatl stood up straight.
    He grew extremely strong.
    He ran and blew lightly.[57]
Instantly, he moved [the sun].   10
Like so, he follows his path.

And when [the sun] was following his path,

The moon was left behind.
When the sun was going to go into
    his entrance again,[58]   15
Like so, the moon came forth.
    In this way, they exchanged with each other.
    They separated from each other.
In this way, the sun emerges once,
    He takes one whole day.   20
And the moon shoulders his work
    for one whole night.[59]
He shoulders his work for one night.

Like so, he appears there.
It is said that, certainly,   25
    He, the moon, Tecuiçiztecatl,
    Would have been the sun
    If he had fallen into the fire first.
Because, indeed, he offered himself first.
With all precious things,   30
    He celebrated the rituals.

Here it ends, this thing:
    The tale,
    The ancient[60] fable,
In this way, they used to tell it,   35
The old ones whose charge it was.

This rich tale telling about the beginning of the Fifth Sun paints ornate word pictures of serial transformation. The Fifth Sun or Age is not created out of nothing in a few short moments. It is the result of a sequence of concrete, destructive events in which one thing changes to create another, each new thing heir to the previous. In these connected sacrifices, various beings are deformed and transformed into the beings that shape the Fifth Sun. First Nanahuatzin and Tecuiçiztecatl burn, followed by the eagle and jaguar. Then the two suns that arise from these paired conflagrations are distinguished from one another when the second is beaten in the face to create the moon. These ruinous acts are succeeded by the sacrifice of all the gods and the chasing of Xolotl, who changes into corn, maguey, and a salamander before he is finally cornered and killed. Only after all these wild steps can Quetzalcoatl gently puff the newly shaped sun and moon into motion on their appropriate paths; only then can the Fifth Sun move.

    These deformative-transformative motions do not occur through irrational or mere brute force but through quite ordinary, biologically based events. Admittedly, these particular experiences may not appeal to those whose selective appetites tend toward the essentially life-enhancing rather than the concrete hunger of mortality. Yet eating, death, and decay are at the core of Mexica realities, not calm or aseptic ideals of spiritual eternity that are unattainable in the gutsy crunch of physical life. Nanahuatzin, Tecuiçiztecatl, and their beastly counterparts, the eagle and jaguar, are not neatly dispatched; they are cooked in an oven, their sizzling flesh eaten by its flames to nourish the new sun (Birth: IV.1–52). Xolotl is not quietly taken away by Death; he is confronted, pursued, and cornered like an animal. And before the quarry finally is hunted down, he transforms himself into major foodstuffs (Birth: VI.37–59). Like a real physical being, this Fifth Sun is born of a well-cooked meal and must hunt its nourishment in field and pond.

Just as eating nourishes new life, so too do death and decay. The second sun is "face-killed" (*conixomictique*) (Birth: I.8, VI.19) in order to transform him into the moon. Nanahuatzin, whose name means "Honorable Venereal Sickness" (Birth: II.29, n. 1:25, 26), used the flaking scabs from his skin lesions for the aromatic incense necessary to his own ritual transformation. All these acts, while they may be seen today as overly violent, are also part of biological life, even in the present. No organism can exist without eating, none will exist forever, and when an organism dies, its remains rot and change into that which nourishes other organisms. Destruction does indeed create, even now.

This narrative's ornate images are historical and communal as well as biological. All destructive acts create the place and age, the *space-time* of the Nahua. The first light dawns in that cosmos's watery eastern sky, and the age's diurnal motions are puffed into action on paths coursing across a space marked by the four cardinal directions (Birth: V.54–56). Space and time are now on the move. Moreover, these early historical events of the Fifth Sun do not create themselves by themselves; they have help from a greater community. Actors in this drama "take counsel" and "discuss" things before they decide what to do when and where (Birth: II, VI.1–13). Only by group determination can effective action take place. Nothing ever happens because of a lone individual whose singular heroism saves the day; one cannot volunteer for glory. Group counsel chose the tale's hero, Nanahuatzin, while the self-selected Tecuiçiztecatl failed to accomplish the task he so wanted to perform (Birth: II.14–44). And even Nanahuatzin's heroism could not suffice, for he was only one part of a long process that eventuated in everyone's sacrificial death (Birth: VI.31–36).

A sacrificially destructive-creative process also patterns this book. Old ideas stressing creation above all else must be destroyed to understand how destruction creates. This new conceptual image of deformative transformation will be constructed by a series of spiraling documentations beginning with the Fifth Sun's birth story just recounted. This book's narrative will return to that narrative many times, but for the moment, a flashback is in order. "The Birth of the Fifth Sun" tells its listeners that "the gods did all this at Teotihuacan" (Birth: II.7). Nanahuatzin and Tecuiçiztecatl ritually celebrated for four nights at the city's "pyramid-mountains" called the Sun and the Moon (Birth: III.35–37). Teotihuacan's urban center created an enormously influential paradigm. It therefore offers concrete instruction on how Mesoamerican cities often shaped themselves to link with terrestrial and celestial patterns. By linking with these patterns, Teotihuacan and its heir Tenochtitlan presented *spatio-temporal* equations that made transformation a most logical deduction.

Birth Place: Teotihuacan

Teotihuacan still exists today. It lies, reduced to the dead ruins of an archaeological site called "las Pirámides," just to the northeast of present-day Mexico City. Here, rhythmically echoing the shapes of the mountains around them, two very tall, human-constructed "mountains" rise from the Valley of Mexico's floor. Even though they are dwarfed by their natural geographic counterparts, to a small and insignificant human being they nevertheless appear to loom large against the sky. These are the two mountains that the Mexica dubbed the Pyramid of the Sun and the Pyramid of the Moon in their tale about the Fifth Sun's mythic beginnings (Birth: III.35–37). The site itself they called Teotihuacan, or "The Place Where the Gods Were Created." Since the city's first inhabitants (unknown predecessors of the Mexica-Tenochca) had disappeared long before the Mexica even discovered Teotihuacan, no one knows what its original name was.[61]

As a vital urban center, Teotihuacan (ca. 200 B.C.E.–650 or 750 C.E.) enjoyed one of the longest lives, widest domains, and greatest influence of any city in Mesoamerica. Approximately eight hundred years after its decline, the Mexica-Tenochca gave the remains of this city's once-great buildings a kind of creative transformation, a new life-form, by telling mythic stories about its history. Not only did the beginning of the Fifth

Sun occur there with the birth of the two celestial bodies whose motions marked that age's temporal boundaries; Tamoanchan, the place of origin for people, corn, and the Mexica themselves, was situated there as well (CC 1992a, 146–47 or 1992b, fol. 77:2–26, 89–90; FC, bk. 10, pt. 11, chap. 29:191). Thus, Mexica *space-time* gained light after its "dark place-time" (Birth: II.2), the motion of its days, its inhabitants, and their food— all of that at Teotihuacan.

Myths were not all that gave life and form to the uninhabited but still standing "mountains" at Teotihuacan. The Mexica also directed their own paths toward the city's then desolate pyramids in order to perform rituals there; previous generations before them, after all, had put this abandoned archaic site to similar ceremonial use.[62] Motecuhzuma II, the Mexica-Tenochca ruler living at the time of the Conquest, is said to have visited Teotihuacan every twenty days (or once every Mexica month) to partici-pate in sacrifices. This same source says that on the Pyramid of the Sun's summit, facing west, was a stone sculpture of the deity Tonacatecuhtli, the Lord of Produce. In front of this pyramid, on a low platform, sat Mictlantecuhtli, the Lord of the Dead. Mexica wrongdoers were ceremo-niously punished in a great plaza between these two pyramids ("Relación de Tequizistlan y su partido," 1986, 1:235–36). Even in death, Teotihuacan was alive for its heirs.

This mytho-ritual use of Teotihuacan appears to reflect a potent Mexica-Tenochca attitude toward their history, for the long-dead inhabitants of Teotihuacan were considered ancestors. Although "The Birth of the Fifth Sun" did not speak specifically of any genetic relationship between the Mexica and their ancestors at Teotihuacan, Mexica archaeological re-mains embody it. The remains of the Mexica-Tenochca's own ritual cen-ter, the Templo Mayor at Tenochtitlan, show their ties to past ancestors. The Tenochca collected antiquities from the abandoned sites of several long-dead civilizations, including Teotihuacan, and brought them to their pyramid (Umberger 1987a). An Olmec jade as much as three thousand years old, for example, has been found buried in one of its royal layers as well as a greenstone bowl and a pottery candle holder with the face of Tlaloc (the rain god) carved on it, both taken from Teotihuacan (Bonifaz Nuño, 1981, figs. 22, 55, 78). Hundreds of other items from different ages and origins also have been unearthed from the caches at the Templo Mayor. Moreover, the Mexica did not limit themselves to collecting an-tiquities from long-abandoned cities. Copies of ancestral artifacts were executed by Mexica artisans as well. A very good Mexica replica of a bench at Tula (ca. 750–1100 c.e.), another urban center that had long disappeared by the time of Mexica hegemony, has been unearthed in the Temple of the Eagle Warriors at the Templo Mayor.

Tula's inhabitants were called *Toltecs*, but that term can take on a far broader significance than just the residents of that one city. More often, *toltecs* generically describes the inhabitants of any number of ancient cities that were in ruins by the time of the Mexica, including Teotihuacan (Umberger 1987a, 87). The deceased residents of these once-great urban centers were considered somehow ancestral,[63] and they and their now-ruined buildings took on a cosmological potency for the living Mexica. As did all ancient Mesoamericans, both the Teotihuacaners and the Mexica-Tenochca constructed their buildings in layers. But the Mexica-Tenochca buried not only the cremated remains of their own ancestral elite there but also items belonging to esteemed toltecs like those at Teotihuacan. Gathering and copying powerful objects from these desolated spots allowed the Mexica to maintain concrete links with their ancient ancestors.

Out of all these ancestral habitations, Teotihuacan played a special role. A story is told of how, before they founded their capital of Tenochtitlan, the Mexica stayed for a time at Tamoanchan, which lay close to Teotihuacan. While there, they devised the calendar, made offerings at Teotihuacan, and raised the twin pyramids to the sun and moon. Teotihuacan was so named, or so this story says, because there Mexica rulers were both elected to office and buried. Those rulers were not considered really dead but alive in some sense; some of them became the sun and some the moon upon their earthly death (FC, bk. 10, pt. 11, chap. 29:191–92). Like their inhabitants, these ancestral cities also were not dead; they too lived in some way. Their ruined, skeletal dwellings continued to house previous generations of Mexica toltecs who, having lived in earlier times, now continued to participate in the ongoing temporal reality of the cosmos (FC, bk. 10, pt. 11, chap. 29:190–92).

The Nahuatl word *chalchiuitl* (greenstone or jade, and precious) indicates some of the depth of these ancestral concepts. Greenstone refers to the centrality of history, the importance of dead ancestors, and the significance of burying artifacts and bodies in the earthly foundations of living buildings. Hundreds of greenstone items have been found buried in the caches at the Templo Mayor of Tenochtitlan, caches that also included the skulls and skeletons of human sacrificial offerings.[64] A myth telling about the creation of people in the Fifth Sun offers a hint of what greenstone may have meant. This myth relates how the god Quetzalcoatl went to Mictlan (Land of the Dead) to gather the dead bones of past people so that presently living people might be created. Those bones were called *chalchiuhomitl,* or "greenstone-precious bones" (CC 1992a, 145–46; 1992b, fol. 76:18–77:1, 88–89). Perhaps both greenstone and bones had similar ancestral potencies that were important if the living were to continue. As will be seen, both the fertile underworld and the dead ancestors had unique relationships with those living up on Tlalticpac (Earth's Surface).

The location in which all this ancestral activity took place had great significance. Mexica mythohistorical time was shaped by the human-constructed and natural imagery of archaic toltec sites like Teotihuacan. Teotihuacan's original builders aligned the city's architecture[65] so that it conformed to both the natural mountains surrounding the city and specific celestial events (Aveni 1977, 3–5). They oriented their city to mark the solar equinoxes[66] and even diverted a river to correspond to a pattern which was constructed around a major axis oriented to 15°28' east of north (the Street of the Dead). A baseline drawn between two markers, one by the Pyramid of the Sun and the other on a nearby hill, runs perpendicular to the Street of the Dead.[67] The Pleiades underwent a heliacal rising along this line on the same day that the sun passed across the zenith. Anthony Aveni suggests that Teotihuacan created a paradigm for other urban centers. The sites of Tula and Xochicalco, among others, reflect its influence (Aveni and Gibbs 1976, 510, 513).

Many centuries later, Teotihuacan's ancestral paradigm reappears at Tenochtitlan. Even though the astronomical orientations of this site are not yet fully understood, it is clear that the Pleiades and equinoxes also played important roles in Mexica-Tenochca ceremonial life.[68] In Tenochtitlan, the disappearance of the Pleiades heralded both the sun's zenith and the coming of the rainy season around the end of April. The Pleiades' constant appearance in the night sky heralded, in turn, the sun's nadir and the beginning of the dry season around November and December. Both of these contrary celestial and seasonal events figured prominently in their ritual calendar. And, although the Templo Mayor was designed differently from Teotihuacan's temples,[69] it was deliberately oriented, like Teotihuacan's, toward the equinoctial sunrise that occurred during the festival month of Tlacaxipehualiztli. For an observer situated 142 meters away at the Temple of Quetzalcoatl, the rising of the equinoctial sun was framed in the notch between the twin temples on top of the pyramid (Aveni and Gibbs 1976, 510–16; Aveni 1977, 7).

Both the Teotihuacaners and the Mexica used horizon-line astronomy to align their celestial and terrestrial topographies.[70] Horizon-line as-tronomy uses the horizon as a line or graph along which the motions of the heavens can be marked and mapped. This habit of coordinating the earth with the sky is a worldwide practice, not just Native American. But a tropical orientation, such as that of Mesoamerica, lends itself to further elaborations, which can be seen at Tenochtitlan and its toltec centers. In the tropics, the horizon line serves as a fundamental reference circle, and the sun's zenith and nadir serves as northerly and southerly demar-cations (Aveni l981, 161–71). In Mesoamerica, therefore, horizon-line astronomy provides a way simultaneously to calculate time and create spatial boundaries by directly linking localized terrains with celestial motions.

Such terrestrial-celestial intimacy creates a rationale for change that is all the more compelling because it is wholly natural. First, linking natu-ral mountains and their human-constructed echoes with the sun, moon, and stars meant that earthly geographic formations marked temporal-celestial motions. In other words, coordinating the horizon with build-ings kept track of time. Second, the reverse logic also was true: moving celestial objects marked off local terrains with their regular appearances behind particular landmarks. In this way, earthly space kept track of time, and time kept the boundaries of earthly space.

If one lived in such an environment, an environment in which earthly shapes and spaces demarcated the motions of celestial shapes and spaces, it simply would be impossible to separate time and space. In other words, that oft-noted equation of time and space in Mesoamerican thought is a logical correlate to horizon-line astronomy. If time delimits the bound-aries of space, which delimit the boundaries of time, it is but a small step of logic to see the two equated. Mexica *space-time*, then, is an inevitable result of time defining space defining time.

And if one accepts the fully natural inevitability of *space-time*, it is but another small step to see that transformation must govern all things. For if time equals space, then the shapes that occupy space must embody time as an inherent characteristic. And if shapes embody time, then all things, all shapes that occupy space in this cosmos must be timed. By their very nature, timed shapes must change and transform. The sky, the earth, the mountains, buildings, food, even people—all must continu-ally change; for all things, no matter how apparently stable in the short term, are timed in the long term.

This is why the changing faces of ancestral histories, as storied ways of timing things, delineate the core of reality; the motion of transformation is necessarily inherent to all. The buildings at urban centers like Tenoch-titlan and its toltec ancestor, Teotihuacan, depict in concrete form a naturally transformative reality, which also is narrated in the stories of their various inhabitants. The pyramids of these ancient cities are stone and mortar images of geographical, astronomical, and ancestral change; they embody a history of Mexica human and nonhuman heritage in which all things transform into the ancestors of those that follow.

The Mexica-Tenochca named the Fifth Sun "4-Movement" (Naui Ollin) for good reason. In this sun things moved, transforming continually, rather like presently living people transforming into past but still living ancestors who, at Teotihuacan, transformed into the sun and the moon, which then followed their appropriate paths through the sky. "The Birth of the Fifth Sun" and toltec celestial-terrestrial alignments are two mythic and architectural examples of Mexica biologically historical metaphors.

That buildings can be considered both biological and historical may seem odd to people living in the twentieth century. Such things generally are not considered the same as plants, animals, and humans in contemporary universes; they neither eat nor count their life's rhythms with their blood's flow, if for no other reason than that they have neither teeth with which to eat nor blood to flow. But as will be seen, in the Mexica cosmos, all (even buildings) are alive; all eat and pump blood even if one cannot immediately see that. There is no distinction between animate and inanimate. Therefore, it makes sense to talk of architecture as both "biological" and "historical."

Many more examples of biological-historical beings exist. Exploring nine chronologically arranged myths will help give living shape and form to this Mexica transformative logic. As with the Fifth Sun's birth story and place, we will spiral back to these myths again and again to develop (bit by bit) the depth and meaning of Mexica time and sacrifice, whose structures bear the same transformative logic expressed in the *space-time* of the Fifth Sun's birth among Teotihuacan's living buildings. This logic slowly emerges from the myths as entirely natural and often based on quite ordinary events like the weather, eating, aging, death, decay, and the limited capacities of gods, people, and other beings.

Nine Biologically and Historically Transformative Myths

Mythic examples of both biological and historical change abound. Over and over again, physically generative change occurs in ancestral-sexual or destructive-corruptive modes, or combinations of both. Ancestors create heirs, all of whom eat, die, and rot. Again and again, these biologically based transformations take place in history in a sequence of events that involve the human and nonhuman beings dwelling together in the Fifth Sun's community. Never is anything created out of nothing and never does anything act alone. Images appearing in the *space-time* of the Fifth Sun's birth, moreover, continue to appear throughout the sun's life.

Such biological transformations were not accomplished in any willy-nilly manner. Each thing had an allotted time or life span which needed to be completed for the next new thing to be formed. In the Mexica world, things kept on ending in order for new things to keep on beginning. Nanahuatzin's and Tecuiçiztecatl's time spans, for example, ended so that the Fifth Sun's might begin. Thus Mexica transformation can be characterized as a process of ongoing completions or "continuing eschatologies," to re-present or transform a term from Western religious traditions.[71]

Calculated, transformative endings meant that gods' and people's lives and personal capacities also were temporally bounded. While Nanahuatzin and Tecuiçiztecatl may live on in some sense as the sun and the moon, they do not live on as Nanahuatzin and Tecuiçiztecatl; those two have disappeared completely. Moreover, although Nanahuatzin was successful with his sacrificial actions while Tecuiçiztecatl (though he tried and tried) failed to jump into the fire first (Birth: IV.1–52), both gods were transformed. In their limited lives, people and gods sometimes succeed and sometimes make mistakes, some of which are irreparable as was Tecuiçiztecatl's. Yet transformation is nonetheless inevitable. Beings are seen as capable of neither preventing their own deaths nor assuring success during their life spans. They are unable to alter the fact of their own ends; their lives, in due course, will be completed, for they too are timed regardless of how well they perform. In the end, the wise and the foolish alike will become ancestral to new beings who appear from their transformed and vanished bodies.

These chronologically arranged myths describe a series of transformative moments bounding the edges of Nahua and Mexica history. Five of the nine come from "The Legend of the Suns,"[72] a rich Nahuatl text that moves from cosmic beginnings and endings to the beginnings of the Mexica and other people living in the current sun.[73] The legend's structure will help organize these nine myths. But because of its length and richness, one story from another source will be substituted for the legend's rather brief version of the same, and four more will be added to the set in order to complete what the legend only begins. Stories from the legend will tell how the first four suns were begun, how fire was created, and how the first couple was turned into dogs (*chichime*). Then, with the telling of how bones were stolen from the land of the dead and turned into people and how corn was stolen from the Mountain of Produce, the legend relates how the Fifth Sun was born, what earlier generations did, and finally, how the Mexica-Tenochca rulers arrived. Fray Diego Durán helps fill out this picture of the Mexica by telling how the greatest of those rulers, Motecuhzuma I, returned to the Mexica place of origin in Aztlan to learn of the Mexica's future demise. Finally, the Fifth Sun's demise is predicted in a short verse found in a companion text to the legend. This set of nine begins where "The Legend of the Suns" begins, by first telling how the four suns preceding the Fifth lived and died.

1. The Four Suns[74]

I.

Here is the wise, traditional tale.[75]	1
It was done long ago in this way.	
They divided the earth into one portion each.	
They apportioned it.	
In this way, it began.	5

Thus it is known how all those things originated.
Everything existed as the Sun's time and place
    for 2,513 years.
Now, [the tale] is recounted
    on the 22nd of May, 1558.[76]   10

This one, 4-Jaguar Sun, was 676 years long.
Those who were stretched out here together
    were eaten by jaguars on [the date],
        4-Jaguar sun.

Then they were eating 7-Grass as their food.[77]   15
In this way, they lived for 676 years.

Then, like so, they were eaten by man-eaters
    for 13 years.

Like so, they were destroyed.[78]
Then, when the sun perished, their year was 1-Reed.   20

On one whole day of the sun's heat, 4-Jaguar,
    They [the man-eaters] began to devour them.
Right away, thus they went to their end.
    Thus they completely perished.

II.

This sun's name was 4-Wind.   1
These suns had stretched out two times.
At that time, on [the date] 4-Wind,
    They were blown away by the wind.
And thus they perished.   5
At that time, they were blown away by the wind.

They turned themselves into monkeys.
Their houses, their trees,
    All were blown away by the wind.
Right away then, this sun was blown away   10
    by the wind.
Then they were eating 12-Snake as their food.
In this way, then, they had lived for 364 years.

In this way, they perished:
For only one whole day, 4-Wind,   15
    They were blown by the wind.
In one whole day of the sun's heat,
    Like so, they perished.
Their year, then, was 1-Knife.

III.

This sun, 4-Rainstorm, was number three.   1
In the third sun, 4-Rainstorm, they had lived.

Then, like so they perished,
    They were rained upon by fire.[79]
They turned themselves into turkeys.   5
At that time, the sun burned up.
Their house, everything, burned up.

When they had lived for 312 years,[80]
Then they perished.
It rained fire for one whole day.   10

At that time, they were eating 7-Knife
    as their food.
Then their year was 1-Knife.
Then, the day of the sun's heat was 4-Rainstorm.
    In this way, those who were nobles perished.   15

Because of that,
   now children are called "noble ones."

IV.

This sun's name was 4-Water.   1
   At that time, the water spread out for 52 years.
Those years had lived, arranged in four parts,[81]
   When the sun was 4-Water.
At that time, they had lived for 676 years.[82]   5

Then, this is the way:
   They perished,
   They were flooded,
   They turned themselves into fishes.
In just one day they perished.   10

At that time, they were eating 4-Flower
   as their food.
   Then their year was 1-House.
At that time,
   the day of the sun's heat was 4-Water.   15
Thus they perished.
   All of the mountains perished.

Then, in this way,
   the water spread out for 52 years.
Their sun is completed.   20

This myth about the first four suns is a story about cosmic beginnings resulting from cosmic endings. It is a story about multiple transformations. Each sun's life span is carefully counted out. Then each sun has its own unique inhabitants who live in unique houses and eat their own particular food. And each sun draws its name from its own particular manner of destruction. Just as the beaten and destroyed bodies of Nanahuatzin and Tecuiçiztecatl were transformed into the primary celestial objects of the Fifth Sun, each destroyed sun transforms into the next sun. The first becomes the second, the second the third, and so on. Just as Xolotl transformed himself into important foodstuffs of the Fifth Sun, the inhabitants of each previous sun also transformed themselves into the new inhabitants of each new sun: monkeys became turkeys which became fish. And just as destruction's creative acts gave the Fifth Sun's sun and moon their characters and days to count, so too destruction gave each sun its own character and count. Each sun perished in order that the next might begin. In this way, each sun's years were completed.

Creation occurs sequentially, as it did in the "Birth of the Fifth Sun."
No mention of a time before time is made. Instead, a series of transformations occur; multiples of twenty-six count out each sun's life span.[83]
Each life is punctuated by a cataclysmic death. The first is eaten; the
other three are blasted into disarray by wind, volcanic action, and flood,
all forms of natural disasters.

But these potent acts of earth and weather just happen; they are not
acts of an angry god or the result of terrible misdeeds. No great moral
lies behind these destructions. The remains of each sun simply change
into the forms of the next according to a schedule. Transformation is
naturally described and historically circumscribed, not in any way morally prescribed.

With the destructive ending of the Fourth Sun, the legend goes on to
tell what happened to the first couple, Tata and Nene (Papa and Mama),
the first people to inhabit the Fifth Sun. The incompetence of that couple
resulted in their own deformative transformation in this second story.

2. The First Couple[84]

1. With the ending of the Fourth Sun, the sun of people began. The great god,
Titlacahuan,[85] called to the first couple, Tata and Nene, and asked,
   "Children, do you want anything more?"
   "Make a very big hole in an ahuehuetl tree[86] and put us in it when the vigil
begins and the sky falls." This he did. And when he was finished he told them,
   "You will have one cob of corn each to eat. When you have finished all the
kernels, then you will see that the water is all gone and that your ahuehuetl
trunk has stopped rocking."

2. When the corn was gone and the ahuehuetl trunk had stopped rocking,
Tata and Nene emerged and found that they were saved. Using a drill to start
a fire in some small sticks, they roasted a few fish. But this was not appreci-
ated by the gods because it smoked the sky, making it black. Titlacahuan-
Tezcatlipoca bawled them out for their error. He then cut their heads off at
their necks and sewed them back onto their buttocks. This turned them into
dogs (chichime), the first ancestors of all those living in the Fifth Sun.

3. The sky was smoked by these dogs in the year 1-Rabbit. Afterward, it was
dark for twenty-five years. Then [in the twenty-sixth year], which was called
2-Reed, Tezcatlipoca lit the fire drill and smoked the sky once more.

An act of decapitation creates the ancestors of all those living in the
current sun. As in the previous two myths, they were created out of the

remains of what was there before, in this case, the rearranged and transformed bodies of the first parents. These new ancestral beings were constructed by sewing the first couple's heads onto their old bodies, if not
onto the wrong end, then at least onto a different end. There was no
glorious reason for this reshaping. It was brought on by a childish error,
reminding the listener that all Nahua, like their ancestors, are limited by
their own small capacities.

Still, even though it be done badly, the Mexica, like their ancestral
parents, must eat, and to eat, one must have fire. These insignificant,
misbehaving dogs created the situation that created a most significant
event, the first fire that started the count of the Fifth Sun. Hereafter, every
fifty-two years (2 x 26 years) in the year 2-Reed, people will blacken the
skies again in order to create a new sun. In a fire begun with a small drill
such as that used by Tata and Nene, a sacrificial offering will be roasted
(as were their fish [myth 2: 2]) so that a new sun may be nourished and
people may continue to have food to eat. Thus the New Fire ceremony is
born, creating a series of destructive events that transform the age and its
succession of suns so that all can continue to eat and live, so that the
Fifth Sun and all its inhabitants will not die before their time.

In the following story, similar themes of destructive transformation and
incompetence can be found. Here it is told how Quetzalcoatl went to
Mictlan (Land of the Dead) to collect the bones kept there by Mictlanteuctli
(the Lord of the Dead) and Mictlançihuatl (the Lady of the Dead). This
third story says that in spite of Quetzalcoatl's incompetence, these bones
were transformed into the residents of the newly formed Sky-Water
(Ilhuicatl) and Earth Lord (Tlalteuctli).[87]

3. Quetzalcoatl and the Bones[88]

1. And then the gods consulted among themselves. "Who will be the ones to
settle[89] there?" they asked. "The sky has been spread out,[90] the earth lord[91] has
been spread out. O gods, who will settle there?" Çitlallinicue, Çitlallatonac,
Apanteuctli, Tepanquizque, Tlallamanqui, Huictlolinqui, Quetzalcoatl, and
Titlacahuan were not happy.

2. Then Quetzalcoatl went to Mictlan (Land of the Dead). Upon arriving, [he
met] Mictlanteuctli and Mictlançihuatl (the Lord and Lady of Death). He said,
indeed he [spoke] like so:
   "I have come for the precious greenstone bones (*chalchiuhomitl*) that you
are guarding. I have come to take them away."
   "What will you do with them, Quetzalcoatl?" [Mictlanteuctli] asked.

He answered once again, indeed he [spoke] like so: "The gods are un-
happy; who will settle there on earth?"

Mictlanteuctli again responded, "Oh, very well! Blow my conch-shell horn[92]
and encircle my precious enclosure four times. And may the shell horn not
have holes."

Immediately [Quetzalcoatl] summoned worms who drilled holes in it.
Then bumblebees and honeybees entered it. When he blew it, Mictlanteuctli
heard it.

"Oh, very well! Take them!" Mictlanteuctli once again replied. Right away
Mictlanteuctli said to his messengers, the Micteca (the People of the Land of
the Dead), "Gods, tell him that he has to leave them here!"

Quetzalcoatl responded, "No, I'm taking them once and for all!"

3. Just then Quetzalcoatl's *nahualli*[93] spoke to him. "You tell him that you
have left them." So [Quetzalcoatl] said to [Mictlanteuctli], he called out to
him, "I've left them!"

Quickly rising, Quetzalcoatl took the precious greenstone bones. A man's
lay in one place and a woman's in another. Immediately, Quetzalcoatl gathered them up, wrapped them up, and carried them off.

4. Once again Mictlanteuctli said to his messengers, "Gods! Quetzalcoatl is
actually taking the greenstone bones! Gods! Quickly, make a pit!" They wanted
to make him fall down.

He fell right into that pit, he whacked himself and the quails startled him.
He passed out from that fall, spilling all the greenstone bones. The quails
chewed them; they ground them to bits.[94]

5. Then, Quetzalcoatl was revived. He howled out, he said to his *nahualli*,
"My *nahualli*, how will they be?"

He told him how it would be: "Really, he messed things up. However it
actually goes, is how it goes."[95]

6. Then [Quetzalcoatl] gathered them up, he picked them up and wrapped
them. Like so, he carried them to Tamoanchan. When he delivered them, the
[goddess] named Quilachtli, who is called Çihuacoatl here,[96] ground them
and bathed them in a greenstone bowl. Quetzalcoatl bled his penis on them.
Then all the gods in that place gave them merit (*tlamahceua*). [These gods]
were named: Apanteuctli, Huictollinqui, Tepanquizqui, Tlallamanac, Tzonte-
moc, [and] the sixth, Quetzalcoatl.

7. And then they said it, "The gods and commoners were born because they
gave us merit (*otopantlamahceuhque*)."[97]

Just as were the first couple, those old inhabitants of the Fourth Sun,
reshaped by destructive acts into the ancestors of the inhabitants of the
Fifth Sun, so too were the bones of the dead ancestors reshaped into the
people living now, the Nahua. These poor bones are scattered, chewed

on by birds, ground like corn, and sacrificially bled upon before being molded into people. As in previous myths, eating appears as one of the ways transformation occurs. And just as the first couple were portrayed as children who sometimes foolishly err, so too was Quetzalcoatl portrayed as somewhat childish in his rather incompetent efforts to gather those bones: dropping them, whacking himself, and even passing out before finally accomplishing his task. He may have been clever enough to trick Mictlanteuctli in order to steal the bones, but that cleverness extended only so far. Like human abilities, godly capacities can be limited.

In the fourth story, it was thanks to this same Quetzalcoatl that people had food to eat. Again this is portrayed as a moderate accomplishment completed in spite of a certain amount of incompetence. Moreover, people (*macehualtin*) are portrayed as though they were babies who must be fed by having food put into their mouths.

4. The Gathering of Corn[98]

1. After the *macehualtin* (commoners) were created, the gods wondered what they would eat. The ant went and got a kernel of corn from inside the Mountain of Produce (Tonacatepetl).

Meeting this ant, Quetzalcoatl asked him, "Tell me where you mean to take that corn you are carrying." But the ant didn't really want to tell him. So Quetzalcoatl questioned him very firmly and eventually the ant gave in. "Over there," he said.

2. Instantly, Quetzalcoatl turned himself into a black ant and followed the red ant, helping him to carry the corn.

He carried the corn to Tamoanchan. It is there that the gods chew it up and place it on our lips. In this manner, we [who live now] grew strong.

3. The gods asked, "What will we do with this Mountain of Produce?" Quetzalcoatl wanted to carry it on his back. He tied it up and tried, but he couldn't do it.

So Oxomoco and Cipactonal cast fortunes with corn (*quitlapolhuia*). They also cast fortunes of the day (*quitonalpolhuia*).[99] They said, "Nanahuatl[100] will be the one who strikes open the Mountain of Produce."[101] They knew this because they had "opened up" the fortune.[102]

4. Immediately, the Tlaloques (the fierce rain and lightning gods of the mountains) piled up:[103] the green Tlaloques, the white Tlaloques, the yellow Tlaloques, and the red Tlaloques.[104] Instantly Nanahuatl struck the mountain and the Tlaloques snatched out all the food—the white, black, yellow, and red corn, beans, chia, and amaranth,[105] all of it they snatched away.

A godly link between this myth and "Birth of the Fifth Sun" equates human sexuality, agricultural fertility, eating, decay, and death. Recall that the Fifth Sun was born from the body of the poor and humble Nanahuatzin, whose name meant "Honorable Venereal Sickness" (Birth: II.29). This deity used the flaking scabs from his skin lesions for the aromatic incense necessary to his own transformation. It surely is no accident that only he (here simply called Nanahuatl or "Venereal Sickness"), and not Quetzalcoatl, could crack open the Mountain of Produce. That mountain held its nourishing foodstuffs as a seed contains an edible kernel. It, like the seed, had to be cracked open and shelled before it could be used. And like the mountain that he opened, Nanahuatzin cracked himself open when he peeled his scabs to burn as incense; he ritually husked himself like corn in order to prepare his edible body for the "God-oven" at Teotihuacan. For it was he who, like corn and roasted meat, would be consumed in order to create and nourish the new sun.[106] Gods and people are not so different from one another; both must eat, and both are like corn to be consumed at appropriate transformational moments. Moreover, both can decay and die.

5. The Birth of the Fifth Sun

The moment for the Fifth Sun has now arrived. The legend presents its own, somewhat shorter version of the tale relating how Nanahuatzin sacrificed himself in the fire at Teotihuacan. Here in this fifth story, Nanahuatl arrives from the same Tamoanchan in which Quetzalcoatl and Cihuacoatl shaped the ancestral greenstone bones into the age's people. After jumping in the fire, he rises to the sky. There, the old creator couple, Tonacateuctli and Tonacaçihuatl, bathe him, set him on a beautiful feathered throne, and bind his head with a red band (CC 1992a, 147–49; 1992b, fol. 77:27–78:23, 90–91). The royal tone of this particular rendition is appropriate, for now the legend moves on to tell of the exploits of hunters, warriors, and the Mexica kings. Later, the close relationship between rulers and the sun will be explored.

With the sixth story, our chronological tale of nine also moves to tales about the Mexica, although not drawn from the legend. If the legend's stories about those who came before the Mexica stressed biological patterns of transformation, the following stories stress historical patterns, for images of communal ancestry and lineage appear more frequently than those of the physically natural. As in all the other stories, destruction and deformation continue to create and transform. We begin with the birth of the Mexica-Tenochca's fatherly patron deity, Huitzilopochtli, as told by Fray Bernardino de Sahagún in the *Florentine Codex*.

6. The Birth of Huitzilopochtli[107]

1. On the top of Snake Mountain (Coatepec), Coatlicue (Snake Skirt)[108] was performing her rituals by carefully sweeping up, keeping the mountain tidy. As she swept, some feathers dropped from above. She picked them up and placed them in her clothing near her waist. But when she had finished sweeping and reached for them, the feathers had disappeared. It was in this manner that she became pregnant.

When her daughter Coyolxauhqui and her four hundred sons from the south (Centzonuitznaua)[109] found out about this mysterious pregnancy, they became very angry and wrathful, accusing their mother of having gravely dishonored them. Calling her wicked, they determined to kill her.

This really frightened the poor woman who had done nothing more than ritually sweep the mountain. But her unborn child, Huitzilopochtli, spoke to her from her womb, comforting her, "Do not fear, I already know what I am going to do about this!"

2. Coyolxauhqui led her brothers in the attack. But a traitor warned Huitzilopochtli about their plans. He told him about every movement Coyolxauhqui and her army made, about each place they passed on their way to Snake Mountain.

Just as this fearsome army with Coyolxauhqui in the lead scaled the heights of Snake Mountain, Huitzilopochtli was born. He was magnificently arrayed! He carried his magical shield, his darts and dart thrower. His faced was painted with diagonal stripes and his upper arms and thighs were striped blue. Feathers were pasted on his forehead and ears. The sole of his one thin left foot also was coated with feathers.[110]

3. Suddenly, the turquoise snake (*xiuhcoatl*)[111] burst into fire. Commanding it, Huitzilopochtli pierced Coyolxauhqui and then quickly chopped off her head. Her body fell over the edge of Snake Mountain and crashed to the ground, breaking apart as it fell; her legs and her arms each came off.

Then Huitzilopochtli charged his four hundred brothers. He plunged after them, scattering them from the top of the mountain. He chased them down and around the mountain four times. He made them turn tail. He destroyed them well (*uelquinpopolo*), he completely enveloped them in clouds (*uelquinmixtlati*) and thoroughly finished them off with smoke (*uelquinpoctlantili*).[112]

Even after all that he continued to chase them. They cried out piteously to him, "Please, let this be enough!" But he continued after them, and only a few escaped back to the south whence they came.

A magical birth that ties Coatlicue with the sky creates a lineage of power. In scenes of political intrigue and might, Huitzilopochtli vanquishes his own relatives to take control of Snake Mountain. This mountain probably was the ancestral mountain of the Mexica, for elsewhere Fray Diego Durán tells how they emerged from just such a mountain, the home of Coatlicue (HI 1984, chaps. 2:21–26, 3:3–33, 4:37–38, 27:215–24; or 1994, 2:12–19, 3:25–27, 4:31–32, 27:212–22). Many interpret this talismanic birth tale from the *Florentine* as the defeat of the moon in the form of Coyolxauhqui by the young sun-god, Huitzilopochtli. While those messages may be true, it also is surely a tale of the defeat of one lineage by another. Just as Nanahuatzin rose as the new royal sun superior to Tecuiçiztecatl the Moon, so the male lineage of Huitzilopochtli rises superior to that of the female Coyolxauhqui.[113] And because of this deformative birth, the Mexica-Tenochca lineage now is transformed into fierce warriors able to overcome many enemies, just as could their mythic ancestor.

Now that their patron god has been born, it is time to tell about the Mexica themselves. In his history of the Mexicans, Durán relates their story of emergence, which he says took place at Chicomoztoc (Place of Seven Caves). Led by Huitzilopochtli, the Tenochca traveled for many years, moving from place to place, before they settled down on their island in Lake Texcoco and founded their city, Tenochtitlan.[114] The following incident from this long, seventh tale of ancient wanderings tells how the actual site of Tenochtitlan was secured for future use by Huitzilopochtli in a second political conquest over another sister.

7. The Sacrifice of Copil[115]

1. [Early in their journeys, the Mexicans were presented with a problem]. Their god, Huitzilopochtli had a sister called Malinalxochitl. This woman was very beautiful, had a charming disposition, and was so intelligent that she became skilled in the magical arts. She was very cunning, however, and did harm to the people, causing them great fear. They suffered her presence and gave her respect only because she was the sister of Huitzilopochtli. [Eventually, however, things became so bad that] they decided to ask their god to rid them of her for everyone's sake.

2. In the usual manner, the priests consulted Huitzilopochtli through dreaming[116] and passed on these revelations to the people:
    "Your god sees your affliction. He says that his sister, with her cunning ways and bad talk, endangers you. He is disturbed and very angry to see the

powers she has acquired by illicit means. She has power over fierce and dangerous beasts. She kills all who anger her by magically sending snakes, scorpions, centipedes, or deadly spiders to bite them.

"Since she is so dangerous, and since your god loves you so much and has no wish to bewitch or harm you, he says you should leave her. After she has fallen asleep, you should depart, leaving no one behind to tell her the way."

So all of those who were not Malinalxochitl's followers went away. They abandoned her and her attendants while they slept.

3. Malinalxochitl, not being able to follow the departed Mexicans because she did not know where they had gone, went on to found the town of Malinalco.[117] There she bore a son she named Copil. When Copil was old enough, she told him the story of how she was so cruelly abandoned by the followers of her brother, Huitzilopochtli. Her son was moved by his mother's tears, and his heart was so filled with wrath that he promised to seek revenge.

Seeing Copil's determination, she helped him to prepare by inciting all the nations against the Mexicans and teaching Copil her own wicked tricks and sorcery.

4. While the Mexicans camped at Chapultepec,[118] Copil set out, passing from town to town, turning many hearts against the Mexicans, and inciting the nations to destroy them with their most fiendish skills and cunning.

But events came out exactly opposite to what Copil had hoped. His uncle, Huitzilopochtli, learned of Copil's bad intentions and warned the Mexicans. He told them that, before Copil had a chance to surround their hill, they must take him by surprise, kill him, and give his heart to him, their god.

5. Shouldering their idol [Huitzilopochtli],[119] the Mexicans successfully stalked and slayed Copil. But when the Mexican priest presented the captured heart to Huitzilopochtli, he was told to cast it as far as he could into Lake Texcoco. It is said that the heart landed in a place called Tlalcocomoco, where a prickly pear cactus sprouted out of it. It is in that same spot that Mexico City [Tenochtitlan] was later built. It also is said that hot water began to gush forth from the place in which Copil was killed. These springs are now called Acopilco, or "Water of Copil."[120]

By means of violent sacrificial acts of death, a second female line of ancestry was creatively changed into the capital city of the Mexica-Tenochca. This transformation is similar to Coyolxauhqui's defeat by Huitzilopochtli and Tecuiçiztecatl the Moon's defeat by Nanahuatzin the Sun.[121] In all three cases, past ancestors were ruined in order to shape others into the presently powerful.

Even the presently powerful, however, will eventually be deformatively transformed into the less powerful, into those who, like the moon, will not "follow the same road" or "shine in the same way" (Birth: VI.6–21). Stories about the Mexica's rise to power are balanced by another story found in Durán's history, "The Return to Aztlan." This eighth tale prophesies the Mexica's eventual demise, the completion and destruction of their own years.

8. The Return to Aztlan.[122]

1. After the king, Motecuhzuma I, had established himself in his office and was very rich and well off, he wanted to find the home of his ancestors. He had heard that Huitzilopochtli's mother, Coatlicue, was still alive and living there. Since he wanted to find her and give her a fine present, he called his associate, Tlacaellel. Tlacaellel told him that he would need many priest-shamans[123] because, according to history, this place of seven caves was very well hidden by huge rock roses, thorny and tangled plants, and lagoons with thick reed beds. Moreover, it was a place inhabited by their fathers and grandfathers, who were described not only as agreeable and delightful but also as very vicious.

2. The life in this place was said to be quite pleasant. No one grew old or tired, and no one needed to do any duties. It was said in these histories that when the Tenochca left this place, everything turned into thorns and thistles. The rocks became pointed and sharp in order to hurt them, the grass became spiny, and the trees turned to brambles. Everything turned against them, and they were not able to return.

3. Motecuhzuma called his royal historian, who told him that this place was called Aztlan. He also was told that, in its middle, there was a large hill called Colhuacan (Place of the Grandparents) that was surrounded by water. Here were numerous "mouths"[124] and caves in which their fathers and grandfathers lived for many years. There were many wonderful things there: ducks of all kinds, herons, cormorants, coots, little birds with red and yellow heads, many different kinds of beautiful and big fish, trees shading its banks, and springs of water surrounded by groves of cedars, willows, and alders. Nor was there any lack of food; maize, chili, tomatoes, amaranth, and beans could be found in abundance.

4. So Motecuhzuma gathered a quantity of mantles, women's clothing, rich rocks, precious jewels, much cocoa, the aromatic *teonacaztli* plant,[125] cotton, flowers of the vanilla plant, and the biggest, most beautiful, and finest feathers he could find. He sent his priest-shamans off with these gifts to look for Aztlan. When they arrived at the hill called Coatepec in the province of Tula, they drew circles around themselves and anointed their bodies with salves[126] so they might call down the gods and be changed into birds and fierce beasts, into lions and tigers and terrible cats. In these forms, they arrived on the banks of the place of their ancestors. There they changed themselves back into human beings.

5. A number of people of the earth were there fishing from their canoes and farming. Upon encountering them, these strange people of the earth asked in the Mexica-Tenochca's own language what the newcomers were doing there.

"Sirs, we are from Mexico and we have been sent by our lords to look for the place of our ancestors."

"Whom do you worship?"

"We worship the great Huitzilopochtli. The great Motecuhzuma and his associate, Tlacaellel, have sent us to search for the mother of Huitzilopochtli, whose name is Coatlicue, and for the place of our ancestors, which is called Chicomoztoc (Place of Seven Caves). We have presents for her, if she still lives, and if not, for the fathers and tutors who served her." The people told the Mexicans to wait and then went to the tutor of Huitzilopochtli's mother.

6. "O venerable sir, some people have arrived at the shore who say they are Mexicans sent by a great lord called Motecuhzuma and another called Tlacaellel. They say they have gifts for the mother of their god, Huitzilopochtli, and that they have been sent to present them to her personally."

The ancient one replied, "It is good they have come. Go back and bring them here."

7. So in canoes they were brought to the island. There they went to the foot of the hill of Colhuacan, where the house of the ancient one stood. It is said that in the middle of the top of this hill there was a tiny sandy spot that could not be mounted because it was so soft and so deep.

"O venerable aged one and sir, here we have arrived, your servants, at the place where your word is obeyed and the desires of your mouth are revered."

"It is good you have come, my children. Who has sent you?"

"We have been sent by Motecuhzuma and his associate, Tlacaellel, whose other name is Cihuacoatl."

8. "Who is this Motecuhzuma and who is Tlacaellel? No one by those names left here. Those who left here were called Tezacatetl, Acacitli, Ocelopan, Ahatl, Xomimitl, Ahuexotl, Huicton, and Tenoch. These seven[127] went out as leaders of each *barrio* (group or neighborhood). Four marvelous tutors of Huitzilo-pochtli also left here who were called Cuauhtloquezqui, Axolohua, and two others."

"Sir, we must confess that we do not know these gentlemen. We have never seen them. We have only a memory of them, for they have died. I have heard them mentioned."

9. The ancient one was amazed. "O lord of the born! What killed them? Why are all of us whom they left behind still living? Why has none died? Who are those that live now?"

"We are their grandsons."

"Who then is now the father and tutor of Huitzilopochtli?"

"A great priest whose name is Cuauhcoatl."

"Have you spoken with Huitzilopochtli?" the ancient one asked.

"No, we were sent by our king and his associate."

"When will Huitzilopochtli return? He told his mother that he would, and the poor woman spends each day waiting and crying with no one to console her."

"We only have been sent by our lords. But we have a present for the great lady, and we would like to give it to her and bring her our greetings. We want to bring her the loot and riches that her son enjoys."

"All right then, get it and follow me." And he moved off with such great agility that they had difficulty in keeping up with him.

10. When they reached the sandy place at the top of the hill, the Mexicans sank into it, first to their knees and then to their waists, as they struggled forward. Finally, they could not move.

The old one returned to where they were stuck and asked, "What have you been doing, Mexicans? How have you made yourselves so heavy? What do you eat there in your country?"

"We eat the food that is grown there and we drink cocoa."

"These foods have made you heavy. They do not allow you to visit the place of your fathers and they have resulted in death. And these riches that you carry, we don't use them here. We are poor and simple folk. Now, give them to me and wait while I go and see if the lady of this house, the mother of Huitzilopochtli, will see you." He took their ample gifts, carrying them on his shoulders as though they were no more than a tiny straw, and climbed the hill with ease.

11. When he returned they were able to continue to the top because they were no longer weighed down by all their goods. There Coatlicue appeared. She was a lady of great age, her face was blackened, and she was as ugly and dirty as one could imagine. Crying bitterly, she said, "It is good that you have come, my children."

Full of fear and trembling, they replied, "Great and powerful lady, we have been sent by our lords and your servants, the king, Motecuhzuma, and his associate, Tlacaellel Cihuacoatl, to search for the place where our ancestors lived. We bring you kisses for your hands. Motecuhzuma is not the first king. The first was Acamapichtli; the second, Huitzilihuitl; the third, Chimalpopoca; the fourth, Itzcoatl; and Huehue Motecuhzuma (Ancient Motecuhzuma) is the fifth, and he remains in your service.

12. "These four previous kings have suffered much hardship, hunger, and work. They paid tribute to other provinces, but now they have their own city and are prosperous and free. They have opened roads to the seacoast and all of the earth. And now Mexico is the lord and prince, the head and queen of all the cities. They have discovered mines of gold and silver and of precious rocks, and they have found the house of rich feathers. And as you can see, we have been sent with these things, which are the goods and riches of your marvelous son, Huitzilopochtli, who is brave and strong with a good head and heart, the lord of the born and of the day and the night. And with these gifts, we have completed our mission."

13. Her weeping somewhat assuaged, she replied, "I congratulate you, my

children. I greet you, my children. Tell me, are those who left with my son still living?"

"Madam, they are not of this world any longer. They are dead and we did not know them. We only have them in our memory."

Her weeping returned. "What killed them? Here all their companions are still living! And tell me, children, this that you carry, is it food?"

"Madam, it is eaten and it is drunk. The cocoa is drunk, and the rest of it is mixed with it and, at times, eaten."[128]

"You have become attached to it, my children, and this is the reason you could not climb up here. But tell me, my children, is the clothing of my son the same as these rich, feathered mantles?"

"Yes, madam. They are crafted elegantly and are richly arrayed, for he is the lord of us all."

14. "This is very good, my children. My heart is at peace. But I tell you, I am in much sorrow because it is difficult to be without him. Look at me now, a penitent who fasts for your cause. He told me when he left:

'Dear Mother, I will be gone only as long as it takes me to establish the seven *barrios* in the places that have been promised them so that they can live on and populate this earth. And then I will return. The assigned years of my migration will expire after I have waged war against all the provinces, cities, villages, and hamlets and have placed them in my service. But then I will lose them to strangers in the same order that I won them, and I will be expelled from this earth.

15. 'I will return after that because those whom I have subjected with my sword and shield will turn against me, and I will be turned on my head, and my weapons will be thrown on the ground. Whereupon, Mother dear, I will return to your lap. But until then, do not feel sorrow. Give me two pairs of sandals, one to go with and one to come back with; four sandals, two with which to leave and two with which to return.'

16. "I congratulated him and told him that he should not linger so that the time would be completed and he could return. But I think he must be happy there, for he does not remember the sadness of his mother. So tell him that his period is now completed and it is time for him to come home. To help him remember his mother, please give him this mantle and loincloth made of maguey fiber."

17. They took the mantle and loincloth and descended the hill. When they had arrived at its skirt, she called to them:

"Wait a minute and see how, in this land, no one grows old! Watch my old tutor!"

The ancient one descended the hill; the lower he got, the younger he became. Then he turned to ascend. And as he climbed he grew older.

18. "This is how we live here, my children," he said. "And this is how your ancestors lived. No one dies here. We can rejuvenate ourselves whenever we want. Now look, your problems have been caused by the cocoa you drink

and the food you eat. They corrupt you and rot you. And these rich clothes and feathers, they ruin you. But because you cannot take this manner of attire back with you, come and take from what we have to offer."

And he offered them all the wonderful game and fruits of the earth that grew in that place. Then he gave them two mantles and loincloths of maguey, one each for their king, Motecuhzuma, and his associate, Tlacaellel. Telling them please to forgive them for they had nothing better to offer, he left.

19. They took their presents, drew their circles around themselves, and turned into the same animals as those they had come as. When they arrived at Coatepec, they turned themselves back into human beings. Twenty members, one-third of their party, had been decimated. Some said that the fierce beasts and birds which they had encountered had eaten them.[129]

20. They returned to Mexico and told their story to Motecuhzuma, giving him the gifts. They told him how Coatlicue awaited the return of her son, how his time would be completed when all the towns that he had conquered were lost again in the same order.

21. Motecuhzuma then called Tlacaellel and related the whole story to him; about the abundance of Aztlan and how their own food and things weighed them down, corrupted them, causing death. Crying because they were remembering the ancestors and wanted very much to see this place, they told those who had gone on the mission to rest and then gave them the gifts which they had brought back. Finally, they gave the mantle and loincloth of maguey to Huitzilopochtli because his mother had sent it to him.

The inevitable ending of mortal existence, the reality of ongoing death and destruction, is described over and over again in this sad and wistful story. Even when immortality is imagined, it is denied to the folks living within the temporally bounded histories of particular cities. After he leads his people out of Aztlan, they and their city, Tenochtitlan, will fail and die; then the patron deity of that city, the source of their ancestral line, will take his sandals and go home to Mama. What is biologically transformed also is historically circumscribed; what is born will die after a predetermined span of time. Their lineage, as was their age, will be completed at the appropriate moment. For the Mexica, history is all there is.

Like generations before them, they are temporally bounded both physically and in their abilities. The current inhabitants of Tenochtitlan, like Tata and Nene, are seen as though they were incompetent children who have erred. They are told repeatedly by their ancestral grandmother and her wise old tutor that they have ruined their lives by their mode of existence. They eat inappropriate foods and, like Tecuiçiztecatl, are attached to a rich life. They have become heavy and corrupted. Already they cannot move, already they are falling into decay. But sadly enough, the reparation of this mistake will not really alter much. The die was cast when they first left Aztlan. For then their time was set into motion, and what was gained would be lost in the same order in which it had been gained. Their city's rise to power was doomed to end in failure; its motion would reverse in spite of anything they might do to make things better.

The Mexica-Tenochca are allotted only a limited time. They are born, they eat food which causes them to grow old, they slow down, and they die. Then they disappear into people's old ancestral memories, changed forever. But people in Aztlan do not follow these same rules. There they can grow old or young merely by running up or down the sandy mountain belonging to the Mexica's ancient ancestors. The Mexica bog down in that same sand; they are powerless to move anywhere, up or down. And like their individual lives—lives that are doomed to destruction, death, and disappearance—their city also can look forward only to failure. It is as if the city itself will bog down in the sands of time. But Huitzilopochtli, even though he too is bound by time, can swing back and forth between youth and age; while his children, bound irrevocably to the mortal level of existence, can only progress irreversibly from youth toward age. They are mere *macehualtin* (commoners), constrained by their weak abilities and limited by the inevitability of their own deaths. It seems that although both people and gods are temporally limited, they are not bound in quite the same way.

Yet not all gods are saved from total destruction, as this tale about Huitzilopochtli suggests, for temporal destruction occurs on more than the human level. Remember how Nanahuatzin, Tecuiçiztecatl, Xolotl, and all the gods died to make the things of the Fifth Sun and how each of the previous four ages was transformed into the next. As are humans, cities, and toltec ancestors, gods and ages also are altered and transformed according to human, godly, or cosmic schedules. The Fifth Sun is no exception. As the ninth and final story tells us, the transformative motion of that age will, in due time, perish.

9. The Destruction of the Fifth Sun[130]

Like so is the Fifth Sun.	1
4-Movement is its day sign.[131]	
It is called Moving-Sun because	
It moved,	
It follows a path.	5
The old ones say that,	

On 4-Movement, it will be done like so.
   The earth will quake.
   They will be hungry.
Like so, we will perish.   10

A Logic of Destructive Transformation

The never-ending process of destructive transformation is a logical
result of the Mexica *spatio-temporal* equation. All living beings must
perish, even the Fifth Sun, because time equals space, which means all,
even the Fifth Sun, must have their appropriate time spans. As were the
other four ages, the Fifth Sun was "apportioned" and "divided"; it existed
in its own "time and place" (Birth: I.3–7). Like the Fifth Sun, gods, cities,
and people alike exist in time *and* place; they embody time. All things
must change because all things are timed.

Time cannot be eliminated from one's experience. Change is a given
reality that one cannot even imagine escaping. It makes sense simply to
live with its inevitability. We are born and change radically from infancy
to old age while our world, as we know it, remains absolutely blind to
any of our desires for stability; obstinately it goes on changing in spite of
all. This inevitability of existence's fleeting nature has implications that
may at first seem a bit strange to Western sensibilities, to people accus-
tomed to imagining an escape from the inevitable. Both Nahuatl tales
and toltec buildings send the same two messages: first, destruction is
necessary to fertility and the sustenance of life; and second, it embodies
a sense of historical *completion* that, in its fullness, is never absolutely
final.

First, the inevitability of change means that nothing can be created
without first altering whatever it is being made out of. As I write these
words, I alter the appearance of my computer. By altering its appearance
I also add meaning to its identity with my words; a dark or blank screen
means something different from one with my pictured speech visible on
its surface. And by continually using this machine, I slowly wear its parts
down, eventually bringing about its demise. Even the birth of a child
alters its mother. Her pre-child form disappears, and in our unfortunate
age of revering youthful beauty, some even think her previously virginal
shape has been "destroyed." To make anything, one must change the
concrete materials of the physical world, transforming whatever shapes
were there before.

Mythically rich Nahuatl metaphors suggest a similar process of transformation. Each story forms its imagery around the natural events that move one from birth to death and disappearance. Even the current sun, the Fifth, is slated to disappear, its name derived from its own inevitable future tragedy; the Fifth Sun, called 4-Movement (*4-Ollin*), will collapse in the trembling motion of earthquakes. What began at Teotihuacan in time would end by destruction; the current people in time also would end.[132]

Without deformative transformation, new generations cannot live. Residents for a new sun must be molded from the residents of a past sun. The Fifth Sun itself had been born from the fertile decay of Nanahuatzin's syphilitic sexuality; it was shelled like grain, roasted like the meat filling inside corn tortillas, and, finally, beaten and shaped out of the noble body of Tecuiçiztecatl.

In the Mexica world, fertility simply does not happen without things decaying, rotting, and falling apart or being smashed, broken, and killed. Before corn could be acquired, the rotting Nanahuatzin had to crack open the Mountain of Produce at Tamoanchan in order to release the many beautifully colored grains (myth 4: 2, 3). Before the greenstone bones could be molded into people at that same magical place, they had to be chewed, dropped, ground into flour, and bled upon. And before the Fifth Sun could even move at Teotihuacan, Xolotl was chased by Death, which transformed him into corn, maguey, and edible salamanders (Birth: VI.37–59). Tamoanchan and Teotihuacan are described as the fertile birthplaces for people, their food, and their age; but these cities' fertility is dependent on ruinous transformations. Birth and nourishment can result only from creative change that comes out of destructive acts.

Ruination by eating constitutes the natural part of this destructive reality. Living things must eat. It was at Tamoanchan that the gods masticated corn and fed it to people, making them strong. Why shouldn't the bones of past toltec ancestors be chewed to pieces by dark birds of the underworld? How can Cihuacoatl and Quetzalcoatl not grind them up as though making flour from seed (myth 3: 4, 5)? Eating sustains life, yet one must kill to eat. It makes sense then that people should be born of the same essential nature as their food. As will be seen, like the living grain they eat to live, people are sacrificially consumed in order to nourish other things. In Mexica stories, it is not so much that grains are anthropomorphized, made like humans, but that human nature is made like grain. Unlike much of Western mythology in which nature is reduced to humans, here humans and nature echo each other.

These biological processes are "genetic" in character. They generate all new things, procreating heirs from ancestral sources. And appropriately, such transformative acts never result in exact copies. In "The Myth of the Four Suns," each sun had a house, inhabitants, and food. Yet even though each sun was shaped from the remains of the previous one, it still differed from it. Its house, people, and food were shaped uniquely. Teotihuacan provided the architectural models for the Mexica to imitate but never copy slavishly at Tenochtitlan, and although the bench from Tula was copied precisely, it was only one element in a vast toltec blueprint. Recall also Tata and Nene, those ancient parents of all Nahua peoples, who were decapitated and whose body parts were rearranged to create the unique inhabitants of the Fifth Sun (myth 2: 2).

These genetic transformations take place step by step. Those poor old ancestral bones that Quetzalcoatl stole from Mictlan, like the Fifth Sun's sun and moon, were demolished several times over before being reshaped into people. And as with the shaping of people, it took a series of destructive acts to create the sun they lived in. Out of all these destructive and fatal acts of sacrifice came not only the sun and moon but also the eagle and jaguar (age-old Mesoamerican symbols of sky and underworld) and important foodstuffs—all things critical to existence in the Fifth Sun.

The word root *poliui* appears frequently in Nahuatl myths to describe these progressive acts of destructive creation. *Poliui* means variously "to disappear," "to perish," "to destroy," "to decimate," "to be lost," and "to fail." Many such permutations of the word are made in similar contexts. The gods, for example, were presented with a problem when the burned bodies of Nanahuatzin and Tecuiçiztecatl appeared in the sky as two identical suns, for they both would "follow the same road" (*ontlatocazque*) and therefore would "shine in the same way" (Birth: VI.8–9). To solve this identity crisis, the second sun was face-whipped (*conixuiuitecque*), face-beaten (*conixtlatlatzoque*), face-killed (*conixomictique*), and face-wrecked (*conixpopoloque*) in order to create a new celestial object, the moon (Birth: I.5–10, VI.15–20).

With these last lines, one gets the sense that "face" (*ixtli*) signifies identity or that the form of something seems to indicate its nature. By changing a thing's shape (or face), its identity is changed; by changing the face of a sun, it becomes a moon. To beat and destroy something transforms it into something new and different, gives it a new name and character. Reshaping its outward appearance alters its inward nature.[133]

Second, the timing of shapes means that nothing is ever fully finished, at least not in a Western sense where a thing stops changing. Nahua "completion" does not mean total termination for all time's sake; it means eventuality, the possibility of what will come. This implies that although the Fifth Sun will perish, something else will arise from its ashes just as the eagle and jaguar and eventually the sun and moon rose from Nanahuatzin's and Tecuiçiztecatl's ashes when the Fifth Sun was born. Indeed, it seems that no Nahuatl myth ever records a destruction without some resulting creation. And even the ruined remains of Teotihuacan live on in a transformed state among the Mexica both as a ritual site and a blueprint for *space-time*. *Completion* never ends.

All the cooking, eating, pummeling, rotting, and decaying takes place in history. It takes place in the specific *space-time* of a particular community of human and nonhuman beings. There are many brave and foolish actions, but no one acts alone. As did the gods at the birth of the Fifth Sun, they "take counsel" with one another; they act together for better or for worse. Tata and Nene smoked the sky together. Quetzalcoatl could not create people by himself; he needed Cihuacoatl to mold the bones into the edible human forms they were to become. Nor could he crack open the Mountain of Produce without Nanahuatzin's help. Huitzilopochtli was a singularly powerful warrior, but even he did not triumph without conspiring with a friendly traitor. And as the Templo Mayor at Tenochtitlan so boldly notes, Huitzilopochtli's temple must share this ritual mountain with Tlaloc the rain god.

Nothing can prevent a being's demise, no matter whose community it belongs to or what it does. Mere status or wealth cannot prevent a destructive end. The high-born Tecuiçiztecatl, with his excellent and noble ritual paraphernalia, became only the second sun, the pale moon. His old face was now gone, and a lesser one than he had hoped for was in its place because he had "completed" (Birth: IV.39) his task less well than Nanahuatzin. The jaguar also was "not arranged completely" as was the eagle (Birth: IV.70); he was marked unevenly in a fire that no longer burned well. If one fails properly to *complete* the tasks of one's allotted time span, one's destruction may prove even worse. One may become the dark sun, the incomplete jaguar, or those things that always are eaten.[134] But success and failure alike lead to a destructively new creation (death is, after all, inevitable, as Xolotl so painfully found out [Birth: VI.37]). No matter how great the Mexica become, Huitzilopochtli's mother awaits the moment when their history is *completed*, for then her son will return home. But he will come alone. Like a quail in the Land of the Dead, time chews on all beings (including the Mexica), changing them with every bite.

Mexica stories show a marked concern for how things end, for their moments of *completion* before they become something new in the ongoing march of destruction. According to a precise schedule, each cosmic age was destroyed in order to make the next unique age. Within the boundaries of the Fifth Sun, each of its particular suns must die every fifty-two years so a new one can be birthed. Huitzilopochtli, moreover, will abandon the Mexica's conquered cities in the same order that he helped acquire them; only then can he return to Aztlan. Things don't just change; they embody time like a clock steadily clicking off the moments as they are *completed* and "disappear."

Again the term *poliui* appears in the myths describing this continuing eschatological process. The four suns were decimated, destroyed, and depopulated, and finally they perished and disappeared. Each sun drew its name, its identity, its *face*,[135] from the mode of its destruction. There is never a return to the original beginning, only a carefully kept tempo of almost evolutionary change. Although time periods are marked by their beginnings, their endings are especially noted, as if the final moments of the old are being marked before they *disappear*, changing into the new. Transformation marks the demise of past objects in order to *re-present* them in new forms. *Completion* does not mean the emptiness of finality; it promises the fullness of creation.

The toltec *spatio-temporal* paradigm embodies in its architecture the same message of fertile finality found in myth. Formulated at places like Teotihuacan and Tula and eventually repeated like so many variations on a theme at Tenochtitlan, these human-constructed mountains present a reality of temporal corporeality; these mountainous spaces embody time because they *are* time. The mountains, the cities, the people must change just as the sky changes because they *are* the sky. They track the course of their own demise with their own bodies. And from their rubble rise a new people, the Mexica. If the sky continues to move, then the transformative process must give rise to new creations. Myths and buildings alike say that transformation is ongoing because time *equals* space.

If a spatio-temporal reality governed Mexica cosmology, then so too must a temporo-spatial reality. If space equals time, time must equal space, for equations are reversible. And surely the reverse of the equation makes sense experientially too. If all things embody time, it is important to count out various beings' years. One will want to know when one's age, city, and life might reach the promise of their *completion*. Indeed, the same destructively transformative logic that governed Mexica myth and architecture also governed an elaborate calendrical system. This calendrical tale will now be spun.

SHAPING TIME

Naming Time

An image of a carefully twisted and knotted rope is centered just beneath the reed glyph on the 2-Reed plaque (figure 1.4). This rope referred to that important rite named both the Binding-of-the-Years and New Fire Ceremony. In every solar year named 2-Reed, fifty-two years (having just been *completed*) were "gathered" and "joined" symbolically into a bundle and bound together with two ropes, just like a bundle of fifty-two reeds was bound for transport by Mexica traders (Binding the Years: 4) (figure 5 C). Mesoamericans often imaged date glyphs as burdens borne by woven tumplines on the backs of porters who traveled by foot from one part of Mexico to another (Nicholson 1966) (figure 7). One can see such an image in figure 8.[1] Here a rabbit seems to kneel on the ground to get a better grip on the year glyph, "13-House." Like a porter adjusting a heavy

FIGURE 7A.
Two Mayan date glyphs showing time being borne by tumplines:
(A) 9 Baktuns, Copan D; (B) Glyph B carrying Glyph X, Quirigua B.
After Thompson and Morley and drawn from H. B. Nicholson, "Significance of the 'Looped Cord' Year Symbol in Pre-Hispanic Mexico," 141.

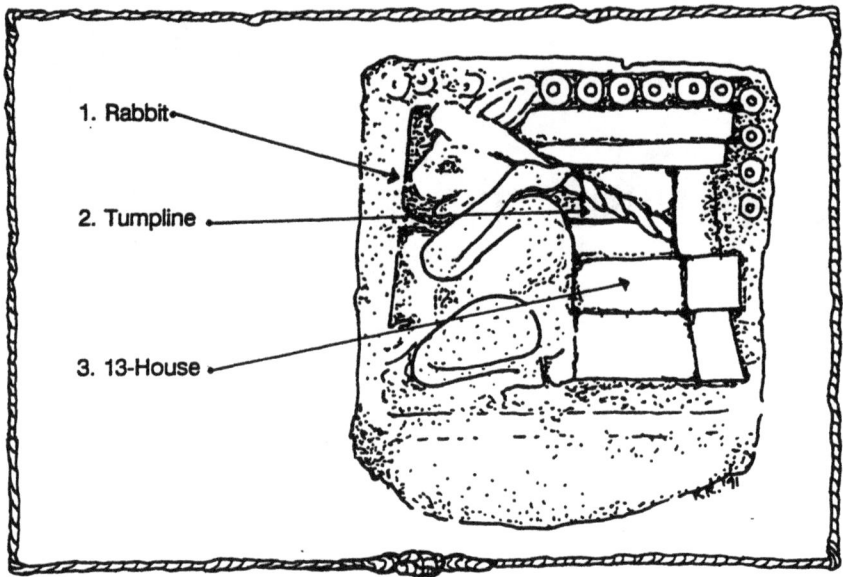

FIGURE 7B.
Toltec-like glyph showing time being borne by a rabbit.
Drawn from a photo of a stone monument in H. B. Nicholson,
"Significance of the 'Looped Cord' Year Symbol in Pre-Hispanic
Mexico," fig. 12.

bundle held on his back with a strap (figure 8), he is perhaps readying it for transport or easing it onto the ground now that his task is *completed*. Calendrical time, a heavy bundle of goods full of potentiality, is carefully borne from one place to another.

Verbal and visual images of this all-important transporting activity are common. Carrying goods with tumplines, after all, was a necessary occupation in pre-Conquest times. Because there were no domesticated beasts of burden prior to the coming of the Spanish, people, not animals, transported the material goods upon which the economic structure of Mexica dominion was founded. The Fifth Age's new sun and moon "follow their paths" and go into their "entrances" when their task is done. Taking turns, they "shoulder their work" and "throw down work or tribute" (Birth: VII.10–22, n. 1:60, chap. 1).[2] The sun and moon are foot porters bearing their burden of time on their own shoulders. At journey's end, their time spans are *completed*, and these traders can throw off their cargo of reeds still bound together by knotted ropes.

FIGURE 8.
Various pre-Conquest and post-Conquest drawings of porters bearing
burdens. Note the tumplines and staffs. (A) after the *Codex Mendoza*,
folio 62; (B) after the *Codex Fejérváry-Mayer*, folio 31; (C) after the
Codex Aubin, 88; (D) after Fray Bernardino de Sahagún, *The Florentine Codex: A History of the Things of New Spain*, bk. 9, pt. 10, no.
13; (E) after the year 1465, found in the "Pichardo Copy" of the
Codex en Cruz, Atlas.

Sahagún describes such an image of time in the following passage about the solar year named "1-Rabbit."

1-Rabbit[3]

It is named [by]   1
    The year-day,[4] "The Place of Thorns."[5]
    The year count is 13.[6]

It carries them [the years].

It makes them walk.   5
It governs them.[7]
It bears them.[8]
    . . . .

And, right away,
1-Rabbit, "The Place of Thorns,"
    Stands up to come this way.   10
When it is standing up,
    It begins its work.

But this passage does more than describe a trader's travels. It also pictures many intertwined temporal and spatial concepts common to Mexica calendrics. 1-Rabbit is both a day name and the name of a year. It also indicates a cardinal direction, for it is called "The Place of Thorns," the name given to the south. Recall how all the gods looked to three directions—the Place of the Dead (north); the Place of the Women (west); and the Place of Thorns (south)—before the two newborn suns finally arose in the Place of Light (east)(Birth: V.27–36). Moreover, 1-Rabbit is the fifty-first in the fifty-two-year round, and the sun visits the south thirteen times, or one quarter of that round, before 1-Rabbit is reached. A pictorial shorthand for this round is graphed in figure 9. This southern year called 1-Rabbit was the dangerous one that came just before the solar round was *completed* in the next year, 2-Reed. Drought, famine, and hardship threatened the Mexica in 1-Rabbit, which were relieved by the lighting of 2-Reed's new fire (FC, bk. 7, pt. 8, chap. 8:23–24). Only when the flame was lit was time *completed* and ready for shaping, ready for binding with spun rope into an orderly bundle, which contained fifty-two carefully counted reed-years and was renamed (*re-presented*) with two dots and a reed plant (figure 5). Only then were the years ready for transport.

All previous ages before the fifth also had been counted out, *com-*

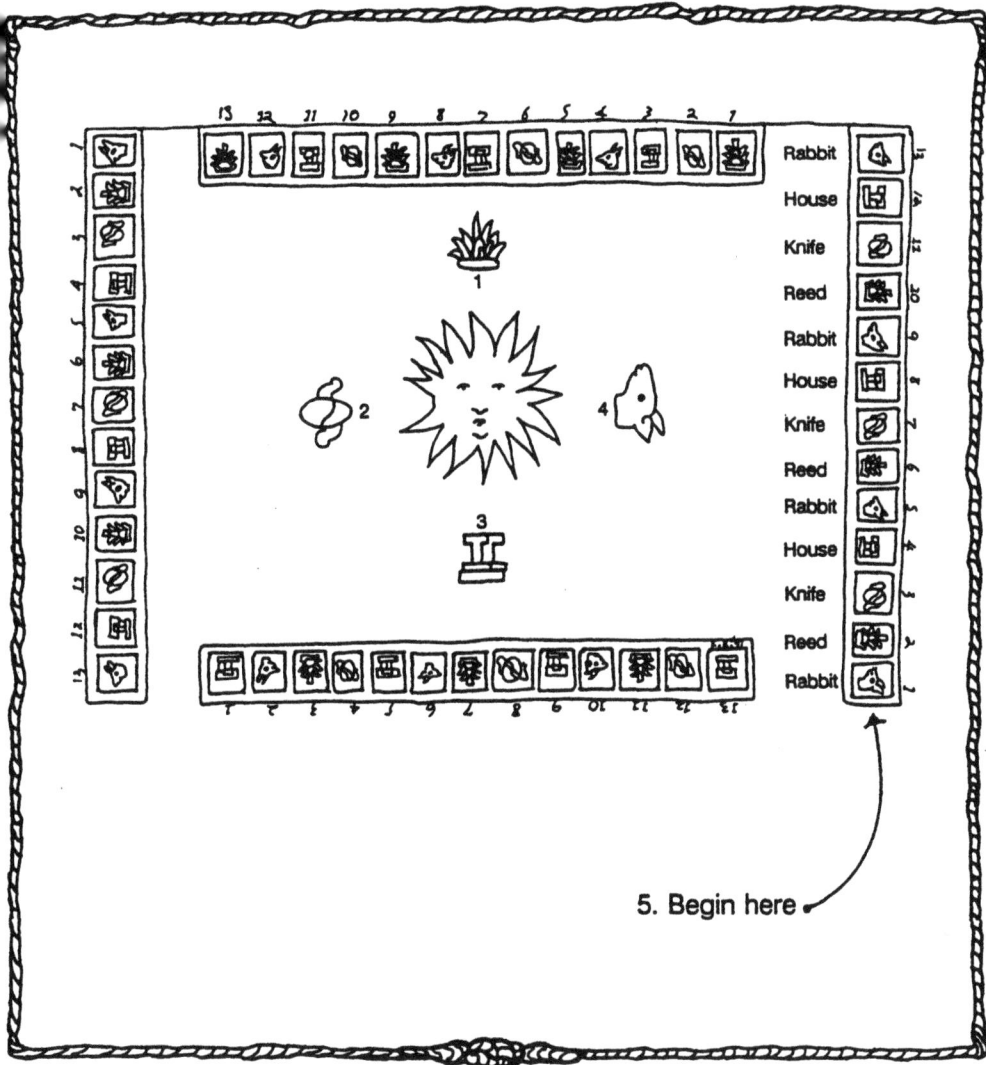

FIGURE 9.

The depiction of the fifty-two-year cycle, from the *Codex Aubin*.
After the Codex Aubin, *2, and the* Códice Aubin: Manuscrito Azteca de la
Biblioteca Royal de Berlin, Anales en Mexicana y geroglificos desde la
salida de las tribus de Aztlan, *11.*

1. East or Reed
2. North or Knife
3. West or House
4. South or Rabbit
5. Begin at 1-Rabbit [d8] and move counterclockwise

pleted, and named by their appropriate images. Recall, for example, this passage from "The Myth of the Four Suns" (myth 1: IV.1–5).

The Fourth Age

This sun's name was 4-Water.	1
At that time, the water spread out for 52 years.	
Those years had lived, arranged in four parts,	
When the sun was 4-Water.	
At that time, they had lived for 676 years.	5

That whole myth spends a great deal of energy on the counting out and marking of time. Each age is calculated for its duration and how long its destruction took, and every age and its food is named by the image of a date glyph. Such a mania for numbers indicates that this myth about the destructive creation of four suns is about more than a concept of transformation. Also hidden within its cryptic verses is the system of calendrical calculations governing that process of moving change.[9] If shapes are timed because space equals time, then it makes tremendous sense to calculate shapes' time spans, for all beings must count their life spans.

All of these intricately intertwined images of space and time make at least one thing clear. Counting is critical, and it does not occur in an easy, one-dimensional form.[10] Although based on simple arithmetic, Mesoamerican calendrical calculations were woven into incredibly complex tapestries (see the explanation of calendrical mechanics in Appendix 2). It should not be surprising that arithmetic was elaborated in such a baroque manner. Counting was the way one kept track of one's trade goods, one's tribute, and the time spans of one's life, one's ancestors, cities, gods, and ages; if all things were timed, then all things in existence had to be counted.

The equation of space and time suggests two things for calendrical calculations: (1) time had a physical shape; and (2) shape was important and was calculated in a way logically consistent with the *spatio-temporal* equation. First, time must have a living shape that occupies space. The above passages hint at the nature of time's shape. The years are alive (and employed); moreover, they occupy the four different cardinal directions. The Fifth Age was borne from the east, but its fifty-two successive suns move through all four points. Time is transported through these directions (east, north, west, south) in the shape of a spiral.

Second, because all things exist for only certain time spans, it is important to calculate those spans accurately. This means that the mathematical structure must be logically consistent with *space-time*; otherwise accuracy will be unattainable. Such complex arithmetical calculations were accomplished using an extraordinary calendrical system whose spiraling motion both accounted for and helped regulate the transformations that constantly shaped the *faces* of all things, naming and renaming them with new identities.

Shaping Time

Like all else in the Mexica cosmos, calendrics had to account for the equation of time and space. Like the earthly structures of a city's landscape, the calculation of time was structured by objects moving through the spaces of a city's sky; the same transformative reality governing urban centers like Teotihuacan also governed calendrics. If this equation of time and space meant that change was inevitable because all things were inherently timed, it might seem preferable to be orderly about this transformative process, to participate in it and manipulate it if one could.

It makes sense, then, that calendrical calculations (shaped by the sky) shaped the time spans of ages, cities, ancestors, people, and corn. These calculations gave order to the inevitable fact of transformation and allowed people to comprehend it, to enter into it, and even to control it a bit. If one did not calculate the quantity of a trader's goods and bind those goods into orderly bundles, how could commerce move efficiently across the changing earthly and celestial topography of a city's dominion?

If calendrical calculations are shaped by the motions of the sky, it also makes sense that time's shape must be as concrete as a city's pyramids. Time must equal space and, like all other things, must have shape and form as part of its inherent nature. What, then, is the shape of time if even the celestial traders' burdens are constantly *re-presented* and transformed according to a calculated schedule? Exactly how is time's face, its *ixtli*, counted out and named, and how is its bundle gathered together, bound, and carried across the topography of earth and sky? What is time's image?

I propose that time was shaped like a complex and multifaceted spiral, rather like the shaping of time's bindings when its ropes were first spun into shape. When rope is made, it is first twisted and spun out of many small individual fibers that are continually added to make the rope longer. Two or more of these twisted cords of many fibers then are spun together in reverse motion to create the finished rope. Often this is accomplished by simply doubling a single cord of spun threads back on itself. In this way, time is spun for the Mexica-Tenochca. One must remember, however, that, unlike the depiction of tribute bundles, it is not entirely clear that the Mexica-Tenochca explicitly used a spiraling and spinning image to describe time. It is important, therefore, to remember that this spiraling image is conceived as no more than a heuristic device. And by using it, I am performing my own act of naming or *re-presentation* in order to give shape and existence to my understanding of the Mexica's carefully calculated mode of transformation. Yet it is a useful analogy, for it can help a stranger to "think with" the Mexica a bit.

It is also an appropriate analogy. For spiraling is quite consistent with the many Mexica images having to do with spatio-temporal themes of curving and twisting that appear in a variety of sources.[11] Spirals twist and bend (*coloa*) like the sun's first rays "spreading in an undulating way" (*monenecuilotimani*) on that early morning of the Fifth Sun's eastern birth (Birth: V.56). They "curve back on themselves" (*coloa*), like the tip of the hill in the name glyph for Culhuacan (Place of the Grandparents), the hill in the center of Aztlan (myth 8: 3)(figure 6.1).[12] Sahagún even depicts the fifty-two-year calendar wheel as a kind of spiral in the *Códice Matritenses* (figure 10).[13] All of these examples show the kinds of contexts spirals and twisted ropes turn up in, contexts almost always having to do with cosmic and ancestral time.[14]

These images of spinning and spiraling are useful. They combine the repetitive motions of cyclical time with the progressive motions of linear time, making it possible to express an otherwise difficult aspect of Mexica transformation. And although others occasionally have noted that the Mexica combined these two temporal elements, few have plumbed the philosophic implications of such combinations, which are both far-reaching and often quite discordant with Western sensibilities.[15] It may be hard for many readers to think comfortably with Mexica images describing past forms which are simultaneously repeated and shaped into new forms for the present and future. It may also be difficult to think of time itself as physically shaped and molded like the rock and stone pyramids of Teotihuacan. For many, this last image may be truly foreign. Yet it need not be entirely so, for a partial sense of déjà vu may be helpful here.

Paul Ricoeur has pointed out that the conceptional framework for time in current use is that time is one-dimensional, like a line in space. He describes this notion of time (an end product of the scientific culture) as

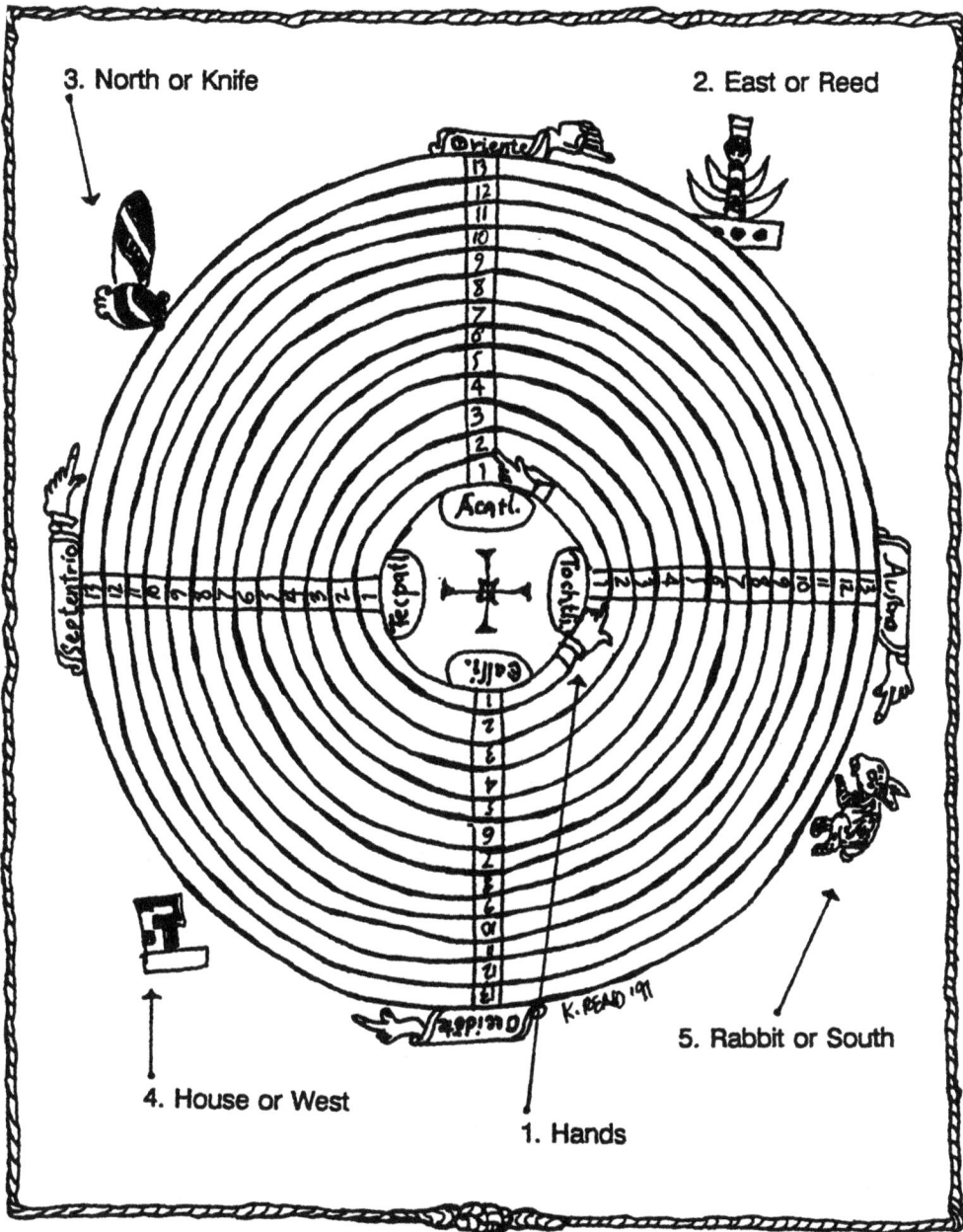

FIGURE 10.
The calendar wheel from Fray Bernardino de Sahagún's *Códice Matritenses.* It shows the division of the fifty-two-year cycle. The hands in the center point out that a counterclockwise motion is to be followed.
Drawn from a photo in Esther Pasztory, Aztec Art, *61.*

an endless continuum that can be interrupted anywhere. These interruptions or "instances" are understood as points on that line. Cyclical time is no more than an oppositional variation on this linear temporal sense, for it is only a line turned back on itself. Although Ricoeur's acceptance of an eternally unchanging reality does not square with an eternally changing and transforming Mexica cosmic reality, a *re-presentation* of his comments on the differing natures of various historical times provides a useful entrée into the shape of Mexica calendrical temporality.

Ricoeur notes, for example, a problematic limitation with conceptions that image time as only either linear or cyclical. This dialectical image overlooks the differences between an "instant," which has no duration, and the multidimensional "experience of nowness," which includes memories of the past and expectations of the future. He suggests that a paradox has arisen in which the source of significance for time is found within the human life span. But in comparison with the enormous time spans of things like geological history, human life spans appear especially insignificant, like very small instances on an enormous time line. Attempts, therefore, are made to integrate this paradox by somehow recapitulating the past in the present and securing the rare experience of "repetition" (Ricoeur 1985, 14–19). He tells his readers: "the pastness of the past is handed down and reoriented toward the future, whereas our expectations are once again rooted in the potentialities inherited from the past" (ibid., 17).

Such repetitive experiences, however, are not the only way to understand time. Ricoeur goes on to suggest that temporality is multilayered. Since such multilayering provides good access to people's experiences of what is religious, he challenges his readers to reassess their own conceptual framework (ibid., 13, 17–19). In order to do this, he suggests that cyclical time must be understood in its own terms, that is, without measuring it against its alleged opposite, the modern concept of linear time. By the same token, noncyclical time also must be understood in its own terms and not hastily compared with that same concept of linearity (ibid., 19).

The shape of spinning, while cyclic, is more than linear time simply turned back on itself. In potentially very complex ways, it is both cyclic and linear at the same time. Much like the twisting motion of rope as it is being spun, new threads are constantly being twisted into Mexica-Tenochca time just as old ones are ending. Time spans partially overlap each other like fibers spinning together, creating an ever longer rope; they reverse their motion by doubling back on themselves, spiraling back to a new beginning by "piling" up their many overlapping threads (Binding the Years: 4). It is this complex, multilayered spiraling motion that structured Mexica calendrical calculations and provided a way for humans to participate in the inevitable process of change. Through ritual divination one controlled the order of one's time span. In that Fifth Age of Movement, it was by the motion of spinning and spiraling that all things existed and died. In this way, the "twisting" and "bending" motion of the sun's rays illuminated its age's transformation very well (Birth: V.56; n. 1:47). If an attempt is made to understand these richly imaged and multilayered cyclical and progressive temporal elements as separate and unique shapes in themselves, and not as necessarily opposed to each other (as Ricoeur suggests they should be understood), it may be feasible to see how Mexica spinning joins them into a single, albeit intricate and even ornate, shape.

The task, then, is first to identify separately the cyclical and progressive elements within the Mexica's temporal conceptions. Then the calendrical system, which operated simultaneously on both cyclical and progressive configurations, may be described. In other words, the shape of time for the Mexica-Tenochca was that of a spiral not just because that moving shape is consistent with common Mexica images but also because Mexica transformative and calendrical conceptions themselves involved coordinated sequential and cyclical elements.

Spinning Time

A complex calendrical system was one of the most central features of Mesoamerican culture (described in full in Appendix 2). Its importance cannot be overemphasized. Calendrical specialists still live in many parts of Mexico today, calculating the needs of their patrons with a system that is probably over twenty-six centuries old.[16] Some continue to coordinate a 365-day cycle with a 260-day cycle, although the way they do this may vary from region to region. Often these two cycles serve different purposes and are computed by different types of specialists. The Mayan Ixil in Highland Guatemala have three such specialists: an elected priest, who determines the days for communal and civil ceremonies; prayer-sayers, who intervene on behalf of the sick; and day keepers or diviners, who help people determine the course of their lives (Colby and Colby 1981, 46).

The ancient Mexica calendar also served a multitude of purposes, ranging from a farmer's need to calculate the seasons to a ruler's desire to calculate the appropriate moments for battle and diplomacy. Events both large and small—birth, marriage, death, the fertility of the land, the motions of the skies—all were calculated and ordered by the calendrical system. Full knowledge of complicated calendrical workings was probably held only by select specialists as is true today in Mesoamerica, for the computing of time was, as it is now, a sophisticated activity with a capability for controlling great social and sacred powers. Still, even the most humble peasants had at least a rudimentary understanding of how time was calculated, for they too needed to manipulate the important events in their lives.

Mesoamerican calendars ordered and controlled the ongoing motions of embodied cosmic powers according to a logic born out of life itself. Time tracks the motion of living beings. If things are alive, they move; if they move, they are timed; if they are timed, they can be calculated; and if they can be calculated, with some luck, they may even be ordered and controlled. Calendrical calculations shaped and reshaped the motions of all living beings as they moved their powers through the paths and roadways of *Ilhuicatl* (Sky-Water), *Tlalticpac* (Earth's Surface), and *Mictlan* (Land of the Dead) and their beings' many and various life spans.

To understand this Mexica cosmos-shaping calendar, one must recognize how different it was from the current Western one. That familiar calendar is a simple affair that stresses complete uniformity. First, just one calendar round exists that rules all activities from train departures to geological ages, from committee meetings and doctors' appointments to the birth and death of earth and other planets, and from marriages and vacations to the creation and demise of the sun and its system. Second, this calendar is calculated by the motions of only one celestial object, the sun. Third, because the Western calendar keeps track of only the sun's motions, it counts the moments as though they were so many beads on a single rope. Everyone rises, eats, works, plays, and sleeps according to the sun's instances: its seconds follow seconds, minutes follow minutes, hours follow hours, days upon days, years upon years, and so on. Instant by instant, time irrevocably marches on, never turning back, never doubling over, and never overlapping. The sun was born once in a fiery burst many long instances ago and eventually will wear out, grow cold, and die many long instances from now. In the meantime each person's life also ticks on in the span of instances allotted it. Often, one can ignore the clock ticking away. On Saturday mornings, one may not set the clock. By concentrating on one's youth, one can pretend one's own clock is not set. And by ruminating on eternity or beautifully timeless values, one may even eliminate the clock.

But mathematics structured just about everything in the Mexica-Tenochca universe. Its clocks were neither simple nor uniform, and no one could ignore them. First, the calendrical system calculated life's events according not just to one but to numerous schedules (see Appendix 2). High state rituals, for example, were often governed by the sun and figured according to a 365-day count. Similar to the way in which contemporary astrological systems govern the events of one's everyday life, Mexica marriages, births, and business deals were calculated by a divinatory calendar which was 260 days long.[17] Second, the Mexica accounted for not just one or even two, but numerous celestial cycles. The most important was that of the sun, which gave the days. Intertwined with this count of 365 days were also the counts of Venus, Mars, constellations, most likely the moon, and perhaps other celestial objects now lost to the modern world. One very important count called the Lords of the Night measured its cycle in nine solar days, but no one really knows the origin of this count or what it originally measured.[18]

Third, because numerous calendars were used simultaneously, their moments of conjunctions and disjunctions were important. Moments did not simply line up like beads on a rope. Instead they arranged themselves more like the rope itself, in which various fibers of differing lengths are spun together, now some overlapping and others not, now others overlapping that had not meshed before. Time spirals and spins around and around, like the rope turning back or doubling over on itself, its fibers now meshing, now not. No sector of the rope was ever exactly like a previous sector. Mexica calendrical mathematics, that many-fibered rope, was like a complicated musical round spinning out its song with numerous parts in ever-changing harmony. At one time the sopranos and tenors might be singing their particular lines; at another, the tenors, altos, and bassos; at yet another, sopranos, contraltos, and tenors; and so on. Each musical line (whether short or long) continues to repeat its simple tune as though each stands alone, yet all these ditties merge and diverge in the most complex and confusing ways, each according to the same steady, never faltering metronomic beat of the days.[19]

Two of these many rounds working together marked the Binding-of-the-Reeds ceremony. The solar round, or *xiuhmolpilli*,[20] combined a count of fifty-two vague solar years with the divinatory calendar, or *tonalpohualli*,[21] which had a count of 260 days (see Appendix 2). After the passing of 18,980 days (52 x 365 days or 73 x 260 days), both of these cycles

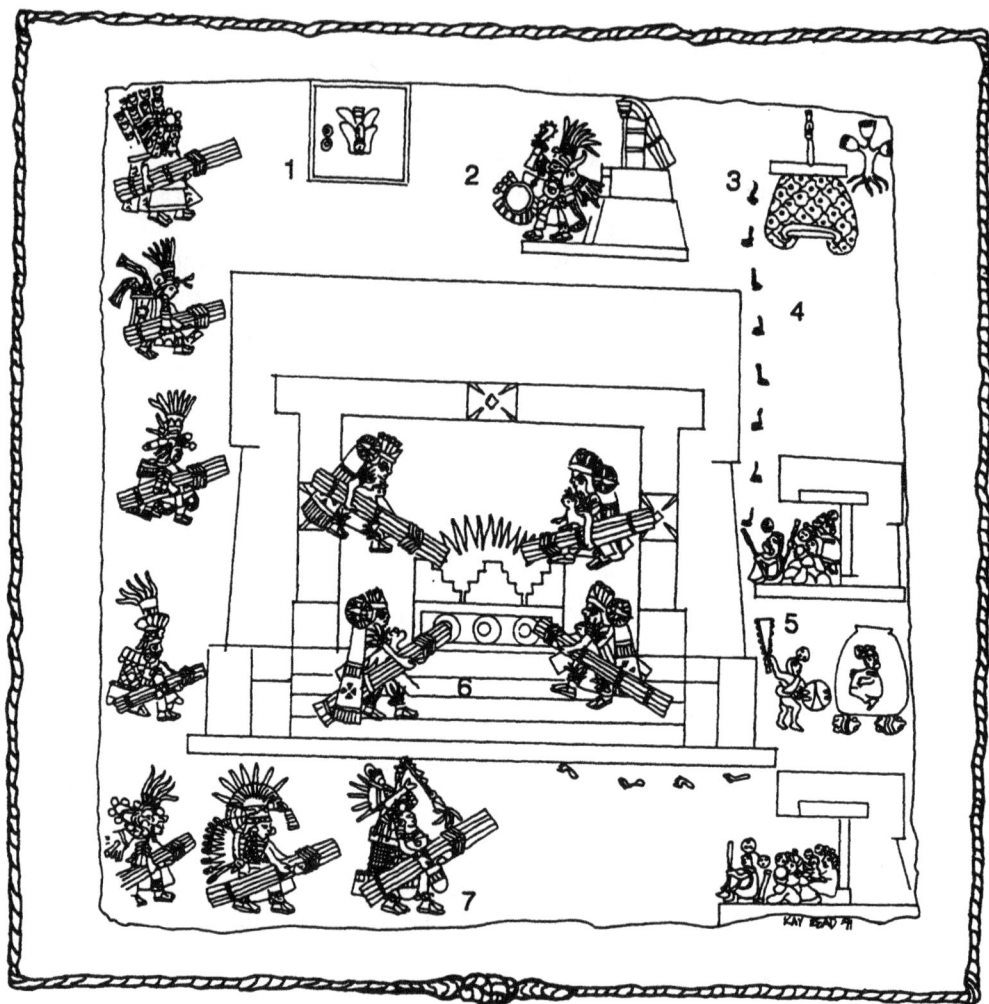

FIGURE 11.

The New Fire ceremony, occurring in the month of Panquetzaliztli.
Drawn from the Codex Borbonicus, *folio 34.*

1. 2-Reed glyph
2. Huitzilopochtli stands in front of a temple decorated with paper banners
3. Place glyph for Uixachtlan shown with a fire drill
4. Footprints depict the way from the hill to the temple
5. A warrior and a pregnant woman who is inside a granary
6. The new fire burns in the temple, stoked with year bundles by four priests of the fire god Xiuhtecuhtli
7. Other deities led by Huitzilopochtli bring more year bundles to burn

simultaneously ended. At that precise moment, the New Fire ceremony had to be performed if the two rounds were to begin spinning together again. The ceremony took place on a high hill called Uixachtlan, overlooking Tenochtitlan (figure 11). Because it occurred in November at the beginning of the Mexica month of Panquetzaliztli, when the Pleiades were at their zenith, the Binding of the Years marked both the beginning of the dry season and the approaching nadir of the sun (FC, bk. 4, pt. 5, app. 143; bk. 7, pt. 8, chaps. 8–12:25–32).[22] All fires were extinguished in the entire domain, all houses swept clean, and all old clothing and household goods thrown out. At midnight, a new fire was sparked on the chest of a human sacrificial offering whose very name contained the word "year" (*xiuitl*) (FC, bk. 7, pt 8, chap. 12:31). His heart was cut from his breast and fed to the fire, which eventually consumed his whole body, as Nanahuatzin's body had been consumed when time in the Fifth Age began (Birth: IV.38–50). It was believed that, if the fire was successfully lighted, a new sun would have the strength to begin spinning again; if not, there would be no sun and all would disappear. If all went well, if all was "well arranged" (Birth: IV.60), time would be made new there on Uixachtlan.

This particular ceremony might appear to be a conspicuous example of an Eliade-like repetitious renewal of time (D. Carrasco 1981). Eliade suggested that religious people renew time by ritually repeating the archetypal paradigms of the primordium. The creative potentialities of that first time of all origination are thereby brought into the present, making continued life possible. For religious people, the shape of "real" time is circular or cyclical, for it returns one to primordial archetypes of the mythic past by ritually repeating those original creations in the present (Eliade 1954). From this point of view, the Binding-of-the-Years rite would be understood as repeating the paradigmatic, mythic events of that first time, when the Fifth Age was born out of the bodies of Nanahuatzin and Tecuiçiztecatl in the fire at Teotihuacan. It would be seen as a rite of renewal which made time "really real" by cyclically repeating creative potentialities of sacred, primordial time, thereby collapsing those past, creative moments with the present. The Binding of the Years would renew time by creating a moment of Ricoeurian nowness.

Many scholars, in fact, have found a circular shape a useful heuristic device for describing this material.[23] The strong repetitious character found in rites like the Binding of the Years and in the calendrical calculations themselves has led Johanna Broda, for example, to suggest that the Mexicans apparently did not have the idea of a progressive historical development, but rather looked upon time as an endless series of great cycles which revolved and interlocked, and which depended upon manifold divine influences. These divine influences were the most important characteristics of a day, and they resulted from its position in the *tonalpohualli*. (Broda 1969, 28)

Repetitions do indeed appear in "The Myth of the Four Ages." Each sun lasted for a multiple of 13 x 52 years, after which that age was destroyed. The year of each age's disappearance, moreover, is named by one of the four-year glyphs (of which Reed is one); these names appear according to their appropriate order in the year-bearer cycle (figure 9).[24] There is a strongly repetitive element apparent in the calculations themselves; for in this myth, a cycle of 676 years is being repeated. Both ages one and four are 676 years long (13 x 52), while ages two and three together (both of which are given the calendrical year sign 1-Knife) add up to the same.[25] The characters of the ages themselves even appear repetitious. They all have a people, a food for them to eat, and a name that comes from their mode of destruction.

A poem recorded by Sahagún aptly describes this strong sense of temporal repetition:

Once Again It Will Be [26]

Once again, it will be like it was then and there.[27]   1
Once again, it will be ordered as it was:
    Sometime, someplace.

That which was being completed[28] long ago
    and far away,[29] no longer is done.
But, once again, it will be done.   5
    Once again, as it was, it will be ordered,
    As it was ordered long ago and far away.
They who live now, once again will live, will exist.

Passages such as this might very well lead one to view time as being shaped like a number of wheels, meshing together like the gears in Renaissance clockworks, an image commonly used by many Mesoamerican scholars to explain the calendrical system. From this viewpoint, Mexica time would be understood as endlessly repeating itself, cycle upon cycle, wheel upon wheel, gears forever interlocking.

There is, however, strong evidence for progressive, sequential, even historically developmental notions of time within this calendrical system, although that evidence may not always be obvious. For example, another element is expressed in "The Myth of the Four Ages" (myth 1) that cannot be described as easily by the heuristic device of endlessly revolving and interlocking gears. This shape is suggested by the developmental progression from one age to the next. A strong break appears between each age, for each is completely destroyed before being transformed into a completely new entity. Even though each age has a people, a food, and a mode of destruction, each of these things is specific to its particular age because all things of each previous age "disappeared" (*polliuhque*).

Moreover, no return to any earlier age or to the beginning of all time is ever mentioned. Entirely new ages are created from old ones, and no old ones ever reappear in exactly the same form. And even though time is begun again at the Binding-of-the-Years ceremony, this new beginning refers back in time only as far as the beginning of the Fifth Age and not as far back as any true Eliadian primordium, a time prior to the beginning of all the ages. The sparking of the new fire at this ceremony represents a repetition that is contained within a specifically limited time span (that of the Fifth Age) and does not refer to all time everywhere. In other words, time not only limits all things, but is itself limited by a certain number of solar rotations.

There is also evidence that a chronological concept of history was present in which time was counted out sequentially, event following event, and year following year. The concept of transformation itself found in mythic sources would suggest this possibility. If things are continually being created new, then time is also moving forward. A sense of historical development, structured by a sequentially ordered count, can be found in the numerous instances of "histories," those stories collected by the Spanish which are now often called the *anales* tradition.[30]

"The Legend of the Suns," whence come myths about the destructions of the four ages and the birth of the Fifth Age, is such a history. Such *anales* tales begin with the mythical and genealogical origins of various Highland Mexican towns, go on to the important events that occurred in each town's history, and often finish with an account of the present ruler's activities. They are laid out according to a chronology based on solar years. Each event of importance is given along with the year in which it occurred. Moreover, each year is carefully counted in sequence whether anything occurred in that year or not. Elizabeth Boone has described the count of the years in these histories as "armatures" that served to tie the events together, to structure them.[31] Such histories calculated, in solar years, the progressive sense of development inherent in the mythically expressed concept of transformation.

Since both sequential and cyclical configurations can be found within Mexica sources, time appears somehow to have been calculated according to a double orientation.[32] Calendrical rounds (such as the solar *xiuhmolpilli* and the divinatory *tonalpohualli*) recurred over and over, punctuated by rites of renewal when the rounds meshed, thereby providing for the strong sense of repetitious time that Broda noted. At the same time, the expressions of progressive transformation (found in mythic sources) and of chronological history (found in the *anales* tradition) provide a developmentally sequential sense. Time, after all, did move sequentially through one age to the next in spite of the repetitiously described calculations of its forward march. Each age repeated but did not copy exactly the last age, just as Tenochtitlan repeated but did not copy Teotihuacan, or a child genetically repeats but does not copy its ancestors. This double nature of time can be thought of as a single spiraling shape, constantly moving with a rotating, spinning motion.

Moreover, as Appendix 2 suggests, mathematically structured calendrical codices graphically depict this spiraling motion of time, suggesting that it was inherent in the workings of the system itself.[33] For while it is true that the calendrical system was structured by great cycles of time revolving and interlocking, a subtle progressive orientation also can be found embedded in the very shape of its math. Like a spinning rope growing longer and longer as new threads are continually added on top of old ones, so too spinning time grows arithmetically longer as time spans are added on top of previous ones.

Some odd elements of the calendrical calculations run counter to an otherwise pristinely perfect system, causing its calculations never fully to mesh. Such odd counts are the dark objects that provide a counter motion to the sun's light, the elements that assure that transformation must continually prevail and that the full potentiality of completion must continue to occur. At least two odd counts appear to force the other evenly counted calendrical rounds forward: the five *nemontemi* and the nine Lords of the Night.[34]

The first count, the *nemontemi*, were five days tacked onto the solar year to bring its otherwise evenly divisible 360 days up to the requisite 365 days. These five days were considered unlucky and "idle." They were not associated with the powers of any god and therefore were not officially "counted" (FC, bk. 4, app., 137). To count them would have been an act of naming, which recognized their identity, thereby increasing their danger. The *nemontemi* cause each year's count to move forward by one day. The second count, the Lords of the Night, was a round of nine days that cycled against the twenty-day round that founded all even rounds. The oddly counted lords are always out of sync with at least one other evenly counted cycle. These two strange counts assured that at no single moment could all cycles end at the same time for an extraordinarily long time, for at least one odd count threw off all the even ones.

These odd counts, in an orderly manner, upset the order of forms. The nine dark Lords of the Night counter the brilliant order of the sun's day. Things of the night were considered to be *tlahtlacolli*, things "spoiled," "rotten," "messed up," "tangled," and "displaced" (Burkhart 1989, 28–29, 82–85). As *tlahtlacolli*, those dark lords "displaced" the orders of other celestial objects. And it may be that, because the *nemontemi* were "idle" and did no work, these resting, unmoving days at the end of each solar year also were considered to be "messed up" and "displaced," for they followed no appropriate path. So too were the unmoving sun twins at the Fifth Age's birth "mixed up," for they "shone in the same way," something clearly out of order (Birth: VI.9, 30). It was the motion of each distinctive sun (*tonatiuh*) or age that gave order to time, but these bright, daily orders are countered by some dark nightly order. Even the order of the physical world can be seen to counter any notion of stability, for just as the sun will rise in the east every morning, so too will it *disappear* in the west every evening to be replaced by the moon. It makes sense, then, that some day Nanahuatzin's time will end and night will prevail; his form no longer will be "well arranged" (Birth: IV.56–66). All things some day will become "rotten" and "messed up."

By countering each other's order, even and odd counts assured that time was transformative in two ways. Time both repeated itself (via its even counts) and moved forward (via its odd counts) in a motion that constantly calculated old shapes into new ones. The disappearance of each sun-age's life on Tlalticpac (Earth's Surface) was limited to a span of 676 years (myth 1). As does the spinning of a rope, time's many threads went around and around while at the same time growing longer and longer. And like the changing shapes of pyramids, this temporal rope also was spatialized, given shape by its own spinning count that traveled through each of the cardinal points until an age had lived out its life. As Huitzilopochtli's mother reminded her visitors in Aztlan, all the Mexica would be destroyed, for they were tied to the foods of a particular age that must end. According to schedule, her son would return home to Aztlan from his journeys (myth 8: 14–18). Once a period completed its schedule, its burden must be thrown down to the ground, its ties loosened, the counted packet of reeds unbound before being bound back up again and marked for further transport. The old bundle must disappear into a new bundle re-presented with a new name.

Spiraling time also held implications for how people were shaped and timed. Because the temporal rope spun forward as it doubled back, people experienced a special sense of repetitious "returns" to the past, which differed from Eliadian returns. And they experienced a very particular sense of "nowness" that was not exactly the same as Ricoeurian nowness. For in both cases, eternity did not exist as a possibility, only historical transformation. Spiraling returns to ancestors who were still somehow present, and experiences of nowness that spun together many past, present, and future moments created a unique transformative anthropology. The Mexica-Tenochca held a very distinctive view of what constituted the spatio-temporal and temporo-spatial nature of human beings.

TIMING AND
SHAPING PEOPLE

Naming People

A particular moment presents its *face* (*ixtli*) on the 2-Reed plaque. For no matter how many other elaborations decorate its surface, the plaque boldly displays the familiar forms of a potent date glyph (figure 1.1, 2, 3). This floral reed glyph dominates the plaque's center; its confining and attention-getting cartouche indicates that the glyph shapes a year, binding it with its name. But this double-dotted plant indicates not just any year, but a year-day-event filled with particular potentialities. And as everyone knew, once this year-day-event was *completed*, its shape *disappeared* into the next moment's *face*, blossoming into a newly named identity.

Like the year 2-Reed, people's shapes also were timed. Their *faces* also *disappeared* into new identities with new names, a process of deformative transformation that both continually molded them and allowed them to mold themselves and the world around them. The nature of Mexica human beings, their sense of anthropology, was characterized by two sides of the same kernel of corn. First, people (like all other beings) were timed; like all else, they existed in *space-time*. A person was born, as was corn, only to experience *"destruction," "death,"* and *"disappearance."* Second, this transformative process was not a one-time affair. It also continually shaped people throughout their life spans, for people also existed in *time-space*. According to one's own particular *mahceua* (merit) or personal composition,[1] one was shaped by one's natural, biological potentialities, which were acted out in history. Moreover, one could participate willfully in this shaping, thereby controlling it to some measure. People were shaped at the same time that they shaped their own selves. Finally, these two sides of the *spatio-temporal* and *temporo-spatial* corn kernel mean that Mexica transformative moments existed only within history. The Mexica both were shaped by history and used history to shape history.

Timing Destruction, Death, and Disappearance

Like all other beings, people were timed by their *spatio-temporal* natures. To be a *macehualli* (a commoner or simple human being) meant that one's life was temporally bounded by a process of change involving destruction, death, and disappearance. All these layers of meaning can be found embedded in the word root *poliui,* that potent verbal image used to describe the deformative transformation of the moon and all the ages. These three layers, moreover, can illuminate what it meant to be human.

The notion of *destruction* entailed the changing of form. Just as the second sun's *face* (*ixtli*) was beaten, destroyed, and killed (Birth: I.4–10, VI.15–20), so too were people's *faces* or identities reshaped. While *ixtli* means *face,* it also can refer to one of the several animistic centers that every Nahua person possessed. The *ixtli* is a locus for perception situated in the head and closely associated with the eyes. This center was for the "complete consciousness that is found in communication with the outside world."[2]

But the *ixtli* was more than one's perception or the means by which a person viewed the outside world. It was also the means by which the outside world viewed a person's *face.* In other words, when the sun's *face* was destroyed and reformed differently, both the way he perceived the outside world and the way the outside world perceived him, his identity, were radically altered. He was no longer the same person or thing; with his new form he also had a new name, a new existence; the sun was now the moon.

Death can be understood as the result of people's bonds with the things of a particular age, bonds that caused people to rot and *disappear.* Alfredo López Austin has suggested that people were bound to earth by two means: ingesting corn and being initiated into the sexual life. This binding resulted in the unavoidable eventuality of *death.* Corn was seen to have sprung from the earth, and by ingesting it, one took the earth into one's own body. To give oneself to sexuality was to give oneself to "the things of the earth" (*tlalticpacayotl*), to "the dust and the filth" (*in teutli, in tlazolli*) (1988b, 313–14).

Only nursing babies were considered free of these two bonds. They had begun neither to eat the food of the earth nor to participate in any sexual life. Once the tie with earth was established with the baby's first taking of corn, the deities of Mictlan (Land of the Dead), that land situated under the earth's surface, would be greedy for the child's body (López Austin 1988b, 311–16).[3] Recall too that it was from Mictlan that Quetzalcoatl retrieved the bones from which people were created. Those bones were ground into flour like maize, the food of the Fifth Sun (Myth 3; CC 1992a, 146; 1992b, 89). People not only were bound to earth by eating corn but, like Nanahuatzin, were corn themselves (Birth, myth 4).

The story about Aztlan also tied *death* to eating the things of an earthly age (myth 8). By leaving Aztlan, the Mexica-Tenochca made their entrance into the Fifth Sun. Readmittance, however, was forever denied them; the elegant food of the Tenochca weighed them down, corrupted them, and brought *death*. While the emergence from Aztlan marked the beginning of the Mexica-Tenochca's history, the beginning of their own time in the Fifth Sun, that same emergence also marked the beginning of bondedness to the food (whether it be corn or cocoa) that would ensure their demise.[4] It marked the beginning of their progress toward *death* and their inability to return to youth. By eating the things of an age (something they must do or die), they incorporated into their own bodies the timing of that age.

Death itself was a process in which various bodily components separated and dispersed to different locations. López Austin describes three different animistic entities that were part of each person's physico-psychic makeup (1988b, 201–36).[5] One such animistic entity, the *teyolia*, went to one of the four lands of the dead, depending on the nature of a person's *death*: (1) if *death* was caused by illness, one went to the Land of the Dead (Mictlan); (2) if *death* was due to water-related causes, to the Land of the Rain God (Tlalocan); (3) for those men and women who fell in war and thus were sacrificed to the sun, and for those women who died in childbirth (also considered to have fallen in war), to the Sky of the Sun (Tonatiuh Ilhuicatl); and (4) for those babies who were still nursing, to the Land of the Breast Tree (Chichiualquauitl).

A second animistic entity, the *tonalli*, fragmented and scattered upon *death*. The *tonalli*'s bits perhaps were gathered by attracting them to a box in which were placed pieces of greenstone, the deceased's cremated remains (its ashes and pieces of bone), bits of its hair or nails, and a wooden effigy. Such burial urns have been unearthed from caches at the

Templo Mayor (Umberger 1987, 428–37). It would seem that the buried greenstone and disintegrated bones of dead ancestors did, indeed, contain some sort of power or force, perhaps like the power and force of Quetzalcoatl's greenstone bones (myth 3: 2).

A third entity, the *ihiyotl*, apparently was a ghost or shadow. Since it was potentially harmful and did not particularly want to give up its bonds with the living, precautions were taken to avoid contact with it and to sever any possible relationships between it and the living (López Austin 1988b, 316–26). Because these entities were part of a person's body, *death* involved a complete *destruction* of the self as a whole, for a self's pieces separated and scattered in many directions, rather like Quetzalcoatl spilling the bones (myth 3: 4).

Finally, to *disappear* meant to cease existing in *death* in the same way one had existed in life. This was not a total evaporation into nothingness, into a black void. It meant, instead, never to return to the same previous visible form. Thus the second sun's shape was forever altered when it became the moon. So too were the parts of Tata and Nene (myth 2) shifted about and Quetzalcoatl's greenstone bones ground into flour and remolded (myth 3: 6).

Contact between the living and at least parts of the dead was, however, maintained. A ruler's bones continued to have some force for the living, for these bones were harbored as relics after the ruler's *death*, probably because of the little bits of powerful *tonalli* that the remains were able to attract. A ruler's heart harbored powerful forces, his *teyolia*. These were returned to and reunited with the divinities whose "fires" it had sheltered during life. The rulers themselves, however, separated and went to different places, to both the Land of the Dead (Mictlan) and the sun (López Austin 1988b, 328–31). For commoners and nobles alike, *death* entailed a separation of the physical and psychic components. Just as a person's material remains rotted and *disappeared*, their many forces scattered and *disappeared*. No longer would they be one coherent entity.

A ruler's ties with the living were maintained even though he himself separated at *death* into many different parts. And in the dwellings of the dead, all people's *teyolias* depended on the living earthly ruler just as they had in life. The fulfillment of the *teyolia's* functions complemented the activity it had on earth. For example, a dead ruler's *teyolia* continued, along with the living ruler, to assist in the tasks of producing fruitful harvests, assuring adequate rain, and, in general, maintaining the cosmos (López Austin 1988b, 342). When Motecuhzuma's priests said to Coatlicue that their ancestors had died and now were only a "memory," they may have meant that they had disintegrated and so now were invisible (myth 8: 8). Nevertheless, the animistic entities of those dead ancestors must have remained among them in concrete and practical ways.

To *disappear* meant that once a person's life-form had ceased, once one's identity, one's *ixtli* had ended, that life-form would never be reconstituted in exactly the same way again. The moon would never again become the sun it had been (Birth: VI.14–21). Tata and Nene were irreversibly changed into dogs (*chichime*) (myth 2). The living Mexica-Tenochca could never return to the deathless Aztlan. They were forever bound to the things of the Fifth Sun, and upon *death*, their animistic entities scattered, never to be rejoined. To be a person was to be limited by one's own human capacities and mortality. Unlike gods, humans could not control their own composition[6] by simply running up and down a sandy hill (myth 8: 10, 17). To be human was a one-time experience.

Any given life-form, however, was doomed to *disappearance* because its fragmented parts were dispersed. Even though existence might continue through the forces of animistic entities making themselves felt on the earth's surface, upon *death*, one no longer was visible in the same way. Thus each person provided the kernels for a number of new creations in a destructive process of *continuing eschatologies*, an ongoing process in which no one form was ever repeated exactly.

In the Mexica-Tenochca world, all forms, including humans, were continually transformed. All forms were limited by their own ends, their own destructive completions. Yet all destructive completions were the fertile sources for new transformations. Like the Templo Mayor's many earthbound ancestral layers, which changed with the seasonal motions of the celestial beings, people's *faces* also change with time. Like a person who is born, eats to continue living, changes a great deal, decays, *dies*, and *disappears*, all forms, human and nonhuman alike, journey through the time spans of their lives. In the words of the Texcocan poet-king Nezahualcoyotl, existence on earth is, at best, fleeting.

The Fleeting Moment [7]

We will exist for just a moment.   1
   Be happy, I say!
Oh, I, Nezahualcoyotl, was traveling.[8]

Is it true that they go on living,
That they are present on earth?   5
   These ones,
   They go on.
   Ohuaye![9]

Not forever on earth.
Only briefly here.   10
   Ohuaye!
   Ohuaye!
Indeed, even greenstone shatters.
Even gold breaks into pieces.
   Oh!   15
Quetzal feathers shred:
   Travelers all.[10]
   Ohuaye!
Not forever on earth.
Only briefly here.   20
   Ohuaye!
   Ohuaye!

Shaping *Mahceua*

Not only were people's shapes timed, but their time spans were shaped by a number of internal and external forces. People's lives and their characters were determined by their *mahceua* (merit), a complex set of elements that constituted their health, personalities, talents, weaknesses, and destinies, which simultaneously formed a person physically and psychically. The *mahceua*, like time, had a doubly coercing and coercible nature. On the one hand, it was as ephemeral as everything else, for it included the shaping of one's biologically based animistic centers, which helped determined the ways in which one would be continually *destroyed*, eventually *die*, and *disappear*. The natural potentialities promised by one's *mahceua*, therefore, were acted out in the fleeting moments of history. On the other hand, since one could participate willfully in this shaping process, one also could control it to some measure.

Included in the *mahceua* along with names, actions, and other forces were those parts of a person's personality and destiny that were developed through their animistic centers. The *tonalli* was lodged within a baby's head during a naming ritual, which took place shortly after birth. The *tonalli* helped define certain ancestral and godly ties as well as her particular temperament that might affect her future conduct. This "thread" that tied one to one's past relatives and deities could be protected and strengthened through various healing rites throughout life. The *teyolia* was lodged in the heart. Probably received during gestation, it gave faculties associated with vitality, memory, will, and reason. It also was associated with the fires of particular deities, which helped determine one's talents and one's death. The *teyolia* could be damaged by sexual misconduct, illness, and sorcery; but it also could be ritually altered and strengthened. Finally, the *ihiyotl* was lodged in the liver and was bathed at birth to ensure its cleanliness, for a virtuous person had a clean liver. It was the seat of strong emotions, both helpful and harmful. The *ihiyotl* had to be revitalized throughout life with healthful air and food (López Austin 1988b, 205–36). Beginning at birth, then, physically based centers that shaped one's health, personality, talents, actions, and destiny were continually shaped by forces both within and beyond one's control.

This transformative process beginning at birth was linked to the divinatory calendar. A newborn was named and given an ordered identity on a day deemed propitious by the divinatory *tonalpohualli*. According to the rules of the divinatory calendar, every day bore both good and bad attributes that were weighed against each other. For example, little girls born on the day 7-Flower in the second *trecena* (or thirteen-day "week")[11] were destined, if they led chaste and honorable lives, to become skilled textile artists, like this day's patroness, Xochiquetzal, a goddess of weaving and sexuality (FC, bk. 4, pt. 5, chap. 2:7). If they did not, they were destined to demise (Read 1986).[12] The day's bird (butterfly), day god (Cinteotl), and night lord (Itztli) also all carried powers that would influence the girl's character and the quality of her life. This *trecena* was governed by Quetzalcoatl and various signs, all of which probably carried forces whose potency could be channeled into the babe on that day. And since the *trecena* also may have been associated with a particular cardinal direction, the characteristics of that topographical point (its gods, tree, bird, and aspects) were drawn into this moment of naming as well. The convergence of all these attributes in a particular moment of naming gave the little girl part of her *mahceua*. A child's *mahceua* could be enhanced further by taking on an ancestor's name that bore powers belonging to the *mahceua* of some esteemed but now dead relative (FC, bk. 6, pt. 7, chap. 37:204). As the Mexica returned to the "Hill of the Grandparents" (myth 8: 3), so too did each child twist back to its ancestors.

However, the naming ceremony was not the only source for the little girl's *mahceua* even though it shaped a significant portion of her identity. Throughout her life, *mahceua* was both received from others acting upon the girl and produced by the actions of the girl herself. Gods of earth, sky, and underworld could decide independently to effect her,[13] causing her to act in unpredictable ways and causing unforeseen things to happen to her. Moreover, the child's own willful acts during her life span also served to effect her personal *mahceua*, her identity; if she chose to remain chaste and pure, one route was open to her, if not, another.[14] Finally, other calendrically timed ritual actions, such as various healing, divinatory, and socially constructive rites, also could alter one's *mahceua*. For example, rulers (along with a host of new names) altered their *mahceua* radically when initiated into office (López Austin 1988b, 396–400). One's *mahceua* was not a completely predestined affair. Like all else, one's *mahceua*-shaped identity was transformed by both one's actions and one's participation in a calendrically shaped existence.

Transformative Moments

Mexica transformative moments existed only in history. These potent moments—these points in *space-time* that reorient the past in the present to reshape the future—have a unique twist to them that is somewhat different from either Ricoeur's idea of nowness or Eliade's idea of returning to the primordium, both of which collapse the present with some sense of eternal sacredness. Ricoeur's and Eliade's ideas must be *re-presented* (transformed) if Mexica *nowness* and *returns* are to be understood. For history (and *only* history) not only made people insignificant by spinning out of the limited sight of humans, it also allowed those same limited, insignificant humans to make history significant by pulling particular transformative moments into their own distinctive present.

Mexica *nowness* is similar but not identical to Ricoeur's nowness. The spiraling, spinning double nature of Mexica time suggests that the past also will be handed down to the present and reoriented to the future with a spiraling, spinning motion; it suggests that any sense of *nowness* will also be shaped in a spiraling manner. If time continually transforms, then history will mold people's repetitive experiences of time, not provide a temporary link to an eternally unchanging reality. Unlike Ricoeur's nowness, this "reorientation" of the "past's potentialities" toward the future (Ricoeur 1985, 17) does not assume that any single thread or even any single part of any one thread in time's rope will continually reappear. At a naming ceremony, for example, a child's *mahceua* did not simply recall a single mythic moment at the beginning of time; it recalled a unique combination of many moments from different temporal periods. Various combinations of calendrical cycles lined up at a given moment, assuring a distinctive *mahceua* or merit of this event. Orderly but changing transformative moments characterize the Mexica cosmos, not temporary periodic moments of eternal stability.

Spiraling time is more like the genetic model of ancestry than an inexact repetition of some sacred past. This is no temporary route to some eternal moment, no transient collapse of the past, present, and future. Although Mexica moments partially repeat each other, they never totally conflate. Unlike a circle that comes around to precisely the same spot at which it began, a spiral comes back to a position that is slightly ahead of its previous point of departure. Each time a cycle is completed, spiraling time returns to its departure point, but the events of the past that occurred at that point can never be repeated entirely in the present, for the repeating rounds never land in exactly the same position. Like the rounds of a coil, the repetitions of temporal rounds are like the children and grandchildren of past ancestors, like but not the same as those from whose bodies they emerged. At its naming, a child drew together all the powers of the particular calendrical event that converged at that particular moment. Because this was a distinctive convergence, different from any other, the child was like all these ancestral moments, but their unique combination assured that the babe would bear its own distinctive character. As new ancestors are followed by even newer ancestors, time moves forward, a rope spinning ever longer as it doubles back on itself.

The divinatory *tonalpohualli* calendar determined which divine influences were most important in each day, thereby making those distinctive forces available to people. Present moments stretched back, picking up all the powers of the particular years, deities, day birds and gods, night lords, and cardinal direction of times past. This was like tying the same points together on a coil of rope. The binding constituted a unique meshing of numerous past moments, just as the binding of all those points on the rope's coil bound a number of unique sets of fibers. During rituals, one collapsed many specific moments (or fibers) into a single moment (or rope sector) in order to activate all those moments' potencies in the present, which then could mold the future. The present moment contained past moments but was identical to no other moment that ever existed, and it could transform moments yet to come. Coordinating human events with past celestial, terrestrial, godly, and other historical events allowed people to use moments of *nowness* to restructure their lives.

Various *mahceua* (merits) characterize these calendrically distinctive moments of Mexica *nowness*. By drawing on the creative potencies of an individual person and her actions, on the forces of outside agents, on the ancestors, and on time itself, one manipulated a person's new future. Each ongoing moment of one's life was a unique temporal confluence filled with possibilities. The Mexica were no more fated than any other human beings who recognize both the forces that restrict their own wills and the powers their own actions have to shape events to come. *Nowness* both limited people and offered them choices; rituals that repeated various cycles of time both bound children with their toltec ancestors' specific heritage and created unique individuals who could transform that heritage.

This means that Mexica ritual *returns* are not identical to Eliadian returns. Unlike Eliadian ritual returns, Mexica *returns* such as the naming ceremony were limited in their possibilities. For although they drew on the powers of the past, they did not draw on the fecundity of all time or on the potencies of a time before time. They drew instead on only particular moments that had special and circumscribed powers. Moreover, each child's naming was the beginning of an ongoing chain of continually new creations as that child's life unfolded. Each moment was an heir to its past, a past limited by its own ever-changing form. Like time itself, Mexica *nowness* was both limited by its repetitious bonds with the past and made expansive by its progressively transformative nature.

This sense of limited yet continuous *nowness* may be seen in the performance of the New Fire ceremony. With the rekindling of all fires in the entire Mexica-Tenochca domain, time was symbolically begun again; it was renewed by creating a new sun as had been done at Teotihuacan when Nanahuatzin leapt into the fire. However, the central imagery in this ceremony harkens only to the beginning of the Fifth Sun at Teotihuacan; it is not a return to the period of all creativity, the time of cosmic origins before the first sun.[15] The New Fire ceremony is no more than a limited return to powers bounded by a single sun.

An Eliadian *illud tempus*, a timeless primordium that sits before time, is not repeated symbolically in this ceremony as some have suggested (D. Carrasco 1981). Only the creation of the beginning of the Fifth Sun is repeated, and that only partially (as will be seen). This sun, moreover, is slated to end just as the previous four suns ended according to calendrical determination. The future toward which the present was reoriented in the New Fire ceremony was one that assured the sun's demise just as a newborn baby's future on earth's surface would eventually include its own *death*.

A concept of spiraling and spinning time reorients and *re-presents* Eliade's myth of eternal returns as a completely new conception of continuing hierophanies. By taking the Fifth Sun's mythic birth out of the primordium's unchanging eternity (something Eliade never did) and placing it into the boundaries of a limited, yet sacred and ever-changing historical present, mythic hierophanies now become continuously transformative; time now is continually renewable. Hierophanous experiences are now ongoing rather than merely periodic as they were in the classic work of Eliade. Time spins simultaneously backward and forward, making the potency of the sacred ever present. Each ordinary moment is a source of extraordinary, sacred creativity, and transformative moments "gathered," "joined," and "met" many past moments of creative potencies like so many threads binding together in time's rope (Binding Year: 1–4).

Continual and ongoing transformations occurring in moments of ritualized *nowness* also are expressed by *poliui*'s creative *destructions*, by those moments of *continuing eschatologies*. The expectations of the present Fifth Sun, based on the past's limited potentialities, included the future *destruction* of all things associated with that sun's existence on earth's surface. Just as the sun and the moon of the Fifth Sun had been created out of the destroyed and transformed bodies of two gods, so things timed by those celestial bodies would be destroyed and transformed. Each child, at the moment of its own *completion* and *death*, would transform into yet more new forms of existence with the scattering of its animistic entities, its various souls. A person's parts, like the shape of the jaguar, eventually would not be "well arranged" (Birth: IV.70). They would spin into *tlahtlacoltin*, "messed up" and "disarrayed." These Mexica *continuing eschatologies*, these continuing endings, give ongoing hierophanies their destructive potentiality.

The creative-destructive potencies of transformative moments could be harnessed to shape people's land and political history as well as people themselves. López Austin also has noted time's complex double nature in Mesoamerican thought, its ability to move historically forward while simultaneously doubling back (1985, 75–79). He suggests that any apparent contradiction that might exist between the historical and the mythical, the progressive and the cyclical, was resolved by the multidimensionality of Mexica mythical time, for cosmic time was composed of many diverse moments. Because cycles became larger and larger, it became impossible, eventually, for any one specialist to have a total knowledge of it. Even the diviners and those skilled in calendrics were limited in their powers to understand the full significance of time. In the cosmic scheme of things, human existence appeared insignificant in practical terms, and social and political events were, in the end, not repeatable. Nevertheless, historical conjunctions offered a chance to make human life significant. López Austin points out that people used historical time to establish the relationships governing things, such as the occupation of land divisions, that would determine a people's hegemony in an area.

People altered their past, present, and future realities by changing how historical events great and small were coordinated. History is therefore the source of creativity, not that which must be momentarily "killed" (as Eliade voiced it) to find some eternal primordium's creativity. History transforms history and that is all there is. By means of calendrically determined rites that created the ongoing identities of people, their land, their deities, and their ages, great mythic rounds of power could be focused upon and drawn into current history and made at least temporarily effective in the impermanent yet concrete forms of an age. People may have seemed insignificant in terms of those great cosmic rounds, but that same spiraling of time—placed, as it was, within the progressive counts of the days and years—also could be used to make their own existence significant. History was all people had, but its spiraling allowed them the chance to form and transform at least partially their own personal, topographical, and political histories.

Sacrifice made all this happen. The land dominated by the Mexica rested on Tlalticpac (Earth's Surface) between Ilhuicatl (Sky-Water) and Mictlan (Land of the Dead). It was a living entity, shaped and bound by time's spinning motion and filled with many beings (human and nonhuman), all of whom shared in its history and were hungry for existence. Living things had to eat, and it was sacrificial consumption that kept all beings alive and warm. At transformative moments of *completion*, sacrifice burned the suns into existence, made the seasons move, and made the divinatory and solar *xiuhmolpilli* spin. Sacrifice fed *returning* moments of *nowness*, gave strength to the porters bearing their burdens of time, and shaped and sustained all glyphic names and *faces*. It sustained the double nature of time, giving it strength to spin its rounds of power onto earth's surface and fashion an ongoing order out of the events arising from human and cosmic history. Now that *time-space's* ropes have been unbound and their bundle of reeds unpacked, that burning shape of fiery sacrificial feeding needs to be spun.

PART 2

BURNING HEARTS

Processes of Sacrificial Transformations

New Fire

1. Like so its face was divided. 2. Only one thing was known; the people on Uixachtlan watched that way; they looked that way; they craned their necks that way. 3. Each person there divined its completion, each expected the drawing of fire when it spreads, bursts forth, shines forth. 4. And when it appeared [and] was sparked well, it was puffed into fire. 5. Later, like so it flickers, it bursts forth everywhere, it appeared, it was seen from far away. (FC, bk. 7, pt. 8, fols. 244v–245r, chap. 10:28)

THE COSMIC
MEAL

Sacrificial Realities

Among the reeds of the 2-Reed plaque's center hides a double image, a visual pun. Therein, rising from the fan of reedlike flames, appears the stemlike stick of a fire drill in action. Just above the stick's point pokes the top of what is possibly a bloodletting thorn, and just beneath its new flame rests the vessel waiting to be filled with sacrificial blood (figure 1.5, 7, 8). The drill is the glyphic sign for the New Fire rite or the Binding-of-the-Years ceremony; the thorn and vessel indicate its sacrificial and consumptive nature. It was this fiery sacrificial ritual that bound *time-space* together, reestablishing the appropriate order of the Fifth Sun for another fifty-two years, allowing the years which had gradually "joined" to "sprout" into life (Binding Years: 4, 9; Birth: IV.49). And once they had blossomed, these hungry new lives were fed with the blood of human and animal offerings.

But before this creative energy was born, a period of frail insecurity existed, for the entangling of the Fifth Sun's normal order was an especially marked threat just prior to the lighting of the new fire. When a full round of fifty-two years came close to its end, people became afraid (FC, bk. 7, pt. 8, chap. 7:21–22; D. Carrasco 1981, 286). The round's last year, 1-Rabbit, brought an inevitable threat of famine and *death*. If people were not prepared, they placed themselves in a state of rottenness or disarray (*motlatlacunamictia*). They caused themselves to become entangled, messed up, or displaced. Just as the Lords of the Night formed the odd counterorder of the even day-signs, so too were such poor and less fortunate people the counterorder of the rich. During famine, those whose lack of success caused them to become the messed-up *tlahtlacolli* were forced to sell themselves into servitude. This unfortunate state of affairs was brought on by either their own or their ancestors' imprudence and resulted in servitude for generations of their heirs to come. When finally paid, this debt reordered and rearranged them. Only after the lighting of a new fire, its distribution, and the relighting of temple and household fires could the dangers of famine be set aside for yet another round. Sacrificing burnt hearts temporarily bound the reed years, keeping the cosmos in a balanced motion.

This sacrificially transformative cosmos is the topic of this chapter. First, I describe the New Fire ceremony and discuss past Western theorizing about why such amazing (and disturbing) events might occur. Then I turn to the Mexica cosmo-logic structuring sacrificial transformation; here two major metaphors for deformative-transformative motion are examined: an eating continuum and the topography of the cosmic house. Finally sacrificial eating and topography are joined into a coherent system of creative-destructive powers that balanced people and other beings traveling throughout this great Nahua dwelling.

Sparking the New Fire

The New Fire ceremony itself took place in the darkness of a November night during the month of Panquetzaliztli, which occurred at the beginning of the dry, warring season. At this moment, the Pleiades, at their zenith, were moving contrary to the sun, which was at its nadir. Then the reed-years were bound by the sacrifice of an individual whose body and heart (the site of the *teyolia*) were consumed completely by the new fire built on his chest. Burned as Nanahuatzin's body had been burned at the beginning of the sun, this offering became the source of energy for a new temporal period. It was from this single fire that all the fires in the entire domain, communal temple, and family hearth alike, were relit. In this way, the Mexica-Tenochca and those whom they governed were given energy to live for another round of fifty-two years. All were given sustenance by this meal of flesh and blood. Ritualized sacrificial meals allowed the Mexica-Tenochca cosmos to function effectively, shaping *spatio-temporal* transformation into orderly motion. Without sacrifice, a state of *tlahtlacolli*, or disarray, would exist for the entire cosmic community.

Yet the person whose flesh and blood sustained the orderly continuation of *time-space* was not an abstract ideal. He was not simply an important cog in a grand mechanical cosmic clock but a real person who lived within a real community of other real persons. Sahagún gives an account of Tenochtitlan's New Fire ceremony held during the *time-space* of Motecuhzuma II (FC, bk. 7, pt. 8, chaps. 7–12:21–32). The offering in this particular event was a "well-bred man" named Xiuhtlamin (FC, bk. 7, pt. 8, chap. 12:31–32), a war captive from the town of Huexotzinco in the Valley of Tlaxcala (a valley to the east of the Valley of Mexico). He may have been fifty-two years old himself since children born during the year of this fifty-two-year rite were given names that included the word *xiuitl* ("year"); to have a name with *xiuitl* in it was a prerequisite for the honored role as sacrificial offering. He had been taken captive in one of the previous "Flowery Wars," battles held between the allied cities of the Valley of Mexico (including Tenochtitlan) and six cities in the Valley of Tlaxcala. These wars occurred during the dry season for no other reason than to capture sacrificial offerings used in both Mexica and Tlaxcalan rituals. Xiuhtlamin had been held prisoner by the Mexica-Tenochca at Tlatilolco, the site of the largest marketplace on the island. His captor's name was Iztcuin, who received the honor of being called "Captor of Xiuhtlamin" (Xiuhtlaminmani).[1]

When it was the moment for the years to come alive, all people in the entire domain "took hold" of them (Binding Years: 8, 10). In preparation for the rite, all fires were extinguished, all wood and stone statues of gods kept in people's homes cast into the water, and all cooking utensils and fire implements thrown away. Everything was swept clean and all rubbish disposed of. The tale tells us that when the ceremonial night finally descended, people were sorely frightened. In this dark period of transition from one sun to the next, they lacked solar protection from the forces of the night. If a fire could not be drawn successfully, the new sun would not be created and nothing could stop those nocturnal powers. No sun darts would exist to shoot the jaguar spirits released from the innards of nocturnal beings.[2] All would be destroyed, eaten by the Tzitzimime, mythical female creatures of the night. The Fifth Sun's light would shine no more.

The ceremony attracted a huge audience of people from near and far. Everywhere people perched on rooftops in the darkened valley; no one was touching the ground. All watched for the fire to be sparked above on an isolated mountaintop called Uixachtlan, jutting suddenly out of the middle of the basin's flat landscape. Children, wearing masks made of maguey leaves, had to remain awake all night or else they would become grain-eating mice. Sitting there on the rooftops with their parents, they were constantly nudged and poked to keep them from quietly nodding off so that such a dire consequence would not happen. Pregnant women, also wearing maguey masks, were placed for safekeeping in granaries, for if the fire was not begun, they would turn into fierce people-eating beasts. Like grain, it seems, the food and future of the next round (corn seed and those ripe with human seed) were stored in houses as the food and future of people to come. Both childbearing women and children (those bearing future ancestors and those who were immature ancestors of people to come) were considered forces of fertility and so were protected, away from the hungry counterforces of earth and night.

A procession of those playing central roles in the performance, the fire priests, snaked its way from the Templo Mayor in the center of Tenochtitlan, across a portion of the lake, and up the mountainside. "Very deliberately, very stately, they proceeded, [they] went spread out." All "were arranged in order, arrayed in and wearing the garb of the gods." Among these godly participants moving so slowly up the mountain were both the rain deity, Tlaloc, and he who blew the Fifth Sun into motion, Quetzalcoatl (FC, bk. 7, pt. 8, chap. 10:27). Present, then, were the wet counterorder of the dry season and the windy forces of motion.

There on the mountaintop, the new fire was first sparked on Xiuhtlamin's chest, a task given to a highly trained fire priest from Copulco. This was an honored and serious job that may have been handed from father to son.[3] Even so, before he sparked it, this skillful firemaker went about constantly practicing his fire-drilling task. Once it was sparked, four priests held Xiuhtlamin down while another removed his heart with an obsidian knife called *ixcuauac* or "he who has an eating face." This knife was so sharp, it is said, that if simply dropped, it would have sliced through his chest as though it were a pomegranate (FC, bk. 7, pt. 8, chap. 10:28; Durán 1971, 91). Such ceremonial knives often bore a face with an open, toothy mouth. Xiuhtlamin's heart, his *teyolia*, was fed to the fire, and once his entire body had been consumed, the flames were distributed to all the regions of Mexica dominion.

As soon as all those sitting apprehensively in the vast darkness on their rooftops saw that first little flame, they cut their ears and spattered the blood in its direction. Even the ears of babies and children were pierced. Thus the fire was ritually fed its merit (*tlamaceua*). Fire brands were lit from it and taken first to the House of Huitzilopochtli on the southern side of the temple and then to the fire priests' house. After this, fire was taken to all the other priests' houses, to the temple of each *calpulli* and to the young men's houses in cities and villages alike. During this distribution of the fires, some hurled themselves at the flames, blistering their bodies. Runners quickly carried flames to all places until everywhere in the domain, fires had sprung up again. This was followed by much rejoicing. All household goods, clothing, reed mats, pestles, and hearth stones were renewed. Sacrificial quails were decapitated, and burning incense was offered to the four directions and then cast into the new fire in each courtyard. Amaranth and honey cakes were eaten, cakes which were considered the flesh and bones of appropriate deities, possibly of Xiuhtlamin himself.[4] Then all fasted until noon, at which point sacrifices of human offerings were made,[5] followed by great feasting and a second laying of new fires in the courtyards. And so ended the ritual of the New Fire.

Theorizing about Sacrifice

What could such incredible rites mean for these individual and communal participants? What possibly could motivate someone to take part in such sacrifices, which to a twentieth-century mentality may seem utterly preposterous and violently barbaric? Surely sacrificial rituals entailed more than vague, abstract notions about ordering *time-space*, about keeping some cosmic clock ticking away. Indeed, these rites were so dramatic that they have spawned a host of theoretical answers to questions such as these. Despite the drama of high state rites such as the New Fire ceremony, however, sacrifice also included a vast array of far less dramatic and mundane rites practiced daily. This complexity has challenged theorizing about the sacrifices for centuries.

Sixteenth-century sources collected and written by Spanish conquerors have tended to overemphasize the number and violent nature of sacrificial rituals. Moreover, Spanish religious orientations were varied, sometimes set in a sixteenth-century, millenarian world and always set in a world which was understood through that century's multiple Catholic views. Spanish authors, for example, variously explained indigenous sacrificial rituals as misguided and ignorant practices originating with the devil, as similar to Christian penitence, or as mere superstition, depending on the author's own background and on the context and nature of the specific rite in question.[6] These Spanish commentators rarely, if ever, fully comprehended indigenous explanations of the many diverse sacrificial rituals. Because the vast majority of our sources come filtered through this sixteenth-century Spanish sieve, comprehension is particularly difficult for the contemporary scholar.

Modern scholarly explanations also have varied widely. Some have seen Mesoamerican sacrifice as a stage in a unilinear process of human evolution. Others, by focusing on its environmental, biological, political, social, or psychological functions, have suggested that it served as a means of population control, a dietary supplement providing protein, a way for the elite to maintain their hegemony, an effective or maladaptive route to political expansion, and a way to maintain an orderly relationship between people's cultural selves and their natural environment. Still others, seeking to uncover the religious and symbolic logic that may have structured these rituals, have focused on sacrifice as a coherent system of belief.[7]

Those who attempt to explain the phenomena of Mexica-Tenochca sacrifice as part of a logically structured religious orientation often have agreed that sacrifices involved the ritual sharing of a variety of plant, animal, and human comestibles. Most believe that the overriding logic included an exchange between human and nonhuman entities, which sustained the cosmos in an ordered state of existence. If one wanted the cosmos to provide food, one had to feed the cosmos.

Many scholars also have noted a close sacrificial bond between death and destruction and life and creation,[8] a bond I suggest correlates with Mexica concepts of transformation. Both the fact that one cannot live without eating (an act that necessarily destroys things) and the idea that all things are timed fit nicely together, for things must continually be destroyed if life's transformative processes are to go on; old things are "eaten" to create new things. Just as a transformative reality fused time inseparably with things of space, so too a hungry cosmos that ate to live fused life and creation inseparably with death and destruction.

Although some of the above theories have lacked adequate support in specific texts and contexts and thus may appear somewhat facile in their conclusions,[9] none alone is sufficient to explain adequately such a complex and widespread phenomenon. The inherent complexity of sacrifice is demonstrated by the description of the New Fire ceremony alone. Foodstuffs of this one sacrificial ritual ranged from the blood and body parts of both animals and humans to figurines made of amaranth and honey. And the ritual itself included the participation of a wide variety of people in a diverse range of activities.

Furthermore, when viewed as a whole, Mexica sacrificial rituals display surprisingly multifarious forms. Quails, jaguars, crocodiles, ducks, salamanders, and amaranth cakes were among the nonhuman offerings used in the many different rites. Although the total destruction of a human offering (as it appears in the New Fire rite) was perhaps one of the most unusual and dramatic examples, one of the most common and widespread practices was the far less dramatic ritual act of autosacrifice. Involving limited ritual bleeding, these acts were performed on numerous occasions ranging from the naming of newborn babies to the corona-tions of kings. Sometimes autosacrifice was one facet in a more complex ritual like the New Fire rite; at other times, it played a central role.

Different sacrificial techniques, furthermore, were utilized in the more extreme forms of human sacrifice, including not only heart extractions but also decapitation, drowning, and shooting the offering with arrows. Neither were the offerings always totally destroyed as in the New Fire rite; instead, they might be consumed ritually by the living participants. The captor, for example, sometimes was given specified parts of the of-fering as a communion feast, and sometimes the heads of offerings were displayed on skull racks. Sacrificial rituals were associated with both war and the agricultural cycle and included both willing and unwilling par-ticipants from many segments of society. Males and females of all ages were sacrificed; sometimes they were foreigners, but often they were not. Finally, the sacrifices were offered to not only celestial foci such as the sun, but also to terrestrial recipients such as the Earth Monster.[10] While this brief survey of many different manifestations of Mexica sacrificial rituals is hardly complete, it gives an idea of the extreme intricacy of the topic.

Two perspectives, both of which view Mexica sacrifice as a coherent religious system, may help explain why people may have participated in these curious and frightening rituals. The first involves an exploration of the cosmology of the Mexica and its sacrificial logic;[11] the second looks at some communal and experiential reasons. For while it may seem im-possible to some living today that anyone could have willingly taken part in such seemingly nasty experiences, nevertheless they did, and there must have been reasons for so doing.

Sacrificial Transformations

Picture, if you can, a carved Mexica-Tenochca *face* or *ixtli* with a very round countenance marked by two eyes staring forward. Its nose is pierced with a bar-shaped ornament, and its ears are punctured by two large jade disks. Set in a prominent and formidable jaw, its open mouth dis-plays an equally formidable set of teeth. Emerging from this mouth and hanging over the lower teeth is a double image, a tongue which is also a sacrificial blade. On this blade, shown upside down, appears a smaller face also with an open, toothy mouth. On each side of this head appear more visual puns, two claws which are simultaneously faces with open fang-filled mouths probably grasping sacrificial hearts in their claw-teeth.

The Fifth Sun's name glyph, *ollin* (motion), surrounds this central head. In each of its four quarters appears one of the four cosmic suns preceding the Fifth (myth 1), each also represented by a face, this time shown in profile (figure 12).

This *face* of the Fifth Sun is in the center of a stone monument dramatically spotlighted and hanging in the Museum of Anthropology in Mexico City. The monument itself is a well-known frieze entitled the "Sun Stone." Colossal in size (with a diameter of 3.6 meters), it was first discovered beneath the main plaza of Mexico City in 1790, when the foundations of the National Cathedral were under repair. It is a complex and sophisticated example of a class of similar solar disks whose full import still is unknown. The subject of much scholarly controversy, the Sun Stone is now generally thought to depict fundamental Mexica cosmological concepts concerning time, space, and sacrifice, and its central figure is thought to represent aspects of the sun, earth, or both. Whoever the central figure is, however, it clearly links eating with sacrifice and *time-space* by repeatedly equating them in a series of related visual puns. What is represented here is the *face* (*ixtli*) or identity of Mexica sacrifice, the binding of *time-space* by eating.

Eating Death: A Transformative Exchange

Eating, for the Mexica, is closely tied to their status as hunters and warriors. Although their early history is shrouded in the misty past, it is thought that the Mexica-Tenochca migrated as nomadic hunter-gatherers from somewhere in the north, acquiring agricultural skills only after settling among the diverse urban populations already in the Valley of Mexico. Domestication of animals never entirely replaced hunting for both historical and environmental reasons.[12] It does not seem particularly surprising, then, that hunting remained an important metaphor for the acquisition of food. Food, no matter what its variety, frequently was equated with wild game, for all were thought of as animated beings. Corn was game that was stalked and captured, and the sacrificial process itself was likened to the act of hunting. War and hunting, after all, involve similar strategies for tracking, capturing, and killing a quarry; as hunting brings food, so too does warfare. And just as eating (the end result of hunting) is a continual part of human life processes, the eating of sacrificial foodstuffs (gained through hunting and warfare) was a continual part of reciprocal cosmic processes. The inhabitants of the Fifth Sun fed each other food that had been hunted and captured.[13]

This sacrificial eating appears in all possible alimentary guises,[14] for a

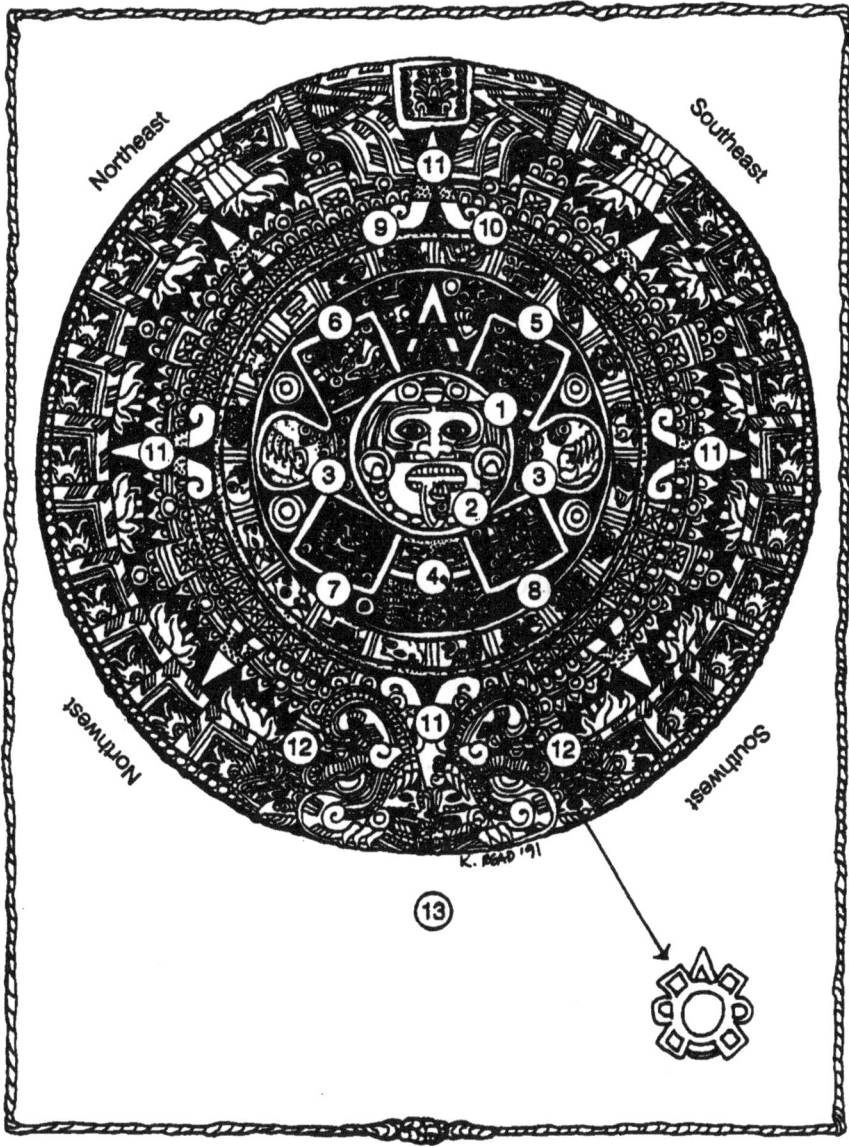

FIGURE 12.
The Sun Stone. *Museo Nacional de Antropología, Mexico City.*

1. Central sun and/or earth deity
2. Tongue depicted as a sacrificial knife
3. Claw-heads grace each side of the central deity
4. 4-Movement, glyph for the Fifth Age
5. 4-Jaguar, the First Age
6. 4-Wind, the Second Age
7. 4-Rainstorm, the Third Age
8. 4-Water, the Fourth Age

9. Crocodile, first day of the twenty day-signs
10. Flower, twentieth day of the twenty day-signs
11. Sun darts, one at each cardinal point
12. Two fire snakes encircling the outer edge of the stone
13. Deities emerging from the mouths of the two fire snakes

comprehensive eating continuum was one of the major metaphoric expressions structuring sacrifice. The capture of sacrificial foodstuffs, their preparation, their consumption, and their final excretion all were pictured in innumerable verbal and visual descriptions of sacrificial acts. And as creative and thus fertile processes, hunting and eating were equated occasionally with sexual intercourse, for all were productive in the most fundamental sense of the word. It was the food of the Fifth Sun that assured the processes of transformation necessary for *time-space's* continuance on Tlalticpac, the Earth's Surface where humans dwelt. Without sacrificial eating, the motion of life would cease.

Examples of this continuum from hunting to excretion abound. Along with the creation of the sun and the moon at Teotihuacan came three major foodstuffs metaphorically described by the hunting of the god Xolotl (Birth: VI.37–59). Unlike a pastoral animal, Xolotl could not be herded willingly into the slaughterhouse. Instead, he was pursued by Death as a quarry. Finally cornered in the water, he was captured and slain. Similarly, people were hunted down, captured, and killed as game for the cosmos. Xiuhtlamin's captor, Xiuhtlaminmani, was considered a hunter who cornered the offering on the battlefield. *Ma*, the verb root of his name, means not only to capture but also "to hunt" and "to fish."

Warriors also were captured, but like corn that was likened to game. In the mid-1400s, the dwellers of the Mexican Highlands were hit by a major drought. Dikes were built in Lake Texcoco to capture fresh water more efficiently, but this tactic was not enough, and it was feared that the cosmos was starving to death as were people. So that the cosmos might be better fed, the Flowery Wars were instituted for the express purpose of gaining sacrificial captives, live warriors from the opposing side (Read 1986). Corn and maguey had the same nature as wild game, and warriors had the same nature as corn, but with a difference. While Xolotl was stalked by Death where corn grows, in the field, these warriors were stalked where corn was sold, in the marketplace. Upon the initiation of the Flowery Wars, the Mexica statesman Tlacaellel said:

> Our god will not be made to wait until new wars appear. He will find a way, a marketplace where he will go with his army to buy victims, men for him to eat. And this will be a good thing, for it will be as if he has his maize cakes hot from the griddle—tortillas from a nearby place, hot and ready to eat whenever he wishes them.
>
> . . . our god does not like the flesh of those barbarous people [who live far away in foreign lands]. They are like hard, yellowish, tasteless bread in his

mouth. Those people are savages and they speak strange languages. Therefore, our marketplace . . . must be in these six cities [which are close to home].
The people from these places will come to our god like warm breads, soft,
tasty, straight from the fire. (HI 1994, chap. 28:231–32)

Perhaps it was for more than convenience's sake that a war captive like
Xiuhtlamin was kept in a market town like Tlatilolco. War, hunting, and
going to market were equivalent acts because they all produced sustenance for the Fifth Sun's various human and nonhuman inhabitants.

Food that is captured and killed must be cooked before eating. Human hearts (their *teyolia*) became warm, tasty tortillas intended to nourish the sun and give it strength. By being eaten, the *teyolia* of the warriors
were incorporated into the sun's land, where they helped fight its daily
battle to rise each morning. And after four years, these *teyolia* transformed
into birds and butterflies sucking the nectar of earthly flowers.

Children, like corn, also were metaphoric foodstuffs to be captured,
cooked, and fed to beings of the hungry cosmos. A midwife gave victory
cries at the birth of a baby, for the mother successfully had captured her
child. And those women who died in childbirth's battle, along with other
female warriors, became the ones who captured the sun at noon from
the male warriors so that it might be brought back to earth by sunset (FC,
bk. 6, pt. 7, chap. 29–30:161–69). At a second naming ceremony, which
took place in the spring during the fourth month of the year, babies captured from the cosmos the year before were taken to the Templo Mayor
by their mothers to be named. With an obsidian knife, a priest made a
small incision in the ear lobes of each baby and, if it was male, in its
penis. These knives were then offered to Huitzilopochtli, the warrior ancestor of the Mexica. Their fathers, at this same time, went into the fields
to capture corn stalks that also were presented to the gods (Durán 1971,
423–24). In the fall during the eighteenth month of the year, a brave
warrior or good woman was sought out as "uncle" or "aunt" for the child.
The child was pierced in the same place as it had been pierced during
the spring rite. A fire was built, and an old man of the *calpulli*'s school
dedicated the baby by holding it over the fire, symbolically singeing it,
preparing it for its role as corn for the cosmos. Then the child was lifted
by the neck so that it "might quickly grow tall" (FC, bk. 2, pt. 3, chap.
37:165–66).

Corn and babies alike were "captured" from the cosmos;[15] both were
symbolically "roasted" over a fire. Children were captured in order to
become cakes for the gods, just as maize was captured from the fields to

become cakes for people. Both children and warriors were corn tortillas for the hungry beings of a living cosmos. The actual sacrifice of some children was required for Tlaloc, the rain god, and was done at the height of the dry season, just before the rainy season began. In this way, warriors were corn captured in the dry warring season while the young were corn captured in anticipation of the coming rainy agricultural season. Sacrifice was not just an act of destroying one thing to make another; it also was an act of eating one thing to create another, an act of living beings in this cosmos reciprocally feeding each other.

Eating's fertile nature can be seen in its close association with sexuality. The syphilitic Nanahuatzin both shelled the Mountain of Produce whence came corn and was shelled at his own roasting in the fire at Teotihuacan (myth 4.3; Birth: III.28–29). And just as a little boy's penis is bled at his various initiations into the Mexica community, so too was Quetzalcoatl's penis bled on the dead's ground bones (myth 3: 6). As though it were cornmeal from which tortillas were to be made, the stuff of people was moistened with his sexually empowered blood to make this bonemeal both fertile and moldable. In both cases, sexual substances are likened to corn.

Much of the Mexica material is supported by contemporary stories, albeit in *re-presented* forms. It is helpful, then, to recount some of these tales. The contemporary Yaonáhuac tell their own version of the "Gathering of Corn" story found in "The Legend of the Suns" (myth 4). As in the ancient Mexica myth, Nanahuatzin is responsible for cracking open the Mountain of Produce, but this time he is the strong Old Thunderbolt, who helps the lightning bolts to get the corn. After they break open this mountainous "granary" and while the Old Thunderbolt is resting from having spent his energies, the lightning bolts steal the corn, leaving him with nothing. Because of the sexual nature of many of the Yaonáhuac tales and the often close association between planting corn and sexuality, James Taggert interprets this as a tale of intercourse between the male Nanahuatzin and a female mountain (1983, 89–92). This is possible, for other historical parallels exist. The earth sometimes (though not always) is seen as female.[16] And, painted on the walls of a building at Tepantitla in Teotihuacan appears a female mountain sprouting flowers and pouring forth water and other good things from her innards (Pasztory 1976); remember, too, the syphilitic nature of Nanahuatzin in "The Birth of the Fifth Sun." If one accepts this sexual interpretation, however, it would have been a violent gang rape, for the Old Thunderbolt and lightning bolts thundered and crashed around to break the mountain open.

Both sexuality and eating are often described in violent terms. In the Mexica "Legend of the Suns," another story is told in which two brothers of the Mixcoa pursue two deer, each with a double head (CC 1992a, 151–52; 1992b, fols. 79:34–80:28, 92–93).[17] After the men abandon the hunt from exhaustion, the deer return, transformed into two seductive women, calling to the men, enticing them to come and "drink their blood." One brother has intercourse with one of the women, causing her to transform her shape and "eat" him (*quallo*). The other brother, frightened, runs from the second enticing woman who follows in pursuit. When she falls on a large cactus and is pinned down by its spines, a *tzitzimitl* (a female nocturnal creature) shoots her with arrows, changing the deer-woman's shape yet again. This series of transformational sacrifices results in four celestial flints springing up from a series of flaming explosions, each a color of one of the four directions. The sky's protective arrows have been born, and the Mixcoa, receiving one of them, now become strong warriors. In this story, sacrifice is equated with both eating and sexuality. By controlling one's sexuality, then, one effectively controls transformative sacrificial actions.

But the fertile, phagocentric imagery of sacrifice does not end with the hunting, capturing, cooking, and eating of game. Even the excretion of food is depicted as part of the sacrificial feeding exchange. Excrement even now is considered an entirely common part of living. The people of present-day San Luis Potosí, for example, tell a tale about long ago when all were sad because they could only smell the good aroma of their meat and tamales but couldn't eat anything. This frustrating problem was solved by the Maize God, who came and gave them all anuses so they could let out what they had taken in by eating. Now everyone is happy (López Austin 1988a, 18–19).

In order to eat, one had also to defecate. What went in also came out but in an altered form whose color and consistency were significant.[18] According to López Austin, the yellowest and creamiest bowel movements were considered the purest, and people were thought to carry *death* in their bellies in the form of excrement (1988a, 16; conversation, 28 August 1990). This is perhaps because the purest form of humanity, a nursing baby, produces such yellow bowel movements. As soon as babies eat solid food, however—that which ties them to the things of earth and to *death*—the color and consistency of their bowel movements change. Moreover, as fertilizer for the crops, human excrement served a practical as well as metaphorical purpose; canoes were kept along the walkways of Tenochtitlan for people to defecate in so that their excrement could be used to fertilize the fields. The castoffs of the eating process recreated that process; the feeding continuum was complete.

All entities that ate produced excrement. Even nonhuman beings defecated, including things of the sky, the earth, and the gods. Precious stones and metals were often described as excrement of various celestial entities. Gold (*coztictecuitlatl*) was the "powerful yellow excrement" produced by the sun, perhaps the purest of bowel movements (FC, bk. 11, pt. 12, chap. 9:233–234).[19] Earth's rain was urine and also likened to gold. Mica (*metzcuitlatl*) and lead (*temetztli*) were both excrement of the moon. A small stone that was thought to grow bigger with time and was used for medicinal purposes was considered Lightning's excrement; it was called the "powerful excrement of rainstorm" (*quiauhteocuitlatl*) (FC, bk. 11, pt. 12, chap. 5:188; 9:234–35). The edible algae which still is eaten today on tostadas is named either "excrement of rocks" (*tecuitlatl*) or "excrement of water" (*acuitlatl*). The smell of a skunk was the god Tezcatlipoca passing gas and an omen of *death* under the right circumstances (Ibid., bk. 5, pt. 6, chap. 19:171).

Mictlan (Land of the Dead) appears as a metaphorically balanced inversion of the eating process found in the sky and on Tlalticpac (Earth's Surface). Its lord, Mictlantecutli, appears in pictorial codices as a figure with a skull-head endowed with a strong jaw and teeth. He is the one who "soaked things" with his tongue (*omjtzalmopalti*)[20] and "built a watery foundation" (*omitzalmotetzonti*) for the dead (FC, bk. 3, pt. 4, app. 1:41–42). A passage from Sahagún's *Primeros Memoriales* describes the food of this place. Mictlantecutli and Mictlancihuatl (lord and lady of the Land of the Dead) eat the feet and hands of people. Their stew is made of beetles who live in moist places, their tamales are imbued with gas also passed by beetles, and their atole is made of pus which they drink from a skull. There they eat pits of fruit, spiny herbs, and thistles (López Austin 1988a, 49). The inhabitants of Mictlan eat things not normally consumed by those on Tlalticpac; they eat the cast-off refuse of the Ilhuicatl (Sky-Water) and Tlalticpac.

Death necessarily is accentuated in an eating environment such as the Mexica's, because for one thing to eat, another must die. It is fitting, then, that Quetzalcoatl retrieved from Mictlan the bones used to make people. These bones were the excrement of past life and, as such, went to fertilize new life. What is food in one place is excrement in the other and vice versa, allowing a dynamic exchange to occur in what is an ecological balancing act. To eat enmeshes one in a transformational process which conserves life-giving substances by continually recycling them. This notion of reciprocal conservation is repeated in the cosmic topography.

The Cosmic House: A Topography of Transformative Exchange

The cosmos provided a container, a kind of metaphoric terrarium, in whose topography the Fifth Sun's inhabitants lived out their lives.[21] Here they hunted, killed, cooked, ate, and defecated other lives in order to couple with and fertilize each other, giving birth to new lives. All life was contained within this cosmos's boundaries. Like the water and gases cycling through a terrarium's space, water, beings, and powers flowed through the Mexica cosmic space. And like a terrarium's plants, beings sprouted, grew, blossomed, died, and rotted to nourish the beings who sprouted behind them. Life continually cycled through this house, *disappearing* only to appear in a new form. Existence spun forward, but it did so by cycling round and round a confined space in a pre-Conquest version of the conservation of matter.[22] Eventually, as had the houses of the previous four suns (myth 1), this dwelling space would collapse when its time span was *completed*.

The Mexica cosmic house, although a *re-presentation* of general, ancient Mesoamerican patterns, was also a correlate to their own particular physical and seasonal geography.[23] Its metaphoric imagery depicted a balanced recycling of cosmic resources and reflected both actual topography and the reality of living in it. It was within a house and among a group of relatives that the reciprocal sharing of food occurred. "The Myth of the Four Suns" described each of the previous suns as having a "house" occupied by some living beings who ate a particular food (myth 1). The Fifth Sun also had a house with occupants who ate something.

Each of the five suns was ordered by an act of "spreading out" created by either the motion one uses to pat out tortillas (*mana*) or that of water spreading out in a pan (*mani*). Both terms are fitting. The former, *mana*, describes the horizontality of the Tlalticpac (Earth's Surface), which was divided into four quarters.[24] The latter, *mani*, describes the spreading of the heavenly waters surrounding this earthly "tortilla." Even today, similar imagery forms various Mesoamerican cosmoses. The Nahua of San Miguel Tzinacapan describe the earth's surface as a *comal*, the flat pan virtually all Mexicans use for roasting tortillas. The sun above this earthly comal produces corn with its heat, while the sun under the comal is the hearth fire that cooks tortillas made from that corn (Lok 1987, 218–19). And for the twentieth-century Panajachel Maya, the watery sea spread out to the horizon until it joined with the sky (Tax, forthcoming).

The Mexica heavens were said to look like a house with walls that reached everywhere. The sea was called *teoatl*, godly water, not because it was a deity but because it bore special power. The name of this *teoatl* was Ilhuicaatl, or Sky-Water because the walls of the heavenly house were made of sea water extending upward (FC, bk. 11, pt. 12, chap. 12:247). As with the Panajachel, the watery sea spread to the sky.

The codex *Vaticano Latino* elaborates on this picture (lámina 1, 2). It describes the skies as "heavens," which were divided first into seven levels, each called an Ilhuicatl, and inhabited by first the moon, stars, the sun, and then salt. These four are followed by a sky in which a gyrating motion took place and two more of particular colors. Second came a place that had corners of obsidian followed by three places of specific divine powers, each called *teotl* and attributed, again, to a different color. The last was a spot called the "Time and Place of Twoness" (Yomeyocan).[25]

The traditional way of understanding these "heavenly" levels is the way in which the codex itself presents them: as thirteen vertically ordered layers, one on top of the other. But the codex also mistranslates the Nahuatl name, the "Place of Twoness" as the "Place of the Trinity."[26] Furthermore, in a nice Platonic style, it describes the sky-waters as "heavens" and "causes," quoting St. Paul to suggest that the invisible things of God have reached even the lost souls of New Spain. These clearly sixteenth-century Spanish interpretations should warn us that a bit of caution needs to be employed, that perhaps this comfortable complementarity between the two texts comes too easily. The commentator of the codex is fairly explicit in his comparison with a classic medieval universe. Several lower "heavens" are said to be occupied by the moon, comets and stars, and the sun. Beyond these extend further "heavens," reaching eventually, to the first cause. Whether the Nahua conceived of this heavenly topography in a like vertical manner is unclear, though the particularity of the names and their iconographical depictions would suggest that some sort of celestial topography or topographies were present at the point of contact with the Spanish, if not precisely this one.

The waters are muddied even further, so to speak, when we consider the topography of the earth. Here the Spanish codex describes a Dantesque series of eight "hells" descending deep into the ground, which are peopled by various "doctors of the devil." Nahuatl passages describing the journey of the dead to Mictlan in the *Florentine Codex* also describe eight different places which are very similar, though not identical, to these eight earthly locations.

The *Florentine* text, however, has a strongly ritualistic tone and easily can be read as a pilgrimage for the dead or extended *death* rites occurring at specific sites on Earth's Surface. Here, the final geographic goal, Mictlan, is described as a house walled by water and containing no smoke holes. The dead were borne across the "Place of Nine Waters" (also called Tlalocan) (FC, bk. 11, pt. 12, chap. 12:248) on the backs of yellow dogs to Mictlan, where they finally "completely *disappeared*" (*ocempopoliooa*). Since the Tlaloques (rain deities) were situated both above and below Tlalticpac (Earth's Surface) and also stood at each corner of the cosmos, reaching between Ilhuicatl (Sky-Water) and Mictlan (López Austin, conversation, 28 August 1990), the entrance to Mictlan may have been situated at the horizon's edge where the sky meets the sea and mountains. In the passage above describing the watery celestial walls, it also is said that the speaker will cross over the sea and die there (FC, bk. 11, pt. 12, chap. 12:247).[27] Again, the verticality of this geographic arrangement may be questioned. Perhaps the strong horizontality of those spreading words (*mana* and *mani*), which also described the ordering of each sun, needs to be remembered. The dead may be *disappearing* outward as well as downward.[28]

Descriptions of the earth and land are various. In one source, the cosmos is created from a great, female, aquatic monster (Atlalteutli) on whose joints appear eyes and deadly toothy mouths ("Histoyre du Mechique," 28).[29] Two gods, Tezcatlipoca and probably Quetzalcoatl (Calcoatl), turn into snakes. As the monster lies floating on the water, one grabs its right hand and left foot and the other grabs its left hand and right foot. Squeezing it hard, they tear it in half. One half produces the earth, the other the sky. From its hair and hide come the trees, flowers, and plants. From its eyes and nostrils come the springs and caves, and from its mouth, the valleys and mountains. This sacrificial dismemberment, however, demands a return sacrifice, for it will not cease crying unless it is fed human hearts, and it will not produce fruit unless it is watered with human blood.

Iconographically, this figure is represented in a number of different guises (figure 13). The beast is shown in a squatting position that could be one of parturition, intercourse, defecation, or that of a crouching toad or lizard, and its *face* (*ixtli*) is depicted in three distinct ways: as a humanoid, as crocodile-like, or as that of Tlaloc, the rain god.[30] Its gender is

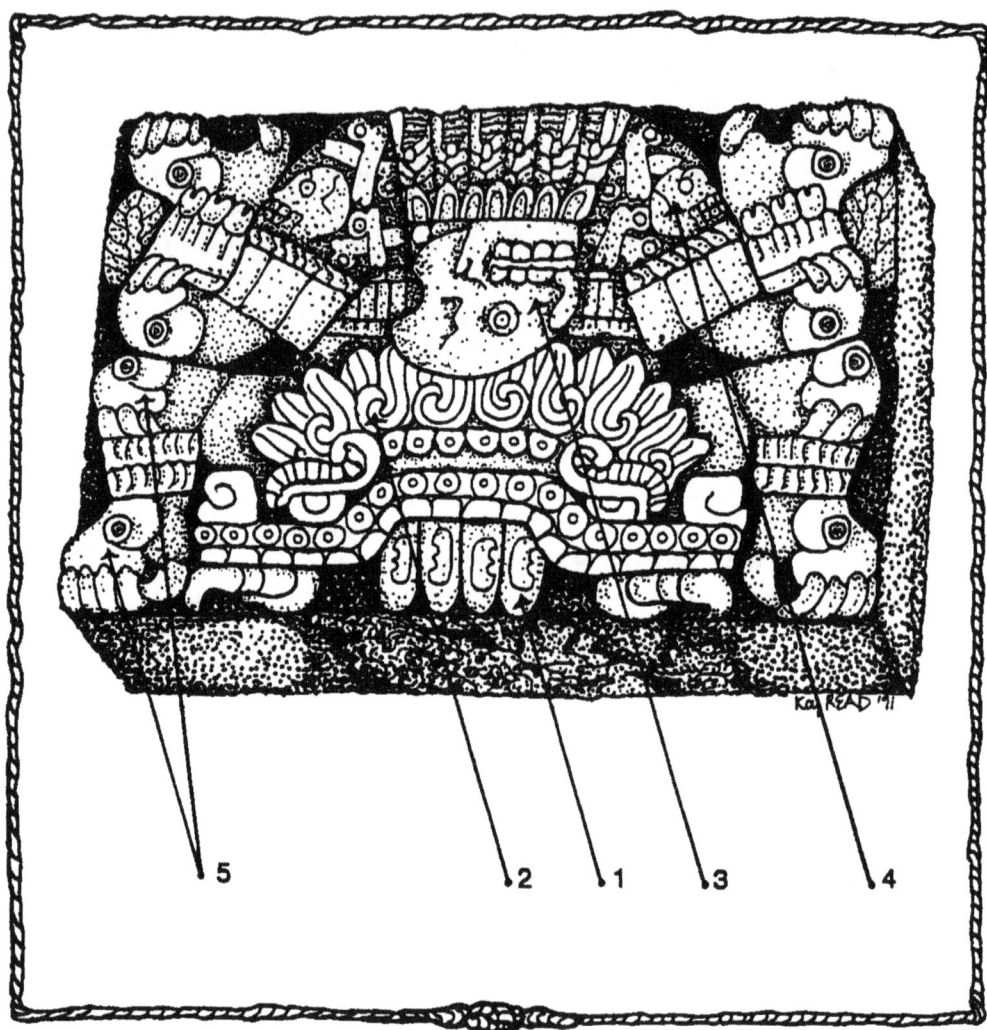

FIGURE 13.
Relief of a descending earth monster. Found under the base of a stone box housed in the Hamburgisches Museum für Völkerkunde und Vorgeschichte. *Drawn from a photo in Esther Pasztory,* Aztec Art, *256.*

1. Crocodile-like face displaying an open mouth filled with fangs and teeth which are shaped like sacrificial blades
2. Its hair
3. Skull ornament decorating its back
4. Skull and crossbones embroidering its clothing
5. Claws which are simultaneously mouths, and claw-mouths depicted on its knees

not readily identifiable, although it is clearly associated with the things of the earth. Its hair is full of insects, its teeth and tongue are sacrificial blades, and its joints are dressed with human skulls, all things reminiscent of Mictlan. Often snakes are knotted around its waist, wrists, and ankles, and its hands and feet are the same claw-mouths found gracing the Sun Stone's central head (figure 12.3). Its gaping bestial mouth even appears alone as a sign for the earth and the demand for sacrifice. Just as the gender of the earth monster is not entirely clear iconographically, neither is the actual earth's gender always clear. It usually appears as female in creation stories, but elsewhere is often given both male and female characteristics, as in Mictlan, a world clearly associated with terrestrial terrain.[31]

When one focuses instead on the actions of gods, the motion of celestial objects, and the flow of water, however, one finds a quite coherent picture, one that effectively draws earth and sky together into a moving pattern of ordered conservation and balanced dualisms. Tlalticpac (Earth's Surface) was the home of the Fifth Sun's inhabitants. This horizontal slice of land divided the Sky-Water's house from the bestial earth. Sometimes imaged as a four-part flower, its center was made of jade and was inhabited by Xiuhtecutli, the old fire god,[32] or a closely associated figure, Huehueteotl, the ancient and wise mother-father of all who dwelt there.

Running water (atoyatl) coursed through the entire Mexica-Tenochca landscape from top to bottom. Mountains, like houses or pots, held the water that was released from Tlalocan by the goddess Chalchiuhtlicue in the form of rain or rivers. It was said that if the mountains dissolved, the whole world would drown. People even called their settlements "Water-Mountain" (altepetl) because they relied on these vessels of moisture. Water came from the sea through underground rivers to the mountains, changing from salt to fresh water as it moved into the land. Thence it burst forth in lakes, springs, streams, and rivers to return eventually to the sea, where it formed the celestial walls of the cosmic house (FC, bk. 11, pt. 12, chap. 12:247–48).

Above and below Tlalticpac (Earth's Surface) were the Tlaloques, rain deities, surrounding all human habitation. They also stood as trees at the four corners of the cosmic house, holding up Ilhuicatl (Sky-Water) and linking it with earth (López Austin 1993). From them came rainstorms. With spiraling trunks, these trees served to funnel the influences of the various gods from the upper and lower realms toward the center of the cosmos. Across the Sky-Water's central axis ran the "paths" of various deities and their forces (López Austin 1988b, 58–61; 1990, 91–106; and conversation, 17 August 1988 and 28 August 1990). It was along this axis that male warriors captured the sun from the earth with a great clamor each morning. It was here that, at noon, the sun was delivered to female warriors who, with great shouts of joy, carried it back down to the *Micteca* (the inhabitants of Mictlan). These dark folk then bore this solar burden to their home in Mictlan for its turn to have daylight (FC, bk. 3, pt. 4, app. 3:49; bk. 6, pt. 7, chap. 29:161–65).[33]

In this way, both powerful forces and water were continually recycled through a great cosmic vessel. Not only was the cosmic house apportioned or "spread out" like water and tortillas, but also its topography was marked by the continual and orderly following of paths. Water was said to "run" (*totoca*) along its inner and outer courses, and the sun and moon were made to "follow their paths" (*otlatoca*) at the beginning of the Fifth Sun. Like traders bearing their burdens of *time-space*, they traversed the well-known roads of their territory.

Created here is a picture of a great cosmic vessel containing a process of ongoing production. The aquatic earth monster is dismembered in order to create arable land. Even its name is based on a word meaning a type of cultivable dirt, *atlalli*.[34] This act is not unlike dredging up the rotting lake bottom to remold Tenochtitlan's island surface into rich gardens. And water is recycled through the whole cosmos in a continuous process of irrigation. Sky, earth, and water all provided for the continuing sustenance of the Fifth Sun's creatures. And so the dark lower world balanced the bright upper world with Earth's Surface spreading between and out to the edge, where sea and sky become one.

Similar images still appear in contemporary Mesoamerican cosmologies. The Nahua of San Miguel Tzinacapan describe the underworld as a mirror image of the upper. There are villages, rivers, and mountains just like theirs under the earth and "'in Mexico-City there are sky-scrapers: 40 floors high and 40 deep' (into the earth)" (Lok 1987, 219). In the 1930s the Panajachel Maya described the sky as a great round bowl separated from earth by large pillars. Beyond where the sea and sky become one lay some land on which dwelt people with no anuses; the sun ate one of these people (who could not eat) each morning as it rose in the East and another as it set in the West. The Panajachel were made of earth, and when they died they went to a town inside a volcano. The Devil lived inside a hill where he lured people to eat. When he needed laborers, either he bribed weak souls to come work for him or he asked God for them; then there was much sickness (Tax, forthcoming).

Such contemporary images of sky, earth, and underworld help one imagine what the richness of the now lost Mexica tradition may have looked like. Today's Quiché Maya, for example, describe the underworld as a dark place honeycombed with mountainous chasms and watery channels named Pus River and Blood River. It is peopled by a host of unpleasant characters bearing such gripping names as 1-Death, 7-Death, Blood Gatherer, Pus Master, Jaundice Master, Bone Scepter, Skull Scepter, Trash Master, and Stab Master. Daily, the sun and moon travel through both this world and the sky above Earth's Surface. What happens below affects what goes on above and vice versa (D. Tedlock 1985).

A Mexica-Tenochca pattern of balanced cosmological dualisms is created through the coordination of wet and dry elements. Johanna Broda has shown the symbolic marking of the Highlands biseasonal structure by coordinating the seasonal cycle with the eighteen-month annual ritual cycle given in the *Florentine Codex* (Broda 1983). Corn was generally sown between the end of April and the beginning of June, just as the dry period gave way to the wet; the wet season gave way to the dry when the harvests took place, around the end of October to the end of November or beginning of December. Hunting was practiced during this dry season after the animals had finished their breeding period. The ritual cycle reflected these seasonal cycles of weather and production.

A period called Xopan (green *time-place*) spanned the wettest period from June through September (months 7 to 11). This period was symbolically associated with the night, moon, Venus, the Pleiades, and Tlaloc, one of the primary deities who released the rain from the mountains. It was to Tlaloc that the north side of the Templo Mayor in Tenochtitlan was dedicated. Overlapping this period was one spanning the period between the two zenith passages of the sun, a period including the summer solstice, 17 May to 27 July.[35] During this *time-space* the sun was said to be in Mictlan and monthly rituals celebrated the birth and growth of corn. On 19 November (during Panquetzaliztli, month 15) war was initiated along with the dry season, called Tonalco (in the *time-place* of heat). Huizilopochtli, the Mexica war god to whom the south side of the Templo Mayor was dedicated, was the focus of ritual just before the winter solstice. This period was symbolically associated with the sun, war, hunting, and the mountains that held back the rains inside their bowels. Children were dedicated during this period, but some also were sacrificed to the mountains, which needed them for strength to produce rain. In both rituals, children were likened to corn.

The seasons were thus divided between the wet summer months in which agriculture produced food and the dry winter months in which war, hunting, and sacrifice produced those only too necessary comestibles. During the summer, the period when corn ate human excrement and drank rain in order to grow, the sun lived in the moist land of Mictlan, where its inhabitants ate the human dead, the excrement of life on Earth's Surface. Hunting for animals and hunting for people took place during the winter, when the sun was in the dry season of Tonalco. Corn was captured to be eaten at the end of the growing season, which coincided with the rites of Quecholli (month 14, October to November), in which Camaxtli, a god of hunting, was celebrated. And the mountains, sources of rain and irrigation in the summer, required food and drink from sacrificial offerings at the driest point of winter.

The same wet and dry coordination is implicit in the figures of the female and male warriors who carried the sun on its daily path. Just as the cold, wet Mictlan was the inversion of the warm, dry, sun-filled sky and Earth's Surface, so too it was the inversion of Tonalco.[36] Summer, when the sun was at its zenith, was the inversion of winter; afternoon, when the sun moved toward Mictlan, the inversion of morning; and women, the agents of that motion, the inversion of men.[37] Water was not only recycled continually through this cosmos but also recycled (as was just about everything else) according to a schedule regulated by the motions of spatially defining celestial objects. In a delicately balanced ecological system, the earth went on eating and drinking the sky, who went on eating and drinking the earth, just as people went on eating and drinking cosmic entities, who went on eating and drinking people. This process was made possible by the careful *spatio-temporal* regulation of a precious commodity in a dry landscape, fresh water.[38]

The Cosmic Meal: The Moving Powers of Transformative Exchanges

Sacrifice made this delicate process of exchange possible by feeding the living entities of the cosmic house. It did so in order to keep a flow of various powers in motion. Fray Alonso de Molina, in his sixteenth-century dictionary (1970), lists two Nahuatl terms for the Spanish words *sacrificar* (to sacrifice) and *offrecer* (to offer): *uemmana* and *tlamana*. The first is built on two roots: "offering" (*huentli*) and "to spread out" (*mana*); the second means simply "to spread something out" (*tla* + *mana*). Other words involving sacrificial acts are largely built on the same roots but also may involve the way in which sacrifice occurred, such as burning (*uentlatlatilli*, "offering which is burned") or bloodletting (*izo*, "to slice or bloody"). What is called "sacrifice" in English or Spanish, then, simply means the "spreading out of an offering" in Nahuatl.

The spreading itself is the same kind of action that arranges and orders the five suns of the cosmos (myth 1) and involves the motion employed in patting out tortillas. There were a number of ways in which this spreading out of an offering could happen. Burning and hunting, for example, spread the things of the Fifth Sun, while blowing on those altered offerings made them move on their paths. When things are spread out, they not only are formed and arranged but also put into motion. They are animated with living powers through the destruction of old forms just as tortillas are spread out of the crushed and ground seeds of life-sustaining corn. Transformative sacrificial acts destroy in order to create, but they also cause life-giving powers to flow. The powers that sacrifice caused to flow also can be better understood if their Nahuatl expressions are considered.

A number of authors have noted the sense of power expressed by the word *teotl*. Walter Krickeberg used the German term *kraft* (power) (1966, 183–84), and Arild Hvidfeldt compared it to the Polynesian concept of *mana* (1958, 25–35). Jorge Klor de Alva expanded on these ideas by coining the word "teoyoism" to mean "the complex of theological belief systems, ritual practices, and emotions which constituted Nahua religiosity," for he saw *teotl* as absolutely central to Nahua religious understandings (1980, 66). Often translated simply as "god," *teotl* can be rendered with more depth if one includes some sense of animistic force or vitality. Its nature can be gleaned from the following passages:

> It is called *teuatl* [teo-water, or the sea], not that it is a god [*teotl*, teo-noun end], only that it means esteemed [or begetting awe], a great marvel [or miracle]. (FC, bk. 11, pt. 12, chap. 12:247)

> . . . any creature whatsoever they see to be good or bad. They call it "teutl," which means "god," in such wise that they call the sun "teutl," because of its beauty, or at least because of its frightening disposition and fierceness. From this it can be inferred that this word "teutl" can be taken for a good quality or for a bad one. This is much better recognized when it is compounded in this name, "teupilzintli," "very pretty child," "teuhpiltontli," "very terrible or bad boy." Many other terms are compounded in this same way, from the meaning of which one can conjecture that this term "teutl" means a "thing extremely good or bad."[39]

Teotl may be described as potent, honored, and sometimes beyond normal human understanding. It also seems to permeate almost any creature, including objects Westerners call inanimate, like the ocean, and although it can be extreme in its potency, it need not be. The personalities of children as well as the awesome qualities of the sea and sun are all described by this term. Moreover, it is potentially both good and bad in character.

Teotl's animating powers were like the natural forces that operate according to given sets of rules or laws in the way that gravity, electricity, or bacterial infections might operate in the modern world. And like natural forces, they both controlled people and could be controlled by them. As the largely invisible electrical forces of the modern world can be used to operate things but will cause harm if mishandled, so too the largely invisible forces of *teotl* could be used to make things work effectively and efficiently if handled well but could also cause grave harm if mishandled. And just as a lightning bolt can strike with no warning, so the powers of the Mexica-Tenochca world could operate beyond human abilities to predict or control them.[40]

The Mexica, along with many other Native Americans, saw the entities in their world as animated by various powers or forces. Clara Sue Kidwell suggests that in many parts of ancient Native America "[e]very outer form or active physical phenomenon had its inner form that motivated it. All living and moving things, thus, had a spiritual sanction" (1992, 396). Richard Townsend has noted that everything in the Mexica world, "things, animals, people, transitory phenomena had the capacity to manifest some aspect of the sacred" (Townsend 1979, 28). Everything was, in some sense, alive. Because these animating powers operated according to a defined system and were, at the same time, individually distinctive and context specific, I use the word *teoyotl* for a singular power and *teoyome* for plural powers.[41]

As the celestial beings marked their cosmic territories with their travels, as water formed the cosmic boundaries and marked its innards with its flow, so the flow of powers marked and wove the shape of the cosmos together. These powers, originating in the sky and underworld, constantly flowed back and forth between the upper and lower worlds, passing through all the things of Earth's Surface. The various beings of the Mexica-Tenochca universe were intimately bound by diverse and distinctive powers continually flowing between them, rather as the years were bound every fifty-two solar cycles by the channeling of those particular temporal powers in the New Fire ceremony.

This means that when a person donned a ritual costume to climb the mountain of Uixachtlan, that person became the god. It was no longer a person climbing the hill, but Quetzalcoatl or Tlaloc. Every mask, costume, effigy, and object embodied a particular force (Townsend 1979, 28). To wear it meant to take on its *face* (*ixtli*), to become its identity.[42] To cast something out of one's house and replace it with something new meant to exchange one kind of *teoyotl* for another, to make a new force. To have a particular name meant to be shaped by a particular potency. To live in this cosmos meant constantly to plug into or to unplug oneself from various and specific powers affecting one's life in concrete ways. When a woodcutter needed to chop down a tree, for example, he told that tree not to drink his blood. If he did not disconnect his animistic force from the tree's, once cut, it would fall on him (Alarcón 1984, 82–83; López Austin, conversation, 29 August 1990; López Austin, 1990, 177).

The beings of the Mexica cosmic house participated in a systematic, sacrificially destructive interchange of powers. Humans and nonhumans alike in the supercharged Mexica world can be arranged in a series of five domains that move, like both calendric *time-space* and *space-time* in "The Legend of the Suns," from great ranges of cosmic spans to the intimacy of humble, historic moments. Each domain is characterized by its temporal endurance and the degree to which it controlled or was controlled by other domains.[43] And differences between humans and nonhumans are more a matter of the quality and degree of their powers than of categorical distinctions, for all beings in this cosmos were alive with *teoyome* and were necessarily interrelated.

In the first and greatest cosmic domain appear the deities that have endured through all the suns. Quetzalcoatl and Tezcatlipoca, for example, return again and again as formative figures in all five suns. One of the other versions of the "Four Ages" myth tells how they were among the first four gods, all children of the creator couple Tonacateuctli and Tonacacihuatl, who existed before any of the suns came into being (*Historia de los Mexicanos por sus pinturas* 1968, 23–38).[44] In this myth, Quetzalcoatl and Tezcatlipoca take turns overcoming each other in agonistic battles that end and begin each sun. Although they never die, there is a pendulumlike swing between them, for first one (like the moon [Birth: VI.14–20]) is sacrificially beaten in order to create the next sun, and then the other is beaten. It is this back-and-forth, destructive swinging that drives the ages forward: as each beats up the other, each sun is destroyed to create a new one. They demolish and shape the cosmic houses over and over again, even though neither of the two gods holds power for more than a limited time. Sacrificial acts deformatively transform in rhythmic motion.

In the second domain appear the humanlike original inhabitants of each of those large cosmic suns and their particular houses. A continuity of existence is implied. The first human couple did not die but, through decapitation, were sacrificially transformed into the ancestors of the Nahua (myth 2) just as the various other inhabitants of each sun sacrificially deformed into the beings of the next (myth 1). Included here are gods such as Nanahuatzin and Tecuiçiztecatl, who were transformed so a particular sun might exist. Existence is continual, but specific forms are not. Animating powers endure, but because of deformative, transformative, sacrificial processes, they serve different beings.

In the third domain are the gods of the Fifth Sun, such as the patron or tutelary deities (*calpulteteoh*) like Huitzilopochtli. These deities were the founding ancestors of the kinship-linked social groups called *calpullies* (López Austin 1988b, 68–72; 1973) and an important source of *teoyome* for their heirs. Gaining strength through sacrificial battles with his sister and another sister's son (myths 6 and 7), Huitzilopochtli issued forth from Chicomoztoc or Aztlan (as did other patron gods), leading his people to hegemony in the Valley of Mexico. Recall, though, that "The Return to Aztlan" tells about the limited nature of Tenochtitlan's hegemony; it is "assigned" only a few years, after which Huitzilopochtli abandons it and returns home (myth 8: 14–15). Although the city and its rulers, magicians, and inhabitants will *disappear*, Huitzilopochtli himself will not suffer such a fate. He can grow young and old at will, for in Aztlan, the food they eat does not cause *death*. Unlike the Mexica commoners (*macehualtin*), he is not doomed to a limited life span progressing from birth to *death*. These founding ancestors do not *disappear* into the bowels of Mictlan; they do not become sacrificial excrement for the Fifth Sun's continuing processes of life. In this domain, the animating power is enduring life, unfettered by corruption and *death*. The inversion of Mictlan (Land of the Dead) to Tlalticpac and Ilhuicatl, of *death*'s dark vitality to life's light, does not apply. Transformation here is reversible.

The fourth domain is inhabited by special mortals, human beings who live on Earth's Surface, eat the Fifth Sun's foods, but still retain special powers, the *pipiltin*, or noble class (López Austin 1988b, 388–400). Their powers come from their kinship link with their patron deity, the *teoyome* they receive from Huitzilopochtli. Literally forming a "thread" of ancestral lineage (*tlacamecayotl*, "cord of men"), *pipiltin* were established as the governing class before the birth of people. According to López Austin, *pipiltin* could eat certain things not available to commoners: the flesh of sacrifices, cacao, pulque, and psychotropic drugs, for example. They also could smell fragrant flowers, burn incense, and use precious stones. All these things embodied various animating powers which strengthened them and made them physically warmer, allowing them to govern more effectively. The king was transformed at his coronation into the bearer of the heart belonging to the group's tutelary god, thereby funneling some of that god's power into earthly governance. Although *pipiltin* mediated between some particular cosmic powers and commoners, they did not hold responsibility for all events on Earth's Surface. Life was difficult and people were held responsible for their own actions.

All people, even *pipiltin*, were tied to the things of the Fifth Sun. It was exactly those things *pipiltin* were privileged to ingest, the things that strengthened them also weakened them and led to their eventual *death*. The magicians who ingested drugs in order to take their magical flight to Aztlan, King Motecuhzuma I and Tlacaellel, were told by Huitzilopoch-tli's old tutor that their rich life would lead to their abandonment and city's sacrificial demise. As mortals, their lives were temporarily bounded. They were all created from the excrement of Mictlan, the pulverized bones of the dead stolen by Quetzalcoatl (myth 3), and it was to the Land of the Dead that they would at least partially return upon their own *deaths*.

It is said that when the dead crossed over the waters to Mictlan, "they completely *disappeared*" (*ocempopoliooa*) (FC, bk. 3, pt. 4, app.:41–46). As is done in the transformation of each cosmic sun into the next (myth 1) and of Tecuiçiztecatl into the moon (Birth: VI:14–20), this text makes a play on the word *poliui*. Transformation is a kind of *disappearance*. And as in the sacrificial *disappearance* of Nanahuatzin into the fire at the Fifth Sun's birth (Birth: IV.38–50), a dead person's body was carefully, perhaps even lovingly, burned, and its flesh "sizzled" (*tzotzoioca*), "crackled" (*cuecuepoca*), and even "stank" (*tzoiaia*) (FC, bk. 3, pt. 4, app.: 44). The remaining bones were gathered into a pot, a greenstone "heart" was placed with them, the pot was buried, and offerings were made thereafter to the bones to preserve and channel their powers to the deceased's offspring, the "poor orphans" (*icnotl*) they left behind (Ibid.:42). Although endowed with special powers, nobles also paid a price for their privileges. As was true of all things of the Fifth Sun, their *time-space* on Earth's Surface was limited, and they were promised no everlasting rewards. Having *completed* their life spans, they too would simply *disappear*; their various animating centers would scatter and their bodies would disintegrate.[45] Gods, on the other hand, had control over the composition of their *temporo-spatial* structures. They could change forms and reverse their aging processes; they were not at the mercy of a particular age.

Commoners occupy the fifth and most humble domain. As the poor of society, they were denied the privileges of the rich. Yet they were not without recourse to various powers flowing through the cosmos. All human beings, nobles (*pipiltin*) and commoners (*macehualtin*) alike, could bind themselves to a variety of powers through divination which manipulated the *tonalpohualli,* or divinatory calendar. The professionals able to control cosmic powers performed a variety of tasks ranging from healing to taking magical flights and creating successful thieves. These diverse powers varied with the social class and could come from a variety of sources, such as the outside will of a god or the force of one's *tonalli* (head soul) or naming. One might be designated for shamanistic skills because of some illness. Or one might seek them by artificial means, such as cranial deformation, a particular costume, or body painting which placed one under the domination of a specific god (López Austin 1988b, 360–62). In all cases, the profession required extensive and rigorous training, and as is the case with shamans elsewhere, they were both loved and hated. They were needed for their capacity to manipulate great powers but were distrusted because of those same abilities.

Although mortals were limited to one life span and controlled by a host of forces, divination at least allowed them to control the limited temporal period at their disposal. *Teoyome* varied and were incremental in nature. Such powers were specific to particular actions and occurred according to the *spatio-temporal* schedule of the multiple, intermeshing cosmic rounds. By manipulating life's events in order to coordinate them with the calendrical system, one could determine propitious moments in which to act. A child's naming day, for example, could be moved according to a fairly flexible set of rules if the actual day of birth was not a good one. Days bore varying degrees of good and bad *teoyome,* allowing a skilled diviner to calculate the best combination. This gave some control over the *mahceua* (merit), the inherent nature, of one's offspring. Divination also was used as an interpretive device for understanding the correct moves to make in specific situations. The calendar determined the correct day to wage war, and merchants sought diviners for advice on good days to travel or when to make business deals. Of course, divinatory rituals gave their potencies through sacrificial acts such as ritual bleeding or the killing of animals.

Because the calendar was set in motion at the beginning of a particular sun, divination linked people with that sun's realities. And since each sun was also timed according to preordained principles dependent on the agonistic swinging back and forth of Quetzalcoatl and Tezcatlipoca as they created the suns, mortals' daily lives also tied themselves to that highest cosmic domain of existence. In this way, existence in the humble, historic present (domain 5) bonded with existence in the great deathless cosmic domain (domain 1). *Death* itself was fated, but life's events could be manipulated to coordinate them with the positive, more creative, aspects of all existence. The inherent limitations of people's capabilities could be overcome at least a little, just as Oxomoco and Cipactonal overcame Quetzalcoatl's inability to crack open the Mountain of Produce by casting lots to find out who could accomplish the task better than he (myth 4).

Merit figures into this systematic interchange of powers, for *mahceua* refers to more than the merit of humans. Often mistakenly translated as "to do penance,"[46] *mahceua* has more to do with the who, how, why, where, and when of the flowing of powers (*teoyome*) within the cosmic house than with any ritual atonement for one's sins. This term is complex and very difficult to translate accurately because it describes the controlling of and the being controlled by these animating forces. Therefore, it sometimes requires different translations in different circumstances. In its genetic aspect, *mahceua* gave a being its inborn nature, which controlled its outer form, actions, and destiny. In the case of a child, this *mahceua* was drawn from a variety of sources, including the forces of the day on which it was named, a past ancestor's name, and the child's own behavior. To this can be added the actions of relatives and the various influences of deities and events throughout a person's life. Even the geographic area of domicile is included in *mahceua*, for land rights also flow through the spun threads of the ancestral cord. In other words, merit is determined by the flow of diverse, animating powers into a person's being, an ongoing process that never ceases, extending even beyond the boundaries of her own life span. *Tlamahceua* gives the term even more depth (n. 2:19). This word describes sacrificial rituals like those performed by Nanahuatzin and Tecuiçiztecatl at the birth of the Fifth Sun, whose focus is on controlling the flow of powers. Finally, in some places today, *mahceua* refers to eating or the first meal of the day (Karttunen 1983, 279), a use that recalls the ancient sacrificial acts of eating that regulated the cosmic flow of powers. The first meal of the day occurs at the *time-space* of the rising of the sun, a celestial body that gained life through sacrifice.

Who someone or something is, then, is a matter of the kind of powers that one's *mahceua* has. And while in the course of a person's life she is given a great deal of merit that helps determine her nature, she also can determine to some degree her own merit through her actions and the rituals performed at appropriate times and places. And because all five domains in the cosmic house spin together through sacrificial rituals, people's morally negative and morally positive activities interact with other beings to cause imbalances and balances. As *time-space* spirals forward, it doubles back on itself in a swinging motion. It is possible to upset its rhythm by balancing it wrong. Just as the sun moves along the horizon to the north in the summer, doubling back south in the winter; just as even counts balance odd counts in the calendrical system; so too people must calculate their actions so that they do not upset their family's, city's, or sun's spiraling motion.

Morally negative behaviors, transgressions were excesses caused by failures to maintain appropriate balances. Such excesses needed counterbalancing. Minor transgressions were dealt with through autosacrificial offerings made to the appropriate deity (López Austin 1988a; 1988b; Burkhart 1989). Gods had the power both to give and to take back that which they controlled. Tlazolteotl, the goddess of filth and a cause of people's poor behavior, was said also to remove people's bad actions if the appropriate ritual procedures were followed (FC, bk. 1, pt. 2, chap. 12:23–27). Various forms of servitude were the standard official punishment for people's greater excesses, and these varied with the transgression's degree of seriousness. Many forms of servitude lasted only until the debt was paid and did not have any further ramifications either for the wrongdoer or for his family.[47]

But really excessive transgressions received harsher forms of servitude. Then the transgressor was shackled with a huge collar and sold in the marketplace. Things like adultery, serious thievery, too many debts, too much gambling, and murder, for example, could earn the transgressor servitude not only for himself but also for individuals from one or more generations of his family. Those displaying an excessive lack of economic and domestic success in a famine were required to send at least one member of their family into servitude for an unlimited number of generations.

Certain numbers of these servants, as well as war captives, became food offerings to sustain cosmic powers. Such a servant was called a *tlacotli*, a word formed on the root *tlacoa*, "to damage." Servants were *tlahtlacolli*, things that were spoiled, rotten, and messed up (Burkhart

1989, 28–30). Like the Lords of the Night, they were the counterbalance to the diurnal order found on Earth's Surface. The servant was placed into balance with his surroundings. His excesses had to be paid off like bad debts before the exchange was made even again, before the rhythm of his own spiraling *returns* could become regular again. The greater the excess was, the greater the debt to be paid. And the greatest excess was the inability to share with the cosmos one's success at sustaining one's family. Sacrifice was a way of re-forming things in order to create an appropriate order again. Like Tata and Nene, who were re-formed into dogs because they smoked the heavens (myth 2); or Tecuiçiztecatl, who failed to leap into the fire and so became the moon; transgressors were re-formed as well (Birth: IV.1–32; VI.14–20).

Excrement, the completion of the feeding cycle and counterbalance for eating, also balanced people's behavior, keeping *space-time's* rhythm beating at an even pace. One avenue to freedom from collared servitude was escape. If a *tlacotli* could flee from the market compound and step in some excrement, he was automatically freed. The act of escape was even somewhat encouraged, for people were required to get out of the way of an escaping *tlacotli* or risk becoming one themselves. After stepping in the excrement, the *tlacotli* went to a special ritual practitioner who bathed him and then took him to the palace, where he was praised for his spirit and often employed by the ruler (Durán 1971, chap. 20:284–85). It appears that his transgression caused physical damage to his body and the excrement repaired that damage. A *tlacotli's* heart was excessively hot and had been "cooked," while its opposite, a free man's heart, was green, raw, and uncooked (López Austin 1988b, 400–405).[48] Through its association with Mictlan, excrement, along with other forms of filth and rottenness, was cold. Thus the overly hot physical condition of a *tlacotli* was counter-balanced by means of something cold, bringing it closer to the desired state of freedom.

People's behavior was balanced in the same way the whole cosmos was balanced, by the constant process of eating. Like Nanahuatzin, a *tlacotli* was cooked as food for the cosmos. But if, unlike Xolotl, he could successfully flee from *death*, he would transform into young corn fertilized by human excrement. As the moist Land of the Dead was the balanced inversion of dry sky and Earth's Surface, the cool, strengthening excrement was the balance of the hot, cooked heart. Transgressions, as excrement, fed corn which, when sacrificially cooked, became tortillas which transformed into excrement when eaten. Sacrificial rituals were a form of morally positive behavior that maintained balance.

The role of sacrifice was to coordinate various powers so that imbalances would not occur, thereby maintaining a healthy, undamaged cosmos community. In this way, sacrificial rituals regulated the timed flow of power in all domains of the cosmic house. Each individual, because she unavoidably was connected with all other beings in this dynamic cosmological structure, was personally responsible for its health. Since life could not continue without sustenance, each person's responsibility was to sustain all other beings. Since shapes are timed and time is shaped, sacrificial rituals formed the *time-space* of the present and future by drawing on various powers of existence and funneling them in appropriate ways.

Sacrificial ritual moments of *nowness* transformed the past and present to reorient the future. A good person took her sacrificial duties seriously, for the weight of the universe rested on her shoulders. Like the sun and the moon, each person had a burden to bear throughout her individual life on behalf of the greater family with all its ancestors who went before and its offspring to come. It is not surprising, then, that another term describing sacrificial ritual actions was *neixtlahualiztli*, "the payment of a debt." Sacrificial action was inherently reciprocal in nature.

The comestible, digestive, and excrementative processes of sacrifice regulated the flow of a huge variety of powers through the cosmic house's five intertwined domains. The great Quetzalcoatl and Tecuiçiztecatl sacrificially beat each other to produce the power-filled suns in which other beings like the first couple lived. Tata and Nene were sacrificially decapitated when their powers became unbalanced by their misdeeds. Patron gods such as Huitzilopochtli sacrificially created their own births so that they could lead their people to both victory and demise. Nobles led sacrificial wars to maintain the powers of their ancestral cord, only to be sacrificially burned upon their *deaths* so that the cord might continue to be powerful. And humble commoners participated in the sacrificial rituals of the divinatory *tonalpohualli* calendar in order to link with the moments of *nowness* that had "piled up" their powers, ready to mold the present.

A definition of Mexica-Tenochca sacrifice from a religious perspective as it occurred on Earth's Surface may now be offered:

Mexica-Tenochca sacrifice, in which human and nonhuman beings participated, was regarded as the systematized manipulation of various life-giving powers via their feeding, which served to: (1) sustain, strengthen, and transform those powers; and (2) maintain an orderly and balanced cosmic ecosystem consisting of many and diverse animated entities which were intimately, inherently, and reciprocally related with each other.

And so the mundaneness of human activity—birth, eating, growth, sex, decay, and *death*—gave shape to Mexica sacrifice. Through eating, things were born, ate, grew, decayed, and died, thereby feeding others with their rotting corpses. But what was it like to live in this community that appears so violent to many contemporary eyes; how did such experiences motivate people to participate in this logical but scary sacrificial system? The coherency and power of those *faces* (*ixtli*) belonging to ordinary experiences may present some possible answers.

BURNING AND
BINDING FIRES

Sparks and Spots

Flames for reeds, stick for stem, the fire drill sparking its little flame is visually equated with the reed plant emerging behind it. Below this visual pun in the 2-Reed plaque lies the image of the knotted rope, and just beneath that are spattered some jaguar spots, inconspicuously hidden in the recess between it and the sacrificial vessel (figure 1.4–7). Just as the images intertwine with each other, so too they recall a number of intertwined messages, many woven around ancestry. The spots probably signify the deity Tezcatlipoca. It was he who became angry with Tata and Nene when, to prepare some fish, that childish couple sparked the first smoky cooking fire of the Fifth Sun (myth 2). And it is he who is often associated with Huitzilopochtli, the Mexica's ancestral patron deity.[1] The reeds rising out of the fire drill were a sign of Tula, the city of royal lineage. Through marriage, a family was required to bind its ancestral cord to these particular toltecs if it hoped to gain political leverage. And like generation upon generation of Mesoamerican rulers before, Mexica rulers also sat on jaguar pelts spread over woven reed mats.

Sparking fires both consume and create the ropes, reeds, and spots of ancestry that mark the years. Tezcatlipoca's "children," Tata and Nene, were the parental cooks for the Fifth Sun's people; Xiuhtlamin engendered his captor-son, Xiuhtlaminmani, whose heart fed the new sun; and Huitzilopochtli-Tezcatlipoca, the great warrior and creator of fire, fathered the Mexica-Tenochca royal line, his special heart (*teyolia*) borne within progressively engendered rulers. Just as fire bound the last round to the current, so Xiuhtlamin's burnt heart tied the threads of past ancestry to the present, while his name tied present ancestry to the future, giving it birth. Both the sparking of cooking fires and the ancestral spots and cords were based on natural, biological models in which each new thing consumed the powers of the old to create new identities which were similar to but not exactly like previous identities; both operated on a genetic model. Cooking transformed inedible raw fish into dinner, and ancestry transformed ancestors into heirs who were *re-presentations* of their earlier forms. Likewise, ancestry bound the ages together, burning into motion the nutritious and generative powers (*teoyome*) of hearts and names.

Why did people participate in these rituals? First, four concepts structured by cosmological processes made it metaphorically logical and analogically reasonable to participate in sacrificial rites. Second, these analogies were embedded in ritual actions and visions; the New Fire ritual speaks images of all four concepts, especially of sacrificially transformative orders and counterorders. Third, a potent reality founded upon mundane communal experiences created and confirmed those same four concepts, and experiences of ritual participation both marked and developed them. Sacrificial sparks of new fires and jaguar spots of Tezcatlipoca's ancestry engendered transformative realities because the logic for so doing was rooted not in transcendent, extraordinary paradigms, but in experiences of an immanently real and thoroughly ordinary world.

Burning Fires: The Logic of Sacrifice

The cosmic house, with its constant transformative flow of powers, shapes four concepts pertinent to sacrificial logic: (1) the sacred equaled the profane, creating a situation of profane sacrality; (2) history was eternal because history was all there was; (3) death gave life; and (4) the cosmic community operated on a sense of limited reciprocity. All of this can be understood only if a number of related Western concepts are able to accommodate some potentially foreign ideas. For if one is going to negotiate between "the familiar and the strange," the strange must be allowed to startle one out of one's comfortable sensibilities (J. Z. Smith 1982, 22–23; Read 1987a). Therefore, in order to understand these four concepts better, each will be used to redraw, *re-present* one or more Western realities.

Profane Sacrality: The Spreading of an Offering

Those acts the Mexica called "spreading an offering" (*uemmana*), Westerners call "sacrificial." Built on the Latin roots of *sacer* (sacred) and

-*ficare* (to make), the English term "to sacrifice," means "to make sacred," assuming that there are things not sacred that can be made so. López Austin offers a Mesoamerican alternative to that Western sacrificial view in which the extraordinarily sacred counters the ordinary profane:

> In the Quiche' myth of man's creation, the gods blurred the eyes of their creatures, which indicates that the southern Maya perceived the supernatural more as a condition brought about by a reduction in man's perception than as a sector of the universe. That is also a deduction dealt with throughout this chapter [on the Nahua body and social structure]. For the Nahuatl man, some of the supernatural beings had a reality as present, as immediate, as daily as he could capture through his senses. The supernatural was judged to be material, potentially visible, tangible, and audible. It was remote from man because of man's limitations, but man was immersed in the supernatural. When the human being believed he could not break his own barriers of perception, he thought the world revealed itself to him more fully. The imperceptible sector, like the perceptible one, was ruled by a struggle of complementary opposites, by alternation of dominion, by hierarchies; there were cravings, wants, a struggle to achieve perfection; there was the possibility of arrangements, payments, of deceiving the opponent. The supernatural part located on the surface of earth was also his world, even if it was hidden from his view. (1988b, 383)

In other words, this highly intimate Nahua world was crowded with constant contacts between various animated beings. It was populated by entities whose powers were often immanent, though sometimes not; tangible, though sometimes invisible; often manipulable, though not always fully understood. To put this into perspective, this same set of characteristics (although operating according to different rules) can be applied to things which populate, for example, the Western microscopic worlds of biology or macroscopic worlds of astronomy. The inhabitants of these worlds also sometimes are immanent, invisible, and manipulable (though not always understood). But that does not make them necessarily sacred or beyond the ordinary to those dealing with them. Neither does "spreading an offering" necessarily separate things sacred from those profane.[2]

In the Mexica world, if any division is to be made at all it must be on some other basis. One important division is embedded in the language, a category that distinguishes between things that could change place and those that could not. For lack of any better terms, I have dubbed these two "animalia" and "animated" objects. Even though not explicitly labeled by Nahuatl terms, these two classes of live entities are marked linguistically. Terms naming various animalia receive a pluralizing suffix while those naming animated objects do not. Animalia seem to be things endowed with independent motion, which can change place by themselves. But even though both animalia and animated objects are alive with various *teoyome* (powers), the latter cannot change their places without outside intervention because they are rooted to particular places. For example, one uses the plural form once the sun and moon have been created out of Nanahuatzin's and Tecuiçiztecatl's bodies. They have become more than simple objects in the sky: they now are living beings which are given the authority through sacrifice to move along prescribed paths. The names of all those things that move (gods, humans, and what the West calls animals) take plural forms while the names of those that cannot (such as rocks, mountains, trees, and plants) do not.

This division cannot be between sacred and profane, for gods are animalia along with people. Neither can it be between people and nature, for pluralized objects also include all animals. Nor can it be between animate or inanimate, for all things in both categories are considered animated; all eat and are eaten. Unlike the West, the Mexica tossed "nature," "God," and "man" into one great, cosmic stew pot of living and, therefore, edible beings. Instead of divisions between sacred and profane, animate and inanimate, or among nature, God, and man, a basic Nahua division is between those things that can change their places and things that cannot, for not all things have authority to move. Movement was the deciding factor in that fifth "Age of Motion" (*4-Ollin*).

Various beings and entities often overlap each other in their human and nonhuman characters, making the nature of animalia complex. The human nobles (*pipiltin*) were endowed with capacities lacked by commoners (*macehualtin*), which allowed them to deal with certain nonhuman powers. Rulers, moreover, were invested with the special powers of their group's simultaneously human and nonhuman ancestral deity, thereby making the ruler himself naturally human and nonhuman. Yet all people, even commoners, could be named for their particular human and nonhuman ancestors and all acquired quantities of both the humblest and greatest cosmic nonhuman powers through the use of divination and other calendric and ritualistic manipulations. Differentiation among various beings or between the particular and cosmic was more a matter of finely tuned gradations than of any broadly conceived kind.

These differences lay in the different food that humans, deities, and other beings ate, which affected their mortality. People, because they ate things of the earth which tied them to its feeding continuum, were limited to a single life span. Upon *death*, their various animistic components dispersed. One's *tonalli* scattered, one's *teyolia* went to one or more lands of the dead, and one's *ihiyotl* roamed the earth. One's own *face* (*ixtli*) or temporal composition *disappeared* forever. The deities also were limited by temporal periods; but unlike humans, they had control over their composition.[3] Once the Mexica's demise came due, Huitzilo-pochtli would return to Aztlan, a place where his aged tutor could run up and down the hill (myth 8: 17–18), reversing at will the *spatio-temporal* direction of his own aging process. Time went on, but it had a mortal effect on only some beings' compositions.[4]

Although it was true that to be human was to be mortal, it also was true that even mortals enjoyed a temporary immortal control over life through their investments of *teoyome*. *Teoyome* were forces that could change various beings' circumstances in all domains of existence and often caused the particular and cosmic to mix and blend. Ancestors, rulers, nobles, and even commoners physically contained quantities of special qualities through their bonds with different ancestral powers. Even though some beings, such as a few gods and the most ancient ancestors, had the potency to overcome *death* and control the feeding cycle, all beings, no matter how humble, had recourse to some powers. *Teoyome* made all things naturally supernatural, creating a state of profane sacrality. What Westerners might call extraordinary powers were ordinary in the Mexica world.

To control the powers around them, people had to manipulate how they and others changed places. The shaman-priests who visited Aztlan on behalf of Motecuhzuma I turned into various wild beasts by entering their bodies (myth 8: 4), for these magicians had the "spirit" (*anima*) and therefore the courage to move in this way (Acosta 1978, 66–67). This enterprise was dangerous because some were "eaten" by the animals whose bodies they had entered (myth 8: 19); their own spirits had been caught inside the beasts' innards. A woodcutter was obliged to talk to the animistic entity of a tree before cutting it down (Alarcón 1984, 82–83). If he did not first break his connection with the tree, it might fall on him. In the first example, magicians bind themselves to other animalia's animistic centers to give them an independent motion that put them in a special place they otherwise could not visit. In the second, an animating bond is broken so that an otherwise immobile but animated object would not be drawn in an unsafe direction when its locative roots were severed. While the ability to independently change place may distinguish animalia from animated objects, it does not distinguish human from non-human or ordinary from extraordinary.

If the prefix *teo-* means "sacred" (*sagrado*) (as Molina often translates it), then the ordinary must be the sacred, for *teo-* appears to be more a matter of degree, nature, and function than of something "out of the ordinary." As various powers coursing through a vast range of entities and objects, following different paths, marking specific territories, making things work, *teoyome* must be manipulated daily. As daily forces, they often are taken for granted and are at least partially under the control of mere mortals who themselves are marked by powers operating within them. This means that any idea of transferring power between distinctive sacred and profane realms must be abandoned in Mexica sacrifice and replaced with the image of a cosmos populated by diverse animate beings interacting with one another by means of a controlled and controlling sacrificial flow of *teoyome*. Whatever else "spreading an offering" meant, it did not mean "making something sacred," for everything already was in this world where the profane *equals* the sacred.[5]

Eternal History: Sacrifice's Transformative Role

If all these many profanely sacred beings share their histories with those of others in the same cosmic house, then a separate state of eternity makes little sense. One way to understand change is to postulate its opposite, no change, the solution of those who contrast an extraordinary and eternal sacred to an ordinary and changing profane. Many have taken this metaphysical position. Along with Rudolf Otto, Mircea Eliade, and Davíd Carrasco, one can include, for example, Platonic visions, the positing of a golden age, or revelatory events that bridge the vast gap between the two contradictory poles of history and eternity. All presume that historical change must be understood in terms of an unchanging eternity. In some cases, the eternal may even become a way to deny the true reality of change. One need only recall the unmoved mover and first cause espoused by the author of the *Codex Vaticano Latino* for such an example. That this codex described the Nahua cosmos in such markedly medieval terms should make one wary of assuming that the Mexica held similar presumptions about change.

For the Mexica-Tenochca, however, ordinary historical change was not contrasted to its opposite, eternity. A different logic operated in this constantly changing world where numerous nonhuman and human beings (both great and humble) spun their powers in and out of each other. Because the ordinary was sacred and nothing profane existed, all things, including the changing forms of everyone's daily history, were sacred. The temporally patterned flow of *teoyome* through various cosmic spaces made time and space equivalent; all things constantly changed because *teoyome* constantly moved. No concept of a motionless eternity is possible here. The only everlasting thing is change itself; *history is eternal.*[6]

Although an apparent paradox between change and no change (i.e., unchanging change) seems to have governed this worldview, in practice, this contradiction did not seem to be much of an issue. In India a number of philosophic schools arose to debate a similar irresolvable state of affairs, but the Nahua often seem to have philosophically considered the permanency of impermanence largely for its pragmatic and experiential affects.[7] Recall Nezahualcoyotl's poem about the "fleeting moment," which emphasized the necessity to endure change's presence while accepting its absolute reality. Though impossible to fully comprehend, change simply is—a statement of fact that is paradoxical only if you are concerned that its opposite might actually exist, something that apparently did not concern the Mexica.

Such a fleeting reality meant that one would want to have, if possible, some control over the inevitably changing flow. This was accomplished by regulating the feeding continuum, for eating caused growth and therefore transformation. Eating, which endowed all beings in all domains with time spans, also allowed them a chance to regulate that calendrical reality because it controlled the forces of life and destruction upon which *teoyome* depended. In that first great cosmic domain, regulation occurred in a pulsating, rhythmic pattern shaped by deities like Quetzalcoatl, Tezcatlipoca, and Huitzilopochtli, who formed the ages, destroyed them, and formed new ones. While these gods rhythmically took turns beating their ages into existence and then losing them, time never repeated itself but creatively forged ahead. Each age was a distinctively new one.

In the second and third domains, gods who went on living in the Fifth Sun constantly changed their characters, creatively fusing in and out of each other as circumstances demanded. When the sun (Tonatiuh) was eaten by the earth monster at sunset, he bore the *face* of Tlaloc (the rain god) (López Austin 1990, 203–210); for Tlaloc's powerful garb (which was often shared with Mictlan's beings) was needed when the sun moved toward that moist underworld of *death*. In the fourth and fifth domains, for mortal nobles and commoners alike, time moved forward progressively through eventful series in which each person and lineage *re-presented* their past ancestral forms through their various *teoyome*. In the first three cosmic domains, nonmortal forms pulsate, regularly creating new shapes as they take turns moving forward through the ages; in the two remaining human domains, mortal forms pulsate with continual returns of ancestral powers, reforming them as they move forward through individual life spans and generations. Both the immortal and mortal move temporal periods and their powers by *re-presenting* them, creating a calendrical spiral. Change may pulsate, yet each new thing retains a unique character; no two ages, gods, or people are exactly alike. Change neither ceases nor gets out of hand.

These pulsating, progressive formations sometimes appeared as rhythmically paired inversions, for while some changes were serial, others moved with appropriate partners, each balancing the other. Every new child was a personal mixture of various powerful bits and pieces coming from previously disintegrated entities. Tecuiçiztecatl, however, that false sun who became the moon, transformed to become the proper sun's necessary but opposite partner.[8] Such partners rhythmically overturned each other through time. Mictlan (Land of the Dead) ate the excrement of Ilhuicatl-Tlalticpac (Sky-Water and Earth's Surface) while Ilhuicatl-Tlalticpac fed on the excrement of Mictlan. Those things classed with Mictlan (Land of the Dead) as the spoiled, rotten, and entangled *tlahtlacoltin* had an order of their own from which came their counterorder, those things fresh and well arranged. In due course, the well-arranged would reach their *completions* and transform into the not-so-well-arranged. As these inversions swung back and forth, *time-space* spiraled forward, just as did Tezcatlipoca's and Quetzalcoatl's creative battles. Order was the inverse of a creative counterorder; each was potentially chaotic for the other. Yet chaos occurred according to an orderly plan.

This is not a case in which order holds the chaotic at bay. At issue here is the meaning of "chaos." Students of world religious traditions often describe chaos as a double-sided affair: on one side is extreme disorder, things disintegrating so much that they are out of control; on the other is a state in which no change at all takes place.[9] As many have pointed out, both extremes are uncreative and must be avoided if life's changing rhythms are to continue. By avoiding the extremes, however, chaos can become a creative source for orderly cosmic formations. Creation of the world from nothing but water, on the one hand, or by ferocious deities who smash things into existence, on the other, has been suggested as mythic examples of chaos's creative counterorder in a variety of cultural settings.

For the Mexica, the reality of continual transformation makes neither the danger of no change nor that of extreme disorder a concern, for such oppositions have no meaning in their world. The counterorder of chaos is a creative option, not dangerously uncreative. Although ordering takes place both by spreading out and by marking the world's forms, it is chaotic violence, the destructive essence of transformation that makes this happen. Endings, not beginnings, of things are marked because the *completion* of something automatically pushes the process forward to a new beginning. In this violent world, one must recognize destruction's inherent orderly nature, for creation comes from destruction in a highly regulated fashion. Because it avoids the extreme possibilities of chaos, the Mexica cosmos may be described as moderate despite all its violence. Chaos's order (not its disorder) is the reason that people actively sought sacrificial participation.

Sacrificial transformations were accomplished in direct and unmediated ways; one form was simply altered to become a new one. From the moment of his own naming at birth, the New Fire offering bore in his own person some of the sacred powers needed for the rite. As a war captive of good character, Xiuhtlamin was corn, and his heart (*teyolia*) was, like grain, endowed with the forces required for both germination and divination. His name lent further *mahceua* (merit). Named for the year itself (*xiuh*), he was likely born during the year of the last ceremony and therefore held within the temporal power of the calendar. All this made him a seed ripe for germination, corn ripe for harvest and consumption, and the ancestor of the new fifty-two-year round to come.

Xiuhtlamin's honorable behavior, furthermore, had earned him more *mahceua*, which was shared with his captor. When Iztcuin changed his name to Xiuhtlaminmani, he now had some of his captive's *teoyome*. By sharing names, a concrete genetic relationship was established between them, making Xiuhtlaminmani the son of Xiuhtlamin. Xiuhtlaminmani did not eat his catch because he already had incorporated his powers by means of inheritance.[10] And like all animalia and animated beings, the *teoyome* Xiuhtlamin embodied linked him with other beings, making consecration unnecessary because he was already in a state of sacrality.

Xiuhtlamin was the nourishing knot that tied together the two ends of the old and new fifty-two-year rounds. A priest gently blew the new fire built on his chest into life as one blows gently to start a cooking fire. His heart was fed to it and his body consumed. From this, the fifty-two years "blossomed." As corn, Xiuhtlamin fed and germinated the next temporal round. As the ancestor of that round, he transformed old into new. As with Nanahuatzin's transformation into the sun, Xiuhtlamin's is a direct, unmediated reformation of his body into the sun of the next round through the nurture of feeding. Hence it was not a "person" (as someone today might think of him) being sacrificed but corn and good *mahceua*, the ancestors and time.

While Xiuhtlamin's sacrifice was an especially marked one, other animated beings were not any less profane or more sacred than he. They simply held different varieties and combinations of merit. All beings, whoever they were, participated somehow in the sacrificial process that enabled transformation. All humans, for example, were like Xiuhtlamin, a bundle of comestible, meritorious, ancestral, and temporal potencies. As corn, all people fed the cosmos as they were fed.

Mexica sacrificial events included both daily and special occurrences periodically marked by calendrical cycling. Sacrifice never ceased even when an age ceased. Rather than a one-time sacrifice (as is observed by the Christian tradition, for example) or a sacrifice that overcame disorderly chaos by temporarily unifying an eternal sacred with a changing profane (as Eliade or D. Carrasco would have it), sacrificial transformation was constantly happening in all domains from the great to the humble. Both the ages and those who went to the Land of the Dead simply *disappeared*, and warriors who died as sacrificial offerings transformed into birds and butterflies after four years. This suggests that the sun born in a New Fire rite was not merely renewed but made *entirely new*, just as a baby does not renew its parents but is an entirely new person in its own right.[11] Nothing was forever in this orderly process moderating chaos, this eternally historical process of continuously creative hierophanies that are naturally profanely sacred.

Life-Giving Death: *The Morality of Destruction*

Rhythmic inversions often spoke of life and *death* on the feeding continuum. Both life and *death* were necessary because both gave life by making vital moves in the cosmos's sustaining and fertile processes. Eating as the inversion of excrement and wet summer as the inversion of dry winter express much of the same intention that the upperworld and upperworld pair (Mictlan and Ilhuicatl-Tlalticpac or Land of the Dead and Sky-Water, Earth's Surface) expressed. In each case, one partner needed the other, for together they accomplished the regulated destructive-creative process in which *death* eats one thing to create life-giving food for another.

There are moral elements in the destructive-creative pairing of life and *death*. Life and *death* meant that success and failure continually overcame each other. Because all things were inextricably connected, one agent's effective or ineffective actions would necessarily affect another's. For example, failures were those people who suffered from a lack of powers (*teoyome*), creating a damaging imbalance. Hence, during famine, the poor suffered the most enduring form of servitude. As *tlahtlacotin* (messed-up beings) at a time when the cosmos itself was in this same state of damage, they were the ones who had to undergo the longest period of rebalancing, for it was they who "had eaten themselves" (*moquaque*), thereby situating themselves as excrement in the feeding continuum (FC bk. 7, pt. 8, chap. 8:24).

Success and failure are expressed by the ability or inability to complete a task (*tlayecoa*). Nanahuatzin successfully finished his sacrificial task while Tecuiçiztecatl could not. For this reason, unlike the jaguar, the eagle was well arranged (*uellalac*) and, unlike the secondary moon, the sun came first (Birth: IV, V.64–70, VII.25–31). Like Tecuiçiztecatl, the *tlahtlacotin* also fail and are entangled, messed up, and not completely well arranged. Not only are they lesser because of their failure, but they also now are positioned in the feeding continuum to redress their poor arrangement, the damaged state of imbalance which their actions helped cause.

The New Fire rite demonstrates such a pattern of morally paired inversions positioned as points on the feeding continuum. Two paired human sacrifices occurred, the initial sacrifice of Xiuhtlamin on the mountaintop and the final sacrifice of *tlahtlacotin* by people in their courtyards. Xiuhtlamin's *mahceua* was successful: he was a willing sacrifice, at least to the degree that sacrifice was one of the possible hazards of his chosen occupation, and he had been selected, like Nanahuatzin, for a special honor. The *tlahtlacotin*, like Tecuiçiztecatl, met their fate because of their own failure to meet certain standards, and while they were not exactly willing sacrifices, they had brought this on themselves. Both had chosen in some way to become sacrifices.

Because of their respective *mahceua*, Xiuhtlamin was the sacred seed who became the new sun of the new age, and the *tlahtlacotin* became the sacred excrement who fertilized this new sun. Xiuhtlamin *disappeared* into the new fire, which then was distributed to all parts of the empire before its solar appearance. He was an offering spread out at the midpoint of the night in anticipation of the sun's rising, just as was Nanahuatzin. The *tlahtlacotin* were spread out at noon, the midpoint of day, in anticipation of the moon's rising. Similarly, pregnant women were guarded in the granaries along with the corn that people ate, as if to guard the success of life to come, for they were seen as life-giving inversions of the people-eating monsters they would transform into should Xiuhtlamin's sacrificial *completion* fail.

By reenacting key points of success and failure on the feeding continuum, the next temporal round is efficiently engendered. The new age and its sacrificially active inhabitants are now endowed with their corporate *mahceua*. Life in this form will continue for fifty-two years, until its period is finished and a new planting is required. And just as Nanahuatzin *completed* his sacrificial act so that now the eagle is well arranged and the sun of the Fifth Sun placed in motion, so too the old sun, bearing its bundle of years, has *completed* its journey. And now its ancestral power, in Xiuhtlamin's form, will transform into a new sun with a well-arranged new bundle of years.

These paired inversions form no simple oppositions. Many authors, both classical and contemporary, have suggested that, in sacrificial rituals, life is juxtaposed to *death* so that the former might overcome the latter.[12] But such an intimate pairing does not go quite far enough by itself, either in describing the complex feeding process or in illuminating the role that animated entities played in this intertwined cosmic house. Eating and excreting food are not direct opposites of each other. While excretion is the *completion* of eating, the reverse is true only after several intermediary steps, all of which are symbolically marked: sexual fertilization and growth, hunting, capture, *death*, and cooking. Eating and its results are embedded in a detailed process; life and *death*, while crucial foci, are only parts of this larger and complex picture. As a life-giving act, the sacrificial *death* of eating moves entities from one kind of sacrality to another, from failure to success to failure (and so on), from *completion* to incompletion to *completion* (and so on), from the old age's forms to those of the new (and so on), and from one order to its paired counterorder, *returning* to a spot slightly ahead of and not quite like the old one. By controlling such sequentially arranged destructive inversions, the whole complicated process of transformation is regulated.

This is not a case of simple avoidance, of an intense fear of chaos. It is not just that the Mexica don't want night to last forever, but that the order of night needs to be used so that the order of day may be created. This means that killing is a natural part of transformation, for only destruction can repair the imbalances and damage incurred by people's failures. Success feeds on failure, eventually transforming it into success, which eventually will fail.

Nor is this a case in which all killing is right, for some killing was considered immoral. Murder was inappropriate because it was done for reasons other than promoting the cosmic order upon which everything depended. Murderers, therefore, were considered *tlahtlacotin* (messed-up beings) and became slaves to the deceased's family to balance their loss.[13] But the natural transformative flow of *teoyome* was neither morally good nor morally bad. Rather, it was an amoral, unavoidable reality; the flow simply was. To ignore it, however, was morally bad, for then one endangered the whole corporate body of a cosmos inhabited by thousands of beings. This meant that moral valuation depended on the circumstances; what was considered morally good or morally bad was necessarily context specific. Both the sun and the moon were valued for the particular "burden" each bore, but only when following their appropriate paths (Birth: VII). It was not good that both should "shine in the same way" (Birth: VI.9); such a circumstance indicated a bad imbalance.

Nor is this a case of good versus evil. By their inborn nature and by acting inappropriately or responding properly to others' inappropriate behavior, all things are potentially both pleasantly good and unpleasantly nasty. Recall that the sun was called *teutl* (god or powerful being) not just because of its "beauty"; it also had a "frightening disposition" and was known for its "fierceness."[14] Drought came from too much sun, and the fire that gave birth to that mixed solar force of the Fifth Sun was a thing that "could not be faced" or "tolerated" (Birth: IV.8–11). Recall also that the grandfathers and fathers dwelling in Aztlan were considered both "delightfully agreeable" and "very vicious" (myth 8: 1). And anyone (even rulers and nobles) could fail by not acting correctly, thereby turning themselves into things needed for their feeding properties. One lived with any number of beings who, on the one hand, were valued for their pleasantly creative characters and, on the other, carried some very scary possibilities for creative harm. Both the pleasant and unpleasant were good when they were appropriate. Evil was not an issue in the Western sense of demonic actions versus saintly ones, nor were all unpleasant actions necessarily always bad, much less evil. Rather, inappropriate actions were differentiated from appropriate on the basis of context; and these inappropriate actions could be made appropriate through a sacrificial eating that was not always pleasant. Not all death was considered the same; the death that was inappropriate because it did not create life was considered murder and had to be balanced by an appropriate, life-giving, but nevertheless unpleasant sacrificial death.

Limited Reciprocity

Animalia and animated objects had need of each other in this cosmic house, making reciprocity a requirement for all. Just as all the gods cooperated in the sacrificial creation of the Fifth Sun, so all people, from infants to the elderly, cooperated in the sacrificial creation of each new sun marking that age. The appropriate acts of animated beings had to be properly reciprocated by those animated beings who followed, or else the ecological balance would collapse and the appropriate destructive counterorder would take over to rebalance the cosmos.

Calendrical patterns regulated and limited these reciprocal relations between gods and other animated entities. The enduring gods, such as Quetzalcoatl and Tezcatlipoca, took agonistic turns with each other to create each age. Although they fought one another, they won their battles according to a balanced pattern. And even though they did not die in the same way mortal beings tied to a particular sun did, that pattern imposed on them tight temporal limits. While it may have been true that "that which was being completed long ago and far away" would be done "once again" (Once Again: 1–4), the reverse also was true: that which is being done here and now, at some point in time, will no longer be done in the future.

The pulsating, progressive temporal patterns of Mexica realities suggest that something like limited contracts structured sacrificial exchanges. No party, whether human or nonhuman, held omnipotence here. Even Huitzilopochtli would return home to his mother in Aztlan; Quetzalcoatl could not open the Mountain of Produce without Nanahuatzin; and although he could and did beat Tezcatlipoca into the background, this periodic hegemony was balanced by Tezcatlipoca's chances to return the favor. Nor could any one person hold extreme hegemony for any length of time. Even rulers constantly had to negotiate their relationships with others, for circumstances kept shifting. In spite of their special *teoyome* (powers) rulers were limited to only those *teoyome* they actually held, which forced them to reckon with the possibly stronger *teoyome* of others. Rulers also had to face the fact that their own poor decisions and unwise actions might bring failure. Thus, the Mexica cosmos constantly balanced and intermeshed social and political powers in the most complex ways.[15] Each animated entity (human and nonhuman) was limited by its particular type of powers, the temporal authority those powers gave it, and the absolute necessity of reciprocity.

The New Fire Ritual: An Ongoing Rite of Transformation

The New Fire rite demonstrates each of the above four concepts—profane sacrality, eternal history, life-giving death, and limited reciprocity—although it is particularly instructive on the second concept, historical transformation. As did the birthing of the Fifth Sun, so the making of the New Fire performs a complex message of eternal history. These two related but distinct mythic and ritual messages say that morally charged orders counter each other and sacrificial actions create new beginnings again and again. In both, a "try, try again" motion eventually molds the new sun's form. The final message of both myth and rite is that, although nothing is final, sacrifice helps give order to the endless change of existence because it *completes* living entities's life spans so that new life can arise.

Profane Sacrality: The Spreading of an Offering: The ritual's main task was to spread the offerings of Xiuhtlamin and the *tlahtlacotin*, the former as a captured meal of animalia for the new sun and the latter as the rotting fertilizer that will help it grow. These direct and unmediated consumptive acts used the distinctive *teoyome* of each sacredly profane offering to create a wholly new sun.

Eternal History: The Transformative Role of Sacrificial Orders and Counterorders: The rite structures a series of ongoing transformations that *re-present* events of the First Sun's birth. This is made apparent when the ritual event and its mythic partner, the story of the Fifth Sun's birth, are compared and contrasted to a classic rite-of-passage model. The elegance of this comparative model is its simplicity, flexibility, and apparent universality.[16] Its ritual structure almost guarantees instant recognition for many, if for no other reason than its close affiliation with contemporary dramatic productions such as the three-act play. Even more fundamental might be the idea of beginning something, doing it, and then finishing it, which may constitute a basic human experience embedded in this three-part structure. One often feels that an activity is unfinished, for example, when it lacks a marked closure of some sort, something saying, "Now it is done."

Yet it is exactly the final stage of finishing that is downplayed in both the "Birth of the Fifth Sun" myth and its ritual echo, the New Fire ceremony, which underscores their fundamental structures of ongoing transformation.[17] Four things create a sense of continuous hierophanies in this paired myth and ceremony: (1) complex mythic and ritual structures that emphasize beginnings while de-emphasizing endings; (2) several metaphoric re-presentations; and (3) a series of metaphoric inversions that (4) express an ongoing process of uncompleted and completed actions. First, although they do so in different ways, both the myth and the rite structure their individual events into three major phases, each focused on sacrificial beginnings. But rather than following the three stages of a classic rite of passage, each phase constitutes its own arena of action (though related to the other two by a developmentally transformational process). And, although the rite as a whole doesn't incorporate a beginning entrance, a sacrificial climax, or a final exit, each individual phase does. The motion from sacrifice to sacrifice is accomplished by eliminating the exit phase of the previous stage, thereby emphasizing the entrance of the next. Remarkably, the structures of both myth and rite begin and end with a beginning.

In both the myth and the rite, phase (a) begins in darkness with the gods. In mythic form, they are simply there; ritually, they file from the Templo Mayor to the top of the hill. As part of this entrance into action, various preparations occur. Nanahuatzin and Tecuiçiztecatl ready their costumes, bleed themselves, and burn incense while the fire priest from Copulco practices lighting fires. These beginning stages then move abruptly to their sacrificial climaxes, the leaping into the flames of both gods, followed immediately by the rising of the eagle and jaguar in the former case and the immolation of Xiuhtlamin in the latter. Then comes a transition in both, a simultaneous exit from phase (a) and entrance into phase (b). In the myth, they wait for and then observe the spreading of the two suns across the sky. In the rite, the two gods' sacrificial fire is distributed and spread across the entire dominion, followed by the renewal of all household goods.

The myth's phase (b) focuses on the second sacrifice of Tecuiçiztecatl with the smashing of his *face* and transformation into the moon. The rite focuses upon the sacrifice of quail and consumption of Xiuhtlamin's body formed in amaranth cakes. These sacrificial actions are again followed by transitional stages combining the exit from phase (b) and the entrance into phase (c). In the myth, the edible Xolotl is given chase; in the rite, a period of fasting occurs from sunrise to noon.

Phase (c) climaxes with the sacrifices of both Xolotl and the other gods in the myth, followed by Ehecatl blowing the Fifth Sun into action, while the rite climaxes with the sacrifice of human *tlahtlacotin*. Here something important happens in both myth and rite. Mythic action abruptly ends with the successfully *completed* sacrifice, which now has resulted in the appropriate continued motion of the sun and moon. In the rite, the human sacrifices are followed by a feast and then a second laying of the fire. Both end with a sense of ongoing action beyond the events just related. In the myth, the sun and moon will continue as they do now. In the rite, the concluding feast doesn't simply end the action as a classic rite of passage would dictate, but the ending itself is *completed* by creating a third new fire as if to say that this fire now will be ongoing just as the sun and moon are in the myth. As this third fire is an entrance into the new fifty-two-year cycle, so too is the whole rite no more than yet another beginning of temporal motion. *Completion* is not final; it is a beginning.

Second, the ritual action of the New Fire ceremony *re-presents* several metaphors similar to those in the myth. Xiuhtlamin repeats, but not exactly, Nanahuatzin's sacrifice, while the *tlahtlacotin* repeat, but not quite, Tecuiçiztecatl's. In the first, both Nanahuatzin and Xiuhtlamin are burned entirely and become the next new sun. However, Nanahuatzin is characterized as a poor, honorable but humble deity with a skin disease, while Xiuhtlamin, although honorable, is not poor but an elite warrior, one of the group represented by the eagle rising from the ashes of Nanahuatzin. And although both Nanahuatzin and Xiuhtlamin were metaphoric corn, Nanahuatzin's flaking skin is the main focus while Xiuhtlamin's heart is the central image. In the myth, Nanahuatzin is rotting like excrement and husked like corn before burning, while Xiuhtlamin's heart goes as food for the fire. Both act as nourishment, but one fertilizes and seeds the age while the other feeds it. One is its beginning, the other its continuation and sustenance.

The *tlahtlacotin* also *re-present* inexactly Tecuiçiztecatl's action. The myth describes that god as rich and perhaps just a bit cocky. Unlike Nanahuatzin, Tecuiçiztecatl fails repeatedly in his attempts to jump into the fire, giving rise to the not-so-well-arranged jaguar. Ultimately he must be smashed to gain his proper authority as the moon. The *tlahtlacotin* also are failed, incomplete, disarrayed individuals who will be violently reformed through sacrifice. But even though both are underworld beings, their imagery is different. Tecuiçiztecatl is associated with the feline forces of night; the *tlahtlacotin* with excrement. Both jaguars and excrement are of the earth and underworld, but each disarray represents different kinds of power; the former are the hungry powers of night, the latter fertile, nourishing powers.

While both the myth's and the rite's task is the creation of a new sun, each performs this re-presentative motion in unique ways. The myth moves from the husking and burning of corn in the form of Nanahuatzin to the creation of light and food, and ends with the formation of daily and nightly temporal authorities. The rite moves from the burning and eating of Xiuhtlamin to the lighting of new fires and a possible second eating of Xiuhtlamin cakes. This is followed by a period of fasting and finally the offering of excremental *tlahtlacotin* and the laying of a new fire. The myth creates the Fifth Sun, putting it into its appropriate order, while the rite continues the process of transformation begun at Teotihuacan by creating a new sun every fifty-two years thereafter.

Although the primordium is not completely reenacted in an Eliade-like "myth of eternal return," similar metaphoric re-presentations structure time at both the beginning of each new fifty-two-year cycle and the beginning of the sun itself. Nanahuatzin is the offering that forms the Fifth Sun, and Xiuhtlamin is just one of fifty-two sacrificial offerings who follow, each of whom forms an entirely new sun equipped with the authority to wage war against the forces of night associated with the jaguar. Xiuhtlamin does not copy Nanahuatzin's actions, but he does creatively knot the last fifty-two-year cycle with the next.

Third, both the myth and the rite share a series of metaphoric inversions, driving home the task of creating a cosmos in a properly balanced motion. Xiuhtlamin is the sky's diurnal light, as is Nanahuatzin, while the *tlahtlacotin* are the forces of the night and underworld, as is Tecuiçiztecatl. The eagle is the inversion of the jaguar in this same set of pairings, as midnight is the inversion of noon. The cosmos and its appropriate inverted orders and counterorders are sequentially developed in both the myth and the following ritual actions. Patterns of continuing hierophanies and nownesses are expressed with their Mexica re-presented sense of ongoing creation. In a spiraling motion, the present only partially returns to the past to create a completely new future. The primordium is ever present because the cosmos is continually created. The present is all one has, but this wholly ordinary present is extraordinary.

Fourth, the morally paired inversion of success and failure, expressed often as completed or uncompleted action, is important in these series of transformative moves. The myth's action moves from the uncompleted state of the Fifth Sun at its beginning to the successful completion of the two gods' ritual preparations. But only Nanahuatzin's sacrifice is successfully completed; Tecuiçiztecatl's is a failure and is followed by a series of semiproductive sacrifices that repeatedly attempt to get it right. Eventually this effort pays off, and the sacrifices are successfully *completed*; the moon is in place and the foodstuff in order. Quetzalcoatl-Ehecatl then blows this new fire into action with an animating breath of life, giving the sun its proper authority. The motion of the new sun and moon will not be finished for a limited period of time. The action moves from incomplete to *completed*, to incomplete, to semicomplete, to *completed*, and back to incomplete. Every successful *completion* results in a transformation that begins another uncompleted state. To fail is to not *complete* something as one should by further sacrifice. Sacrifice is necessary to *completion*.

Thus are created a myth and rite which express the ongoing transformation so foundational to the Mexica world. In each stage, fire is followed by sacrifice, eating, and a move to the next fire. By ending the myth with a fiery puff that blows the cosmos into motion and the rite with yet another fire, the next beginnings are stressed, for things really have not ended; they have been *completed* only to begin something new.

This is not a pattern that builds to a climax and then ends. It begins with a climax and never quite ends. Serial actions drive home the reality of transformative change and the necessity of sacrifice to keep the motion in creative order. The fact that the New Fire ritual reenacts neither the birth of the Fifth Sun nor the primordial beginning of all time before the creation of the First Sun, drives the point even deeper. For the rite merely binds one small span of time to another in a long series of ages. At some point the knot will not hold, the Fifth Sun will *complete* its action, and a new and highly drastic, sacrificial transformation will occur.

By manipulating three basic stages of ritual which begin, create, and finish some new thing, an ongoing motion of transformation is both expressed and acted out. Enacting a series of *continuing hierophanies* sends a message that, although proper preparation may help people enter successfully into activities, those activities can be *completed* only temporarily. The reality of existence is that existence is never done. By not separating sacred from profane or eternity from history, these sacrificial rituals both help control the inevitable changes in the world's animated forms and give form to those animating forces of change.

Life-Giving Death: The Morality of Destruction: It would be immoral not to participate in the destructively creative New Fire ritual, for without it, the Fifth Sun would die along with all its inhabitants. All action was focused in both the myth and rite on the several sacrifices that would transform the old cycle into the new. Clearly Nanahuatzin sets the pattern for morally positive action. The weak, such as Tecuçiztecatl and Xolotl, are forced into sacrificial action by social pressure and, if that doesn't work, physical pressure. Xiuhtlamin, like Nanahuatzin and all the other gods who gave their lives to birth the new sun, represented the moral high ground. Those humans who took the moral low ground, such as the *Tlahlacotin*, helped restore balance with their sacrificial participation, no matter how unwilling it was. The morally charged successes and failures of the gods, Xiuhtlamin, and the *tlahtlacotin* all create the new suns, giving them motion and maintaining life for the larger community in the Fifth Age.

Limited Reciprocity: Finally, reciprocity is crucial to the rite's success. Not just Xiuhtlamin and the *tlahtlacotin* make this rite happen, but all people—young and old, rich and poor, successful and unsuccessful— feed their blood to the new sun. People come from all over the domain to take part in the ceremony. Grandparents, parents, children, and pregnant women wearing their masks of maguey leaves prick their ears to offer their own bit of sacrificial blood. Even the ears of infants offer their blood to give the new sun life. All will benefit from the sun's controlled warmth, and therefore all have a "debt" to pay. Even quail and amaranth cakes do their part. But as with all meals, this is only a temporary and limited sustenance. In fifty-two years another breakfast must be cooked so that a new fiery sun may rise and the Fifth Sun continue its motion.

Binding Fires: The Power of the Mundane

But isn't something missing here? For even though the grand-scale logic of this worldview may be both wondrous in its imagery and compelling in its apparent coherency, was it sufficient to motivate individuals to participate, often willingly, in these demanding, frequently rather grisly sacrificial rites? Few future rewards and no mediation or substitute sacrifices were used to lessen people's potential fears of *death*. Nor was eternal life a possibility after sacrificial fires consumed them. Why agree to take part?

The Mexica sacrificial reality embedded itself in events ranging from markedly spectacular rites like the New Fire ritual to a multitude of un- marked and unquestioned daily occurrences binding life and lives to-

gether. It was the latter that gave sacrifice its real force. Numerous profanely or "ordinarily sacred" events created and sustained a transformative reality so potent that it could make sense of sacrifice not just metaphorically and philosophically but experientially as well.[18] The wondrous
images of and compelling reasons for sacrificial participation were not
simply abstract ideas; people lived those logical images every day.

Profane Sacrality: Sacrifice's Ordinarily Sacred Force

Daily participation in ordinary life gave sacrifice its true power; for
just as the sacred is ordinary, so too Mexica sacrificial realities rest in an
immanent daily order so close that no one questions its power to mold
lives. Often ordinary and not well-remembered events mold and shape
reality most permanently. The unusual (and therefore memorable) may
or may not deeply affect one's life; such effects depend on how that
experience, that break in routine, challenges or supports one's unquestioned sense of the ordinary and routine world. A smoker may be pushed
to kick her habit by the loss of a parent to lung cancer, but only if she is
convinced that smoking caused her parent's death and she can alter all
the little daily patterns structuring her own habit. The shocking or special, when it does happen, accomplishes change only when it becomes
ordinary. Indeed, the oft-assumed extraordinariness of Eliadian
hierophanies is exactly what needs to be overcome if change is to be
lasting. Hierophanies have the greatest effect when they are close and
continuous, not when they appear only once in a while.

Countless examples of common occurrences repeat the Mexica sacrificial reality. Every house formed around a four-sided courtyard repeated
the cosmic house in some sense, and every family's *comal*, used to roast
each day's tortillas, recalled the feeding continuum. Corn, that most common of food, was a many-layered metaphor for sacrificial eating. As nourishment for people, it was the symbolic sustenance for all living entities,
and even people were metaphoric corn for other beings. The sacrificial
nature of all of corn's phases was noted: when it was a seedling; when it
was young, mature, and harvested; and when it was ground into flour,
molded into dough, cooked, and finally eaten. Throughout, corn was
excrement's natural counterorder until it itself spoiled; then it too became rotten fertilizer for yet another round of corn. Corn was even equated
with the sun, life's very substance, that which grew corn and gave it
motion. Like the cosmic terrarium in which it lived, corn fed itself.

On a social level, corn metaphorically formed people in the most intimate ways. Children, when they were in their first year of life, were symbolically captured like corn from the fields and cooked over a fire in order to prepare them properly as little tortillas for the cosmos. On the flip side, concern was expressed that these babes might become "smutty," rotten ears of corn, turning themselves into excrement (FC, bk. 6, pt. 7, chap. 30:168). And finally, children were ritually stretched, by grasping them at the neck, so that they "might quickly grow tall" (FC, bk. 2, pt. 3, chap. 37:165–66).

In this way, rituals instilled the truth of the sacrificial tradition. Repeatedly correlating physical realities with cosmological and social ones gave coherence to the patterns of existence, producing a predictability that made order itself possible.[19] Rituals, even if they themselves change or express conditions of change, often are endowed with the authority of an apparently unchanging tradition. The more something is repeated, the less it seemingly changes and the more "given" it appears. And the more formal a rite is, the less it invites open reflection. Because Mexica rituals formally repeated daily experiences, they created an air of immutable authority.

Such deep authority rested on social and philosophical-cosmological structures, which closely correlated with the things one necessarily encountered each day: weather and people's aging patterns, definite topographical places, and other physical actualities. When drought occurred in their valley in the mid-fifteenth century, sacrifice became one solution. At first, nonsacrificial routes were sought. Dikes were built to hold back the basin's saline water from fresh spring-fed areas, and irrigation was expanded on the surrounding hillsides to increase production (Read 1986). But this was not enough to feed the valley's high population. Such severe drought, moreover, affected not only the Mexica but also others to whom they were socially and cosmologically tied. For while their cosmos was bounded by the particular mountains and skies surrounding them, they also were connected to other areas and, ultimately, all living beings in the universe.

There were two sacrificial responses to this drought: the sacrificial offering of young children to the rain gods (Tlaloques) and the Flowery Wars (Durán 1971, 154–71; HI 1984, chap. 29:235–36; 1992, 29:233–35). The first was already an annual ritual performed normally at the end of the dry season, for sacrificed children gave their watery tears to the raingods so that they might release badly needed rain. The second was an innovation that made sense because, for centuries, human blood and flesh gained on the battlefield had been drink and food sustaining the deities who, because they were sustained, could assure the water and soil consumed by the corn that sustained people.[20] By harvesting people who were corn in war, corn for people in the fields would have the nourishment to grow; the Fifth Sun, with all its hungry inhabitants, could be saved from starvation. Thus, the very real demands of a difficult physical environment were given meaningful order by repeatedly correlating them in a multitude of ways with human society and the metaphorical feeding continuum.

The "practice makes perfect" style of many Mexica rituals allowed people to overcome what fears they might hold of sacrificial *death*. And given Tecuiçiztecatl's nerves over jumping into the fire, the Mexica appear as humanly feeble as anyone might be with such a task. By participating in sacrificial rituals from birth on, however, many must have become familiar with *death* so that the task of sacrifice was made somewhat natural. Repetition can help people overcome both fear and pain, rather as a child may overcome fear of unavoidable surgery by visiting the hospital or "playing" doctor beforehand. Each new exposure to a scary, painful, or terrible act often makes the next exposure easier. Sacrificial rituals may also have allowed people to take control of the uncontrollable through direct participation, thereby jumping the gun on their own inevitable *deaths*.[21] In times of crisis, like extreme drought, it may have been preferable to die in a nice, clean, swift ritual than be devoured by the prolonged sufferings of the beasts of famine. By participating in rituals that dramatically escalated the number of sacrificial killings, people could "practice" both their own end and that of their cosmos.

This suggests that it is only a matter of necessity's style and the degree of necessity that separates daily rituals from high state rites or mundane activities from ritual ones. By repeating the same cosmological scheme represented in a child's house, in the city and the valley environment in which it lives, in its own naming and curing ceremonies, and in high state functions in which that scheme may participate, the givenness of the realities reenacted in child sacrifices, ritual warfare, or the New Fire rite could hardly be questioned. One's real world is formed by what Ray Birdwhistell called multiple channels of perception (1970, 10). People received the message that sacrificial transformation was true over and over again in many different ways; it was learned through constant and continued exposure to it. Nonreflection on those realities with which one lives begins in the cradle.

Eternal History: Transformative Repetitions

Changing daily realities can remind people that the historical is endless, always demanding and effecting transformations in them. One's very sense of mortality is closely bound to this fact of existence, to the reality of temporal change. All people are born, grow old, and die, a process during which a great number of changes are necessarily experienced. Nothing ever stays the same. It should be no surprise that, for many, temporal change is the only reality.[22] After all, what in daily human experience presents one with anything else; why should a state of no change, such as eternity, even be considered a possibility?

If there is no eternity to overcome the vagaries of change, then it is not enough simply to repeat the truth over and over again. Truth must continue to make sense with changing physical and social realities, with the slipperiness and fleeting unpredictability of life.[23] People do come equipped for this demand, for their creative, imaginative abilities allow them to adapt pragmatically to changing circumstances. The Mexica were no exception.

Nahuatl speech patterns, for example, recognized the developmentally creative possibilities of repetition, for it was used as a common literary device linguists call parallelism. This device used verbal couplets in storytelling and ritualized speeches, the halves of which were only slightly distinguished from each other. Nahua orators were especially skilled in using this stylistic tool.[24] In "The Birth of the Fifth Sun," the moon's *face* was both face-whipped (*conixuiuitecque*) and face-beaten (*conixtlatlazoque*), face-wrecked (*conixpopoloque*) and face-wounded (*conixomictique*) (Birth: I.5–8). And the sun upon its rising was described with a couplet: his shimmering rays (*tonameyo*), his warm rays (*tonalmiyo*) (Birth: V.61–63). Such repetitious pairings helped both drive home a message's importance and expand it in subtle ways. The moon's *face* was progressively deformed until it *disappeared.* The sun's primary potencies were light which produced heat. As with the reoccurring sacrifices of the New Fire rite, everyday language used sequential repetitions to develop new messages and give birth to new ideas.

Both speaking and rituals allowed people to adapt to changing realities because they could *re-present* events as they happened and provide arenas for exploring different possibilities. The "try, try again" manner of sacrifices in "The Birth of the Fifth Sun" mythically expresses such experimentation. And other techniques besides verbal parallelisms could creatively structure a situation. Such innovations occurred in any number of circumstances ranging from small, slowly implemented changes to suddenly produced large ones.

Variations on themes provided for slow, controlled creativity. On a mundane level, for example, the birth of a baby introduced elements into family life that required different arrangements; a new (and very demanding) person had altered significantly the previous family relationships. The divinatory naming ceremony shaped not only the characteristics of the child but also the new family paradigm. As a variation on the theme of its ancestors and time of birth, this new thread was thereby woven into the familial fabric. And so this rite helped people restructure their personal lives by incorporating significant changes into their daily lives.

Sometimes, however, circumstances were such that rites themselves needed restructuring to meet new demands. In response to the fifteenth-century drought, two new rituals were begun which radically *re-presented* older sacrificial rites. First, under normal conditions, two children were offered annually to the rain gods (Tlaloques) at the end of the dry season to give them strength for their watery task to come. In one year of this drought, however, it seems that forty-two children between the ages of two and six were offered.[25] A drought-ridden world that lies "slavering," "panting," "crying out," one that "burns" and "crackles" required more than just a little sip; it needed gallons to bring it back to life.[26] Never before or after was this innovative ritual performed. Second, the introduction of the Flowery Wars was a radical revision of an ancient Mesoamerican sacrificial tradition. Formalized almost as a kind of sport, the Mexica version stressed an absolute necessity for numerically massive sacrifices gained through ritualized hunting. In other words, the greater the introduction of difference, the greater the demand for change and innovation.

The Mexica sacrificial reality responded appropriately to changing needs. Small changes required small sacrifices; naming a baby required little more than some bloodletting. But the creation of a new temporal round required both total immolation of a human offering and sacrificial participation from the entire Mexica dominion, just as the creation of the sun itself required total immolation and the complete *disappearance* of almost all the gods. Drought upped the ante even more, for the life of the entire sun was now threatened. Not only did sacrifice need to be practiced on a larger scale, but the ritual practices themselves were transformed to ensure continued control over the very process of transformation. As Tlacaellel announced, a new marketplace must be found, one with fresh tortillas that quickly can be fed to a hungry, starving god who can wait no longer for dinner (HI 1984, chap. 28:232–33; 1992, chap. 28:231–32). And as many have noted, this shift in the use of sacrifice provided the Mexica with a tool for political expansion (see, e.g., Conrad and Demerest 1984). Sacrifice, thereafter, played no small role in the ensuing rise of Mexica-Tenochca hegemony.

In this way, cosmological responses to changing historical and physical actualities further changed those realities, starting the processes all over again. A large shift in water resources demanded a response to the feeding continuum which then worked on physical and social environments through political expansion. A family needed to respond only a bit to resituate parents and the new little corn plant in their particular familial topography. Cosmological structures are never static, abstract entities divorced from other, more real and dynamic physical and social worlds. Rather, they are ongoing experiences of actually lived and fundamentally creative realities, from which they arise and which they form.

The Templo Mayor, then, was no locus of stability in a changing landscape. Davíd Carrasco has called it a "vision of place in which change and transformation (were) the sustained pattern" (1991, 33). But contrary to what he suggests, this shifting vision was never stabilized via momentary experiences of ritual synesthesia, sudden sensations of the "unity of meaning" (ibid., 38, 42, 51–52). Rather, constantly controlled innovative change constituted its ritual core. The Templo Mayor was not a locus for temporarily banishing chaos or overcoming instability with periodic experiences of a unified stability; such oppositions were not issues. It was the center for managing how the age's beings changed places, how one order countered another, and how essentially organic and biological mutations would form. Children and warriors left home and battlefield for its temple caches so that, as food and drink, they might counter drought's dry order, thereby turning on life's moisture.

Life-Giving Death: The Moral Community

Life-giving *deaths*, like all else, were woven into the fiber of daily life. These creative destructions were confirmed by common human experiences ranging from the destruction of life in order to eat and live to the destruction of the forms of rocks and trees to create sculptures, houses, and cooking fires. The feeding continuum was repeated in actual experience. Destroying the identifying *faces* (*ixtli*) of all hungry mortal beings created new things. Such ecological approaches to moral valuation create a world in which all are dependent on one another, for life's destructions bind them.

Because *death* gave life, the Mexica moral community was predicated on creating appropriate life-giving destructions. What they considered morally good or morally bad depended on the positive or negative value an act held in a particular situation. All living entities, furthermore, shared ethical responsibilities, assuring that all could affect an enormous number of beings with their good or bad actions, for the community included far more than people. Mexica cosmic society was like a spider's web; when a fly's struggles ripped a hole in one small section, it was felt all over the web. Only by eating the fly (an appropriate action), could the spider remain alive and have strength to repair the web. The common good extended well beyond human society, no one acted alone, and destruction was unavoidable if society was to remain in good health.

Mexica moral messages of creative successes and destructive failures are expressed in many Nahuatl metaphoric passages concerning the duties of rulers and their people. Using parallelisms, these messages develop progressively in a literary style similar to the sequentially structured New Fire rite. A paired set of metaphors begins each moral passage, which is then used to build a message step by step. The strange couplet "you cast down your face, you cast down your teeth" begins one such passage (FC, bk. 6, pt. 7, chap. 43:247–48, Read 1994c). First the verse tells the ruler that if he is not "straight" or forthright, he will cast his face down, thereby changing his eating identity. It then says that he must stop doing this, or that identity will "dirty" and "damage his life and words." Each line of the metaphoric passage progressively moves from the initial identity crisis to its solution, then to its deeper nature and dire outcome if the ruler does not do what he should. Each reworks the previous line to expand on the old message and create a new. In the end, the foolish ruler is warned that he must be honest and open; if he is not, he will become a *death* that creates a new life different from his own.

Such an interdependent ecology of values operates on biological models. Expiatory acts are not found in Mexica sacrifice, for such killing was considered neither evil nor the source of disease. Rather, sacrifice allowed growth to occur. Sometimes a sacrificial offering was washed with water. Some offerings were even called "Bathed or Watered Ones" (*tlaaltiltin*), and the merchant who sold them, "He who Bathes or Waters" (*tealtiani*). But this was not necessarily an act of cleansing. When it occurred, the bathing preceded the rite for an extended period so that the offering could be prepared in a manner appropriate to its recipient. Since *tlahtlacotin*, as failures, were not quite adequate, they had to be conditioned for their cosmic duty. The transgressor, as rotting excrement, was being prepared as fertilizer, a process accomplished with water.[27]

This process, which kept the cosmic house healthy and its inhabitants moving appropriately within its watery walls, created a shifting topography of values. Innovation itself was a valued tool because it meant one could change to a better place when circumstances demanded. But such shifts also created shifts in the worth of things. The sacrifice of forty-two children during an extreme crisis was a short-term solution that was never repeated in that form; perhaps the price was too high to pay. The Flowery Wars, however, remained long after the initial crisis was over, becoming one of several tools for hegemony with long-lasting effects on the social and political landscape of Mesoamerica.[28] The first shift in ritual valuation, while shocking, was only temporary, never entering ordinary life. However, the second, the Flowery Wars, occurred each winter thereafter; by becoming a part of the normal seasonal cycle, it took its appropriate place in the feeding continuum.

Limited Reciprocity: Communal Ties and Sacrificial Duties

In the reciprocal life of the cosmic house, both animalia and animated objects held communal value. People did not live in this cosmic house alone but necessarily shared their particular *teoyome* (powers) with the powers of a host of other beings, a situation that may seem quite foreign to contemporary folks from an era often based on individualism.

Imagine, then, that you are standing at the beginning of a very broad avenue. This avenue extends into the distance until it reaches a gigantic pyramid which mimics in miniature the mountain that stands behind it. Easily as broad as a city block, this corridor is so long that it is almost impossible to make out the people near the distant pyramid, which stands a good twenty- to thirty-minute brisk hike away. On the right, about half way up the avenue, towers a second pyramid. People climbing on it appear like ants swarming over its surface. Smaller buildings, closer to a more comfortable, human scale, line the sides of this expansive alameda. Spreading out from its sides are the remains of many stone dwellings and structures which at one time were populated by thousands of people. You are standing on the Avenue of the Dead, and this is the vision of stately grandeur that once was Teotihuacan.

Imagine again that you are standing on a humble pyramid atop a small mountain. Having just ascended on a road passing through pleasant, cool forests filled with thick undergrowth, a high, flat mountain park ringed by hills now spreads beneath for miles and miles. Rich farmland and marshlands stretch out majestically. Around their edge, the hills form tall walls reaching to the sky; mist and clouds hang over their tops. Somewhere in the distant haze shrouding much of the valley lies Teotihuacan, hidden from view. Below, the center of the city juts up into the valley's air, like a town built of children's building blocks. You are standing on Uixachtlan, the mountain where the New Fire ceremony took place. Beneath you lies the Valley of Mexico with the once-grand Tenochtitlan buried under the high-rises of Mexico City. At one time you could have seen the four sectors of that earlier urban center with its magnificent Templo Mayor rising from the crossroad of its two main causeways. The ritual district housing the temple was then as stunning as its ancestor, Teotihuacan's Avenue of the Dead. Each visually pronounced a forceful dominion, the energies of the state, and the powers of particular places.

The Mexica-Tenochca lived in this land and skyscape, their existence bounded and defined by it, their lives filled with the endless possibilities of its many potent *teoyome*. The mountains, hills, rivers, lakes, and celestial objects all pulsed with tangible powers. Pyramids, like those of the Sun and the Moon, the Templo Mayor, or the little one on Uixachtlan, were bound to these *teoyome* by means of their topographical orientations. And in this at once ever-changing and ever-bounded world, each family had its own house, set within a sector of the state house which was set within the even larger cosmic house. Each family interacted with other families and living beings within these intermeshing dwellings. Like the temple that buried potent buildings within potent buildings through time, the cosmic house held potent, smaller houses within ever larger ones. Actions taking place within the daily and special events of human life, in the home and in the temple, directly bound people with other people, the powers of the state and the powers of numerous living beings of this knotted and woven cosmos.

And just as each animated being's powers were limited in their authoritative scope, so too were people's, a reality experienced in everyday life. No person can live by his or her own resources alone; all rely on others whether desired or not. So too with the beings of the Mexica world; these experiences are described in their histories and extolled in their moral writings.

Stories tell of the harsh life on the northern deserts led by the early Chichimeca hunter-gatherer ancestors of the Mexica warrior-farmers.

Durán describes them eating only what they hunted, "like a dog in a dung heap with natural instincts to look for something to gnaw." When they left each day seeking to kill whatever they could find to eat—rabbits, deer, rats, lizards, snakes, birds, worms, plants, and roots—the women hung their babes, sleepily engorged with breast milk, in reed baskets to wait their return, for the men alone could not feed all (HI 1984, chap. 2:24; 1992 2:16). Metaphorical moral reminders tell the Mexica ruler that neither can he act alone. His subjects, the *macehualtin* (commoners), are "the tail and the wing" of his city (FC, bk. 6, pt. 7, chap. 43:244); they are the parts of a bird that allow it to fly. Rulers have need of noble folks as well. "Together, close to one another, they cut morsels for one another, gather close to one another" (ibid., 251). Together with nobles and commoners, rulers form a tight, interdependent community in which they feed and give motion to each other, everyone limited by what each can and cannot give (Read 1994c).

Ancestral ties of *mahceua* (merit) both increased the necessity for active participation in this sacrificially fed world and reduced the importance of an individual's *death*. That strong sense of community, begun with the Chichimeca hunters and continued with Mexica warriors, overrode most individual concerns, for any one person could not be divorced from the ancestral "thread." In Mexica genetic theory, individuals both drew their own *mahceua* from the ancestral line and gave *mahceua* to it by their actions. If a person seriously transgressed the societal norms, she not only could be either sold into servitude or possibly sacrificed but also could plunge her whole family into a debt of servitude for generations to come. Individuals did not act alone because their personal acts conditioned the merit and thus the very identity of their familial community.

This means that one might become a willing sacrificial offering, as had Nanahuatzin, for the sake of one's family. Just as one's bad actions could create long-lasting bad merit for one's family, good actions could do the opposite. By offering oneself to the cosmos to be eaten, one became an ancestor from whom merit could be drawn to improve familial chances at successes, thereby avoiding failure. Sahagún tells the story of a young warrior from Huexotzinco, named Mixcoatl, who died in war. Because he had given his heart, he would live again among Huexotzinco's drums and once again would burn or blossom on earth (*tixotlaz tlalticpac*) (FC, bk. 6, pt. 7, chap. 21:114–15). Because one's family extended to include the state, Huexotzinco was more than a family line, it was a center with civic face and heart. And because family was equated with both small communities and grand societal units, Mixcoatl's warrior *death* strengthened both the ties of his parents and grandparents and those of the entire society to which he was genetically linked.

This concept places "[people]-in-society," for it is similar to what Richard Shweder and Edmund Bourne called the "concrete-relational" style of social relations. In such a view an individual is "regulated by strict rules of interdependence that are context-specific and particularistic, rules governing exchanges of services, rules governing behavior to kinsmen, rules governing marriage, etc." (1984). The Mexica were regulated and governed in this way. Children were to be prudent, honest, humble, and benign, they were to have an understanding of their sacrificial duty (FC, bk. 6, pt. 7; Read 1986, 130). Numerous regulations governing sexual activities were aimed at ensuring appropriate communal and family ties (López Austin 1988b, 290–312). Even the ways in which people addressed each other in polite conversation regulated social structure; one often turned natural kin terms upside down or avoided them all together to underscore deference (Karttunen 1986). These sources present a curious picture to the contemporary reader inclined to think of the Mexica as violent and barbarous, for they paint an image of people carefully restricted in their behavior by extremely high standards of personal responsibility to the community.

This orderly and carefully moderated social image is magnified a thousandfold when one remembers that people were not just related to one small community or even simply to a large human society but in some sense biologically related to all animated beings in the entire cosmos. Mixcoatl was a "person-in-cosmic society," and his responsibilities extended from his immediate family and the state to the whole universe. Like the interlocking dwellings in the Fifth Sun's cosmic house or the nesting layers of the Templo Mayor, Mixcoatl's responsibilities also interlocked with nesting layers of expectations.

In order to fulfill a demand of moral goodness under the right conditions, individuals could be subordinated to greater cosmic needs, for reciprocity was demanded by the community without which the individual could not exist. It was the stuff of *death* that Mictlancihuatl ate. This female partner to the Lord of the Dead (Mictlanteuctli) often was shown with open mouth upturned hungrily waiting for what was due her from those living on Earth's Surface (figure 13). The Avenue of the Dead, the Templo Mayor, and Uixachtlan all were alive. One's place, one's dwelling, one's house—all were living entities and therefore part of one's social responsibility.

Because *death* gives life, reciprocity requires sacrifice, which was likened to paying a debt (*neixtlahualiztli*). If one ate something, one needed to kill something of oneself in return. Only suckling babies were not yet tied to *death*, for they did not eat the things of the earth; they stayed home napping when their mothers hung them in a tree to go hunting. In a world where "people-are-in-cosmic-society," an enormous burden lies upon each person. As though caught in a spider's web, an entangled human fly sent waves through the entire cosmic net, and each individual had to account for the societal and cosmic effect of her battles. Along with the cosmic house's ordinary sacrificial truth, a moral requirement upon which the communal cosmic good rested propelled people into sacrificial participation.

Ongoing Rituals of Sacrificial Transformation

People of all ages and all walks of life participated in sacrificial rituals. This is especially clear when one remembers that not just the *deaths* of great warriors were sacrifices but such things as bloodletting, beating, and offering animals also were sacrificial acts. Everyone joined in state rituals like the New Fire ceremony, and even babies had their ears pierced. But the appeal of such large public dramas developed first in far more intimate circumstances. Remember, each day's first meal of tortillas recalled the sacrificial nature of the universe.

Sacrifice began at birth with the sacrificial capturing of the newborn by its warrior mother (FC, bk. 6, pt. 7, chap. 33:179). And in its naming ceremony, a child was raised to the skies, while the midwife declared that it had been created to provide food and drink (FC, bk. 6, pt. 7, chap. 37:203). Naming was followed by a series of sacrificial ceremonies which transformed a child's identity and ushered it into communal life. A child's transgressions were sometimes punished with bloodletting or beating, both acts used in sacrificial rites involving *tlahtlacotin*. Bad children also might be held in the noxious smoke of burning chili peppers, bound hand and foot and stretched out on a damp floor, or wakened at night and made to work (*Codex Mendoza*, fol. 59, 60). All these experiences would not only deter them from misbehaving but also harden them to pain and encourage an unquestioned acceptance of particular violences as simply part of life. Thus, children might be developmentally transformed into the little edible corn plants they were meant to be.

The Mexica sacrificial world both created and rested on the power of the ordinary. Some have noted that participation in sacrificial rituals involved various forms of physical and psychological coercions;[29] while that may be true, such coercion alone is not enough to explain why people took part in sacrificial rituals. Willing participation also must have been rooted in the Mexica world's ability both to make reasonable sense of existence through sacrifice and to ground that sacrificial logic in communally shared experiences that joined physical realities with truths of everyday life. The cosmos survived because it depended on sacrificial acts to control and moderate existence, acts echoing real human experiences of killing and eating, death and life, and inevitable needs to control destructive-creative changes. This sacrificial world invented what seem to modern sensibilities to be painful and brutal experiences. Even more strange, these experiences both gave order to and received order from people's everyday lives. The Mexica world's fundamental need and one of its most remarkable accomplishments was the normalization of sacrificial violence. Life was "fleeting" because intimately ordinary sacrificial moments made it so.

EPILOGUE
2-Reed: A Sacrificial Completion

The elegant but rather ordinary date plaque hanging in its Plexiglas box on the museum's wall encompasses the entire Mexica-Tenochca cosmos. Its date, 2-Reed, binds the powers of a limited period of time that sacrificially spins itself into the rope of all Mexica existence. By binding the years, the Mexica ritually bound temporal transformation into order and brought some measure of control over the inevitable change in their lives' *space-time* (figure 1.1–4). The fire drill sparked the sacrificial flame that cooked, fed, and strengthened those ties. By ritually setting that new fire, the Mexica sacrificially burned old ancestral forms into their new heirs by participating in their *time-space's* transformative process (figure 1.5–8). Thus, this sacrificial ceremony, occurring in the year 2-Reed, marked the *completion* of the year 1-Rabbit and was followed by the birth of its fresh young heir, a new calendrical round ordering existence.

This book also comes to its *completion*. And as with all Mexica *completions*, the end is never final; it must lead to fresh sacrificial beginnings. The tale has spun its conclusion, and now it comes time to transform this yarn into something new. Indeed, the story itself has been shaped by a spiraling motion, moving from concepts of deformative transformation to transformations' moving calculations to the calculated transformative reality of people to people and other beings' timed transformative sacrifices in the cosmic house and, finally, to a transformation of Western concepts in order to better understand this strange Mexica world. Each turn "doubled back" to pick up some threads from earlier turns, each time "piling up" a slightly different selection of earlier Mexica concepts in order to build a new imaged moment of Mexica time and sacrifice. But now the reed-chapters are done and the bundle needs to be set down so that new ones can be picked up. To do this I will, by way of summary, double back and pile up Mexica concepts of time and sacrifice and their *re-presentations* of various Western concepts. Second, I will *complete* those spinning *returns* in order to spiral forward toward the book's young heirs, some new questions and possibilities.

Doubling Back and Piling Up

Time-space worked like spinning rope. Drawing fibers into its rotations, it constantly doubled back on itself in order to spiral forward. With each rotation, the days and years piled up, creating changing and unique power-filled moments. This story also must double back before its *completion* can be successfully moved onward. On the first rotation, I will double back to Mexica concepts of burning hearts and binding reeds in order to pile up concepts of sacrifice and time. On the second rotation, I will double back to pile up various Mexica *re-presentations* of Western ideas, ideas which originally spun out of the sacred and profane dichotomy.

Burning Hearts and Binding Reeds

Sacrifice made transformation happen in the *time-space* of a complex, crowded, and dynamic universe. The Mexica lived with a host of other beings in a cosmic house called the Fifth Sun, which was the fifth house in a series of five. The Mexica and their moving and unmoving housemates (human and nonhuman) continually deformed and transformed themselves and each other. For all was alive in this terrariumlike dwelling, moistened by the flow of water and charged with multiple and shifting *teoyome* (powers) that made things happen. Its upperworld was bordered by the watery walls of Ilhuicatl (Sky-Water) through which the sun, moon, Venus, the Pleiades, and other celestial objects traveled along their appropriate paths. The four corners of this house were supported by four great trees and the Tlaloques (rain gods); various godly *teoyome* spiraled up and down the tree trunks, and all manner of precipitation flowed from the rain gods. Spread out below like a four-petaled flower lay Tlalticpac (Earth's Surface), upon which all lived out their life spans.

Tenochtitlan spread out in the center of this Mexica-Tenochca world, claiming its own particular *space-time*, which was bounded by mountain ranges on all four sides, nourished by wetlands surrounding their island home, and governed by the travels of their particular celestial beings. In the center of the island rose the great double-sided Templo Mayor with its homes to Tlaloc (the rain god) on the north and Huitzilopochtli (the Mexica ancestral god) on the south. These houses marked the path of the sun as it traveled along the horizon from the wet of summer farming to the dry of winter warring and back again. The temple's many-layered body swallowed earlier royal periods into its multiple bellies, just as Mictlan (Land of the Dead) swallowed and ate the dead and decayed from the world above. Below Tlalticpac (Earth's Surface) lay the underworld with its moist load of rotting forms, the fertilizing feed for the upperworld's beings. The sun was born from its innards every day, caught by male warriors clamoring and shouting in the morning air. Every noon, female warriors captured the sun from the males and delivered it back to Mictlan by evening. There it traveled through that dank, excremental world to the next day's new battles.

Ceaseless sacrificial eating allowed the inhabitants of this cosmic house to continue living. All living beings both partook of this comestible process and moved through their own eating continuum. People ate corn, digested it, excreted it back out in a new form, and threw it on their fields to feed the new corn they would eat. As in war and hunting, sacrificial acts cornered and captured their tasty meals in marsh and field. And like sexuality, eating created the living ancestors and beings dwelling in the Fifth Sun's house. But people themselves were corn; they were born, ate, grew, aged, decayed, died, and rotted to become fertilizing feed for something else to eat, grow, age, decay, die, and rot. Fires sacrificially cooked these tender meals into new lives moving unavoidably to their own sacrificial demise. Sacrifice both birthed and sustained all inhabitants of the Fifth Sun's house.

Sacrificial powers, however, varied among different domains occupied by various beings. Commoners (*macehualtin*), nobles (*pipiltin*), toltec ancestors like Tata and Nene, and sometimes celestial beings like Nanahuatzin and Tecuiçiztecatl were bound by the food they ate to particular life spans that calculated their years with stunning accuracy. But some gods from the greater domains such as Huitzilopochtli, Quetzalcoatl, and Tezcatlipoca, because they ate foods like the aroma of roasted hearts, could control their forms so that they never quite *disappeared*. Nevertheless, the strength of their *teoyome* was limited by the same calendrical system that controlled all else; these gods' powers swung back and forth like *time-space's* rope, doubling round as it spun forward. Because their sacrificial sustenance differed, the humble *disappeared* when their time spans were *completed*; but, for the great, only their *teoyome* (powers) *disappeared* on schedule.

All beings in the Fifth Sun, from the greatest to the most humble, found their lives bound to the reed years of calendrically counted time spans.

For all moved through their life spans to the rhythm of their changing *mahceua* (merit). These individually identifying bundles created a being's own customized *space-time*. *Mahceua* constituted beings' health, personalities, talents, weaknesses, and destinies; it determined who would move their *teoyome* in what way, why, and where. People's various *mahceua*, with its power-filled bonds to the calendrical schedule, shaped their deformative-transformative *destructions*, *deaths*, and *disappearances*. It shaped how their identifying *faces* (*ixtli*) were successfully or unsuccessfully remolded into new identities. Not all was fated, however. People's morally good and morally bad behavior in combination with their particular *mahceua* determined the triumphs and failures of their time spans.

Nevertheless, each being, no matter how successful, lived for only a particular time span. Once that period was *completed*, a sacrificially deformative transformation *destroyed* it, causing its *death* and *disappearance* into some new being or beings. The calendar's spiral shape allowed the progress of transformation's destructive-creative process; its many cycles' odd and even counts created a spinning motion for *time-space*. Mexica-Tenochca transformation was wholly natural, occurring in biological ways. Ages and their cosmic houses, gods, cities, and people alike were deformed to be transformed via the processes of natural existence: eating, sexuality and ancestry, death and decay. Transformation thus was "generative" because one thing changed to generate another. Nothing was ever born of nothing, and nothing ever stayed the same.

Sacrificial Re-presentations

This new Mexica-Tenochca terrain has demanded some new maps. In order to understand Mexica time and sacrifice, it has been necessary to redraw various Western concepts. These concepts have been *re-presented* in the manner of an artist depicting reality in her own way. Such *re-presentations* are always tied to real things, but no matter how realistic they may appear, they also are never an exact equivalent of reality. Of course, true *re-presentations* cannot occur unless one is sure of the terrain; map-making requires a keen eye. How else can we be certain that we are not simply redrawing maps based on familiar Western terrain or that the old maps have been truly challenged by this strange territory? Theoretical maps chart nothing if they are not based on the careful observation of a terrain's real shape. Therefore, the theoretical maps in this book have been based on some very detailed studies of the Mexica context.

All these *re-presented* Western theories originally spun out of an old dichotomy between the sacred and profane. This dualistic contradiction does not match very well with Mexica biological realities, and the world changes radically when we cease to separate the sacred from the profane. If the new terrain offers a view in which the sacred *equals* the profane, a number of world-forming visions must be readjusted at root levels; they must be sacrificially completed because the usefulness of their life span has ended, and new visions now are needed.

First, if the profane *is* sacred, then history *equals* eternity. The temporal flow of social life in the cosmic house is all one has, for timelessness does not exist; history is eternal because change is endless. In a world with no other options, moreover, this is more a simple fact of existence than a paradoxical problem. Second, a profanely sacred world also means that everlasting life can never overcome death because life cannot exist without *death*'s creative potencies. Third, life in such a historically sacred cosmos might stretch Western ideas about social realities. Beings living in the Fifth Sun's house hold constantly shifting and differing *teoyome* (powers). This means that no being (whether age, god, city, human, or animal) can claim omnipotence, for each being's powers are too specific, too individualistic. Such limitations force all into reciprocal relationships with others (both great and humble). One can expect no more than partial, temporary control over anyone. An intermeshing system of checks and balances governed the Fifth Sun's many-faceted society, not simply the fated, hierarchically ordained control of gods or certain privileged human beings.

Finally, the transformative nature of the Fifth Sun demanded a *re-presentation* of certain Eliadian and Ricoeurian concepts. First, because no transcendent, eternally unchanging sacred realm exists in the Mexica world, Eliade's returns to a prehistorical primordium cannot happen, and Ricoeur's moments of nowness cannot collapse enduring elements of the past into the present, lending unchanging continuity to the future. Instead, because history is all one has, Mexica ritual *returns* are limited in nature, creating a limited sense of *nowness*; they pull into the present only selected threads from the past, piling up only certain *teoyome* which are capable of reshaping only limited and very particular futures. Second, unlike Eliadian hierophanies, Mexica potent moments do not join the sacred and profane only temporarily. Instead, because the sacred equals the profane, multitudinous powers continually course through everything. A situation of profane sacralities is, therefore, always present. The intermeshing and intertwining of these powers creates an ongoing process of *continuing hierophanies* pushed forward by ever-present continuing eschatologies in which beings first destruct and die before disappearing into some new profanely sacred being.

This cosmos is dynamic on all fronts. History is all one has, but history is all one needs to transform the shape of existence, for sacrality is always here and now. The ordinary *is* the extraordinary. As Motecuhzuma's magicians learned in Aztlan, sacrifice's power rests in the shifting sands of mundane existence and on the shoulders of a god who, at least for the moment, is fully present among them, not somewhere beyond. The Mexica may not hope for unlimited power, but they can hope to order and reorder what they can while they exist, especially if they remember the importance of ordinary humility.

Spinning Sacrificial *Completions*

This book is now *complete*. The fullness of its existence has arrived, and its *destruction, death,* and *disappearance* loom ahead. A sacrificial transformation must now rearrange it afresh, drawing on selected threads that have been appearing, *disappearing,* and reappearing throughout. It has come time for some new questions and possibilities. Reconsiderations of our theoretical maps allow us to learn something new that may be useful for our own lives; such is the power of *re-presentation*. In spite of all its violence, then, how can the Mexica offer new possibilities for reshaping contemporary life? Five interconnected issues (among others, I'm sure) beg exploration.

Power is the first such issue. The constant presence of *teoyome* in the Mexica cosmic house raises broader questions about power and hegemony. How does one understand power in a world governed by checks and balances, where powers are as concrete as the folk who embody and enact them? Drawing on a number of theorists as well as on this volume's definition of sacrifice, I have suggested elsewhere that Mexica power is "(a) an efficient but limited ability to (b) effect change (c) within a moral community that (d) is structured by interactive and relative differences" (1994a, 58).

This definition offers four possibilities for a Western rethinking of power, something pertinent to the diverse, heterogeneous reality of today's communal life: (1) Change is an essential and unavoidable element of power, for even those who wish to maintain the status quo must change those who wish to change it. (2) If change is an essential element of power, then negotiation is not aimed at getting everyone to agree to a single standard of truth, for that is impossible. Cooperation is built on the momentary intertwining of differences, not on complete agreement. (3) Not all powers are open to everyone, nor does anyone have access to all powers. This means that power must be understood in all its context-specific complexities. And (4) power therefore operates in a system of relative differences in which the contenders may not share the same resources, much less the same goals. This is different from a model built on the presumption that complete equality is the universal measure, for equality is not possible nor even desirable. Instead, both resistance and cooperation are based on particular goals that must be balanced with other particular goals (ibid., 67–69).

Unfortunately, this model raises real issues for the disenfranchised that are not easily addressed. Yet ideas of complete equality have not addressed those issues either, for equality necessarily demands impossible comparisons that override potentially useful differences. No one lives in a world in which all are exactly alike; like the Mexica, we all bear unique *merits*. Race, gender, ethnicity, health, talents, intelligence, age, and geographic location are but a few of the differences marking people. Such differences sometimes have forced those beholden to complete equality to make claims for a false equality that favors some merits over others; if the differences are unavoidable, the only way to achieve equality is to ignore them. This may leave one wondering what useful differences are being washed over. What might distinctions in gender, health, and so on, offer to communal life? In other words, what is lost when the values of one sector are seen as the values for all?

Second, the nature of Mexica rulership and community might offer some possibilities for understanding these seemingly intractable issues of power and diversity. Contrary to what some have suggested (e.g., D. Carrasco 1982, 1987a; Gillespie 1989), the Mexica ruler was no sacred king, at least not in the classic sense. Rulers had to operate within the realities of their own limited world. And in a profanely sacred world, a ruler could be no more than a "sacred commoner," for in spite of his noble status, rulers were commoners in reference to other more potent forces (Read 1994a, 52–57). This means that a ruler:

> tries to manipulate power (a) effectively (but with only limited abilities) in order (b) to effect the motion of change in such a way that various cosmic powers will remain fed and the human community will be generously provided for. These are (c) moral tasks because they are necessary to communal

survival and are among the particular responsibilities of the ruler because of his unique place in the group. And finally, these moral tasks are circumscribed by (d) the various and differing people and groups with which he is bound and interacts in his cosmic and human communities. (ibid., 67)

Is this a model that is applicable to present leadership? Would it be useful to think about leaders as "sacred commoners" whose status bears only limited possibilities? These questions raise a number of further ethical issues.

Third, how rulers altered and controlled their worlds through imagery is an important issue. In the Mexica world, power is tied closely with objects like the plaque itself. Since *teoyome* operated because they were embodied forms, what were Mexica notions of beautiful forms? What could aesthetics mean in such a profanely sacred world, especially for rulers who must present the images of certain *faces* in order to control the flow of powers? Three possibilities come to mind: (1) Good form cannot be transcendent, for it is embodied in and operates on the ordinary world. Power *equals* form. Well-arranged form, then, is the stuff of beauty, for it is by means of form that identities are shaped. The ruler must be ever conscious of the *faces* he presents to others. (2) Because a profanely sacred world is a constantly changing one, Mexica beauty cannot be eternal or always nice. Changing the arrangements of form "was both a transformational tool of rulers and a barometer of their powers' efficacy, an efficacy that admitted the necessity of destruction for creation, perhaps even destruction of the rulers themselves." (3) Beautiful forms must be concrete, but that does not mean that they must be visible, for their powers may rely on not being seen. Hence the Templo Mayor swallowed the things of dead rulers into its invisible innards in order to incorporate their powers (Read 1995a, 382–83). Good form depends on its inherent and shifting powers, not on being seen. Beauty was a tool in the Mexica world, not a goal; and as such, it carried social responsibilities. Is this true today? For both good and ill, form manipulates others with its powers, an issue that bears real ethical import in today's world of film, video, and television. How do current *faces* or images gloss the differences in a heterogeneous society? Whose powers do they really promote? To affect us, must they always be in front of one's eyes, or do their powers extend beyond the act of seeing them?

Fourth, can the functioning of ethics in such a dynamic and complex system as the Mexica offer any solutions to the problem of equality? Michael Walzer's (1983, 3–30) notion of "complex equalities" may help partially answer this question. Walzer describes "complex equalities" as a system in which social goods or justice is distributed via local, interlocked spheres of influence interacting with each other. Clearly the Mexica-Tenochca social system was not egalitarian, but this is not what Walzer means, at least not the simple egalitarianism mentioned above (ibid., 13–17). He is talking about a system of complex differences, and he demonstrates how this works even in situations of apparent hierarchy similar to that of the Mexica nobles. Each sphere creates its own distinctive identity; harmony is maintained as long as the boundaries surrounding the spheres are maintained. But because the spheres are necessarily different from one another, boundary conflicts are almost endemic (ibid., 318). In other words, Mexica morality shifted with the specified powers and concerns of each distinct context. Moreover, it shifted according to some well-worn rules involving things like kinship; the social independence of material resources; flexible and complex ideas over what actually constituted nobles and commoners, the interlocking of quite a wide variety of social spheres; and, finally, the absolute necessity for communal decision making (Read 1995b). This was an ethically flexible situation; moral actions were in no way built on ideas of unchanging value grounded in eternal truth. Although this model seems to work well for describing Mexica social relations, it raises problems for us. Are we, as Walzer suggests, caught in our own historically defined spheres of influence (ibid., xiv)? If so, what does that mean for our own ethical reasoning?

Fifth, what then does a profanely sacred world mean for today's ethical decision making, carried out as it must be in a world governed by differences that is not unlike the Mexica world? It is possible that the definition of sacrifice given in chapter 4 can be sacrificially transformed into a nonviolent but sacrificially re-presented approach to today's ethical reasoning (Read, 1994b). Three suggestions may prove useful.

1. *A sacrificially ethical process involves acts of reciprocity in which both human and nonhuman beings participate.* As with the Mexica, one's identity is meaningful only inasmuch as one cooperates with and is limited by others. And community must include more than humans, for life will not continue if other life is not accounted for. Moreover, Western images (our *faces* or *ixtli*) of rugged individualism are out in this communally oriented universe, and those of divine prophets, rational philosophers, and accepting humanists are made problematic by their claims to essential knowledge. In a profanely sacred world, essentialism of any kind is not possible because eternal truth is not an option.

2. *This reciprocity transforms by destroying things to create new things (acts recognizing that life is linked to death).* If one lives in a world that is profanely sacred, everlasting life cannot overcome death because it does not exist as a possibility. Creativity requires some destruction, even if that is as seemingly benign as destroying an old value or ideological *face* in order to create a new. Even nonviolent traditions like Buddhism and Jainism have recognized this. Since destruction is inevitable, the best one can do is control it.

3. *Transformation is aimed at the current state of affairs for purposes that the culture regards as morally good and conducive to cosmic order.* This is not a suggestion for any hopeless relativism, for decisions come back to limited yet related communities, living in bounded circumstances which both constrain and shape moral valuations. As with the Mexica, one can never expect full consensus within such a complex web of interests. Arguing it out, allowing one counterorder to moderate another, may be one of the few ways through which agreement may be hoped for. But this task is not hopeless. History is all one has, but history may be all one needs because, in a profanely sacred world, history itself is sacred.

With this spinning of the Mexica world into the present one, this tale's completion has spiraled forward to some new possibilities. Yet neither the Mexica nor we are left with a stable, good order, for things necessarily have moved on to an incomplete condition. The Mexica were born only to eat, grow old, and die, their pieces scattering out into the cosmos to perform other duties. And our contemporary dilemmas over diversity have not been measurably eased by passing through this window into another world; if anything, old problems have been further confirmed and new problems created. Yet, strangely enough, it may be the metaphorically re-presentational possibilities produced by sacrificially transformational processes that offer the most. For only by traveling that creative middle ground of ordered chaos—that area ordinarily existing between the extraordinary poles of transcendent eternity and total chaos—can one even hope to have an effect on the problems.

APPENDIX 1
Glossary of Mexica Names and Terms

1-Rabbit The last year in a fifty-two-year round, which preceded the first year 2-Reed. Its cardinal direction was south or the Place of Thorns. This year was considered unlucky, bringing potential famine and death. The lighting of the new fire in 2-Reed completed the round and brought an end to 1-Rabbit's danger. See 2-Reed, the Binding of the Years, Four Year Bearers.

2-Reed (2-Acatl) The first year in a fifty-two-year round. Its glyph was a young reed plant with two dots (figure 1). Often a knotted rope appeared just below a fire drill that was encased within the reed plant because the Binding-of-the-Years or New Fire ceremony took place in November in 2-Reed. At this time, the years were bound and a new fire begun. See 1-Rabbit, the Binding-of-the-Years, the Four Year-Bearers.

Aztlan The mythical place of origin for the Mexica-Tenochca (myth 8). A lush island in the midst of marshes and lagoons, it was hidden entirely by thorny bushes and brambles. Aztlan was a place of leisure where healthful food came easily. People living there could move at will from youth to age to youth again because they ate simple food like corn, fish, and marsh birds. It also was the home of the Mexica patron god Huitzilopochtli and his mother, Coatlicue. When the Mexica left this paradisical home, carrying Huitzilopochtli on their backs, everything turned against them, stones wounded them and prickly trees and bushes stung them. During the reign of Motecuhzuma the Elder (1424–1440 or 1445), priests took a dangerous magical flight to Aztlan to visit with Coatlicue. She told them that Huitzilopochtli would eventually abandon the Mexica, losing all the towns over which he held hegemony in the same order that he conquered them. She also told them that they were doomed because they had grown heavy with their fancy food and riches. See Chicomoztoc, Coatlicue, Huitzilopochtli, Motecuhzuma the Elder.

Binding-of-the-Years, New Fire ceremony A sacrificial ceremony that took place every fifty-two years in November in the year 2-Reed. Its purpose was to give birth to a new sun that would move on its path for another fifty-two years. This coincided with the beginning of the dry season, and when the Pleiades (which were at the zenith) was moving contrary to the sun (which was at its nadir). At this time all the fires in the Mexica domain were extinguished. On a hill rising above Tenochtitlan called Uixachtlan, a fire was sparked in the chest of a human sacrificial offering; if the fire priest was unsuccessful in sparking the flame, the land would be eaten by the forces of night. A runner carried the fire to the Templo Mayor, and from there runners distributed fire to local temples throughout the land; people received fire from their temples to start their own household fires. See 1-Rabbit, 2-Reed, Templo Mayor, Tenochtitlan.

Calpulli A social group that was formed on the basis of biological parentage, friendship, or, perhaps, business loyalties. All within the group traced their kinship to an ancestral deity or patron god. A *calpulli* held land (distributed among its member families) and constituted an economic, military, political, and jurisdictional unit. There were four *calpullies* in Tenochtitlan, each holding one quarter of the city. Each of these traced their heritage, first, to their patron deity and then to Huitzilopochtli, the patron of the entire city. See Huitzilopochtli, Tenochtitlan.

Chalchiuitl, chalchiuhomitl *Chalchiuitl* was greenstone or jade and metaphorically meant "precious," perhaps because it was thought that it could attract moisture in a semi-arid land. These stones were considered the property of nobles (*pipiltin*). *Chalchiuhomitl* means "greenstone or precious bones." Quetzalcoatl stole these bones from Mictlan so that he and Cihuacoatl could make people from them. See Quetzalcoatl, Cihuacoatl.

Chichimeca A term referring to all barbaric hunting and gathering groups. The Mexica-Tenochca were *chichimeca* in their early history. Some think the term derives from the word for "dog" (*chichi*), something suggested by the story about Tata and Nene (myth 2). Others suggest, for linguistic reasons, that it may derive from the word for "suckle" (*chíchí*). See Tata and Nene.

Chicomoztoc The Place of Seven Caves; the origin place of the Mexica-Tenochca. It is probably the same as Aztlan (myth 8). It is said that seven different groups living in the Mexican Highlands emerged from Chicomoztoc, each from a different cave. The Mexica were the last to leave this paradisical home. See Aztlan.

Chinampa Raised-mound agriculture. An extremely efficient system in which land and loam were dredged from the bottom of wetlands and mounded to create areas for growing corn and garden produce. Cypress trees were planted along the edges to prevent erosion. In a good year as many as six crops could be rotated through these rich fields by moving the plants to increasingly larger plots. As one of the most efficient agricultural systems in the world, it has been compared to wetland rice production. Tenochtitlan was ringed by *chinampas*. Raised-mound agriculture was probably first used by the pre-Classic Maya (1500–250 B.C.E.).

Cihuacoatl Snake Woman. She grinds the bones that Quetzalcoatl stole from Mictlan like corn in order to make people (myth 3). She also gives her name to the high-official political office that was second only to the ruler. See Quetzalcoatl, Mictlan.

Coatepec Snake Mountain. Coatepec was one of the places at which the Mexica stayed before they arrived on the spot upon which Tenochtitlan would be built. The Templo Mayor was also called Coatepec; it was surrounded by a snake wall. See Tenochtitlan, Templo Mayor.

Coatlicue Snake Skirt. A goddess who is dressed in a warrior's kilt made of knotted rattlesnakes; her name means "snake skirt." She is the mother of

Huitzilopochtli (myth 6), and awaits his return in Aztlan (myth 8). See Aztlan, Huitzilopochtli.

Copil The son of Malinalxochitl and nephew of Huitzilopochtli. Huitzilopochtli vanquishes Copil, sacrifices him and throws his heart onto the island where Tenochtitlan will be built (myth 7). See Huitzilopochtli, Malinalxochitl.

Coyolxauhqui A sister of Huitzilopochtli who leads an army against their mother, Coatlicue, when Coatlicue becomes pregnant by mysterious means (myth 6). Huitzilopochtli is born in full war regalia and vanquishes Coyolxauhqui and their four hundred brothers of the south. He then sacrifices Coyolxauhqui in the same manner that the Mexica sacrificed warriors. See Huitzilopochtli, Coatlicue.

Eagle and Jaguar Two creatures who rose from the fire at the Fifth Sun's birth. They arose after Nanahuatzin and Tecuiçiztecatl leapt into the fire and before two identical suns appeared on the eastern horizon. The alter ego of Nanahuatzin, the eagle was completely blackened because he had leapt into the fire when it was still burning brightly. The Jaguar was only spotty because he (as Tecuiçiztecatl) had leapt in the fire after it had died down and was burning unevenly. The eagle is associated with the daytime sun, the jaguar with the night. See Fifth Sun, Nanahuatzin, Tecuiçiztecatl.

Fifth Sun, 4-Movement (4-Ollin) The fifth in a series of five ages or suns. Each of the preceding suns was destroyed by some cataclysmic event; the Fifth Sun would be destroyed by famine and the motion of earthquake. It was the sun belonging to the Mexica-Tenochca and would live for 676 years. When 4-Movement ended, it would be eaten by the forces of night. No mention is ever made of a sixth age, perhaps because it is a moot point to discuss what one will not survive to witness. See Four Suns.

Flowery Wars Wars fought on a pre-arranged battlefield whose sole purpose was to capture offerings for warrior sacrifices. However, there appears to have been little difference between these wars and regular warfare, for often the warriors overstepped these boundaries by allowing the battles to degenerate into all-out warfare in which deaths occurred on the field. They were held during the dry season, and were originally a response to drought. Tlacaellel is said to have invented the Flowery Wars as a solution to the problems of drought-induced famine in the mid-fifteenth century. It was then that he called for a battlefield "marketplace" that was close to home, where they might buy hot warrior "tortillas" fresh from the oven to feed to the starving beings of the then impoverished cosmos. Tenochtitlan had six warring partners to the east in the Tlaxcalan area. The offering at the Binding of the Years that occurred just before the Spanish Conquest was captured in such a war. See Binding-of-the-Years, Tenochtitlan, Tlacaellel, Tonalco, Xiuhtlamin.

Four Suns: 4-Jaguar, 4-Wind, 4-Fire Rain, 4-Water Four ages called suns that existed before the Fifth Sun (Myth of the Four Suns). Each had a house, someone to inhabit the house, and something to eat. They had carefully calculated time spans, which were multiples of 13 x 52 years (676 years, table 5). Each was destroyed by the same thing for which it was named. See Fifth Sun.

Four Year-Bearers: Reed (Acatl), Knife (Tecpatl), House (Calli), Rabbit (Tochtli) In the calendrical system, the solar years (365 days each) are named by four year-bearers. They rotate in order against a cycle of 13: 1-Reed, 2-Knife, 3-House, 4-Rabbit, 5-Reed, 6-Knife, until 13-Reed is reached, then a new rotation of thirteen starts with 1-Knife and so on until the fifty-second year is reached, which is 13-Rabbit. Each year-bearer also traveled through its appropriate cardinal direction: Reed through the east, Knife through the north, House through the west, and Rabbit through the south (figure 11, table 4). See *Xiuhmolpilli*.

Huitzilopochtli Hummingbird on the Left. The patron, ancestral deity of the Mexica-Tenochca. In one myth he is born on Coatepec from Coatlicue (myth 6), where he immediately vanquishes his malevolent sister Coyolxauhqui. Later he conquers a dangerous nephew, Copil (myth 7), sacrificing Copil's heart to the future Tenochtitlan. He was one of the major sources of power for war and political conquest, which would be lost when his time span was up (myth 8). He was housed on the southern side of the Templo Mayor, which was coordinated with the winter and the season of war. Huitzilopochtli was closely associated with the great god Tezcatlipoca and was one of four gods lodged in a ruler's heart at his coronation. See Coatepec, Coatlicue, Copil, Coyolxauhqui, Tamoanchan, Templo Mayor, Tenochtitlan, Tezcatlipoca.

Ihiyotl One of three animistic entities that inhabited the body. The *ihiyotl* was centered in a person's liver and was linked to strong emotions; hence it helped form people's merit (*mahceua*). At death it went to the forests to become a ghostlike shadow that people wished to avoid. See *Mahceua*, *Teyolia*, *Tonalli*.

Ilhuicatl (Sky-Water) The sky walls of the cosmic house; they arched over Tlalticpac (Earth's Surface) and Mictlan (Land of the Dead). The walls were made of water, and the sun, moon, and other celestial objects followed their appropriate paths through them. See Mictlan, Tlalticpac.

Ixtli Both one's external face and inner identity. To change one's *ixtli* was to change one's identity because form was inherently endowed with meaning and power. Hence when the second sun's face was smashed by a rabbit, its identity changed from the sun to the moon (Birth I.4–10; VI.14–20).

Lords of the Night, Night Lords Nine calendrical figures that rotated in the *tonalpohualli* round. They were associated with the "messed up" night. They are one of the odd counts that counters the even calendrical counts, thereby forcing the calendrical cycles to move forward. See *Tlahtlacolli*, *Tonalpohualli*.

Macehualtin Commoners or ordinary people. This could be understood in two different ways: as a class of people beneath the nobles (*pipiltin*), or as a state of common humanity beneath more powerful beings in the Mexica cosmos. See *Pipiltin*.

Mahceua, Tlamaceua *Mahceua* is a complex word having to do with the who, how, why, where, and when of the flowing of powers (*teoyome*) within the cosmic house. It could be manipulated in rituals to affect the identities (*ixtli*) of things and make things effectively happen. *Mahceua* (merit) shaped people's personalities, fates, and their identity. People's *mahceua* were constituted by a variety of things, from the animistic entities contained within their bodies, to special names, to gods acting upon them, to their own actions. *Tlamaceua* refers simultaneously to the eating of the first meal at sunrise and the sacrifice of Nanahuatzin and Tecuiçiztecatl at the Fifth Sun's birth. See *Ihiyotl, Ixtli, Teoyome, Teyolia*.

Malinalxochitl The mother of Copil and sister of Huitzilopochtli (myth 7). After Huitzilopochtli abandoned her, she set her son against his uncle. Huitzilopochtli, however, stalked and killed Copil before he got him. His heart was tossed onto the place where later Tenochtitlan was built. See Copil, Huitzilopochtli, Tenochtitlan.

Mana, Mani Two of several words describing differing actions of spatial ordering. Used to describe the shaping of cosmic space, *mana* describes the action one uses when one pats out a tortilla; *mani* describes the action of water spreading in a pan. Hence the moon was "spread out flat" (*mana* [Birth I.10; chap. 1, n. 9]) when he was face-beaten and face-killed but the sun "spread in an undulating way" (*mani* [Birth V.56, chap. 1, n. 47]) through the watery walls of Ilhuicatl (Sky-Water) when it rose for the first time. See Ilhuicatl.

Maya, Classic (ca. 200–850 or 900 C.E.) One of the major civilizations preceding the Mexica-Tenochca. They were located in numerous urban centers in the Yucatan, Southern Mexico, Belize, Guatemala, Nicaragua, and El Salvador. See Mexica-Tenochca.

Mexica-Tenochca, Mexica (ca. 1325–1521) The group of people genealogically linked to the city of Tenochtitlan. The commonly known term "Aztecs" is a somewhat imprecise term for the Mexica made popular by nineteenth-century scholars. See Nahua, Tenochtitlan.

Mexican Highlands (Central Mexico, Mesa Central) The area surrounding Tenochtitlan, Teotihuacan, and the Valley of Mexico. It is bordered on the west, south, and east by mountains, and extends north to the border of Mesoamerica on the southern edge of grasslands lying between the Lerma and Panuco rivers.

Mictlan: Mictlanteuctli, Mictlancihuatl, Micteca Mictlan is the Land of the Dead that lies beneath Tlalticpac (Earth's Surface). It is a moist place of underground passage, rivers, and rotting things. Mictlanteuctli (Lord of the Mictlan) and Mictlancihuatl (Lady of Mictlan) ruled over this dark world.

The Micteca are the beings who live there. See Ilhuicatl, Quetzalcoatl, Tlalticpac.

Motecuhzuma the Elder (Motecuhzuma I) The Chief Speaker (*tlatoani*) who, according to Durán, ruled the Mexica from 1440 (or 1445) to 1469. It was during his reign that the 2-Reed plaque was made. Motecuhzuma the Elder is the ruler who sent the magicians to Aztlan (myth 8). See Aztlan.

Mountain of Produce The mountain Nanahuatl (Nanahuatzin) cracked open after Quetzalcoatl had failed to carry it (myth 4). As soon as the mountain opened, the Tlaloques (rain deities) snatched all the corn and grain away. See Nanahuatzin, Oxomoco and Cipactonal, Quetzalcoatl.

Nahua, Nahuatl The Nahua are any peoples who speak Nahuatl. The Mexica-Tenochca spoke Nahuatl but so did numerous others in an area roughly covering portions or all of the modern states of Queretaro, Hidalgo, the Federal District (Mexico City), Morelos, Tlaxcala, and Puebla. It was a lingua franca throughout the Mexica domain at the time of the Spanish Conquest and is still spoken by many today. See Mexica-Tenochca.

Nahualli A being or alter ego that can transform itself from one being into another. López Austin identifies the Nahualli as housed in the *ihiyotl*, but able to separate itself from that bodily entity, allowing it to take magical flights (1988b, 362–83). Quezalcoatl's *nahualli* helped him get out of his jam in Mictlan when he dropped the bones and fainted (myth 3). The magicians who traveled to Aztlan probably did so by means of their *nahuallies* (myth 7.4, 19). See Aztlan, *Ihiyotl*, Quetzalcoatl.

Nanahuatzin (Nanahuatl) The poor but humble deity in "The Birth of the Fifth Sun" who bravely leaps into the fire to become the sun (Birth: III, IV). He burns his syphilitic scabs as incense in his ritual preparations for his sacrifice. In another myth, he also arrives from Tamoanchan like a newborn babe at the beginning of the Fifth Sun (myth 5). In yet another, he cracks open the Mountain of Produce (myth 4). See Fifth Sun, Mountain of Produce.

Nemontemi The five dangerous days at the end of a vague solar year (360 + 5 = 365). They were not officially counted for ritual purposes because they would allow dangerous powers to operate. However, they were calculated into the mathematics of the calendrical system. See *Xiuhmolpilli*.

Nezahualcoyotl The poet-ruler of Texcoco to whom "the Fleeting Moment" is attributed. Texcoco was an ally of Tenochtitlan until the Conquest, when they defected to the Spanish. See Tenochtitlan.

Olmecs (ca. 1750–100 B.C.E.) The first major urban civilization in Mesoamerica. They influenced a large portion of the area from Veracruz to the Mexican Highlands to Oaxaca to southern Guatemala and El Salvador. The nature of this influence—whether it be by force, trade, missionizing, or all three— is much debated. The earliest calendars are attributed to them. See Maya, Classic; Mexica-Tenochca; Teotihuacan.

Oxomoco and Cipactonal The old couple who cast fortunes with corn to see who could open the Mountain of Produce (myth 4). The *Codex Borbonicus* shows them doing this (figure 16), suggesting that this act also began the calendar. See Mountain of Produce, Nanahuatzin, Quetzalcoatl.

Pipiltin Nobles or the elite. *Pipiltin* were related by lineages and technically received tribute, ran governmental processes, and enjoyed certain privileges. Not all *pipiltin*, however, were equally powerful or rich. A *pilli* could be poor, sold into slavery, and work for other *pipiltin*, while someone from the *macehualtin* class could be quite well off and apparently wield a certain amount of power because of successful trading. See *Macehualtin*.

Poliui To disappear, perish, be destroyed, decimated, lost, and fail. This word appears in Nahuatl texts describing acts of progressive destruction. For example, the second sun was face-wrecked (*conixpopoloque*) when it was beaten with a rabbit to form it into the moon (Birth: I.5–10; VI.14–20). See Fifth Sun, Four Suns.

Quetzalcoatl, Quetzalcoatl Ehecatl, Topiltzin Quetzalcoatl Quetzalcoatl (Feathered Snake) is a trickster god who goes to Mictlan to retrieve the greenstone bones (*chalchiuhomitl*) so that people can be made (myth 3). In his guise as Quetzalcoatl Ehecatl, he puffs the Fifth Sun into motion after sacrificing all the other gods (Birth: VII.5–7). And as Topiltzin Quetzalcoatl, he is an ancestral lord of Tula who is tricked into leaving; he goes toward the east where, in one of the many myths about him, he becomes Venus, the morning star. See Fifth Sun, Mictlan, Toltec.

Tamoanchan The place of the western tree. Quetzalcoatl brings the bones from Mictlan, Cihuacoatl grinds them like corn, Quetzalcoatl bleeds his penis on them, and the dough is made into people (myth 3). Nanahuatzin come from here as do newborn babies; the implication is that the Fifth Sun is a newborn baby (myth 5). See Cihuacoatl, Fifth sun, Mictlan, Quetzalcoatl.

Tata and Nene Papa and Mama. Tata and Nene are the first couple who light a fire to cook fish after the Fourth Sun is destroyed (myth 2). Titlacahuan-Tezcatlipoca gets angry at them and turns them into dogs by sewing their heads on their rears. See *Chichimeca*, Tezcatlipoca (Titlacahuan).

Tecuiçiztecatl The rich but weak-kneed god who could not bring himself to jump in the fire until after Nanahuatzin had set a good example (Birth: IV.1–52). As a result, Tecuiçiztecatl became the moon rather than the sun (Birth: VII.25–31). See Fifth Sun, Nanahuatzin.

Templo Mayor (Great Temple) The impressive temple in the center of Tenochtitlan. It was double-sided: the left side was oriented to the north, the wet summer and agriculture, and housed the rain god Tlaloc; the right side was oriented to the south, the dry winter and war, and housed the patron war god Huitzilopochtli. It was built in layers, like nesting boxes. Each layer was associated with a particular ruler. Its foundations held numerous caches containing hundreds of items such as jade; pottery; sculptures;

skeletal remains of almost any edible beast of land, lagoon, and sea; and a few human remains. See Huitzilopochtli, Tenochtitlan, Tlaloc.

Tenochtitlan The capital city of the Mexica-Tenochca. It was located on the same spot where Mexico City stands today. A city of 150,000–200,000, it served as the center for a vast domain. This great city was apportioned in four quarters called *calpullies*. Its island domain included *chinampa* fields as well as dwellings. At its center stood the Templo Mayor in a large temple district. See *Calpulli, Chinampa*, Mexica-Tenochca.

Teotihuacan (las Pirámides) (ca. 200 B.C.E.–650 or 750 C.E.) The urban center of one of the most influential of all Mesoamerican civilizations. Its urban pattern, which coordinated its buildings with the motions of celestial objects, provided the paradigm for many other cities, including Tenochtitlan. Its remains were used ritually by the Mexica, who counted its inhabitants as toltec ancestors. Mythically, Teotihuacan is the place where the Fifth Sun (Birth: II.7) was born and is often associated with Tamoanchan, the birth place of people (myth 5). See Fifth Sun, Tamoanchan, Tenochtitlan, Toltec.

***Teoyome (teoyotl*, singular)** The powers that everything in the cosmos embodies. All things—deities, people, trees, cities, mountains, lakes, ages, etc.— embodied multiple powers, which allow things to work and happen. These powers both animate objects and contribute to each thing's particular identity. The powers are gained at birth, through ritual activity, and one's own deeds. At death each power disperses to its appropriate domain. See *Ihiyotl, Ixtli, Teutl, Teyolia, Tonalli.*

Teutl (Teotl) Often translated as "god," it means literally "powerful thing." Fray Bernardino de Sahagún tells his readers that *teutl*, which meant "god," referred to any creature that was seen as very good or bad. This included the sun (which was both beautiful and fierce) and both very pretty and very bad children. "God" has a much broader meaning in the Mexica context than it does in Western settings. Some gods are anthropomorphized beings like Huitzilopochtli and Tlaloc; others are natural objects like mountains, the sea, Lake Texcoco, trees, or celestial objects. See Huitzilopochtli, *Teoyome*, Texcoco, Tlaloc.

Texcoco, Lake Texcoco Texcoco was an allied city of Tenochtitlan until the Conquest, when it defected to the Spanish side. Lake Texcoco was the rich wetlands in which Tenochtitlan's island dwelling lay. The upper portions of it were too salty to be serviceable; the lower portions were spring fed. In a mid-fifteenth-century drought, the Mexica dammed off the upper portion so that the lower portion might be efficiently turned into much needed *chinampas*. See *Chinampa*, Nezahualcoyotl, Tenochtitlan.

Teyolia A potent and centrally important animistic entity concentrated in the heart. Principal activities of consciousness were due to it, and therefore helped form one's merit (*mahceua*). When one died it was claimed by the god or gods whose powers it held. See *Ihiyotl, Mahceua, Tonalli.*

Tezcatlipoca (Titlacahuan) A major deity closely associated with Huitzilopoch-tli (each is portrayed with the same shrunken foot). As Tezcatlipoca-Titla-cahuan, he invented fire and turned Tata and Nene into *chichimeca* (myth 2). See Huitzilopochtli, Tata and Nene.

Tlacaellel A powerful political figure who may have had equivalent although different powers from the Chief-Speaker or ruler. Hence, Motecuhzuma I called upon Tlacaellel for advice and comfort in the story about the return to Aztlan. It is he who is said to have invented the Flowery Wars. See Aztlan, Flowery Wars, Motecuhzuma the Elder.

***Tlahtlacolli* (*tlacotli,* singular)** *Tlahtlacolli* were the messed-up things, the things that were spoiled, rotten, tangled, and displaced. They belong symboli-cally to the night, the underworld, and live at the edges of a city and its society. They are the counter order to order. Hence the Lords of the Night are an odd count that offsets other even counts of the calendrical system. Tecuiçiztecatl became a *tlacotli* when he failed to jump into the fire; hence he suffered the fate of becoming the counterorder to the sun rather than the sun itself (Birth: IV.1–52, VII.25–31). When people are *tlahtlacolli,* it is because they have done things that go counter to the societal order. They may be punished through bad events (e.g., drought, failed careers), re-quired to work off their debts, sold into slavery, or even sacrificed. Under the right conditions, a *tlacotli* could have a family and personal goods and even be freed. See Lords of the Night, Tecuiçiztecatl.

Tlaloc, Tlaloques Tlaloc was the rain god. He was housed on the left side of the Templo Mayor and had enjoyed a very long history in Mesoamerica be-fore the arrival of the Mexica. He controlled the rain that was stored inside the mountains; it was up to him and his henchmen, the Tlaloques, to open up the mountains and release the rain during the wet season. There were four sets of Tlaloques, one at each of the four directions. Hence, the four differently colored Tlaloques stole the grain from the Mountain of Pro-duce when it was opened, for they controlled the rain that fertilized pro-duce (myth 4). See Mountain of Produce, Templo Mayor.

Tlalticpac (Earth's Surface) The surface of earth upon which people, trees, corn, animals, mountains, and so on live. Over Tlalticpac arches Ilhuicatl (Sky-Water), and under Tlalticpac lies Mictlan (the Land of the Dead). It is dry on Tlalticpac but wet in Mictlan and Ilhuicatl. See Ilhuicatl, Mictlan.

Toltec, Tula, *toltec* Toltec means one of two things: either the inhabitants of Tula (Toltecs), a city lying northwest of Tenochtitlan and the residence of Topilt-zin Quetzalcoatl, or inhabitants of any of the numerous cities that had lived and died before the Mexica (*toltec*). In this second sense, *toltec* has the broader meaning of revered ancestors. The inhabitants of Teotihuacan could be considered *toltec*. See Quetzalcoatl, Teotihuacan.

Tonacateuctli, Tonacacihuatl Our Lord and Lady of Sustenance. They appear in the myth about the birth of the Fifth Sun in which it comes as Nanahuatzin from Tamoanchan (myth 5). Tonacateuctli and Tonacacihuatl bathe the new sun and set him on a throne. See Fifth Sun, Nanahuatzin, Tamoanchan.

Tonalco In the time-place of heat. Tonalco is the dry season in which war was waged. It lasted from November to May. Symbolically, it was related to the sun, war, hunting, and the mountains which held back the rains. Children were dedicated during this period but some also were sacrificed to the mountains, which needed them for strength to produce rain. See Flowery Wars, Templo Mayor, Tlaloc, Xopan.

Tonalli A complex animistic entity associated with the head. It was related to solar radiation and heat, the days and their particular signs, and a person's *mahceua* as it was shaped on her naming day. It could spontaneously or accidentally leave one's body, thereby causing some types of illnesses. Because of its solar and temporal associations, it connected one with the entire cosmos. At death bits of the *tonalli* could be collected in a box containing the deceased's ashes. See *Ihiyotl, Mahceua, Teyolia.*

Tonalpohualli **(divinatory calendar, 260-day calendar)** A cycle of 260 days in the Mexica calendrical system, consisting of twenty thirteen-day "weeks" called *trecenas* by the Spanish (20 x 13 = 260). It was used for divination. Everything from the naming of newborns to marriages to business deals to the coronation of rulers, war, and diplomacy was determined by the *tonalpohualli*. It probably is the oldest calendrical cycle in Mesoamerica. Because of its extreme age, it is unknown to what celestial cycle it was related. Seventy-three *tonalpohualli* rounds ended on the same day as fifty-two solar rounds, forming a larger cycle called the *xiuhmolpilli*. The Binding of the Years occurred at that time. See 1-Rabbit, 2-Reed, Binding-of-the-Years, *Xiuhmolpilli.*

Tonatiuh Sun or age. Tonatiuh was the sun as it moved through the sky. It also meant age; the five suns were so called because they represented the life span of a particular age that was determined by solar rotations. Each year was a sun as was one cycle of the *xiuhmolpilli*. A new baby sun was born at the beginning of an age as it was at the beginning of a new fifty-two-year cycle. See Binding-of-the-Years, Fifth Sun, Four Suns, *Xiuhmolpilli.*

Xiuhmolpilli **(solar calendar, 365-day calendar)** A cycle of fifty-two solar years in the Mexica calendrical system. Each solar year consisted of eighteen twenty-day "months" (the *meztli* round) plus five unlucky days called the *nemontemi* ([18 x 20 = 360] + 5 = 365). The four year-bearers marched in sequence through the four cardinal directions to reach the end of the *xiuhmolpilli* cycle, which consisted of the four bearers and a count of thirteen (4 x 13 = 52). Fifty-two solar rounds and seventy-three *tonalpohualli* rounds ended on the same day. The Binding of the Years took place at that time. See Binding-of-the-Years, Four Year-Bearers, *Nemontemi, Tonalpohualli.*

Xiuhtecutli The old fire god also called Huehueteotl. He dwells at the center of the cosmos.

Xiuhtlamin, Xiuhtlaminmani Xiuhtlamin was the sacrificial offering at the New Fire ceremony that was held just before the Spanish Conquest. He was from Huexotzinco, in the Valley of Tlaxcala, probably fifty-two years old, and an honorable man. Xiuhtlaminmani was the person who captured him in one of the Flowery Wars, was seen as his metaphoric brother, and received a special name because of the particular sacrificial role Xiuhtlamin played. See Binding-of-the-Years, Flowery Wars, Tonalco.

Xolotl The god who did not want to die at the birth of the Fifth Sun (Birth: VI.43–59). He was hunted down by death in the cornfield (where he had changed into a young corn shoot), in the maguey field (where he had turned into a maguey plant), and finally cornered and killed in the water (where he had turned into a salamander). Corn, maguey, and salamanders are all major foodstuffs; hence food was created for the new age. See Fifth Sun.

Xopan In the green time-place. The wettest period of the year from May to November. It was symbolically associated with the night, moon, Venus, the Pleiades, and Tlaloc. This was the period of agriculture. During Xopan, the sun went into Mictlan from May to July. Rituals then celebrated birth and growth. See Templo Mayor, Tlaloc, Tonalco.

APPENDIX 2
Calendrical Workings

A complex calendrical system was one of the most central features of early Mesoamerican culture. According to Munro S. Edmonson, the original calendar round was Olmec and begun in Cuicuilco (Valley of Mexico) on the summer solstice in 739 B.C.E. What may be the earliest recorded date, 679 B.C.E., also comes from Cuicuilco; other early dates from the sixth century B.C.E. have been found in the Zapotec area (Oaxaca), (1988, x, 20–21). Edmonson notes that Mesoamericans have been concerned with solar astronomy since 433 B.C.E. in Kaminaljuyu (an Olmec-influenced site in present-day Guatemala); for over 2,726 years they have "calculated the length of a tropical year as accurately as we do" (ibid., x, 277). As will be seen, that period comes very close in length to a period of time embedded in "The Myth of the Four Suns," all the more interesting because the Olmec of Cuicuilco are among the earliest ancestors of the Mexica.

From these early beginnings, several basic calendrical patterns emerged in Mesoamerica. All were based on a count of twenty days, although each had many local variations (Edmonson 1988). Every city or area developed its own version because the calendar was governed by the movements of celestial objects as they appeared above the distinct geography of an area's horizon. Due to the Conquest, the intricacies of the Mesoamerican calendrical system are now difficult to discern. The Spanish destroyed certain calendrical rounds because they regulated state rituals; local versions, however, often remained in use in communities across Mesoamerica, allowing many to function today.

The Mexica-Tenochca calendar was a variant on greater Mesoamerican patterns. Like other calendrical systems, it helped control the transformative changes governing all existence. Hence everything from the changes a birth thrust upon a family to the transforming of a dead ruler's power into that of his successor was shaped by calendrical forces. Calendars gave people a way to manipulate life's events. By manipulating the calendar, one changed reality.

Unlike European calendars, the Mexica calendrical system coordinated a number of calendrical cycles simultaneously in order to control their moments of conjunction and disjunction, when powers would go in and out of influence. Instead of moments lining up like beads on a rope as in European calendrics, Mexica calendrics was shaped more

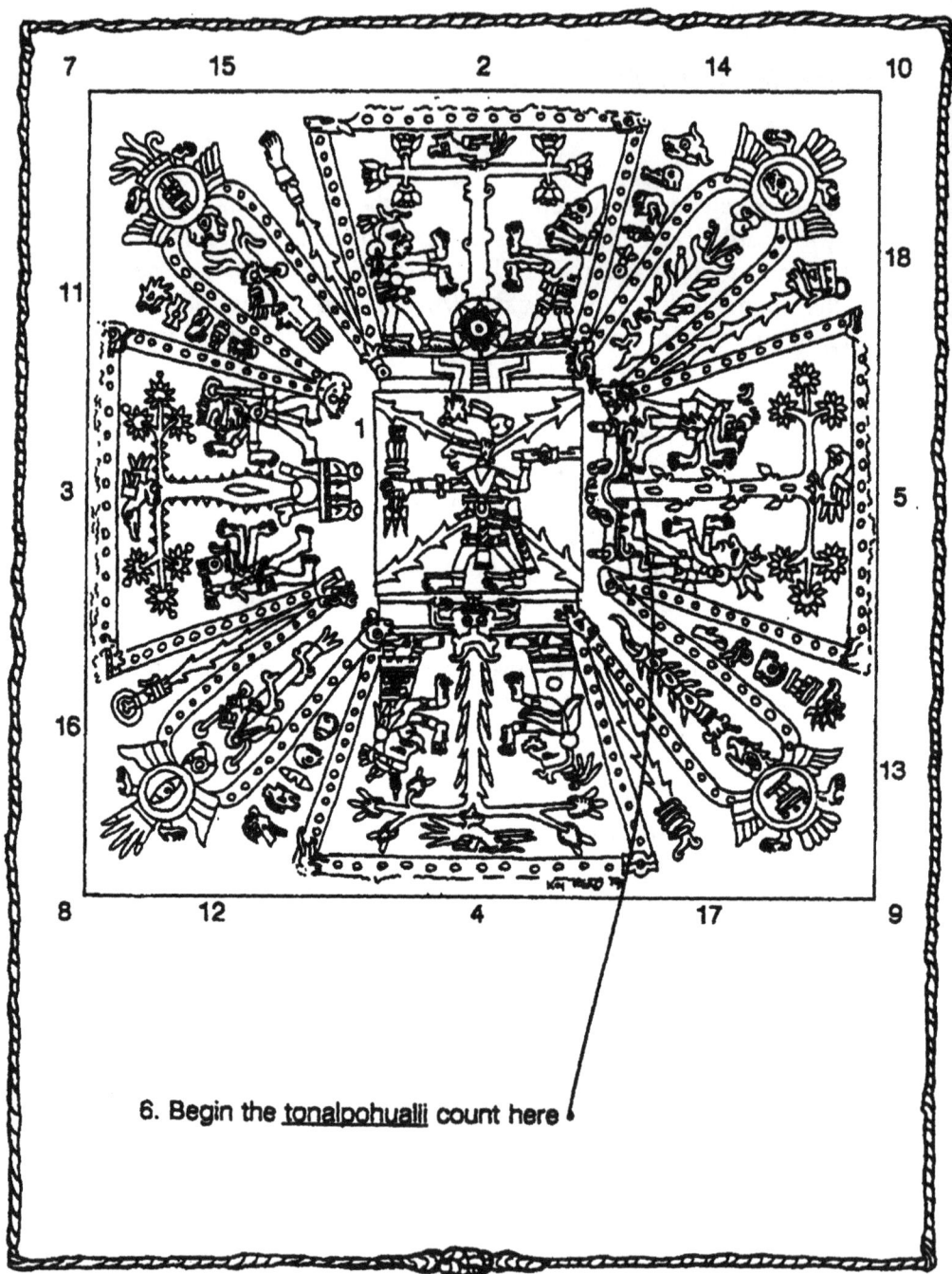

FIGURE 14.
Frontispiece of the *Codex Fejérváry-Mayer,* folio 1.

KEY TO FIGURE 14.

1. Xiuhtecuhtli, the old fire god
2. East, the Place of Light, with its ruling deities, birds, and tree encased within the border of dots. A sun glyph appears at the base of the tree.
3. North, the Place of the Dead, with its ruling deities, birds, and tree
4. West, the Place of Women, with its ruling deities, birds, and tree
5. South, The Place of Thorns, with its ruling deities, birds, and tree
6. Dots depicting the 260 days of the *tonalpohualli* with the beginning glyph for each succeeding *trecena* drawn out. The date 1-Crocodile begins the first *trecena* of the sequence.
7. Reed, the eastern year-sign

8. Knife, the northern year-sign
9. House, the western year-sign
10. Rabbit, the southern year-sign
11. Eastern day-signs (moving from the center out): crocodile [d1], reed [d13], snake [d5], movement [d17], water [d9]
12. Northern day-signs: jaguar [d14], death [d6], knife [d18], dog [d10], wind [d2]
13. Western day-signs: deer [d7], rain [d19], monkey [d11], house [d3], eagle [d15]
14. Southern day-signs: flower [d20], grass [d12], lizard [d4], vulture [d16], rabbit [d8]
15. Arm with flowing blood
16. Leg with flowing blood
17. Ribs with flowing blood
18. Decapitated head with flowing blood

like the rope itself in which various fibers of differing lengths are spun to-gether, now some ends overlapping and others not, now others overlap-ping that had not. During rituals, one collapsed many particular past mo-ments (or fibers) into a single moment (or rope sector) in order to activate all those moments' powers in the present; in this way one effected the future. Present moments stretched back, picking up all the powers of the particular years, deities, days and so on of times past. This was like tieing all the same points together on a coil of rope. The binding constituted a unique meshing of numerous past moments, just as the binding of all those points on the rope's coil bound a number of unique sets of fibers. The present moment contained past moments but was identical to no other moment that ever existed or would exist. By controlling these ca-lendrical bindings, one could control the present and shape the future.

The mechanics of the calendrical system allowed these manipulations because it operated in a spiraling configuration that cycled around as it moved forward. Interlocking cycles ranged from units of nine days to year counts that were astronomically enormous. This appendix will travel from those smallest units of time (which were used to count particular days and nights) to huge year counts that spiraled into vast cosmic realms. First, I examine the frontispiece to *Fejérváry-Mayer* for the spatial ar-rangements governing the calendrical system. Second, using the *Codex Borbonicus*, I will discuss three major calendrical rounds: the *tonalpohu-alli* (the 260-day divinatory calendar), the *meztli* (a monthlike calendar), and the *xiuhmolpilli* (the 52-year solar calendar). Third, I will coordinate the *tonalpohualli* with the *xiuhmolpilli* to demonstrate how, together with the Lords of the Night, the Mexica could have been calculating with precision the years for a very long time. Finally, I show how an even longer count[1] is embedded in "The Myth of the Four Suns."

The Workings of Time in the *Codex Fejérváry-Mayer*

Time-space, dramatically presented by the pyramids of Teotihuacan and Tenochtitlan, also is graphically depicted in the frontispiece of the *Codex Fejérváry-Mayer* (figure 14). This pre-Conquest Mixtec calendrical almanac from the Oaxaca area[2] bases itself on the *tonalpohualli* or divinatory round of 260 days.[3] It depicts the four cardinal directions encapsulated by four sectors spreading from a central area, one toward each direction, like four petals on a flower.[4] Within each petal of the flower, two distinct gods appear flanking a tree with a bird perched on top. Each tree emerges from a glyph indicating a particular aspect of that direction. East is on the top, north is on the left, west is on the bottom, and south is on the right.

This flower is given its shape by a border dotted with 240 circles and twenty glyphs, one each for the 260 days of the *tonalpohualli*. The glyphs represent the twenty day-signs (figure 15 A), each of which is placed strategically among the dots to indicate the proper sequence of the days. These signs represent the round of twenty basic days upon which the whole Mesoamerican calendrical system was based, a little like the round of seven weekdays which form the basis for the Western system. If one follows the appropriate order of these day-signs, one will circle counterclockwise through the dots bordering the flower's space. Recall that one also moved counterclockwise through the cardinal directions described in "The Birth of the Fifth Age" (V.27–40).

The *Codex Fejérváry-Mayer* also spatially portrays the coordination of the *xiuhmolpilli* (fifty-two-year vague solar round) and the *tonalpohualli* (divinatory almanac). Every fifth day of the twenty days, one of the four year-bearers appears (figure 15 A). These four day-signs also named the solar years. A bird in each corner of the frontispiece (figure 14) bears one of these four houses of the sun on its back: Reed (upper left), Knife (lower left), House (lower right), and Rabbit (upper right). A group of five glyphs, each indicating one-fourth of the twenty days, flank the left side of each bird. A body part (a hand, bone, rib cage, and head) with blood flowing from it to the old fire god in the page's center flanks each bird's right side, a graphic reference to sacrifice.[5]

These corners depict the intercardinal points and refer to the extremes to which the sun migrates along the horizon during the course of a year.

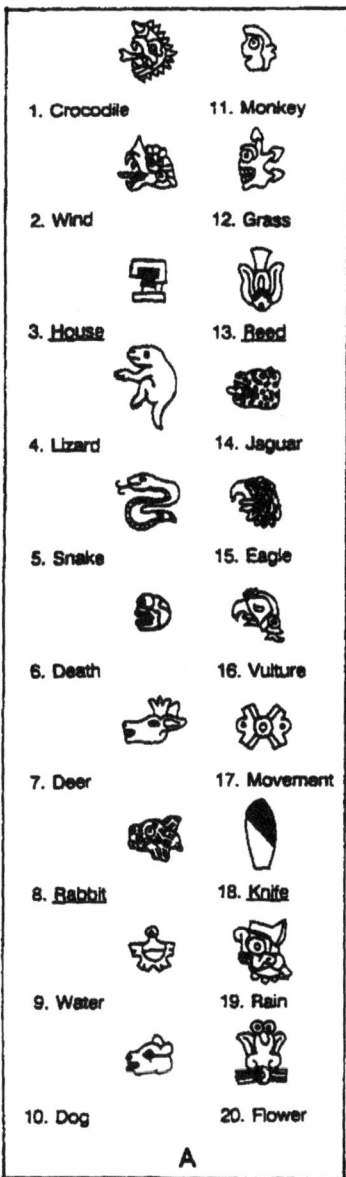

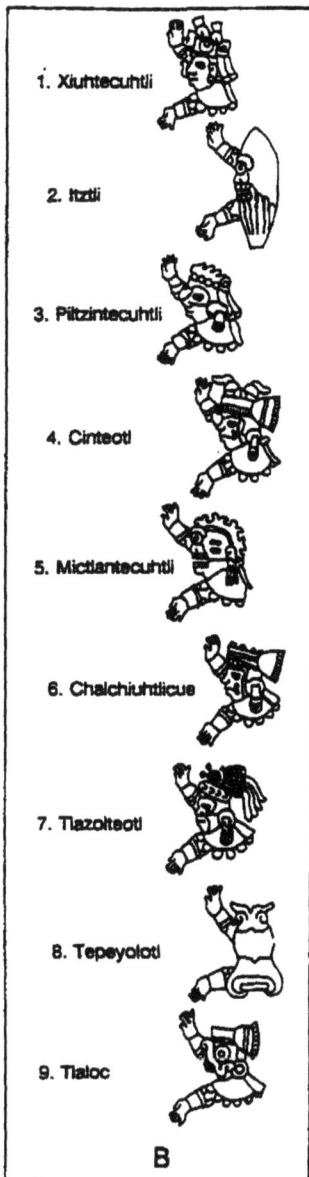

FIGURE 15.
The day-signs and night lords. (A) The twenty day-signs with the four year-signs underlined; (B) the nine night-signs or Lords of the Night. *After the* Codex Borbonicus, *trecenas 8, 20, folios 21, 22.*

Summer-solstice sunrise is shown in the northeastern corner (upper left), and summer-solstice sunset is shown in the northwestern corner (lower left). Winter-solstice sunset is shown in the southwestern corner (lower right) and winter-solstice sunrise is shown in the southeastern corner (upper right). Like a map, this graph marks the motions of the sun on a city's eastern and western horizons. For someone standing in the middle of their urban space, the sun would move along the horizon from south to north in the summer and from north to south in the winter, the solstices marking the most northerly and southerly extremes of its journey.

This folio of the *Codex Fejérváry-Mayer* shapes time into a squared-off circle which is oriented toward the cardinal and intercardinal directions. Each petal of the flower contains exactly one-quarter of the various counts: sixty-five days of the full 260-day count (4 x 65 = 260), five days of the twenty-day count (4 x 5 = 20), and one of four suns.[6]

We can assume that the same four-sided division governed the *Xiuhmolpilli*, for the count of the four year-bearers structured the fifty-two-year round. This is supported by other codical evidence. Another Mixtec codex, the *Codex Aubin* (figure 9),[7] arranges a fifty-two-year count in the shape of a square, dividing its count into four equal parts of thirteen years each (4 x 13 = 52) and orienting its sides to the four cardinal directions, with east at the top.[8] As with the *Codex Fejérváry-Mayer*, one moves counterclockwise around its square.

A four-sided shape also is born out by the workings of the calendrical system itself, for Mexica calendrics operated according to the guidelines of codices like the *Fejérváry-Mayer*. In fact, we can make good sense of how the mathematical calculations worked if we borrow this Mesoamerican shape to think with, if we envision calendrical time as a squared-off circle whose quarters are oriented to the cardinal directions around which the days and years spiral forward in a counterclockwise motion. Mesoamericans used this shape, not the mechanical shape of gears meshing in Renaissance clocks.

The Workings of Time in the *Codex Borbonicus*[9]

There are three calendrical documents contained in the *Codex Borbonicus*: a *tonalpohualli* or weeklike divinatory calendar (figure 4); a monthlike cycle called a *metztli* round (figure 11); and sandwiched between the weekly and monthly cycles, two folios showing a *xiuhmolpilli* round of fifty-two vague solar-years (figures 16 and 17). This codex from Tenochtitlan probably dates to just after the Conquest; both its *tonalpohualli* and its two *xiuhmolpilli* folios are done in a very early style quite

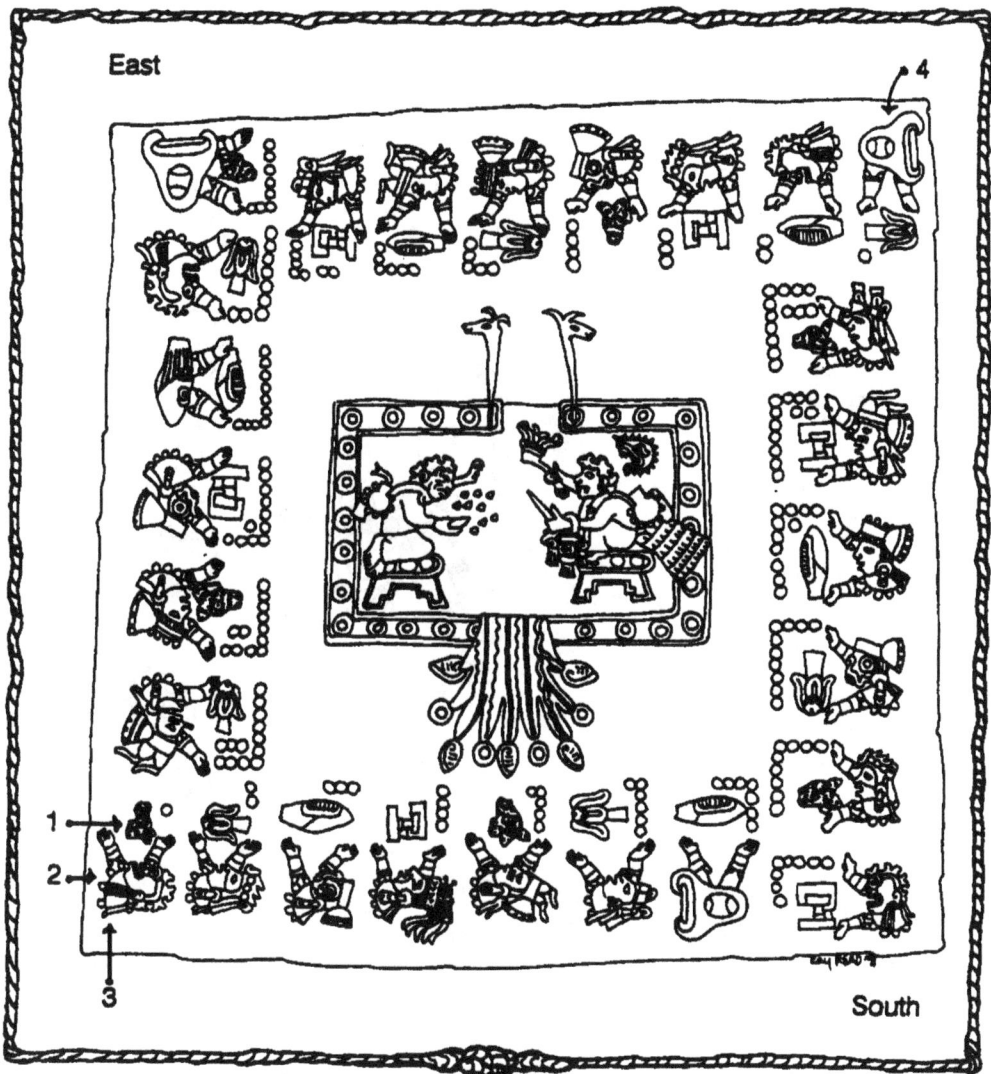

FIGURE 16.
The first two thirteen-year rounds of the fifty-two-year
cycle as depicted in the *Codex Borbonicus*, folio 21.

1. Day-signs with dots marking the *trecena* days
2. Night-signs or Lords of the Night
3. Begin the first cycle at 1-Rabbit [t1, d8], accompanied by
Mictlantecuhtli [n5] and move counterclockwise around the
folio to the second cycle
4. Begin the second cycle at 1-Reed [t1, d13], accompanied by
Tepeyolotl [n8]

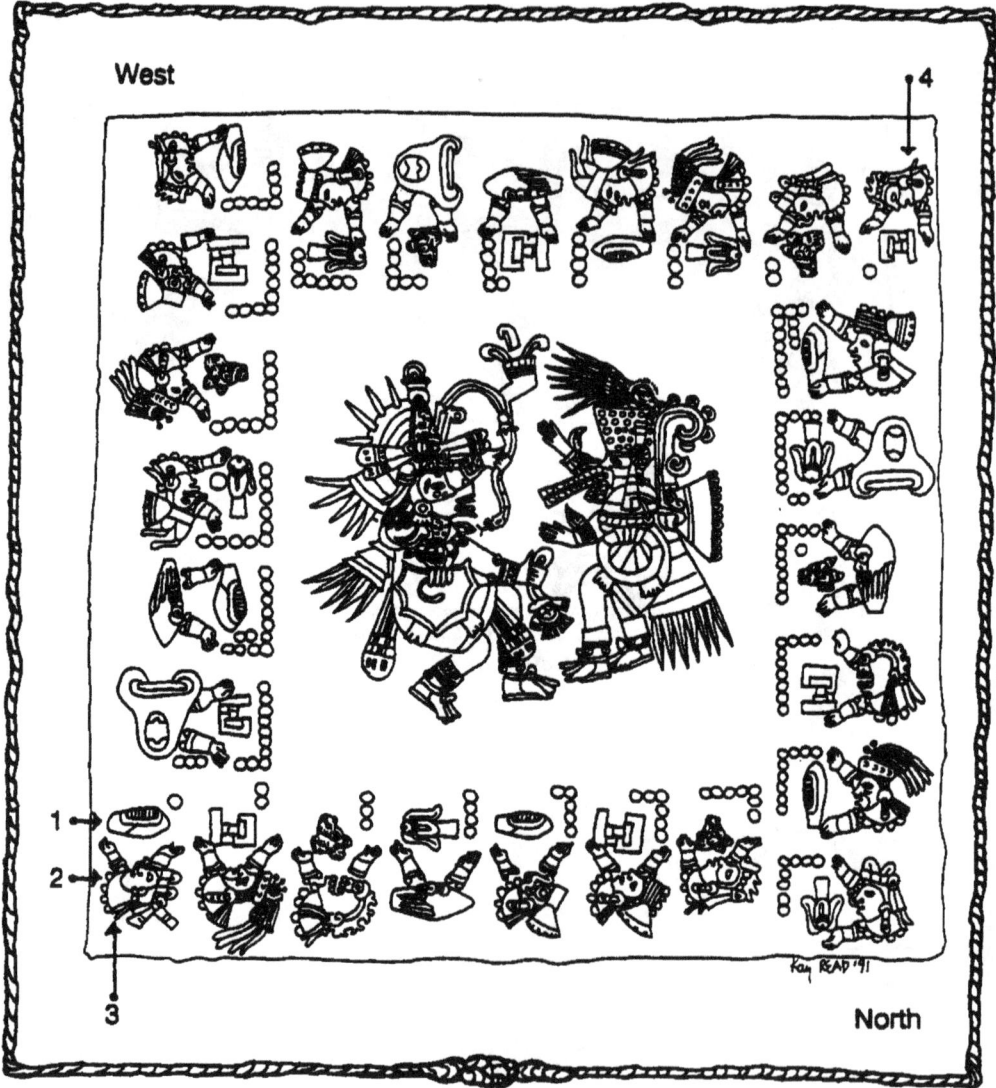

FIGURE 17.

The second two thirteen-year rounds of the fifty-two-year cycle as depicted in the *Codex Borbonicus*, folio 22.

1. Day-signs with dots marking the *trecena* days
2. Night-signs or Lords of the Night
3. Begin the third cycle at 1-Knife [t1, d18], accompanied by Xiuhtecuhtli [n1] and move counterclockwise around the folio to the fourth cycle
4. Begin the fourth cycle at 1-House [t1, d3], accompanied by Piltzintecuhtli [n3]

similar to the Mixtec codices (Robertson 1959, 86–93). The style and mechanics of the calendars found in the Mixtec codices, *Fejérváry-Mayer* and *Aubin*, suggest that they are predecessors to the *Borbonicus*.[10] Since these two sections of the *Borbonicus* are the earliest calendrical manuscripts attributed to the Mexica, they are two of the most important resources for calendrical information. However, the count of the months in the *metztli* round clearly is done in a style different from the other two sections. It is so different that, while there has been disagreement over whether the *tonalpohualli* and *xiuhmolpilli* were pre-Conquest or not, no one has ever assigned this count of the months to anything but the post-Conquest period (Robertson 1959, 69).[11]

The Weeklike Cycles of the Tonalpohualli *Round*

The first document in the *Borbonicus* is a *tonalpohualli*[12] that divides its 260 days and nights into twenty weeks of thirteen each. Both the divinatory calendar and the twenty-day count are fundamental to Mesoamerican calendrical systems. Even today, Quiché, Ixil, and Tepanec diviners perform their duties according to this 260-day round and the twenty days upon which it is based.[13] In the Mexica version of this system, the *tonalpohualli* meshed three basic cycles together: the twenty days, a set of thirteen numbers, and nine Lords of the Night. The sequence of twenty days (its days depicted by twenty distinct glyphs, figure 15 A) rotated against a second cycle of twenty weeks called *trecenas* by the Spanish. Dots numbered each of the thirteen days of each *trecena*, one dot for the first day, two for the second, three for the third, and so on, until the thirteenth day was reached and the round was started over again with the next *trecena* (20 x 13 = 260). Table 1 shows how these two cycles of twenty and thirteen worked together.

The third cycle working within the *tonalpohualli* was the count of the Lords of the Night, a set of nine deities who probably governed the night portion of the day.[14] These, like the day-signs, also were each depicted by a distinct glyph or face (figure 15 B). Table 2 shows this cycle of nine meshed with the twenty-day and *trecena* cycles.

Each of the twenty *trecenas* was governed by one or more particular deities and signs, just as the four quarters in the *Codex Fejérváry-Mayer* were governed by various deities and signs; and, like the cosmic quarters, each *trecena* also was probably associated with one of the four cardinal directions.[15] In addition, each day of each *trecena* was governed by a particular day lord and a bird. All of these deities, directions, signs, and glyphs carried powers and forces that influenced the course of events and were open to manipulation by skillful diviners.

Table 1. The rotation of twenty day-signs and thirteen *trecena* days in the *tonalpohualli*

Day-Signs	Dots, Thirteen Days of each *Trecena*
1. Crocodile	1 dot, *Trecena 1*
2. Wind	2 dots
3. *House*	3 dots
4. Lizard	4 dots
5. Snake	5 dots
6. Death	6 dots
7. Deer	7 dots
8. *Rabbit*	8 dots
9. Water	9 dots
10. Dog	10 dots
11. Monkey	11 dots
12. Grass	12 dots
13. *Reed*	13 dots
14. Jaguar	1 dot, *Trecena 2*
15. Eagle	2 dots
16. Vulture	3 dots
17. Movement	4 dots
18. *Knife*	5 dots
19. Rain	6 dots
20. Flower	7 dots
1. Crocodile, etc.	8 dots, etc.

Originally there were twenty folios in the *tonalpohualli* of the *Borbonicus*, one for each of the twenty *trecenas*, although the first two of these now are missing. Table 3 graphs out information depicted in the eighth *trecena* (figure 4). This particular *trecena* contains the 2-Reed day-sign that served as the year-bearer for the 2-Reed plaque. Using table 3, one can learn to read that folio and perhaps get a better feel for how various cycles of time were spun together. There are six cycles drawn out in this particular *tonalpohualli*: (a) a cycle of thirteen dots numbering each day of each *trecena*; (b) the twenty day-signs (table 3 numbers each with brackets: [d1], [d2], [d3], and so on); (c) the thirteen-day lords associated with each day of the *trecena*; (d) the thirteen birds associated with each day; (e) the nine Lords of the Night (also numbered with brackets: [n1], [n2], [n3], and so on); and (f) the four day-signs serving as year-bearers (Rabbit, Reed, Knife, and House, each in italics).

This *trecena* was governed by the goddess of pulque, Mayahuel. She is shown emerging from a maguey cactus, pulque's source (figure 4.1).[16] Recall that maguey was one of the three food sources which Xolotl turned into at the birth of the Fifth Sun (VI.51–54). Around Mayahuel are the

Table 2. The rotation of twenty days, thirteen *trecena* days,
and the nine Lords of the Night in the *Tonalpohualli*

Day-Signs	Dots, Thirteen Days of	Lords of the Night
1. Crocodile	1 dot, *Trecena 1*	1. Xiuhtecuhtli
2. Wind	2 dots	2. Itzli
3. *House*	3 dots	3. Piltzintecuhtli
4. Lizard	4 dots	4. Cinteotl
5. Snake	5 dots	5. Mictlantecuhtli
6. Death	6 dots	6. Chalchiuhtlicue
7. Deer	7 dots	7. Tlazolteotl
8. *Rabbit*	8 dots	8. Tepeyolotl
9. Water	9 dots	9. Tlaloc
10. Dog	10 dots	1. Xiuhtecuhtli
11. Monkey	11 dots	2. Itzli
12. Grass	12 dots	3. Piltzintecuhtli
13. *Reed*	13 dots	4. Cinteotl
14. Jaguar	1 dot, *Trecena 2*	5. Mictlantecuhtli
15. Eagle	2 dots	6. Chalchiuhtlicue
16. Vulture	3 dots	7. Tlazolteotl
17. Movement	4 dots	8. Tepeyolotl
18. *Knife*	5 dots	9. Tlaloc
19. Rain	6 dots	1. Xiuhtecuhtli
20. Flower	7 dots	2. Itzli
1. Crocodile, etc.	8 dots, etc.	3. Piltzintecuhtli, etc.

various signs of potency associated with this *trecena*. The count of the days begins in the lower left corner, moving right from day 1 to 7; each day is shown in its own square along the bottom of the page (figure 4). The horizontal row of seven squares above the bottom row contains the bird and day lord governing each of the first seven days. Days 8 to 13 appear in the two vertical columns bordering the right side of the page. One reads these columns from bottom to top.

Each individual day was named by both its *trecena* position and its position in the twenty-day cycle. The sixth day of this *trecena*, for example, is called 6-Movement and is represented by six dots and the seventeenth day-sign, called movement [d17] (figure 4.4). Its governing bird (a barn owl, figure 4.2) and day lord (Mictlantecuhtli, figure 4.3) are shown in the square above. It is accompanied by the seventh night lord, a goddess called Tlazolteotl [n7], who appears as though cradling the day-sign in her arms (figure 4.5). The *trecena*'s second day, 2-Reed (in the second square of the bottom horizontal row), is marked by two dots and the thirteenth day-sign called reed [d13]. The third night lord, Pilzintecuhtli

Table 3. *Trecenas 8 and 9 of the tonalpohualli cycle*

	Dots—Day-Sign	Day Lord	Day Bird	Night Lord
Trecena 8	1-Grass [12]	Xiuhtecuhtli	Blue Hummingbird	Itztli [n2]
	2-*Reed* [d13]	Tlaltecuhtli	Green Hummingbird	Pilzintecuhtli [3]
	3-Jaguar [d14]	Chalchiuhtlicue	Falcon	Cinteotl [n4]
	4-Eagle [d15]	Tonatiuh	Quail	Mictlantecuhtli [n5]
	5-Vulture [d16]	Tlazolteotl-Ixcuina	Eagle	Chalchiuhtlicue [n6]
	6-Movement [d17]	Mictlantecuhtli	Barn Owl	Tlazolteotl [n7]
	7-*Knife* [d18]	Cinteotl	Butterfly	Tepeyolotl [n8]
	8-Rain [d19]	Tlaloc	Goshawk	Tlaloc [n9]
	9-Flower [d20]	Quetzalcoatl	Turkey	Xiuhtecuhtli [n1]
	10-Crocodile [d1]	Tezcatlipoca	Horned Owl	Itztli [n2]
	11-Wind [d2]	Yaoltecuhtli	Parakeet	Pilzintecuhtli [n3]
	12-*House* [d3]	Tlauizcalpantecuhtli	Quetzal	Cinteotl [n4]
	13-Lizard [d4]	Omecihuatl	Parrot	Mictlantecuhtli [n5]
Trecena 9	1-Snake [d5]	Xiuhtecuhtli	Blue Hummingbird	Chalchiuhtlicue [n6]
	2-Death [d6]	Tlaltecuhtli	Green Hummingbird	Tlazolteotl [n7]
	3-Deer [d7]	Chalchiuhtlicue	Falcon	Tepeyolotl [n8]
	4-*Rabbit* [d8]	Tonatiuh	Quail	Tlaloc [n9]
	5-Water [d9]	Tlazolteotl-Ixcuina	Eagle	Xiuhtecuhtli [n1]
	6-Dog [d10]	Mictlantecuhtli	Barn Owl	Itztli [n2]
	7-Monkey [d11]	Cinteotl	Butterfly	Pilzintecuhtli [n3]
	8-Grass [d12]	Tlaloc	Goshawk	Cinteotl [n4]
	9-*Reed* [d13]	Quetzalcoatl	Turkey	Mictlantecuhtli [n5]
	10-Jaguar [d14]	Tezcatlipoca	Horned Owl	Chalchiuhtlicue [n6]
	11-Eagle [d15]	Yaoltecuhtli	Parakeet	Tlazolteotl [n7]
	12-Vulture [d16]	Tlauizcalpantecuhtli	Quetzal	Tepeyolotl [8]
	13-Movement [d17]	Omecihuatl	Parrot	Tlaloc [9]

[n3], cradles reed in his arms and the day is governed by the deity Tlalte-cuhtli, and a green hummingbird. The thirteenth day with its bird and day lord appear in the upper right-hand corner of the page. Its thirteen dots are clearly numbering the day, its day-sign is lizard [d4], and, although its night lord, bird, and day lord are too damaged to identify, we know that they are Mictlantecuhtli [n5], Omecihuatl, and a parrot, respectively, simply because these are the figures that must appear in these particular sequences (table 3). If we continue on to *trecena* 9 in the divinatory round (table 3), we can see how each of the five cycles continues rotating against each other. This spinning of seven different fibers together (twenty *trecenas,* thirteen dot-numbers, twenty day-signs, thirteen day lords, thirteen birds, nine night lords, and four year-bearers) continues for all 260 days of the *tonalpohualli.*

The Monthlike Cycles of the Meztli *Round*

Each vague solar-year (365 days) was divided into eighteen months of twenty days each (18 x 20 = 360), with five extra days tacked onto the end. In this third document of the *Borbonicus,* every one of these twenty-day periods is depicted with a drawing showing the major festival of that month (*metztli*). The New Fire ceremony, for example, can be seen as it occurred in Panquetzaliztli, the fifteenth *metztli* of the year (figure 11).[17] The roots of the *metztli* count are both obscure and problematic. Caso felt that this cycle was based on the moon (1967, 34). In Nahuatl, *metztli* means both "moon" and "a count of twenty days," somewhat of a curiosity in itself because it appears more coordinated with solar than lunar motions. The 360th day (not the first or last day) was considered the name day of the year, the day each year's bearer appeared. A year could not be named for its last day because the five following days, the *nemontemi,* were considered unlucky and "idle." They were not associated with the powers of any god and therefore were not officially "counted" (FC, bk. 4, app. 13). To count them would have been an act of naming which recognized their identity, thereby increasing their danger. Nor was the year named for its first day, the day it began. As the five suns were named for the manner in which they were completed and destroyed, so were the years of each sun.[18]

This round had a variety of purposes. Among other things, it established the dates that children were entered into the community and ordered important state rituals, many of them agricultural in nature. And as with the *tonalpohualli* and the pyramids of Tenochtitlan, the *metztli* round was bound to both earth and sky. Broda (1983) has shown how the count of the months coordinated with the seasonal agricultural cycle of the Mexica, the wet and dry seasons, the solstices, and the movements of the Pleiades in the Valley of Mexico in the sixteenth century.[19] Like the *Fejérváry-Mayer*, this calendar served as a map of celestial motions. The highly varied growing seasons of Mesoamerican urban centers made such precise coordination between calendrical calculations and each center's topographical peculiarities absolutely necessary.

Another curiosity of the *metztli* round is that graphically it is depicted in several sources as moving clockwise rather than counterclockwise, as do the *tonalpohualli* and *xiuhmolpilli* rounds. It is possible that it was intended as a counterpoint to the 260-day count, rather like the sun risings that move along the eastern horizon from north to south in the winter and from south to north in the summer.[20]

The count of the *metztli* was used by the elite like Chief Speaker Motecuhzuma both as an expression of national cohesiveness and the means to link his people with the appropriate sacred, creative forces necessary for the maintenance of society. Recall the important role rulers played in sustaining agricultural fertility, so important that it continued even after they had died and disappeared. The *tonalpohualli*, on the other hand, was available to all people for a multitude of reasons, including the calculating of an individual farmer's growing season. The sculptor of the 2-Reed plaque would have used the local day keeper's reading of this calendar to help him decide when to marry and when to name his children. Even today, the Highland Maya use two calendars, a 365-day calendar for coordinating civil affairs and a 260-day divinatory calendar for more personal concerns (B. Tedlock 1982, 88).

The Yearly Cycles of the Xiuhmolpilli Round

Placed between the *tonalpohualli* and *metztli* rounds in the *Codex Borbonicus* are two folios (21 and 22, figures 16, 17, 19) which show three more possible ways of using some of the counts in the *tonalpohualli*. These counts could be used to extend the calendrical calculations beyond 365 days.

First, if one ignores the Lords of the Night (concentrating on only the dot numbers and year-bearers, figure 16.1), folios 21 and 22 depict the same fifty-two-year cycle found in the *Codex Aubin* (figure 9). In both, four counts of the four year-bearers (Rabbit, Reed, Knife, and House) and a series of thirteen dots are shown rotating against each other, just as a series of thirteen dots rotated against all twenty day-signs in the *tonalpohualli*. Two quarters of the round are shown on each page of the *Borbonicus*, the southern and eastern on folio 21 (figure 16), and the northern

Table 4. The 52-year cycle of the *xiuhmolpilli* round

Southern Quarter Dots—Year Sign	Eastern Quarter Dots—Year Sign	Northern Quarter Dots—Year Sign	Western Quarter Dots—Year Sign
1-Rabbit	1-Reed	1-Knife	1-House
2-Reed	2-Knife	2-House	2-Rabbit
3-Knife	3-House	3-Rabbit	3-Reed
4-House	4-Rabbit	4-Reed	4-Knife
5-Rabbit	5-Reed	5-Knife	5-House
6-Reed	6-Knife	6-House	6-Rabbit
7-Knife	7-House	7-Rabbit	7-Reed
8-House	8-Rabbit	8-Reed	8-Knife
9-Rabbit	9-Reed	9-Knife	9-House
10-Reed	10-Knife	10-House	10-Rabbit
11-Knife	11-House	11-Rabbit	11-Reed
12-House	12-Rabbit	12-Reed	12-Knife
13-Rabbit	13-Reed	13-Knife	13-House

Note: Read each column down, beginning with the southern quarter (on the left), move right to the eastern quarter, then the northern quarter, and end with the western quarter. This cycle repeats every fifty-two years.

and western on folio 22 (figure 17). In folio 21, the count begins in the lower left corner with 1-Rabbit (figure 16.1), just as it does in the *Codex Aubin*, and makes a full circle around the page, ending in the same corner with 13-Reed. Folio 22 follows the same pattern, beginning in the lower left corner with 1-Knife (figure 17.1), again circling counterclockwise back to the same corner, ending with 13-House. If we count sequentially forward using repeating cycles of the thirteen dot-numbers and twenty days found in the *tonalpohualli*, each of the fifty-two years (1-Rabbit, 2-Reed, 3-House, 4-Knife, 5-Rabbit, 6-Reed . . . etc.) appears exactly 365 days apart.[21] Table 4 explains this round more fully.

Second, if we also take the nine Lords of the Night into account, folios 21 and 22 of the *Borbonicus* show the thirteen numbered year-bearers with their night lord partners (figure 16.1–2) that belong to each of the cardinally oriented quarters of the *tonalpohualli*. When we sequentially count the days of the *tonalpohualli* round over and over, each set (number, year-bearer, and night lord) presents itself in order every 104 days (or every eight *trecenas*), creating a spatial pattern. Beginning with 1-Rabbit and Mictlantecuhtli (figure 16.2), the thirteen sets of the south appear first, then those of the east and so on. As will be seen, if we graph the 260 days of the *tonalpohualli* out in four directionally oriented quarters of sixty-five days each, this pattern becomes visually obvious (figure 19). In other words, as does the frontispiece to the *Fejérváry-Mayer*, folios 21 and 22 of the *Borbonicus* present a shorthand depiction of the *tonalpo-hualli* carefully coordinated with the *xiuhmolpilli* according to a topo-graphically shaped pattern.

Third, if we ignore the dot numbers in folios 21 and 22, we can calcu-late precisely the fifty-one years that will appear both before and after the year 1-Rabbit accompanied by Mictlantecuhtli.[22] By circling these two folios, beginning at 1-Rabbit and Mictlantecuhtli (figure 16.1–3), every fifth pair (unnumbered year-bearer and night lord) appears exactly 365 days apart. Circling forward gives us the pairs of the next fifty-one vague solar-years and circling backward gives the pairs of the previous fifty-one vague solar-years. After the year Rabbit-Mictlantecuhtli, for ex-ample, the year Reed-Xiuhtecuhtli (five pairs away in the southern quar-ter [2-Reed, figure 20]) will come, then Knife-Chalchiuhtlicue (five pairs further [3-Knife]), House-Pilzintecuhtli (five pairs further into the eastern quarter [4-House]), and so on, for fifty-two years. Preceding Rabbit-Mictlantecuhtli by 365 days, the year House-Tlaloc (five pairs backward into the western quarter [13-House]) appears, preceded by Knife-Cinteotl (five pairs further back [12-Knife]), preceded by Reed-Tepeyolotl (five pairs further back into the northern quarter [11-Reed]), and so on, for fifty-two years. In this way, we could keep track of a span of at least 103 years, which would add up to 104 if we accounted for the next binding ceremony. It was probably this 104-year cycle that Sahagún's informant called the "One Whole Old One." When this round was completed, then "two times they circled around, two times they meet each other at the Binding of the Years" (Binding Years: 13).

The "count of the fifty-two years" structured the *anales* historical tra-dition (figure 6.2). A fire-drill glyph marked each fifty-two-year count in these annals, indicating the year in which that ritual's performance took place (figure 6.4). By repeating the fifty-two-year round over and over again, such tales of ancestors could be extended far back into the past, spanning hundreds of years.[23] And theoretically, if one calculated the years precisely by coordinating them with the Lords-of-the-Night cycle, each individual year could be kept in chronological order for nine fifty-two-year cycles or almost five hundred years.[24]

That the Lords of the Night should form a progressive sequence play-ing counterpoint to the other evenly counted cycles is in keeping with the Mexica sense of transformation and its double temporal nature. If all things indeed were in motion (*olinia*), then it makes sense that the calendrical system itself would have been structured to mirror transfor-mation's progressively repetitious nature—a spiraling and spinning nature that would need to be calculated in some precise manner, especially in a cultural system with such tremendous skill, accuracy, and needs in the area of calendrics. I suggest that the Lords-of-the-Night sequence helped provide such an element. Like the five *nemontemi*, the Lords of the Night were among the odd elements that forced the otherwise pristinely even elements forward, thereby allowing accuracy in calendric manipulations.

Coordinating the *Tonalpohualli* and *Xiuhmolpilli* Rounds

Both the *Borbonicus* and *Fejérváry-Mayer* coordinated the *tonalpohualli* and *xiuhmolpilli* rounds. The three graphs that follow coordinate these two rounds using the information and guidelines provided by these two codices.

Figure 18 depicts an ideal coordination of one divinatory round (260 days) and solar round (365 days) drawing information from the frontispiece of the *Fejérváry-Mayer*. As was done in the *Codex Aubin*, this graph is arranged in four quarters aligned to the cardinal directions; the fifty-two year-bearers appear along the outer edges of each quarter, and the thirteen numbers appear along the inner edges. Between the year-bearers and numbers, 366 twenty-four-hour days (the little squares) are arranged sequentially, rotating counterclockwise around the four quarters; each day's square has the number of the day-sign in its upper left corner, and the number of its night lord in its lower right corner. The count begins with the first day-sign (Cipactli [d1]) and night lord (Xiuhtecuhtli [n1]) in the lower right corner of the eastern quarter (figure 18.1). In each quarter, the *tonapohualli* is outlined in heavy black lines; two extra rows of twenty-four-hour day squares bring the count from 260 to 364, and the last day of the year and first day of the next year appear in a third extra row (near the outer edge of the eastern quarter) (figure 18.3–5). The fifty-two year-bearers' squares also are outlined in black (figure 18.6). The assumption made in this graph was the most obvious to my Western eyes; the *Fejérváry-Mayer*'s frontispiece began at the beginning with all cycles. As will be seen in figure 19, this was not the correct assumption; it provides, however, an instructive exercise.

If we begin spiraling to the right around this four-sided circle, each quarter of the *tonalpohualli* will have sixty-five days in it (4 x 65 = 260). Such an arrangement piles up five rows of thirteen days each (13 x 5 = 65) in sequential order. The first *trecena* of thirteen days appears in the south, the second in the east, the third in the north, fourth in the west, fifth in the south, and so on, until the twenty *trecenas* have been com-

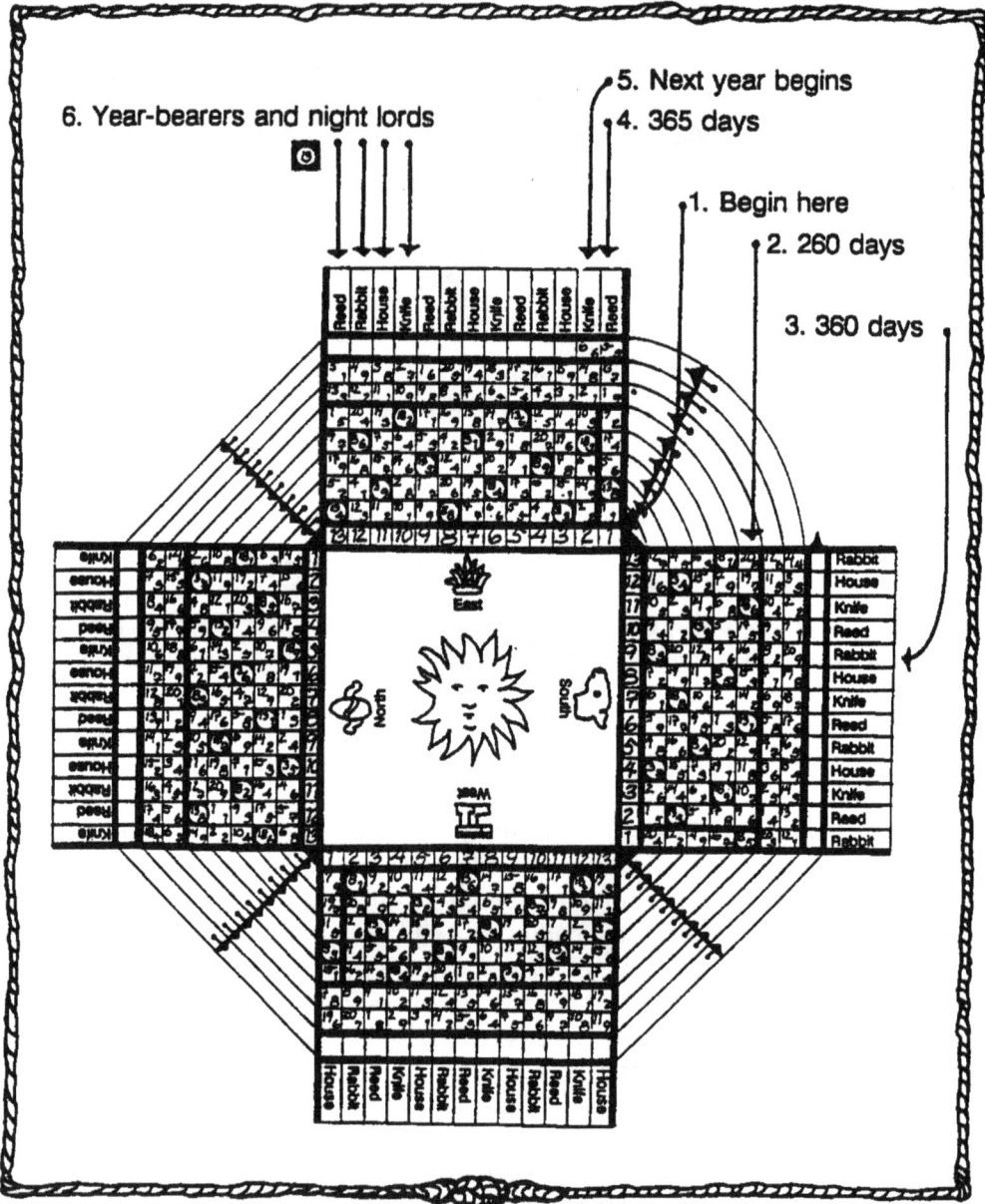

FIGURE 18.

The *tonalpohualli* round (260 days). Coordinated with one solar year (365 days). The thirteen numbers around each side of the inside edge mark the *trecena* count. Each square represents one twenty-four-hour period and contains the number for its day-sign in the upper left-hand corner and the number for its night-sign in the lower right-hand corner.

1. Begin at square 1/1, *trecena* 1, the first square in the lower right-hand corner of the eastern quadrant. This day is 1-Crocodile [t1, d1], accompanied by Xiuhtecuhtli [n1]. Move counterclockwise around the square, spiraling outward.
2. 260 days, 13-Flower [t13, d20], accompanied by Tepeyolotl [n8]: one completed *tonalpohualli* round.
3. 360 days, 9-Flower [t9, d20], accompa-

nied by Tlaloc [n9]: one completed round of eighteen months, each month twenty days long.
4. 365 days, 1-Snake [t1, d5] accompanied by Mictlantecuhtli [n5]: one solar year. The last five days are called *nemontemi*.
5. The next solar year begins at 2-Death [t2, d6], accompanied by Chalchiuhtlicue [n6].
6. The fifty-two year-bearers with their accompanying night lords.

pleted. The five day-signs appearing along the right side of each quarter's *tonalpohualli* (outlined in black) match the five day-signs appearing in the corners of the frontispiece to the *Fejérváry-Mayer* (figure 14.11–14). Peter van der Loo shows a similar arrangement of the *tonalpohualli* in the *Codex Borgia* (1987, 52–53).[25]

Figure 19 shows that it probably is the year 1-Rabbit depicted in the *Fejérváry-Mayer*'s frontispiece. This works extremely well if we do two things: assume that the years are named for their 360th day instead of their first (Edmonson 1988, 103–106), and adjust the graph accordingly. The graph must be aligned so that the *tonapohualli* lines up with the graph's outer edge rather than its inner (beginning in figure 19.1 and outlined in black), and the 360th day placed in the upper right corner of the southern quarter so that it coincides with 1-Rabbit (figure 19.3). 1-Rabbit begins (in Western terms) on 6-Water [d9] accompanied by the night lord Chalchiuhtlicue [n6] (figure 19.1), and its 365th day is 6-Reed [d13] accompanied by Xiuhtecuhtli [n1] (figure 19.4). The next year begins on 7-Jaguar [d14], accompanied by Itztli [n2] (figure 19.5).

Such an arrangement matches this frontispiece very closely and shows how one could easily have read it. The key is the positioning of each year-bearer in the sequence of five day-signs just to each bearer's left (figure 14.7, 11, 8, 12, 9, 13, 10, 14). One begins at *cipactli* [d1] (figure 14.6 or figure 19.1), moves through four *trecenas* (four sets of thirteen dots in figure 14 or four rows around the graph in figure 19) to the reed year-bearer [d13] (figure 14.7), which coincides with the second of five glyphs belonging to the east (figure 14.11 or, in figure 19, the second of the five squares outlined along the eastern quarter's right side). One then moves five more *trecenas* to the year-bearer knife [d18] (figure 14.8), which coincides with third of five glyphs belonging to the north (figure 14.12 or, in figure 19, the third of the five squares outlined along the northern quarter's right side). Next one moves five *trecenas* to the year-bearer house

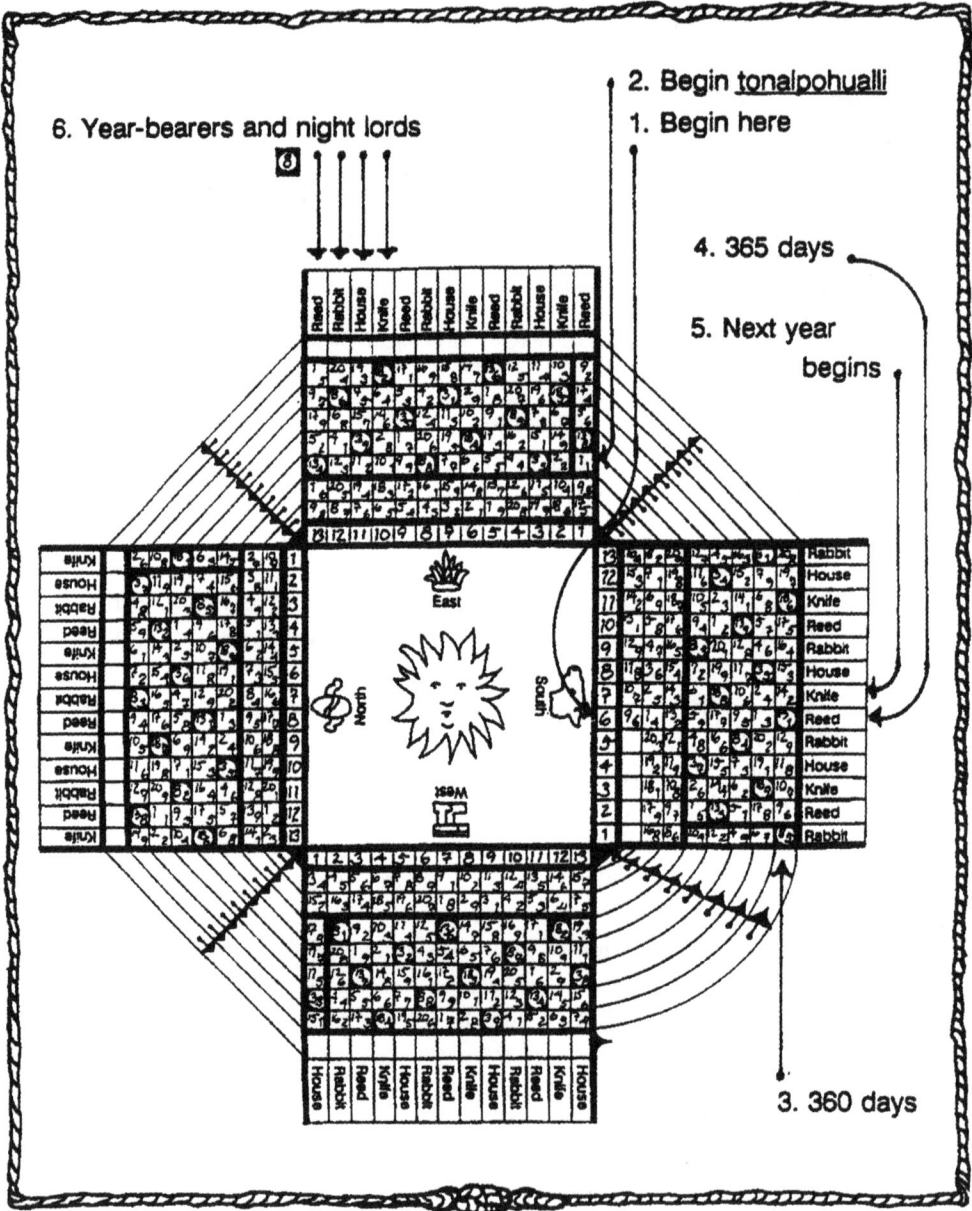

FIGURE 19.

The solar year (365 days) called 1-Rabbit. The thirteen numbers around
each side of the inside edge mark the *trecena* count. Each square
represents one twenty-four-hour period and contains the number for its
day-sign in the upper left-hand corner and the number for its night-sign
in the lower right-hand corner.

KEY TO FIGURE 19.

1. Begin this solar year at 6-Water [t6, d9], accompanied by Chalchiuhtlicue [n6].
2. Begin the *tonalpohualli* at 1-Crocodile [t1, d1], accompanied by Xiuhtecuhtli [n1]. Move counterclockwise around the square, spiraling outward.
3. This year's name day (day 360) is 1-Rabbit [t1, d8], accompanied by Mictlantecuhtli [n5], the same pair that begins the fifty-two-year cycle on folio 21 of the *Codex Borbonicus* (figures 16 and 17).
4. This solar year (365 days) ends on 6-Reed [t6, d13], accompanied by Xiuhtecuhtli [n1].
5. The next solar year begins at 7-Jaguar [t7, d14] accompanied by Itztli [n2].
6. The fifty-two year-bearers with their accompanying night lords.

[d3] (figure 14.9), which coincides with the fourth of five glyphs belonging to the west (figure 14.13 or, in figure 19, the fourth of the five squares outlined along the western quarter's right side). Finally, one moves the last five *trecenas* to the year-bearer rabbit (figure 14.10), which coincides with the fifth of the five glyphs belonging to the south (figure 14.14, or in figure 19, the fifth of the five squares outlined on the southern quarter's right side). This is the 360th day. Each year-bearer's place in its quarter's series of five day-signs locked the days into a particular sequence which indicated a particular year, and the count of five provided the counter to the even count of four.

The *Borbonicus* is marking the same sequence found in figure 19. The thirteen numbers, year-bearers, and night lords found in folios 21 and 22 appear in order in their appropriate quarters (each outlined in black). In the south, 1-Rabbit [d8] is accompanied by night lord Mictlantecutli [d5], 2-Reed is accompanied by night lord Piltzintecuhtli [n3], 3-Knife is accompanied by Tlaloc [n9], 4-House [d3] by Tlazolteotl [n7], 5-Rabbit [d8] by Cinteotl [n4], and so on, through the quarters on both the folios and the graph. Hence the *Borbonicus* may be marking the year 1-Rabbit as the critical year preceding the 2-Reed and the New Fire ceremony.

Figure 20 shows the workings of the next year 2-Reed, the year of the Mexica New Fire ceremony. 1-Rabbit's name day, the 360th, is seen in figure 20.1 [d8, n5] just as it appeared in figure 19.3. 1-Rabbit ended (from a Western viewpoint) on 6-Reed [d13], accompanied by Xiuhtecuhtli [n1] (figure 19.4, figure 20.2); 2-Reed begins on 7-Jaguar [d14], accompanied by Itztli [n2] (figure 19.5, figure 20.3). 2-Reed's name day, the 360th, appears in figure 20.4 (Reed [d13] accompanied by Xiuhtecuhtli, the same pair the year began with). From a Western view, 2-Reed ends on 7-Knife [d18], accompanied by Chalchiuhtlicue [n6] (figure 20.5), and the next year begins on 8-Rain [d19], accompanied by Tlazolteotl [n7] (figure 20.6). Thus one could calculate with extreme precision the sequence of the years for at least nine *xiuhmolpillies*, or 468 years (9 x 52 = 468).

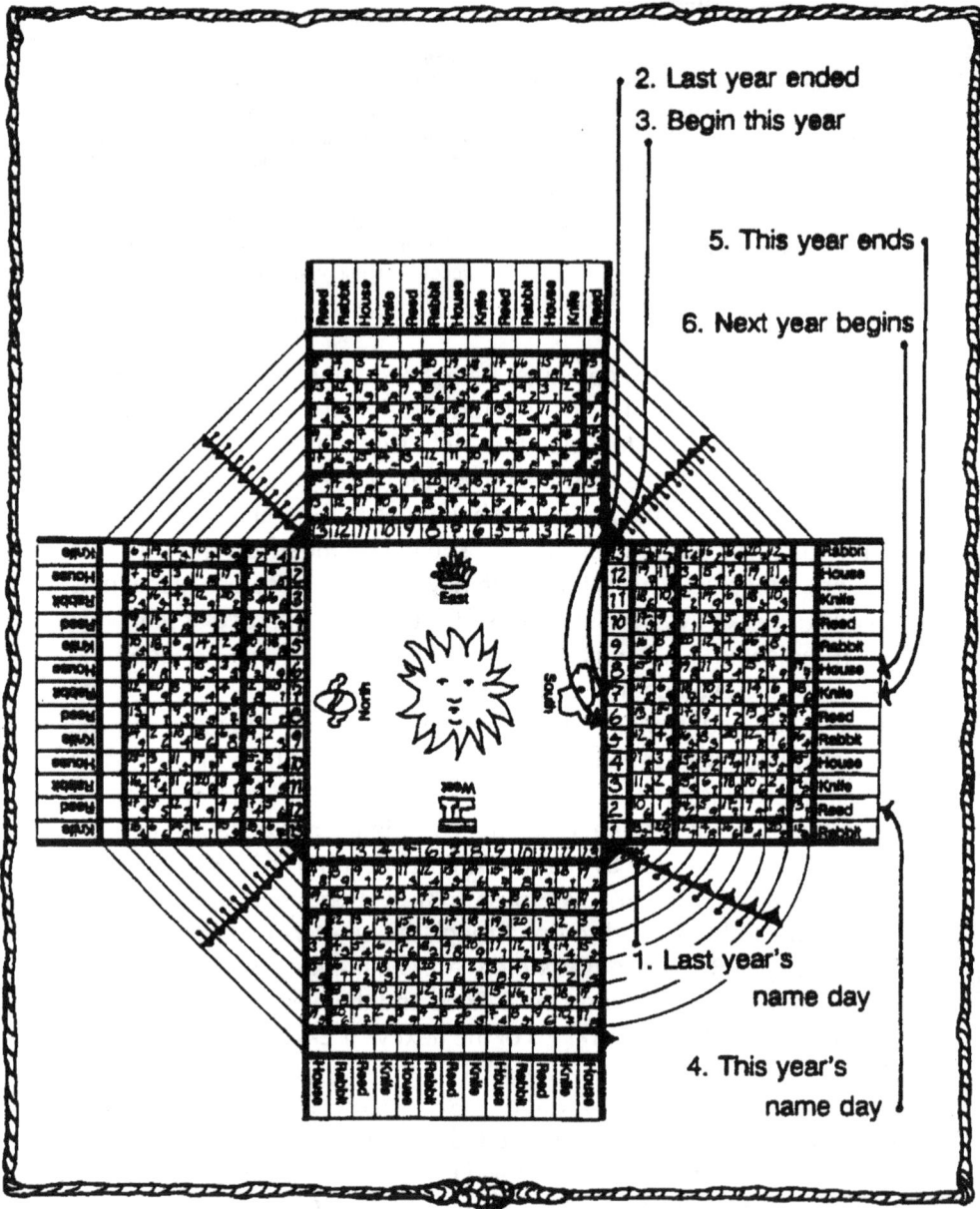

FIGURE 20.
The solar year (365 days) called 2-Reed. The thirteen numbers around each side of the inside edge mark the *trecena* count. Each square represents one twenty-four-hour period and contains the number for its day-sign in the upper left-hand corner and the number for its night-sign in the lower right-hand corner.

KEY TO FIGURE 20.

1. Last year's name day (day 360) fell on 1-Rabbit [t1, d8], accompanied by Mictlantecuhtli [n5] (figure 18).

2. Last year ended on 6-Reed [t6, d14], accompanied by Xiuhtecuhtli [n1] (day 365, figure 18).

3. Begin this solar year (365 days) at 7-Jaguar [t7, d14], accompanied by Itztli [n2].

4. This year's name day (day 360) is 2-Reed [t2, d14], accompanied by Xiuhtecuhtli [n1].

5. This solar year (365 days) ends on 7-Knife [t7, d18] accompanied by Chalchiuhtlicue [n6].

6. The next solar year begins at 8-Rain [t8, d19], accompanied by Tlazolteotl [n7].

The Workings of Time in "The Myth of the Four Suns"

Actually, thousands rather than mere hundreds of years probably were spun and calculated.[26] "The Myth of the Four Ages" hints at great cycles of time, periods of enormous length that also were marked, computed, identified, and given a *face*. In this myth, each age is counted out meticulously according to a pattern of 676 years, the same as thirteen *xiuhmolpilli* rounds (13 x 52 = 676). Table 5 demonstrates this.

Table 5. The count of the five suns

Sun or Age	Date Ended	Year Ended	The Count			Total in Years
one	4-Jaguar	1-Reed	(13 x 52)			= 676
two	4-Wind	1-Knife	(7 x 52)	=	364	
					+	
three	4-Rain	1-Knife	(6 x 52)	=	312	= 676
four	4-Water	1-House	(13 x 52)			= 676
five	4-Movement		(13 x 52)			676
					Total	2,704

There is something a bit strange here though. Although the first four ages are explicitly computed, the Fifth Sun is not. Of course it cannot be; it has not happened yet in the story. But there is more to this mystery than that, for it seems almost as if the year count is manipulated in order to include the Fifth Sun implicitly. Suns two and three are both called by the same name, 1-Knife. Like the two suns who might "shine in the same way" at the beginning of the Fifth Sun (VI.1–9), these two ages are identified as being the same thing, as having the same "appearance" (VI.5), the same *face* (*ixtli*). They are equated so that a total unit of 676 years could be divided between them (364 + 312 = 676), leaving one unit of 676 years for the Fifth Age to endure.

The total of the years of all five ages, 2,704 (4 x 676), adds up to the equivalent of fifty-two Binding-of-the-Years ceremonies (52 x 52 years). Moreover, it calculates out to 26 x 65 cycles of Venus, a celestial object of extreme importance in Mesoamerica.[27] The Quiché Maya include Venus in their calculations today.[28] Venus may be the odd shadowy element here, the celestial object that, like the *nemontemi* and night lords, kept time transforming.

Those odd elements, those dark objects that provide a counter motion to the sun's light, are the elements in the Mexica calendrical system that assure that transformation must continually prevail and that the wholeness of *completion* could never occur permanently; something is always there to force time forward in spite of all the cycles. Each year's count is one day ahead of the previous one's because the *nemontemi*, those five dangerous days at the end of a year, cause the count to move forward by one day. It takes 2,704 years for Venus to mesh with the *tonalpohualli* and the *xiuhmolpilli*. And within this period, the Lords of the Night are always out of synchronization with at least one other cycle.[29]

The characters of both Venus and the lords reflect this orderly manner of upsetting the order of forms.[30] Because Venus closely follows the sun's motions, this morning and evening star is sometimes paired mythologically with that solar object, rather like the pairing of Nanahuatzin and Tecuiçiztecatl.[31] The dark night lords counter the brilliant order of the sun's day. Things of the night were considered to be *tlahtlacolli*, things "spoiled," "rotten," "messed up," "tangled," and "displaced" (Burkhart 1989, 28–29, 82–85). As *tlahtlacolli*, those dark lords displaced the orders of other celestial objects.

While the mathematical inevitability of all those cycles eventually coming together might offer a possibility that "once again" things may be "like it was there and then," the point at which all things will "once again . . . be done" (Once Again: 1, 5) would have been part of such an enormous cycle that its cosmic proportions would have made it almost incomprehensible in everyday temporal terms. In this system, one could count the days in sequence for a very, very long time before such an astronomically huge cycle of convergence would be repeated.

The disappearance of each age's life on the surface of *Tlalticpac* (Earth's Surface) was limited to a span of 676 years. As does the spinning of a rope, time's many threads went around and around while at the same time growing longer and longer. And like the changing shapes of pyramids, this temporal rope also was spatialized, given shape by its own spinning. It was this spinning that gave order to the inevitability of *de-*

struction, death, and *disappearance*; to the fleeting moments of "green-stone" and "quetzal feathers" (Fleeting: 13, 16). As Huitzilopochtli's mother reminded her visitors in Aztlan, all the Mexica would disappear, for they were tied to the foods of a particular age. According to schedule, her son would return home to Aztlan from his journeys (myth 8: 14–18). Once a period completed its schedule, its burden would be thrown down to the ground, its ties loosened, the counted packet of reeds unbound.

NOTES

Preface

1. Although many call the Mexica-Tenochca the Aztecs, this name carries a number of problems; it is both a bit inaccurate and not particularly useful. See A Note on Terminology (p. xxiii) and chapter 1, p. 4 (and n. 4) for the reasons for these problems.

2. The pre-Conquest Huron, for example, had some extremely violent sacrificial practices (Clendinnen 1991, 87–88). A tendency to continue the unfortunate stereotypes of primitives has had its effect on this discussion. Primitives have been seen for centuries as either noble or barbaric savages (Gill 1982a, 1–9; 1982b, 1–13). In recent years, people have described Native Americans historically living north of the Rio Grande in romantic terms by deemphasizing the violence that was present and emphasizing what is sometimes questionably described as "earth-centered spirituality." At the same time, pre-Conquest Mesoamericans have been described in barbaric terms by emphasizing the violence of human sacrifice and political expansion, and deemphasizing the philosophic and moral depth of this often subtle culture.

Thus, in the eyes of both the popular media and many scholarly works, Native Americans north of the Rio Grande become noble savages, while those historic residents south of that river (which so conveniently forms the border between the United States and Mexico) become barbaric savages; currently living indigenous Mesoamericans are seen romantically, which unfortunately implies that it took the Europeans to civilize them. It will help the reader if she or he can abandon these misjudgments in favor of viewing the Mexica as fully human with all the wonderful possibilities and sad imperfections that condition brings to all of us.

3. Kirchhoff placed the boundaries of Mesoamerica at the rivers Sinaloa, Lerma, and Panuco in the north and the mouth of the Motagua river and the Gulf of Nicoya in the south (1966, 7). Mesoamerica's distinctiveness does not negate dividing the Americas up into two parcels, although (as always) any divisions cause problems. When divided into two, North America generally is understood to cease in the south at Panama. Mesoamerica does not extend that far for linguistic, historical, and cultural reasons, although certainly contact did. Corn, for example, possibly went through a rather complicated developmental process in which different strains were shared back and forth between the north and south (Adams 1991, 35–37).

4. For a recent definition of Mesoamerica's boundaries, see chapter 1, n. 3.

5. The Mesoamerican link with the Mississippian Cultures is a hotly debated issue that ranges everywhere from no connection whatsoever to visions of Mesoamericans paddling up the Mississippi River in order to found cities. My own personal sense is that both of these extremes are too extreme, and therefore

are likely unwarranted; the truth probably lies somewhere in the middle. As a Mesoamericanist (although rather an amateur in things Mississippian), I often find the similarities striking. The iconographic depictions at Spiro and the sacrificial emphasis on hands at Cahokia both have Mesoamerican parallels. But the differences also are striking; for example, the calendar that is so central and remained fairly stable for many centuries in Mesoamerica appears to be largely missing in the Mississippian culture; although this could be due to the differences in latitude, other iconographical elements appear to have no Mesoamerican link. At any rate, the mystery is an intriguing one, and does not deny other Mesoamerican connections north of the Rio Grande (Fagen 1991, 1995, 446–50; Jennings 1993, 56–67; Schaffer 1992, Silverberg 1968).

6. A fire drill consisted of two sticks that were spun rapidly together to spark tinder into a flame.

1. Introduction

1. The plaque was unearthed from phase 7a of the temple, which dates it to before 1502 (conversation with Alfredo López Austin, 17 May 1989). As will be seen, it is marking a rite called the New Fire ceremony and, since the last New Fire ceremony to take place before 1502 was in 1455 (Caso 1971, table 5), this plaque must have been made to commemorate that ceremony.

2. I borrow this phrase from Paul Ricoeur, who used it in his class "Speaking, Writing, and Discourse," jointly taught by David Tracy, University of Chicago, Divinity School, 4 October 1984. My conversational approach to iconographic interpretation should not be confused with either Ricoeur's or Tracy's dialogical approaches, however, for it is fundamentally different.

3. Mesoamerica is a historically and culturally defined area whose northern border is roughly the Sinaloa River in the northwest and the Soto la Marina River in the northeast, taking a dip in the middle to exclude the central deserts of Chihuahua, Nuevo Leon, and Coahuila. The southern border ran from the mouth of the Ulua River in Honduras, angling south into El Salvador, ending at the Gulf of Fonseca on the Pacific Ocean. The Gulf Coast formed its eastern boundaries. Its area has a very long history that extends back possibly 40,000 years (some even claim up to 100,000 years), with carbon–14 dating of human habitation up to 25,000 years ago (Adams 1991, 12–13, 23–27). Its cultural ending is marked symbolically by the Spanish Conquest in 1521, although many contemporary indigenous peoples continue to live in Mexico and Central America in ways that can be traced directly to pre-Conquest periods.

4. The sixteenth-century historian Fray Diego Durán notes that the people I am calling Mexica or Mexica-Tenochca were at first called the Aztecs (Azteca) because they came from a place called Aztlan. They were also called Mecitin or Mexicans (Mexicanos), after their leader, whose name was Meci. Moreover, in Durán's time, they had yet another name acquired after taking their land, the Tenochca (Tenuchca), which refers to the prickly pear cactus that sprang from a

rock on the site of their future city. Throughout his lengthy history, Durán consistently refers to the Mexica as los Mexicanos (HI 1984, 3:28–29). It is probably no accident that the Spanish renamed Tenochtitlan as Mexico City. Even today, that huge metropolis is referred to simply as "Mexico" and the cactus and rock appear on the Mexican flag. Given the imprecision of the nineteenth-century term *Aztecs* and the apparently more widespread use of either *Mecitin* (*Mexicanos*) and/or *Tenochca* in the sixteenth century (and even today), it seems appropriate to abandon the first in favor of the latter two.

5. Mexica rulers were called *Tlatoani* or, literally, "he who speaks it." By scholarly convention, this title has come to be "Chief Speaker" in English.

6. For historical information see Townsend (1992), Adams (1991), Davies (1973), Katz (1969), Wolf (1959), and Vaillent (1944, reprint 1966).

7. See, for example, Fray Diego Durán's reporting of the Mexica's early migration story (HI 1984, chaps. 1–5, 13–54 or 1994, 1–5, 3–50).

8. See HI 1984 (chaps. 1–5:13–53) or 1994 (1–5:3–50); and the *Codex Boturini* 1831–48 for the story of its founding. The date is not really known for sure; Edmonson lists a series of dates attributed to its founding (1988, 50–54).

9. This system was very old and very widespread. For example, raised-mound agricultural systems similar to those used by the Mexica have been uncovered in Belize in Mayan territory and date to the late pre-Classic period (ca. 400 B.C.E.–250 C.E.). Teotihuacan was also using a *chinampa* system (Adams 1991, 145, 205).

10. Although the Nahua were not pastoralists, E. Hunn claims that they could have domesticated a variety of herbivores such as "peccary, pronghorn antelope, tapir, agouti, and muscovy duck. Instead they deliberately chose more efficient means of providing nutrients through intensive agriculture" (cited by Ortiz de Montellano 1990, 85).

11. One shouldn't underestimate the value of these alternative resources no matter how strange they may seem to Western palates. I can personally attest that tacos made of the algae *tecuitlatl* (*Spirulina geitlerii*) are very tasty. And a water beetle called *axayacatl* (*Corisella sp.* and *Krizousacorixa femorata*) is said to taste a bit like shrimp. Both the beetle and its eggs are eaten (the eggs can be dried and stored for months). This beetle not only provides protein but also is rich in minerals and vitamins. Moreover, it reproduces at a fantastic rate. Ortiz de Montellano estimates that Lake Texcoco could produce over 2,000 tons of protein from just this one source. For a fascinating discussion of the agricultural and dietary practices of the ancient Mexica, see Ortiz de Montellano (1990).

12. See Clendinnen (1991, 15–83) for a rich and wonderful description of Tenochtitlan in both its public and private aspects.

13. The powers animating all things in the Mexica cosmos will be discussed at length later.

14. The Mexica cosmos will be discussed in detail in chapter 4.

15. For further information on the colonial period in Mexico, see Jacques La

Faye's *Quetzalcoatl and Guadalupe: The Formation of National Consciousness, 1531–1813* (1976), Robert Ricard's *Spiritual Conquest of New Spain* (1966), and Charles Gibson's *Aztecs under Spanish Rule* (1964).

16. There remain four pre-Conquest Mayan pictorial codices, five Mixtec from Western Oaxaca, and six from a disputed area (probably Southern Puebla, Western Oaxaca, or the Gulf Coast).

17. This was not the first time the whereabouts of the temple were explored. Manuel Gamio, for example, worked on probes into the southwestern corner of the temple in 1913 and 1915 (López Luján 1993, 25). It was not until recent decades that the climate was right for extensive excavations; the current interest in pre-Conquest history has helped promote this and other archaeological projects.

18. According to hearsay, the manuscript quite possibly was destroyed when an airplane crashed on the side of Mount Popocatepetl, killing scholar Salvador Toscano. At any rate, it has been missing from the Museum of Anthropology in Mexico City since 1949 (conversation with Wayne Ruwet, 22 and 26 May 1991). The codex also includes an unrelated manuscript in Spanish by the sixteenth-century Indian cleric Pedro Ponce de León called "Breve relación de los dioses y ritos de la gentilidad."

19. For example, the presence of the deity Mixcoatl suggests at least one Nahua-speaking group other than the Mexica (conversation with Alfredo López Austin, 18 August 1989).

20. Sahagún patterned his twelve-volume collection after a medieval European model for encyclopedias. As a European encyclopedia would move hierarchically from the Trinity to natural history, ending with something like mineral forms, so too the *Florentine Codex* moves from the gods to the things of heaven and hell, continues with lordships on through histories of particular peoples, and ends with an earthly, natural history (López Austin 1974).

21. Davíd Carrasco (1982) has explored the "topiltzin question" about Quetzalcoatl's personality.

22. See Wolf (1982) on this issue of the co-opting of the voices of the conquered.

23. Such categories as color, line, texture, shape, mass, pattern, and composition, of course, also are Western defined, although I continue to find them useful tools. One can learn something by noting the visual categories another culture uses that the West ignores. For a discussion of some of these in Mesoamerica, see Read (1995a). For a discussion of Western categories of design, see Arnheim (1954) and Beardsley (1958).

24. See Read (1995a) for a visual interpretation of royal aesthetics in Mesoamerica.

25. For many of my remarks about what is involved in the production of visual artworks, I am drawing on some fifteen years spent as a professional fiberist, illustrator, and teacher in studio art classrooms of various public school and adult education programs.

26. The divinatory calendar in the *Codex Borbonicus* (facsimile, 1974), while probably not pre-Conquest in origin, is done in an early style quite similar to the Mixtec codices (D. Robertson 1959, 86–93) and is therefore a good model for what Mexica manuscript painting might have been like.

27. The Spanish often viewed the Indians of the New World as misguided children in need of their guidance. This was but one of the ways to morally validate the Conquest. For more on Spanish imagery of the inhabitants of the New World, see Baudet (1976), Phelan (1970), and Wolf (1982).

28. See Nicholson (1973) for a discussion of phoneticism and other aspects of Mexica writing.

29. The first five images are easy because they all deal with well-known calendrical materials. Some basic secondary sources that describe these materials, give explanations of the fundamental counting and calendrical systems, and identify the primary sources for this information are Edmonson (1988), Closs (1986), Umberger (1981), Aveni (1980), Caso (1971, 1967), Payne and Closs (1986), Broda (1969, 1989), Satterthwaite (1965).

30. See previous note for references describing the calendrical system.

31. As Miguel León-Portilla has noted, one of the many ways to deal with this complex situation is to recognize that, if something appears repeatedly in the post-Conquest resources, one can be more assured of its accuracy than when it appears only once (1992, 12–13).

32. See Preface, n. 6.

33. This myth is translated by Arthur Anderson and Charles Dibble from the original Nahuatl found in Fray Bernardino de Sahagún's *Florentine Codex* (FC, bk. 7, pt. 8, chap. 2:3–9; app. 42–58). My own translation appears in chapter 2.

34. See Sáenz (1976, 13). Deborah Nagao feels that this stone sculpture may be of Mexica origin (conversation, August 1989). The Binding-of-the-Years ceremony is described in *Florentine Codex* (FC, bk. 7, pt. 8, chaps. 9–10:25–33).

35. Emily Umberger, personal communication, 20 April 1989.

36. Richard Townsend, personal communication, 25 January 1991.

37. Ibid.

38. See Edmonson (1988, 12–13) and Caso (1971, Table 5) for two correlations of Aztec solar years with Julian dates.

39. My use of the term *iconology* should not be confused with Erwin Panofsky's use of the word (1955). Nor should my system for interpreting images be equated entirely with his, for there are some fundamental differences between us. First, Panofsky, following Ernst Cassirer (Holly 1984), presumed that a universal pure presence shows itself through essential tendencies of the human mind, which can be identified. I make no such presumption. Second, because I do not make this presumption, I work from the paradoxical position that (quite possibly) the only unchanging truth is that all things change. Panofsky, however, conceived the ultimately real as eternal and therefore sought cultural continuity as evidence for an unchanging reality that somehow transcended human understanding (although it operated within it by means of symbols). In this sense, he is very

akin to the genealogical line of scholars in religious studies I differentiate myself from (below). Third, I find Panofsky's failure at his pre-iconographical and icono-graphical levels to delineate clearly between the formal, visual elements of an image and its referential elements potentially confusing. To do so seems to me like confusing discrete units of sounds (e.g., phonemes) with full units of mean-ing (e.g., words).

40. See, for example, Johnson (1987, 1993) and Lakoff (1987) for in-depth treatments of analogical thinking as viewed from interdisciplinary approaches based in both cognitive science and philosophy.

41. See Read (1987a and 1991b) for an expansion on the nature of analogi-cal thinking and its centrality to interpretation.

42. My primary aim in this book is to promote understanding of human time and sacrifice within the fifteenth-century Mexica-Tenochca cultural context that is as unclouded by personal attitudes of moral repugnance as possible. At this time, my aim is not to address the very deep and most difficult ethical questions that are raised when cultures clash over moral differences, although those ques-tions are pertinent, fascinating, and natural to the situation.

Any number of ethical issues could be extremely interesting to discuss. For example, should Western or Mexica-Tenochca attitudes toward human sacrifice be extended to everyone? This suggestion is based on an assumption that moral-ity is grounded in universally held standards. Or do differences between West-ern and Mexica moral standards not matter because, given the ancient histori-cal context of the Mexica, the two cultures have never and will never clash? This second attitude may be grounded, like the first, in an idea of universal moral standards, thereby making the Mexica simply wrong. Or it could be grounded in a relativistic position, which sees morality as context specific; the Mexica were not wrong for their place and time, but they would be wrong now. In any case, this second position sees the whole question of Mexica morality as a moot point because they are no longer living.

I do not think it is a moot point, nor do I believe that any single moral stan-dard is universally capable of answering all ethical questions. Neither of those approaches will help resolve our current ethical problems. Instead of asking who is more moral, why, or why one should even care, we ought to be asking what we can learn from this historically and culturally remote context that can assist us now. Scholars need to take challenging possibilities such as those of-fered by the Mexica seriously, drawing on their historical studies for models that could change their own lives. For example, see Read (1994b) for a discussion of how our ethical questions about and problems with diversity might be chal-lenged and transformed by fresh ideas gleaned from Mexica worldviews.

43. Some, like Mary Daly (1973), would argue that dichotomous thinking has led to physical violence against women and others (the Mexica and other "primitives" among them) who are equated with an inadequate and even evil material world because they do not fit a white, youthful, male definition of the

sacred. While I am inclined to be in sympathy with Daly on this issue, my concern in this particular book is not with these damaging visions of power, but with how—if we abandon dichotomous thinking—we might come to a different understanding of Mexica worldviews that can teach us something new.

44. Synesthesia is the cognitive process by which people combine their sensory experiences to gain a fuller experience. It should be noted that one's senses can also *contest* with one another. Given that, and the fact that these processes are still not fully understood, whether or not a true unity is achieved through synesthesia is, as Lawrence Sullivan has said, "the $64,000 question" (conversation, 26 January 1996). My own inclination is to see the temporary joining of sensory experiences in synesthesia as much a form of transformative activity as it is a connecting with some eternal or stable unity. The paired activity of contestation and synesthesia provides a rich and never-ending source for human creativity. At the moment, merely understanding that synesthesia occurs does not explain the reality of change, far less describe its character.

45. D. Carrasco is extending and altering Eliade's notion of a stable, even static ceremonial center by noting two things about Mesoamerican centers. The first is well supported by recent archaeological evidence; the second is an interpretational re-presentation of that evidence and other data: (1) centers are able to "expand and retract, meander and transform"; and (2) they are able to link change with unity (1991, 33). To do this, he is drawing on the work of Jonathan Z. Smith, Lawrence Sullivan, and Rhys Isaac.

46. Linda Sexson is not the first Western thinker to weave the sacred and profane together. Among many others, I have found the pragmatist tradition particularly helpful, for it too recognizes the importance of everyday experience and its shifting character. See, for example, Dewey (1934a, 1934b), and Peirce (1932, 1957).

47. Many other authors have followed an understanding of transformation which sees change as variations on an essentially unchanging theme. One of the most recent versions of this has been proposed for the Aztecs by Inga Clendinnen. In her struggle to define Aztec aesthetics, she describes an enduring sacred Aztec world whose mere shadow is replicated in the "ephemeral" physical world. By so doing, she is not describing (as she claims) a different aesthetics based on Aztec "semblance" rather than Western "structure." Instead, she has found a path that will take her back home to the dichotomy of the sacred and profane, in which divine, eternal structures are replicated as mere semblances in the unenduring profane (1991, 214–216, 223).

Past authors who base their interpretations on similar dichotomies of the sacred and profane besides Clendinnen, Otto, van der Leeuw, Eliade, Ricoeur, and D. Carrasco include the following (to name just a few): Claude Lévi-Strauss (1963 and 1966), Edmund Leach (1976), Stanley Tambiah (1979), David Tracy (1981), Langdon Gilkey (1985), E. Lawrence Sullivan (1988), and Lindsey Jones (1989).

48. See note 44. Mapping and synesthesia may, in fact, be very similar activities, processes that function on a daily basis. But in neither activity is an unchanging reality a logical necessity.

2. Timing Shapes

1. Not all oral traditions are gone from Mesoamerica. Contemporary practices can help us to imagine what may have been five hundred years ago. Dennis Tedlock, for example, draws on the contemporary oral tradition to translate the ancient Quiché Maya text, the *Popol Vuh* (1985).

2. Although linguistic research continues to resolve the difficulties of translating classical Nahuatl, a number of translation problems persist. Sixteenth-century grammars and dictionaries often lack detailed analyses of the language's structure. Moreover, the rules for how it was to be recorded changed throughout early post-Conquest years, adding to the confusion. To compensate for these difficulties, I used a wide variety of resources ranging from early dictionaries and manuals to current works. All translations were joint projects shared with me by Jane Rosenthal. We both are indebted to Alfredo López Austin for checking the accuracy of our final translation drafts. Our resources include Molina (facsimile 1970), Carochi (1790, reprint 1910), Andrews (1975), Siméon (1981), Santamaria (1983), Karttunen (1983), Thelma D. Sullivan (1983, 1988), Bierhorst (1985), and López Austin (1988b).

3. In my English prose style, I have tried to mimic the texts' native quality as much as possible, especially the prominent rhythmic character of many of the Nahuatl verses. For this reason, I frequently have worked the "discourse markers" into the English version. These are short phrases, repeated like a chorus to a song, which indicate changes in the action. Nahua orators often used these for rhythmic purposes, creating a beat that emphasized some points over others. Another quirk of these texts which I have retained is the conscious switching of verb tenses. The present is sometimes switched into from the past to emphasize moments of intense action. Since Nahuatl is a language that relies heavily on metaphoric expression, many phrases are expanded upon in the notes to retain the rich, polysemous nature of their imagery. Much of the meaning of these texts lies in the complex imagery invoked by the speaker's words, and it is a crime not to describe it. The narrator may have included little passages of explanation or excluded well-known details, depending on the sophistication of his audience. These also will be noted whenever necessary. I also tried to retain the clear stylistic differences between the Nahuatl texts. Some, such as "Quetzalcoatl and the Bones," take on the character of a folktale or fable. Others, such as "The Myth of the Four Ages," appear to be highly formalized, intended to impart technical calendrical information.

If not consciously attended to, oral styles are easily lost when translated into writing. Translation styles that mimic contemporary written scriptures (such as biblical texts) or modern poetry and prose may be somewhat inappropriate analogies for English translations of Nahuatl texts. These Nahuatl stories and chants were not "scripture" in the grand religious traditions of the Bible, nor were they always high literature. Closer analogies for "The Birth of the Fifth Sun," for example, might be found in popular forms such as rap or Caribbean music like calypso.

Presentation involved more than simply oration. "The Legend of the Suns" probably was accompanied by a screen-fold manuscript. Often a narration was presented with music and dance. The very marked sense of rhythm inherent in the verses of "The Birth of the Fifth Sun" indicates that this was probably the case. Since these orations involved a wide range of rhythmic, musical, and theatrical elements, a slightly awkward quality in a translation may be good, for it will serve to remind us of what is missing, just as the awkwardness of song lyrics or the flatness of an operatic libretto points out to us that only a fraction of this art form is before us. To choose the wrong analogy in English, no matter how smooth and beautiful to English ears, can only encourage false impressions.

4. Pre-Conquest manuscripts were painted on paper made from either a particular kind of tree bark or deer hide. They were long and folded accordion style. One read all the folios on one side of the document and then turned it over to read the rest. These codices were one of the props used in an oral performance, and discourse markers probably helped point out each new picture. Because skilled orators could rhythmically manipulate these markers, they may have timed their "page turns" to fit the beat.

5. In this chapter, I have translated three myths from Nahuatl in their entirety: "The Birth of the Fifth Sun," "The Myth of the Four Ages," and "Quetzalcoatl and the Bones." Two other short excerpts are also direct translations: the little section describing the ending of the Fifth Sun from the "Anales de Cuauhtitlan," and the poem "the Fleeting Moment" by Nezahualcoyotl. All other stories are retellings rather than translations. This means that they are not quoted word for word and that much has been left out of them. "The Return to Aztlan," for example, is only about one-third of its original length in Spanish, and Tenochtitlan's stories of conquest are mere summaries of long, elaborate narratives told in both Spanish and Nahuatl.

6. "Sun" (*tonatiuh*) also means "age."

7. Each line of the poetry selections and the paragraphs of prose translations have been numbered for easy future reference.

Endnotes expand on the often polysemic nature of the language. This is necessary because, without all the metaphoric imagery that only the Nahuatl can convey, the poetic messages become one-dimensional, conveying only a fraction of their original intention, thereby encouraging misunderstandings.

8. Because of its richness, I used the Nahuatl version from Sahagún's *Florentine Codex* drawing from the following sources: (1) facsimile 1979, fol. 5r, 3:231; (2) 1953–1982, bk. 7, pt. 8, chap. 2:3–9, app. 42–58; and (3) 1978, 131–35.

9. This means "to spread out flat" as one pats out a tortilla (*mana*).

10. The equation of time and space is shown in the language; the suffix used here, -*yan*, indicates both time and place (*iooaian*).

11. If one breaks Teotihuacan into its components, a much richer understanding of the religious context begins to emerge. Teotihuacan means "the place where the gods (*teotl*) were made (*teotia*)." Moveover, the word "god" is formed on a more general notion of power (*teo*), an idea rather different from one of anthropomorphized deities. In other words, not only deities were created at Teotihuacan; a complex system involving powers that make the universe an efficient and effective place also was created. This notion of power is somewhat like Polynesian notions of *mana* and will be discussed at length in chapter 4.

12. "To take counsel" (*ilhuia*) means more than mere discussion, it also means "to imagine," "invent," or "do something by using all of one's powers." A notion of wielding one's powers to make something or make something work is embedded in the idea of counseling.

13. "To carry" (*itqui*) also means "to govern." Many metaphors describe the ruler as governing the city by carrying it on his back as one might carry a child. As will be seen, year dates were borne on the back of the being who governed that particular period of 365 days.

14. This metaphor is one of bearing a burden as a trader would have borne his burden on his back during transport. The burden to be borne will be time itself, and the sun and the moon will be the bearers because they are the ones governing these periods.

15. "To step forth" (*ixquetza*) also means "to offer oneself," which is exactly what Tecuiçiztecatl is doing.

16. "To be" (*ca*) also means location. In other words, one can exist only in time and space.

17. Since time and space are not separated in Mesoamerica, words such as "thing," "there," and "then" must be understood as being equivalent.

18. "Turning tail" literally means "buttocks stand up" (*tzinquetzaya*). In other words, they were ready to run away.

19. "To celebrate the rituals" (*mahceua*) often has been mistranslated as "to do penance," perhaps because the sixteenth-century Nahuatl dictionaries were compiled by Spanish clerics who had a particular understanding of religious life that was not always in tune with their informants. In fact, *mahceua* may be one of the most difficult words in Nahuatl to comprehend fully. It covers a huge range of contexts and carries a variety of intentions. In a superficial way, *mahceua* means variously "to obtain one's merit," "to rob," "to dance," and "to do penance." This latter signification is somewhat problematic, especially in the current context. Because the indefinite article suffix *tla* precedes it, *mahceua* becomes *tlamahceua*, which is usually translated as "doing penance," although Karttunen (1983, 279), notes that in Sierra de la Zacapoaxtla, Puebla, the term refers to eating the day's first meal.

Unfortunately, the word *penance*, in English, carries a sense of atonement for one's sins, of paying a penalty for one's misdeeds in order to achieve "at-one-ment" with God. But this is not appropriate in the Mexica religious context. Rather, the gods are beginning a kind of complex ritual dance in which, through a number of acts (including sacrifice), the sun will be put in motion and the cosmos put into an appropriate order. Not only is sacrifice a central part of this, but so is the creation of foodstuffs. Since sacrifice also is considered an act of feeding and involves eating, the above reference to the first meal of the day makes sense, a meal equated with the sun's rising, which came about as an act of eating.

Because the Mexica rituals are not ones of atonement, I have chosen to use terms less laden with Abrahamic significations when I translate this word. In most cases, I will use the word "merit." As will be seen, ritual actions are manipulating a variety of powers that make things happen efficiently. Merit is produced because of these powers (*teoyome*), and is a bundle of specific powers aimed at accomplishing certain things. *Tlamahceua* literally means "to merit it," meaning to give something merit under ritual circumstances. In this case, because of the awkward sound of "merit" in English, I have chosen instead the words "to ritually celebrate," referring to the ritual actions that shape merit-producing powers. The complexities of merit and powers will be discussed further in chapters 3 and 4. Although none of *mahceua*'s richness is conveyed by these English words, at least one has some hope of avoiding the unconscious expression of non-Mexica religious ideals.

20. This fire pit (*tlecuilitl*) is a cooking fire whose three stones were used, as they still are today in many parts of Mesoamerica, to support cooking vessels.

21. These branches (*acxoyatl*) were extremely precious, for unlike the usual branches made of pine or fir, these are made of quetzal feathers.

22. Gold (*teocuitlac*) means literally "powerful or god's (*teo*) excrement (*cuitlatl*)." The meaning of excrement will be explored in chapter 4.

23. Spines of obsidian, greenstone, or maguey were used to let blood.

24. Balls, usually woven of grass, were used to catch blood flowing out during bloodletting ceremonies.

25. This passage is filled with sexual images. What I have translated as "scab" comes from the word *nanahuatl*, Nanahuatzin's name. This term refers to a class of swellings, lumps, and/or pox involved in venereal disease or other diseases associated with the sexual area, such as swollen glands, tumors, hemorrhoids, chancres, or pustules. The Spanish often translated this as *buboes*. In other words, these are probably the scabs from a skin disease that was considered sexual, such as syphilis.

26. The flaking of Nanahuatzin's own sexually diseased skin is being ritually burned.

27. "To lift up" (*neehualco*), possibly refers to the rising or lifting up of the powers gained through ritual preparation and is intended to ready Nanahuatzin

and Tecuiçiztecatl for sacrifice, although the word's true meaning is a bit obscure.

28. "To arrange" (*mahmaca*) means a lot more than simply to put something in order. They are composing the ritual vestments in order to appropriately apportion their powers. As we will see, such vestments carried various potencies all their own. (This notion of power [*teoyotl*] will be expanded in chapters 4 and 5.) Almost always used in passages describing rituals, *mahmaca* is an extremely rich word with many levels of meaning. It means "to divide something among several people," "to handle something," "to apportion," and (in the form used here) "to give oneself medicine [powers?]," "to give something to someone," "to deliver oneself," or "to confide in someone."

29. A headdress bore on it the glyphic image, or name, belonging to a particular god. As with all names, this image was imbued with that god's power. Hence the name belonged to the god and not to Nanahuatzin.

30. "To spread" (*mani*) is like water covering the surface of a shallow pan. They are spreading around the area like water flowing out, a very fertile image.

31. "Praising" (*motenehua*) also means the ritual calling in of gods and various powers.

32. "To place" (*quimonmanque*) is heavily laden with cosmic significance. The cosmos is properly put in place through an action that is like "patting out a tortilla" (*mana)*. Hence Nanahuatzin and Tecuiçiztecatl are placed in the middle like one shapes the single most important form of sustenance and places it on a griddle to fry. This makes sense, because soon they will be fried in order to create the Mexica cosmos.

33. "To face each other" (*ixnamictia*) also means "to do battle in a fight or dispute." The implication is that there is going to be a contest.

34. "To hurl or throw" (*mayahui*) also means "to dash someone to death," which is what is going to happen.

35. This passage probably means that because Nanahuatzin bears a good heart, he has the power to do the deed he needs to do; his merit (*mahceua*) is of a good variety (see n. 1:19). One's heart (*yolia*) was the seat of one of the animistic centers or souls (*teoyolia*) giving character and power to a person's identity (López Austin 1988b, 229–32). I will expand on these issues of souls, powers, and merit later in this chapter as well as in chapters 3 and 4.

36. In Nahuatl, "to blossom" captures, perhaps, the onomatopoeic character of corn popping. Popcorn was seen as a kind of flower, and today, as in pre-Conquest times, strings of tightly packed popcorn are used to beautifully decorate altars and ritual objects. As will be seen, Nanahuatzin and the sun are very closely associated with corn. "To blossom" (*cueponi*) also means "to shine," "to glow," "to burst into bloom," and "to burst or explode." This rich verb is made even richer here by using a repetitive form (*cuecuepoca*), thereby intensifying its meaning.

37. The Nahuatl songster is skillfully plying his trade in this passage. Sizzling

(*tzotzoyoni*) actually is mimicking the sound of frying. Not only is he employing the onomatopoeic quality of this Nahuatl word, with both this word and "to blossom" (*cuecueponi*), he repeats the syllables twice in order to create a sense of intensity and excitement.

38. Again the skill of the songster emerges in the text. Each one of the three burning words has syllables that are repeated, a poetic device probably intended to show the spottiness or inadequacy of the burning. A literal reading of the repeated syllables gives a sense of spottiness: "burn, burn, fire, fire, burn, burn, fire, burn, burn."

39. This is a very strange passage. It not only lacks the rhythmic and metaphorical style of the previous passages but also contains several mistakes. This passage probably was added later to the original text, perhaps as an explanation for a foreign or untutored audience.

40. "To stretch out" or "to be lying" (*o*) has an existential quality to it. This phrase could be translated as "existed for a long time," but that would lose the essential spatial quality of the verb and the idea that a particular topography is "stretched out" at the time of creation. Another word often used in these contexts of cosmic production is *mana*, which is "to pat something out as a tortilla is patted out." Because English differentiates among time, space, and existence (something Nahuatl does not do), this verb is essentially untranslatable.

41. These two words, which in their simplest sense mean "dawn," are particularly rich in metaphoric imagery. The first, *tlahuizcalli*, describes the lighting of a house because the cosmos was thought of as the house in which people lived. The second, *tlatlauillotl*, describes dawn's first rosy rays as does the color of burning embers, perhaps the embers of the fire from which the new sun has just emerged.

42. These are the cardinal directions, described in an appropriate counterclockwise order beginning with the North (the Place of the Dead), moving to the West (the Place of Women), and then to the South (the Place of Thorns). Appropriate ritual motion may have been counterclockwise.

43. This, as one might expect, is the East (the Place of Light).

44. Again, the songster's skill shines through his choice of words. Using two different distance words he shows how the dawning of light is moving closer to them. First the dawn is far away (*ompa*), then it moves within sight (*oncan*).

45. This name refers metaphorically to the Nahua universe. Mesoamericans conceived their world as ringed by water which formed the walls of the cosmic house.

46. The dawn is metaphorically a red sacrifice, for ink (*tlapalli*) also refers to blood.

47. "Spreading in an undulating way" (*monenecuilotimani*), is a rich metaphor for the growing light of dawn. The sun's rosy hues are twisting and bending like red dye or sacrificial blood spreading out in a body of water. Since the walls of the cosmos were made of water, this seems particularly fitting.

48. In other words, there are now two suns sitting together on the horizon.

49. "To follow a road" (*ohtlatoca*) is often used to describe the motions of the sun and moon. It is a metaphor that also refers to traders who follow roads while they bear their trade goods. So too do the sun and moon bear their burdens of time. This rich word also means "to go along in life," "to be extended," and "to spread as a stain would spread." It fits into a general class of ordering terms that spatially define an area, thereby creating order. However, there are several ways to create cosmic order, each according to its own particular way: spreading like water in a pan (*mani*); patting something out like tortillas (*mana*); lying down or stretching out (*o*); and walking across a territory (*ohtlatoca*).

50. As will be seen, they are destroying his identity in order to create a new one. "They wrecked his face" (*conispopoloque*) is built on the very potent word "to destroy" (*poloa*), which is replete with metaphors for destructive transformation. It also meant "to disappear," "to decimate," "to be lost," "to perish," and "to fail." Its metaphoric import will be discussed at length below.

51. In other words, they spread on the earth's horizon or edge.

52. Gods and people are not supposed to be living together in the same area, something that would literally mess things up. "Mixed up with" (*neloa*) also means "to agitate," "to stir," "to mix things together," or "to make a mess of things."

53. This means more than strengthened, for it has all the connotations of birth and childraising. Like a small babe, the sun is to be born and raised in an appropriate manner. "To revive" (*izcalia*) also means "to hatch," "to restore," "to teach," "to nurture," and (in the form here) "to raise children."

54. Like the good leader, Ehecatl is performing his communal duty. "Work" (*tequitl*) also means "tribute," "labor," "duty," and "term in office."

55. The words give a verbal image of two stalks of corn adorned with the leaves young maize shoots have when they first emerge from the ground, which look like a parrot's dark green chick feathers. "Xolotl of the Fields" (*millaca Xolotl*) means literally "field by means of Xolotl." *Xolotl* also means the "leaves of maize" and is the name given to the feathers of the parrot, *toznene*.

56. Strictly speaking, the *axolotl*, or salamander, is not really a fully developed salamander but is still in the larval stage. This particular variety, known as the mole salamander (*Ambystoma talpoideum*) in the United States, is neotenic when found in Mexico and, therefore, does not transform into the next stage as other varieties do. This means that it never loses its gills and remains fully aquatic. Nevertheless, the creature looks like a full-grown salamander except that it sports huge feathery gills on each side of its head.

57. Ehecatl is gently puffing and coaxing a new, weak spark into a strong fire, for that is the kind of blowing indicated (*ehecac*) (López Austin, conversation, June, 1990).

58. The sun's daily path (ending in the west) is established and he will now continue to set there. From now on, he will enter the earth each night, and travel

through the underground before emerging again in the East. This is reminiscent of Pueblo mythology, which sometimes conceives of the cosmos as four houses arranged according to the cardinal directions. Each house has a door through which various deities and mythic beings pass. This architectural arrangement repeats the four houses around the patio model so fundamental to Mesoamerica. "His entrance" (*icalaquian*) uses the postposition -*yan*, which means "the time and place of some habitual activity."

59. This seems to be a metaphor for finishing the work (*tequitl*) of night. Night's passage may be imagined as a trader shouldering his burden of time for a while and then throwing it down at the end of his journey, his office or duty being finished for the moment. "Shoulders his work" is literally "night work he throws down" (*iooualtequitl quitlaça*).

60. "Ancient" (*in ye huecauh*) also joins time and space, for it means both "a long time" and "something old."

61. Nor does anyone really know who first inhabited Teotihuacan, although it is clear that they were not originally Mexica.

62. Although Teotihuacan's life span as a functioning urban center stretched from approximately 200 B.C.E. to 650 or 750 C.E. (Adams 1991, 201–29), its periphery was reoccupied after its decline, and like most urban centers in Mesoamerica, its ruined buildings continued to be used as a pilgrimage center pretty much continuously after it was abandoned by its original inhabitants. By including this abandoned urban center in their mythology and going there to perform rituals, the Mexica were following an extraordinarily ancient custom that dated back at least to the Olmec, over three thousand years before.

63. Tula is the archaeological site many scholars associate with the toltecs, the paradigmatic royal ancestors of the Mexica. But a number of resources use the term *toltecs* to refer to ancestors originating in other "Tulas" or "Tollans." This would indicate that the terms *toltecs* and *Tollan* are more generic than has been sometimes thought, referring to groups' origins at sites other than simply the archaeological site of Tula. D. Carrasco (1982) has noted the mythic import of some of these other Tollans.

64. The skulls of adult humans and the skeletal remains of children and of numerous animals (many of them from the sea or other aquatic realms) have been unearthed from caches at the Templo Mayor (López Luján 1993).

65. One of Sahagún's informants expressed his amazement over the size of the sun and moon pyramids at Teotihuacan. "And they built the pyramids of the sun and the moon very large, just like mountains. It is unbelievable, as is said, that they made them by hand, but giants lived there then. Such things also appear at Cholollan; they are made of sand and adobe. One can see that they are only constructed, only made" (FC, bk. 10, pt. 11, chap. 29: 192).

66. Aveni (conversation, April 1988). A viewer standing on the Temple of the Sun at the Teotihuacan outpost of Alta Vista also can witness the sunrise at the equinoxes in a due easterly direction (Aveni 1980, 228).

67. The markers, or "pecked crosses," consist of a pair of concentric rings and a cross. One is laid in the stucco floor of a group of buildings adjacent to the Pyramid of the Sun, and the other is on the slope of Cerro Colorado, three kilometers to the west (ibid., 222–28).

68. Johanna Broda (l983, 81–123). Since the Templo Mayor's remains have only recently come to sight from under the center of what is now Mexico City, it is not yet fully known what kind of correlations were made between this building and the sky.

69. The Mexica-Tenochca were the only Mesoamerican peoples to build double pyramids with dual staircases leading up to two temples.

70. All Mesoamerican urban centers aligned their buildings with terrestrial and celestial topographies using horizon-line astronomy, although not all did it exactly the same way that Teotihuacan and Tenochtitlan did.

71. I am using the term *eschatology* in a broad sense to mean the marked endings of things. The Christian eschaton represents only one kind of ending, one characterized as singular and final. Nahua endings represented a different sense of completions, one involving continual processes.

72. For my translations, I used the Nahuatl versions of this story found in *Codex Chimalpopoca* (1938, 322–88) and *Códice Chimalpopoca* (1945, 119–42). The entire legend has been translated into English by John Bierhorst in *Codex Chimalpopoca* (1992a, 139–162).

73. Given the lack of information about the circumstances of this text, it is difficult to know if this story would have been told in this long serial form or whether these stories were gathered together by the post-Conquest collector. Such a progression, whether ever consciously related like this in pre-Conquest times, is implicit in the stories themselves, however. The stories about cosmic ages end with the beginning of the current age, the birth of the predecessors of living populations is situated in this most current age, and each group's migration story begins with its own first ancestors. Moreover, other Mesoamerican stories exist, such as the Mayan Quiché story of creation, the *Popol Vuh*, which is told in a similar lengthy sequence (D. Tedlock 1985).

74. This is a translation of only one version of an extraordinarily widespread Mesoamerican myth (*Codex Chimalpopoca* 1938, 322–27; *Códice Chimalpopoca* 1945 and 1992b, fol. 75:1–45, 87–88). For a discussion of a number of other versions see Moreno de los Arcos (1967).

75. This text may have been intended to be told with pictorial illustrations. Unlike "The Birth of the Fifth Sun," this passage uses relatively few discourse markers, giving it a far less notable rhythmic sense, something which may be due to its original manner of delivery. The word *inin* ("this one") at the beginning of passages may indicate it was meant as an oral explanatory supplement to a series of pictures as is true of "Historia de los Mexicanos por sus pinturas" (translation 1968). Given that the codex from which this text is taken is laid out on a clear, sequentially ordered year line, as was that one, this theory seems quite

plausible. If this is so, then these pictures are lost to us today as in the case of the "pinturas" text.

76. The numbers of years given in this document add up to 485 years short of 2,513 years. This may be because they were still counting years into the Fifth Sun up to 22 May 1558. This particular count of the ages is discussed in Appendix 2.

77. The word rendered here as "food" (*tonacayotl*) has the active sense of something being made like a "crop" or "produce" instead of the rather inactive sense of "sustenance" that has been its traditional translation.

This is a particularly cryptic line, one that is repeated with a different "food" in each of the four different ages. The food in this age is called "7-Grass," which is a day-sign designating a particular date. Such day-signs, however, served as one of the many names for people and gods and carried divinatory import. There are several ways to understand this "food." It could be referring to something they actually ate. It could be the name of a god or carry special significance according to its divinatory aspects. It could be a specific period of time that was passing, hence being eaten metaphorically. Some authors have noted what they believe is an evolutionary progression in the foodstuffs mentioned, moving from grass to snakes to seeds to corn. Interestingly, this grass is the kind used to bind the frames of houses together. Since houses also could be a metaphor for the heavens (hence the motion of time), this passage may have as much a temporal sense as anything else. The presently told Mayan creation story, the *Popol Vuh* (D. Tedlock 1985), has astronomical and calendrical information hidden in its imagery. And it could, of course, be all of the above, for none excludes any of the others.

78. As in "The Birth of the Fifth Sun," the terms "to destroy," "to disappear," "to be lost," "to fail," and "to perish" all are formed on the root *poliui*. This particular permutation of *poliui* is used in its frequentative form (*popoliuhqui*), giving the augmented sense of "depopulation," "decimation from pestilence," or "to perish completely." Various permutations of the term *poliui* are used each time an age is destroyed.

79. In the "Anales de Cuauhtitlan," one of the other texts contained in the *Codex Chimalpopoca*, it is said that it rained both fire (*tlequiauh*) and pebbles (*xaltequiyauh*) during this age. In other words, fire-rain refers to volcanic action (CC 1945, 62; CC 1938, 5).

80. The length of the second age (364) plus the length of this one (312) adds up to the same period of time as the first age, 676 years. Both the second and third ages, moreover, are named by the same year sign, 1-Knife. In other words, these two short ages add up to the same as each of the other two.

81. Each fifty-two-year cycle was divided into four parts of thirteen years each.

82. The total for one age of 676 years is equivalent to thirteen fifty-two-year cycles.

83. There is, of course, a reason for counting the suns in multiples of twenty-six. The logic behind this will be explained in chapter 2, but see Appendix 2 for a mathematical explanation of the calendrical system.

84. This retelling of the story was drawn from the *Codex Chimalpopoca* (1938, 328–30) and *Códice Chimalpopoca* (1945 and 1992b, fols. 75:45–76:18, 88).

85. This is one of the many names of the god Tezcatlipoca, a major god sometimes balanced with Quetzalcoatl and sometimes identified as the Tenochca god Huitzilopochtli.

86. Ahuehuetl trees, a type of cedar, are enormous and can live for hundreds of years. They are a symbol for rulership. This may imply the beginning of genealogical lines that originate with royalty, for rulers were seen in a parenting role with regard to their cities. They carried the cities on their backs as a parent would carry its child, and they protected this child as an ahuehuetl tree spreads its wide branches in protection (FC, bk. 6, pt. 7, chap. 5:22 and 43:252).

87. Note the difference between Tlalticpac (Earth's Surface) and Tlalteuctli (Earth Lord). In this story, the earth is given a godlike nature.

88. This translation of the story comes from *Codex Chimalpopoca* (1938, 330–38) and *Códice Chimalpopoca* (1945 and 1992b, 76:18–77:2, 88–89).

89. They are asking, "Who will lie down in this space and occupy it, who will settle themselves here?"

90. The sky and earth have been patted out into shape like one pats out a tortilla, for *mana* again appears, meaning "to spread out something like a tortilla."

91. The earth is being personified as a male and given special characteristics, for the word contains the word "lord" (*teuctli*).

92. Such horns were made out of carved conch shells.

93. *Nahualli* is a complex term referring, in its most simple sense, either to a "magician" (or shaman) or to the transfiguration of that magician into some other form. In this passage, the *nahualli* would appear to be an extra soul or alter ego that could act independently of the magician himself. For a fuller discussion of nahualism, see López Austin (1988b, 1:362–75, 2:283–84).

94. This passage creates a metaphoric link between eating and the decay that happens to bones in the underground, painting a picture of how the underground eats dead matter (this will be expanded in chapter 4). "They ground them to bits" also includes the meanings "to shatter something," "to grind something to bits," "to nibble bones," "to decay or crumble."

95. A bit of fatalism seems to be creeping in. "However it actually goes, is how it goes" (*maço nel yuhqui yauh*) appears to be a Nahuatl form of "que será, será."

96. This bit of added information indicates that the narrator was from out of town.

97. It would seem that both gods and commoners were created by the gods' acts at Tamoanchan. This is consistent with a cosmos in which all things were imbued with power, in which the sacred was not separated radically from the

profane or humans from gods, something that will be discussed at length in chapter 4. This sentence has been translated variously by different authors. It literally means "they were born, the gods, the commoners, because they merited (*tlamaçeuhque*) on us (*topan*)" (see n. 19, this chapter).

98. This shortened retelling of the story comes from *Codex Chimalpopoca* (1938, 338–40) and *Códice Chimalpopoca* (1945) and is translated into English in full by Bierhorst (1992a, 146–147).

99. Oxomoco and Cipactonal are pictured casting fortunes with corn in the center of folio 21 of the *Codex Borbonicus* (figure 16). They are surrounded by a count of the years which was based on the count of days. Corn still is used today to cast fortunes, and calendrical divination is as central a part of Mesoamerican life as it ever was (B. Tedlock 1982). Much more will be said about this in later chapters.

100. *Nanahuatl* is simply the noun form of *Nanahuatzin*, the syphilitic sacrifice in the "Birth of the Fifth Sun." The latter is a much more polite form of address, meaning the "Honorable Nanahuatl."

101. In modern versions of this myth told by the Yoanáhuac and the Huitzilan, Nanahuatzin is lightning, and he strikes the mountain open with his head (Taggert 1983, 88–92).

102. "To cast fortunes" (*tlapolhuia*) also means "to open something," a most interesting extra layer of meaning. It implies that the future can be opened.

103. The Tlaloques are piling up like rain clouds over the tops of mountains.

104. As in the "Birth of the Fifth Sun," these are the four directions. There were four sets of Tlaloques, one for each direction.

105. This is a listing of basic foodstuffs found in the largely vegetarian Mesoamerican diet. Corn came in several varieties, each a different color. Chia and amaranth are both indigenous varieties of seed-bearing plants; the latter is very rich in protein. Note that the colors repeat almost exactly the colors of the four Tlaloques. Corn may be associated with the directions as well.

106. These passages present the listener with a classic complex of Mesoamerican images from both the past and present. The young god is corn, which is the sun. To give just one example (for there are many), in the *Popol Vuh* (D. Tedlock 1985), the presently living Quiché Maya tell a story about the Hero Twins. When they descend to the underworld, each plants a corn seed in the center of their house. These seeds grow into corn plants which live, die, and live as the twin's individual fortunes change. After a series of sacrifices (as with Nanahuatzin and Tecuiçiztecatl) one twin is transformed into the sun and one the moon. This twentieth-century story has ancient roots; a written copy was collected in the sixteenth century, and a number of pre-Conquest iconographic representations of the same story have been found at Mayan archaeological sites.

107. This shortened retelling of the story comes from the *Florentine Codex* (FC, bk. 3, pt. 4, chap. 1:1–5).

108. Coatlicue (Snake Skirt) is not a sweet-appearing lady. She is depicted with a warrior's kilt knotted from rattle snakes. In one famous sculpture in the Museum of Anthropology in Mexico City, she is portrayed as an old woman dressed like a warrior. Her hands and head are snakes, her feet are jaguar claws, and she wears a necklace of human hands and hearts. On her back is tied a human skull. On the bottom of her base appears the Earth Monster. She is not a mother many would long for.

109. Literally, *Centzonuitznaua* means the four hundred who are close to spines. *Uitznauac* could be referring to several levels of meaning here. The south was The Place of Thorns, hence the southerly direction. It also referred to a group of people, supposedly of Colhua heritage, who entered the Valley of Mexico when the Mexica did. So there may be a reference to a political conquest embedded in this myth.

110. Huitzilopochtli, like his close counterpart Tezcatlipoca, is shown iconographically with one small or oddly shaped foot. Sacrificial offerings sometimes also were stripped, painted blue, and pasted with feathers.

111. This weapon, *xiuhcoatl*, includes the meanings "greenstone," "turquoise," "heat," "comet," "grass," "year," and "snake."

112. This imagery depicts a powerful mountain storm with Huitzilopochtli wielding a comet or lightninglike weapon and throwing up huge storm clouds to defeat his enemies.

113. Cities were defined by lineages. When defeated, a lineage was described in feminine terms (Read forthcoming).

114. The word *Tenochtitlan* may create a scene that now appears on the Mexican national flag, the foundation of Tenochtitlan, which involved a prickly pear growing from a rock (HI 1984, chap. 5:47–53; 1994, 5:42–50). Tenochtitlan is derived from *tetl* (rock) and *nochtli* (prickly pear cactus) and refers to a particular species of prickly pear.

115. This is a shortened retelling of a story found in Durán's *Historia* (HI 1984, chaps. 3:30–32, 4:37–38; 1994 3:24–25, 4:31–33).

116. Dreaming is probably analogous to the long-standing tradition of vision questing of Native North American peoples in which religious practitioners, sometimes called shamans or medicine people, sought visions by "dreaming." These visions might be thought of as extrasensory visual experiences by Westerners. They were acquired through a wide variety of ritual practices. In Mesoamerica, sometimes visions were induced by fasting, bloodletting, dancing, or the use of hallucinatory drugs. Linda Schele and David Freidel have noted correctly, I think, the close relationship between these royal practices and shamanism (1990), though that comparison could have been drawn out quite a bit more to mark both the unique nature of the Mesoamerican traditions and the differences between rulers and other kinds of healers.

117. The remains of Malinalco lie in the mountains to the west of Mexico City. A most remarkable structure can be seen there, a round house built into the side

of a mountain that is reminiscent of the kivas built by the Pueblo peoples of the southwestern United States. This house is entered through a door in its side, shaped like a serpent's mouth. Before passing under the creature's fangs and into the dark interior of the mountain, one must walk on the snake's tongue, as though one were walking on a red carpet carved into the porch floor. Part of a ruler's coronation ceremony may have occurred here (Townsend 1987).

118. Chapultepec lies in some rock outcroppings on the shore of Lake Texcoco, just to the west of Tenochtitlan, and now is the site of Chapultepec Park and Zoo. In pre-Conquest times, it was also a magnificent garden. Then springs flowed from the rocks, and Mexica rulers visited there.

119. An effigy, or concrete image of the god, was carried in a bundle on a priest's back during this journey. Durán mentions this, and it is shown in the *Codex Boturini* (fol. 2). Such a bundle may be likened to the medicine bundles used by Native North American peoples. These bundles are filled with various objects, carvings, bones, feathers, etc., that embody particular potencies used to make things happen or to give strength or special powers to their owners.

120. Acopilco was a hot spring in Lake Texcoco just to the east of Tenochtitlan's island (Gonzalez Aparicio 1980).

121. One way to understand this overcoming of female ancestry might be to see it as a result of a male-dominated society. However, when dealing with cultural situations different from one's own, one needs to be cautious before making such judgments.

There were, for example, instances of female rulership, of female warriors, and of female conquest over males. The *Códice Garcia Granados* depicts five women seated in the pose of rulership (Mercader Martinez 1979, cover photo). Torquemada speaks of female warriors (reprint 1975–83, vol. 3, bk. 10, chap. 35:426–27); Coyolxauhqui (like her mother, Coatlicue) is depicted in warrior garb (Pasztory 1983, plates 102–103); and there were two different types of females who, upon death, became goddesses charged with carrying the sun to its western entrance: "women who died in war and precious/quetzal women [those who died in childbirth and who died in war]" (*in jaomjcque cioa ioan in mocioaquetzque*) (FC, bk. 7, pt. 8, chap. 29:162–63). Moreover, under certain instances, female sexuality and war appear to have been equated as modes of both conquest and fertility (Read and Rosenthal 1988; Read, forthcoming).

In the particular mythic instances cited here, it seems quite possible that the workings of a kinship system in which the female line played an important role is being described metaphorically; i.e., in order to conquer another group, one conquered the female line. Huitzilopochtli may have conquered two sisters so that his own line, through his mother, would be in power.

122. This is an abbreviated retelling of a story told in Spanish by Durán (HI, chap. 27:215–24; 1994, 27:212–22). Its counterpart story, the story of the Tenochca's departure from this place, can also be found there (HI 1984 chap. 2:21–6; 1994, 2:12–19).

123. The often made distinction between shaman (one who practices magic in order to control directly the sacred for the purposes of individual needs) and priest (an intermediary who, as a member of a religious institution, supplicates the sacred for the purposes of resolving communal problems) does not apply in this situation. These terms ultimately rest on a distinction made by early-twentieth-century British historian Sir James George Frazer in his landmark book *The Golden Bough* (1992, rpt. 1963). But the terms are inadequate to the whole Mesoamerican context. The Mexica case is much closer to the one Barbara Tedlock found when she studied the present diviners of the Quiché Maya in Momostenango, Guatemala (1982, 47–53). These people served functions from both categories. Therefore, I am borrowing her terms here, "priest-shaman" or "shaman-priest."

124. Recall here the mouth of the cave-house at Malinalco (n. 117).

125. This is a beautiful plant with yellow flowers and a lovely aroma that was used to perfume cocoa when it was made into a drink.

126. An ointment was made by mixing the ashes of burned scorpions, spiders, vipers, centipedes, and gila monsters with tobacco. This was then kneaded with a few live spiders and scorpions and ground seeds of the ololiuhqui plant. Finally, the ashes of black and hairy worms were blended into this delightful mixture. The hairs of the latter are poisonous, while the seeds of the ololiuhqui plant are hallucinogenic and were used to obtain visions. The Spanish author tells us that this salve helped priests to lose any fear they might have and to acquire a great courage (*grande ánimo*). This spirit (*espíritu*) helped them to perform sacrifices and to turn into "witches" who spoke with the "devil." It is said they went in the night to the mountains where there were lions, tigers, wolves, and serpents to transform into the "devil" (Acosta, reprint 1978, 66–67).

127. There is a discrepancy between the number of names given and the total that follows. Durán has apparently made a mistake. In the *Codex Boturini*, eight leaders are shown with four more leaders in front (fol. 1). But elsewhere, in *Historia Tolteca Chichimeca: Anales de Quauhtinchan* (1947, fol. 7), seven tribes are said to have migrated from Chicomoztoc and seven is the number used through out the rest of this story. So it is difficult to tell which is correct.

128. This may be referring to the *teonacaztli* plant that was mixed with cocoa and was listed earlier as one of the gifts.

129. These references suggest that the shaman-priests gained souls that entered the bodies of various animals. If this were so, then one danger might be that these souls would not return at the end of the journey and thus be seen as having been eaten. This is reminiscent of the many sculptural images of little heads appearing from within the mouths of the same types of animals listed here: snakes, birds, and jaguars.

130. This verse comes from the "Anales de Cuauhtitlan," one of two other texts contained along with "The Legend of the Suns" in the *Codex Chimalpopoca* (1938, 63) and *Códice Chimalpopoca* (1992b, fol. 2:42–45, 5).

131. "Its day sign" (*itonal*) also means its "warmth of the sun," "day," "summertime," and "animistic spirit."

132. There may never be a mention of a sixth age for the simple reason that it is pointless to discuss the forms of the age to come if it is the forms of one's own age (including one's own personal age) that are ending. If one's self disappears, it is difficult to know what takes one's place next.

133. Clara Sue Kidwell has noted that in many parts of ancient Native America, things bore both an outer and an inner nature (1992, 396). It makes sense then that changing a thing's outer appearance will change its inner nature.

134. All these things resulting from failure—moons, jaguars, and food—also are associated with the decaying and dark underworld. More on these kinds of cosmological metaphors will be discussed in chapter 4.

135. On the Sun Stone (figure 12), each of the five ages is represented by a pictographic glyph of a head depicting that age's name and destruction. The first is a jaguar head, the second is the head of Ehecatl (the wind god), the third is the head of Tlaloc (the water and mountain god), the fourth is probably that of Chalchiuhtlicue (the water goddess), and the fifth is a large face with an open mouth filled with many teeth and a tongue in the shape of a sacrificial knife. The identity of this figure is the subject of much discussion.

3. Shaping Time

1. A tumpline is a kind of sling that is thrown around one's forehead to support bundles carried on one's back (see figures 8 and 9). People have been known to carry burdens over a hundred pounds using tumplines. In figure 9, "Toltec" refers to the inhabitants of either the city of Tula during its hegemony or one of the cities influenced by it.

2. "Its work" (*itequiuh*) also means "tribute."

3. FC, bk. 7, pt. 8, chap. 7:21–22.

4. "Year-day" refers to both a day-sign and date glyph, which is also one of the four year signs. The word refers to something more that is important, for included in this word is *tonalli*, which means "the heat," "the day," and "the summertime." The *tonalli* was one of the animated entities making up a living person. Upon a person's death, bits and pieces of the *tonalli* could be gathered up and kept in a box along with greenstones and chunks of bone. Perhaps a living being was "heated" by a temporal entity which gave her force and power in life, a power which, because it was temporal in nature, did not totally disappear at death. Time, after all, kept on going.

5. "The Place of Thorns" is the South (see Birth: V.30). Since time and space were one entity, time was given a spatial orientation.

6. The way numbers are translated literally indicates their mathematical logic: 13 (*matlactli omei*) is 10 + 3; 52 years (*ompohualxihuitl om matlactliomome*) is (2 x 20 years) + (10 + 2); and 676 (*centzonxihuitl ipan matlacpohualxihuitl ipan yepohualxihuitl ipan ye no caxtolxihuitl oze*) is 400 years + (10

x 20 years) + (3 x 20 years) + 15 years + 1. The numbers used for calculations also may be written by means of number glyphs (Closs 1986, 213–36).

7. "It governs them" (*tlatqui*) also means "to raise up" and "to carry."

8. Rulers governed for a particular period of time just as the sun bore its burden for a set period. "It bears them" (*tlamama*) means both "to bear something on one's shoulders" and "to govern." This together with "it governs them" (*tlatqui*) suggests a confluence of terms describing this close relationship between political governance and time.

9. This particular verse is less subtle about its calendrical information than some others. Only after working with a living Quiché time keeper, for example, did Dennis Tedlock (1985) learn of the esoteric calendrical counts hidden behind the metaphoric imagery of the *Popol Vuh*. A whole cosmological system calculated by the cycles of Venus and other celestial bodies was indicated by the actions of various gods and such innocent metaphors as a net bag. Because no numbers were given in this story, the only way he could learn this was by being trained in the calendrical system itself. The lesson to be learned from this is that the centrality and pervasive nature of Mesoamerican calendrics easily may be missed in sixteenth-century sources, especially because much was collected under the highly critical eye of conquest.

10. The Mexica calendar consisted of many, many rounds all simultaneously intermeshed.

11. Describing time as "linear" or repetitiously "cyclical" are also heuristic devices.

12. The word root for *Culhuacan* is the passive form of *colli*, which means "grandfather." The related word root *coloa* means variously "to twist," "to encircle," "to curve," "to bend," "to fold," "to double back," "to change direction," and "to detour around." The name glyph for Culhuacan may refer to the twisting of time that appears in concepts of ancestry, perhaps meaning "place in which things are twisted" or "place in which ancestors are curved back to." The meaning is deepened when one learns that spun ropes depicted ancestry and the place glyph for Colhuacan was a hill with a curled or curved top (figure 7.1), images reminding one of the ancestors living at the hill of Aztlan and their ability to change the direction of their time spans.

13. A similar spiral format for this calendrical spinning helps structure the *Codex en Cruz* (1981).

14. Once I heard a gentleman from Guatemala explain that "time is like a spiral, it keeps coming back." This man, who was describing what it meant to be Maya to an undergraduate class on religious studies at DePaul University, drew a spiral on the blackboard to explain this concept. Later, while discussing the Maya cosmogonic myth they called the "Pop' Vuh," his companion and teacher explained to me that the sacrifice of creatures such as chickens helps the cosmos to continue living by returning "life for life." These two statements are in close keeping with what I am suggesting here about sixteenth-century Mexica-

Tenochca concepts of time and sacrifice. Time spirals forward while returning to the past, and sacrifice keeps it spiraling by giving "life for life."

Spun rope, with its twists usually clearly marked, frequently appears as an iconographic element associated with temporal issues in Mesoamerican and specifically Mexica-Tenochca sources. Several small clay disks, for example, each imprinted with a five-layered spiral, have been unearthed from the Templo Mayor excavations (The Templo Mayor Museum in Mexico City). One disk displays, in its center, a cord knotted into a loop that is similar to the looped cords appearing in the *Papers of Itzcuintepec*. Here, looped and spun cords are associated with year glyphs and joined genealogical bonds (Nicholson 1966, 141–43). See also Cecelia Klein (1982, 1–35) for many examples of spinning and fiber arts representing Mesoamerican cosmological and temporal conceptions.

15. Susan Gillespie, for example, notes that Mexica time had both linear and cyclical elements. But then, citing David Carrasco, she goes on to reconcile these two configurations in a way commensurate with Eliade. This allows her to ignore (to borrow Eliade's term, perhaps even "kill") historical time by concentrating almost exclusively on its cyclical elements. Mexica time, for Gillespie, periodically reshaped the present and future by equating it with deified moments in the past, thereby making it possible for both a cosmic "mandate" to reassert itself and the present to repeat that mandate's powers. Hence the "pictographic 'books'" were "very sketchy," for greater precision would not have allowed the "variation and modification" necessary to this repetitive process in which the present was made the same as the past in order to shape the future (1989 xxii–xxvi).

Gillespie is comfortably in line with the school of thought that has spawned Eliade, Ricoeur, and D. Carrasco. I, however, will be *re-presenting* this school in order to bring it in line with the tremendous precision I believe many of the pre-Conquest books actually often carried and the concepts of ongoing transformation I believe those books expressed. The present did not repeat the past, but reworked it. History was not periodically ignored in order to return to any "mandate" of the *primordium*, but history was all there was, and history, not an eternally unchanging *primordium*, was the source of authoritative creation. Finally, it was the very existence of two carefully coordinated motions—cyclical and linear—that made all this possible. One did not overcome the other; together they created a transformative reality.

16. Edmonson places the first calendric documentation in the Mexican Highlands at Cuicuilco in 739 B.C.E. (1988, x, 116–17). Some of the oldest archaeological evidence is found on stela 12 at Monte Albán, Oaxaca, dating, according to Edmonson, to 542 B.C.E. (ibid. 268). See Gossen (1974), Colby and Colby (1981), van der Loo (1981), and B. Tedlock (1982) for examples of the continuation of ancient calendrical orientations in use among modern groups.

17. It is unclear what celestial motions structured the divinatory calendar; everything from agricultural seasons in Honduras to human gestation to the

moon's cycle have been suggested. This lack of clarity is due to its age, which is so ancient that its origin is now lost. Moreover, its ancient venerability has been extended, for this calendar continues to thrive in many parts of Mexico today.

18. Besides Appendix 2, see Anthony Aveni (1980, 1989) for introductory discussions on Mesoamerican calendrics.

19. Munro Edmonson (1988) presents strong evidence for the foundational role played by the days in all Mesoamerican calendrics.

20. *Xiuhmolpilli* is formed from the word root *xiuitl*, which means "year," "turquoise," "comet," "grass," "herb," and "leaf." Karttunen reports that it is used as an intensifier for heat in much the same way that "white" or "blue" are in English. By combining *xiuitl* with *molpia* (to be bound), the word means literally "bound years." This suggests that the solar years were associated with plants and strong heat much the way that *tonalli* also included a notion of time as fertility and heat. It was binding that ordered that fertility and heat. Edmonson (1988, ix) views this fifty-two-year count as the most constant and basic cycle in all Mesoamerican calendrical systems.

21. *Tonalpohualli* is based on two word roots, *tonal* and *pohua*. *Tonal* is a complex root which means "heat of the sun," "summertime," "soul," "spirit," "sign of birth," and "that part or portion which is the destiny of someone." *Pohua* means variously "to count," "to estimate," "to evaluate," "to predict," or "to divine" and in its bound form, *-pohualli*, "a unit of twenty" or "something countable." This suggests that the sun's heat is equated with existence and calculated by a calendrical system. As will be seen, this calendar (which is based on a set of twenty days) is the basis for divination in Mesoamerica.

22. For astronomical information on the New Fire rite, see Aveni (1980, 33–34) and Broda (1983, 145–64).

23. A circle and a spiral, while both cyclical, constitute very different configurations. The former always returns to the exact same point while the latter does not. Spinning, moreover, adds a dimension to spiraling by including the possibility of multiple counts being constantly introduced, overlapping with other counts and then ending. Spun rope also allows an image of doubling back to create a fatter group of threads or a larger set of cycles.

24. Figure 9 depicts the four year-signs: Reed (*acatl*), Knife (*tecpatl*), House (*calli*), and Rabbit (*tochtli*). These names are used to designate solar year, and they appear in a sequence that is repeated over and over again. One year would be called Reed, the next Knife, the next House, Rabbit, Reed, Knife, House, Rabbit, and so on. In "The Myth of the Four Ages," the first age ends on 1-Reed, the second and third each on 1-Knife, and the fourth on 1-House. This leaves 1-Rabbit for the Fifth Age, whose story comes later in the text (CC 1992a, 147–49; 1992b, fols. 77:27–78:23, 90).

25. Age Two: (7 x 52) 364 years long

$$+$$

Age Three: (6 x 52) 312 years long

(13 x 52) 676 years long

Three of the major calendrical rounds of the Mexica system are coordinated in this myth, rounds that are discussed in more detail in Appendix 2. By joining ages two and three numerically and having them share the same calendrical sign for the year of their destruction, the myth is anticipating the Fifth Age (myth 1: I. 11–18; II. 10–13; III. 8–10; IV. 1–5), an event that occurs after the four ages and the creation of people and corn in "The Legend of the Suns."

26. This is drawn from a section on adages in the *Florentine Codex*. The first passage is the adage itself; the second is a somewhat more poetic explanation of it (FC, bk. 6, pt. 7, chap. 41: 235).

27. Again, Nahuatl does not separate what English does. A single word (*iuhcan*) indicates what English must use a whole phrase for, "like so there and then."

28. Notions of wholeness and completion are often used in situations involving action which has ended and begun again. The idea of completed and uncompleted actions is one of fulfillment; time, actions, and things are unfulfilled, fulfilled, then unfulfilled again. In chapters 4 and 5, this same sense of uncompleted completion will appear in actions involving moral transgressions and again in the ritual pattern of the New Fire ceremony itself. "Was being completed" (*mochioaia cenca*) means literally "to occur/come about completely" and is in the imperfective tense, giving it a sense of ongoing action.

29. Again, time and place are not distinguished so that when time is discussed, space and matter are simultaneously considered. "Long ago and far away" (*uehcauh*) means both something that is old and a long period of time. It means "to attain a great age" or "to remain in one place for a long time." The form used here, *ye huehcauh*, has the highly suggestive meaning of "on the other side" (Karttunen 1983, 82, 336). While rather enigmatic, this last intention may refer to a spatial understanding of time periods.

30. Given (a) that this tradition seems to be a very widespread tradition; (b) that some examples of it come to us recorded not only in Spanish but also in two indigenous forms of communication, Nahuatl and graphic representation; (c) that the Mixtec also had a pre-Conquest form of history which, while distinctively Mixtec, also bears some resemblance to that of the Highlands and may be directly ancestral to it; and (d) that a genre of histories telling about the origins and past events of various groups of people can be found in the form of migration stories all over the Americas, it appears likely that these histories predate the Spanish, at least in their general format. In other words, it seems to me to be very unlikely that the *anales* tradition was totally a European introduction. Rather, the Mesoamericans sequentially ordered narrations about their past long before the Spanish ever arrived.

31. Boone notes a number of very interesting regional variations in the painted manuscripts of the Aztec Empire, manuscripts which also depict attitudes toward time and history. The *anales* tradition, which utilizes the continuous year count, may have been developed primarily by the Culhua Mexica of Tenochtitlan, who focused on a particular kind of royal history. The Mixtec appear to have developed a different style which focused on the deeds done by particular people

(1987, 5–7, 10–20). To be fair, Boone is not entirely convinced that her suggestions are fully supportable, for she feels that not all the data have been collected yet (in conversation, 2 August 1988). If she is right, however, it would indicate an indigenous sense of sequential time that had been rooted long enough in the culture to develop different regional styles by the time the Spanish arrived.

32. The *Codex en Cruz*, a codex containing pre-Conquest historical references to both Texcoco and Tenochtitlan, pictures time with just this double orientation. While showing the fifty-two years spiraling around, it also shows the important events of each sequential year in an *anales*-style depiction.

33. See Appendix 2 for a detailed discussion of the workings of the calendrical system in terms of its math, its shape, and how those mesh with the philosophic picture I am painting here.

34. Venus may also have been an odd countercount. See Appendix 2.

4. Timing and Shaping People

1. *Mahceua* repeatedly appears in contexts describing the who, how, why, where, and when of the flowing of powerful influences, not, as many think, in the context of doing penance. This will be expanded in chapter 4. See chapter 1, note 19 for a discussion of the complexities of translating this word.

2. An excellent discussion of the various bodily animistic centers, animistic entities, and concepts about death can be found in López Austin (1988b). An animistic center was a place within the body in which animistic forces or vital substances were concentrated. It was here that basic impulses originated for directing the processes that gave life and movement to the organism. These forces also permitted the fulfillment of psychic functions. *Ixtli* was part of the *ix* group, which focused on knowledge and could be reduced to the functions of perception. Thus, to take on *ixtli* may have meant to acquire complete control of an organ of perception, one of the manifestations of a conscious state. López Austin notes that *ixtli* can mean either "face" or "eye." Given the context of *ixtli* in the myth about the birth of the Fifth Sun, I would suggest that its intent is that of the former and means "that part of man where sensation, perception, understanding, and feeling unite in order to integrate a complete consciousness that is found in communication with the outside world" (1988b, 197).

3. If a baby died before eating corn, it went to Chichiualquauitl, one of the four lands of the dead. There it sucked milk from breasts that hung on a tree as oranges hang from an orange tree. It is said that these children were to repopulate the world after it was destroyed (*Códice Vaticano Latino 3738*, reproduction 1964, 3:fol. 4).

4. As may have been noticed, corn seems to have a somewhat confusing role in these sources. In the first, the references to babies, corn appears as the substance that ties people to the earth. In the second, the story about the Mexica's visit to Aztlan, corn is the food of a land where immortality appears to be possible, and chocolate is the item specifically mentioned as the substance that ties

people to death. There is often confusion of this sort over details within the sources, confusion which may have as much to do with the manner in which the sources were collected as with anything else. The earlier collectors may not have gotten it right, or the two versions may have come from different peoples. Or the meaning here may be that corn ties one to an age in general so that babies who die while still nursing are born into the next age and not into the current one. Chocolate may be a food identified specifically with the Mexica-Tenochca, one of many groups living in the Fifth Sun. All this must be conjecture, however, since there appears little in the sources to give us a definitive answer.

5. It is important to remember that this is not in any way comparable to Christian soul concepts, nor can these concepts be compared to notions concerning a division between the material body and the nonmaterial spirit, a concept logically impossible in a system which does not distinguish between space and time. It should also be noted that it is quite common to find notions similar to this Nahua concept of multiple animistic entities in other Native American contexts.

6. López Austin, conversation, 30 August 1990.

7. This has been translated from the Nahuatl given in Bierhorst (1985, 184, folio 17, lines 15–19). These are just a few lines from a poem attributed to the sixteenth-century "poet-ruler" of Texcoco, Nezahualcoyotl. It is contained in a manuscript which, if not collected by Sahagún, was known to him. Bierhorst believes that this manuscript can be dated no earlier than 1585, since the selections contained therein show a number of influences ranging from various pre-Conquest sources to Christian. Each piece in this collection is difficult to date, however. While many accept that at least some of the material is pre-Conquest in origin, Bierhorst suggests that all of it is representative of a single post-Conquest revitalization movement. To confuse the issue further, the actual poethood of Nezahualcoyotl himself is difficult to establish and may be a post-Conquest fabrication of the Mestizo historian from Texcoco, Ixtlilxochitl (1985, 3–5, 7–8, 103–104, 106–109; Wauchope 1964–76, 15:329, 337, 352).

8. "Traveling" appears to be emphasizing a fleeting sense of time in both people and things. It is based on "to go" (*ya*), which has a sense of motion rather like journeying.

9. This is an exclamation which is being used rhythmically in the song and is untranslatable.

10. The moving sense of "go" suggests people traveling on a long trip or peregrination. Because a sense of transformation is fairly strong in this passage, I used the term "travel" in this and the above phrase concerning Nezahualcoyotl to emphasize this sense. "Travelers all" comes from *yahui*, which means "someone who has been on a long journey."

11. For the days of each thirteen-day *trecena* or "week," there were thirteen signs, one for each day. Each sign carried good and bad qualities it would im-

part to the child. A few signs were largely good, a few largely bad, and most contained both. Apparently the naming of a child could take place on any of the thirteen days of the week in which it was born. Generally, one named a child on the fourth day after birth if the signs were propitious; if not, another day could be chosen. Since a naming ceremony was an expensive affair, the poor often had less choice, for if a full-blown ceremony could not be afforded, then the child had to be named on the fourth day after birth no matter what the merit of that day might mean (FC, bk. 4, pt. 5; bk. 6, pt. 7, chap. 36:197–99).

12. If textile artists did not control their sexuality, they would become harlots and contract sexually related diseases. The diseases associated directly or indirectly with Xochiquetzal (acquired by promiscuity and relieved by sacrificial rituals) were all, categorically, sexual in nature, all of them skin lesions appearing in the body's sexual area such as buboes, piles, and chancres (FC, bk. 1, pt 2, chap. 14:31; Durán 1971, 246; *Codex Telleriano Remensis*, 3rd Trecena).

13. López Austin suggests that gods "influenced [people's] conduct so their death would come as a consequence of the act they themselves inspired" (1988b, 331–32). In other words, one's actions might bring on one's death or a god could influence those actions. Or, by the appropriate behavior, one could influence a god to act more favorably toward oneself.

14. In a moving passage from the *Florentine Codex*, a mother gives words of advice to her daughter. The child is told that she descends from her ancestors and that her actions can alter the effect of the *mahceua* (merit) received on her naming day. She is warned that poor behavior will bring dishonor and good behavior can help overturn the bad draw of a poor divinatory sign (FC, bk. 6, pt. 7, chap. 18:94–95).

15. To further draw out the unique sense of Mexica time and sacrifice, an analytic comparison between myth and rite will be detailed in chapter 6.

5. The Cosmic Meal

1. The name Xiuhtlaminmani indicates many of the active forces involved in giving birth to a fifty-two-year cycle and suggests the message that hunting and war give motion and life to the new sun. Included in this word are "to capture," "hunt," "fish" (*ma*), and "to shoot a bow and arrow or harpoon" (*tlamina*); and "year," "turquoise," "comet," and "herb" (*xiuihtl*). Comets were often equated with arrows and years were said "to blossom" like plants (Karttunen 1983; Molina 1970; López Austin, conversation, 28 August 1990).

2. According to López Austin, the sun equaled comet-arrows intended to shoot jaguar spirits released by things of the night, something that makes the actual moment of sacrifice especially dangerous. Xiuhtlamin, as his name suggests, was equated with those protective arrows (conversation, 28 August 1990).

3. According to Durán, at least some priestly offices involving sacrificial duties were handed from father to son as in "primogeniture" (Durán 1971, 90–91).

4. Although the text is not specific, the metaphoric consumption of gods and Xiuhtlamin is possible. Amaranth cakes in the shape of the sacrificial offerings frequently were consumed at other rites. Durán, for example, tells us that *tzoalli* (amaranth dough) "was always used to make images of the gods—the 'flesh' and 'bones' of the deities" (1971, 203).

5. Although this text does not say anything specific about the matter, the humans being sacrificed were possibly slaves bought in the marketplace. Slaves were considered tlahtlacotin (messed-up or disarrayed ones) because they were people who had failed in some way. Tlahtlacotin fell into this state because of such things as murder, theft, bad debts, or adultery. Chapter 6 will expand on this.

6. Fray Diego Durán and Fray Bernardino de Sahagún, for example, seem to hold somewhat different personal attitudes toward the many diverse sacrificial rituals they observed. Whereas Sahagún often calls it a "debt," occasionally brings up an iconoclastic issue of idolatry, and holds reflections about the devil to a minimum, Durán often makes comparisons between Mexica and Catholic practices on the theory that the Indians were originally Hebrews who were led astray by that satanical figure. Ruiz de Alarcón, however, observed far less dramatic folk practices and tends to see such bloodletting rites as mere superstition. Given the centrality of sacrifice to Christianity, it is not surprising that Mexica practices would greatly concern the Spanish clergy.

7. A selected bibliography including both specialist and generalist treatments of human sacrifice may be roughly grouped according to the following categories. Those setting sacrifice into some sort of evolutionary schema include Alfonso Caso (1953), Sir James George Frazer (1922, reprint 1963), René Girard (1977), William Robertson Smith (1886), and Edward Burnett Tylor (1874, reprint 1970). Those who focus on environmental, biological, political, social, or psychological functions include Geoffrey Conrad and Arthur Demerest (1984), Yolotl Gonzalez Torres (1985), Michael Harner (1977, 117–35), Marvin Harris (1977), and Peggy Reeves Sanday (1986). Those focusing on religious and symbolic reasons include Nigel Davies (1981), Christian Duverger (1983), A. M. Hocart (1936, reprint 1970), Henri Hubert and Marcel Mauss (1898, 29–138; reprints 1964, 1981), Marcel Mauss (1925, trans. 1967), Bernard Ortiz de Montellano (1978, 611–617), and Valerio Valeri (1985). Each author has his or her own distinctive orientation within these categories and several could be placed in more than one. Finally, Elizabeth P. Benson and Elizabeth H. Boone (1984) have edited a useful collection of diverse articles on Mesoamerican sacrifice from a wide geographic and cultural area.

8. For example, see Caso (1953), López Austin (1988b), and Eduardo Matos Moctezuma (1987, 185–207) for three different variations on the bond between life and death in Aztec rituals. My contribution on this is yet another variation on this classic sacrificial theme and is discussed at length below.

9. The textual situation in Mesoamerican studies is especially tricky, making

it difficult for specialists and nonspecialists alike to find sufficiently sophisticated research methods. Nonspecialists, in particular, have encountered problems, frequently failing to recognize, for example, the fragmented condition of the sources or the complicated issues involved in accounting for the Spanish voices. Interpretation in the Mexica case depends heavily on a huge range of materials, a knowledge of the indigenous language, and an ability for iconographic interpretations, all things difficult for nonspecialists to accomplish without becoming specialists. As Edmund Leach noted (1976), the essence of interpretation lies in the details (see also López Austin 1988b, 1–48). Unfortunately, many nonspecialists often have tended to ignore significant details, treating the materials in a naive and superficial manner. For these reasons, past comparative studies often either tended to avoid Mesoamerican materials or lacked an adequate base in them. As I hope to demonstrate, while the essence of interpretation lies in the details, the details do not deny comparison but make it possible by means of a process of *re-presentation*.

10. Michel Graulich (1988, 393–404) discusses double offerings.

11. To many readers, "logic" might have a static quality because of its natural link with "reason" in Western philosophy. Here, however, I must emphasize that whatever logic I endow the Mexica cosmos with is set firmly in a particular context and at a particular moment, that of the sixteenth-century Mexica-Tenochca as they appear in the materials available to us. This cosmo-logic in no way should be construed as representative of all Mesoamericans for all time.

12. While domestication of such things as fish, dogs, and turkeys certainly made significant contributions to the Mexica diet, herding anything larger was never a real possibility, for there were no animals to herd. Some Mayan groups may have had partially domesticated deer (Adams 1991, 143), but these animals have never lent themselves to full domestication. Hence, hunting both small and large wild game remained important.

13. These remarks do not in any way imply a direct cause-and-effect relationship between the environment and religious structures. Nevertheless, metaphoric thinking is interdependent with its environmental and semantic contexts, even though one does not necessarily precede or result in the other. No one develops her spiritual or religious sensitivities in a vacuum, for all are deeply affected by their interrelationships with their physical and cultural contexts.

14. Many before have noted the phagocentric character of the Mexica sacrificial cosmos. The work presented here is based on the extensive treatment of the topic in my dissertation for the Ph.D. (1991). Recently Davíd Carrasco has offered a brief treatment of the same topic (1995).

15. Both corn and children came from the same place to which Quetzalcoatl took the bones to be ground into dough for people, the cosmic tree in the west, Tamoanchan (CC 1992a, 146; 1992b, fol. 76:51, 89; FC, bk. 6, pt. 7: 167).

16. The complex and confusing gender of the earth is discussed further below.

17. The word *mixcoatl* means clouds that spin or turn, such as tornadoes or hurricanes. *Mixcoa* means "cloud-snake."

18. Bowel movements also are a sign of one's state of health.

19. Eduard Seler said the yellow bands across Huitzilopochtli's face were made of babies' excrement (López Austin 1988a, 54).

20. This is the kind of soaking given by licking things with one's tongue (*paltia*) (conversation with López Austin, 28 August 1990), something curiously appropriate to a figure depicted by a skull with a strong jaw and teeth.

21. For additional (and somewhat different) comments on cosmology, see Cecelia Klein (1982, 1–35); and López Austin (1988a, 49–88).

22. In other words, existence continues to spiral forward through history, but it does so within a confined space. This is somewhat like karmic cycling within a Hindu cosmos. All is contained in Brahman, yet all continues to flow through time in the samsaric world. The major difference is that there is absolutely no concept of either moksha or nirvana here. The cycling simply continues.

23. It is always a danger when mapping out spatial relationships to presume that they have a kind of timelessness they probably do not deserve. What follows is a sketch of sixteenth-century Mexica-Tenochca cosmological structures which, while related to general Mesoamerican patterns, cannot be presumed to have existed in exactly this form for all of Mesoamerican history. Mesoamerica was a richly diverse culture area providing many options for cosmological structuring. Since spatial cosmologies were connected intimately with specific, physical topographies, they necessarily would have to vary from place to place and from time to time.

24. The Mixtec calendrical codex *Fejérváry-Mayer* depicts the four-sided division of the cosmos (see figure 15 in Appendix 2).

25. Yomeyocan or Omeyocan means "the place and time of twoness." This place was inhabited by a male/female couple, Ometecutli (Two Lord) and Omecihuatl (Two Lady), who engendered four major gods before the first sun was created. Thus this "twoness" is one of male/female fertility. Yomeyocan was probably meant to read *in omeyocan*. It is built on the word for "two" (*ome*), the suffix, *-yo-*, and the postposition, *-can*, meaning place and time. *Yo* is added to a word to stress a quality or state of being. Hence, *omeyotl* would mean "twoness."

26. These two pages of the *Códice Vaticano Latino* have had more influence than any other single text in formulating current descriptions of Mexica cosmology. Therefore, it is all the more important to consider carefully the voices that may be part of past conversations concerning this text, for those voices are also very much a part of present conversations.

27. The codex *Fejérváry-Mayer* places Mictlan in the north (see figure 15).

28. Several other sources (probably from other areas) list different skies and underworlds, something indicating their indigenous nature. If these skies and underworlds were actually ritual or pilgrimage sites on the earth's surface (as is suggested by the *Florentine Codex*), they would have to differ according to local

physical topography and custom. Like the many calendrical variations, such local variation is common. Even if these skies and underworlds were layered, one still should not overlook the essential horizontality of the Mexica cosmos, a cosmology otherwise quite comparable to others in the southwestern United States. There, levels of underworlds are spoken about, but again, the stress is on two worlds, an upper and a lower with the earth's surface spreading out between. Various openings allow the two worlds to communicate. This is especially true of Pueblo mythology, a more appropriate analogy than anything from medieval Europe. See López Austin (1988b, 54–55), who takes an alternative view yet nevertheless has created an interesting synthesis of the various sources.

29. There is a problem with the translation of the earth monster's name, Atlalteutli. This is a sixteenth-century French translation of a lost Spanish text. The names for the deities are given in Nahuatl, although nothing else is. Its twentieth-century publisher glosses this deity as Tlalteutli, although direct evidence for this is lacking. Moreover, in the *Pinturas* version of the story, this earthly beast is equated with a crocodile-like figure called Cipactli (*Historia de los Mexicanos por sus pinturas*, 26) who also is the glyph for the first day-sign, something commensurate with the beginning of time and the mythic import of the tale. Whatever its various possible associations, however, the particular monster in this myth is a metaphor for the creation of cultivable land whose name it includes (*atlalli*).

30. H. B. Nicholson as cited in Pasztory (1983, 82).

31. The earth is called Lord (Tlalteuctli) in the *Codex Chimalpopoca* (1992b, fol. 76:19, 88). And, while gold is called the excrement of the sun, which, if it is attributed any gender at all, is usually considered male, it is also the urine of its mother, the earth (FC, bk. 11, pt. 12, chap. 9:233). López Austin suggests that the upper half of the fully female Cipactli became the earth's surface, and the lower half, the underworld. He also pairs the sky with male and earth with female while noting the contradictions in the sources (1988b, 53–56; conversation, 29 August 1990). In spite of the problems, I have found this pairing useful below. My only caution is not to assume too quickly that all things associated with the earth are automatically considered female. The underworld, after all, is populated by many nasty male deities while a number of both good and bad female deities come from the sky.

32. The old fire god is shown in the center of the cosmic graph found in the frontispiece to the Codex *Fejérváry-Mayer* (see figure 15).

33. This also suggests that the entrance to Mictlan was located at the edge of the universe, where sky and earth meet, something comparable to the cosmology of the Tewa, another member of the Uto-Aztecan language group (Ortiz 1969).

34. Interesting associations belong to deities whose names include *atlalli*. For example, Atlatonan was a goddess of the maimed, lepers, and those with sores (Durán 1971, 223, 228), which echoes both the dismemberment of the

earth monster and the natural state of decay of things of the earth. Atlalteotl was a deity of both water and earth, again a reasonable association (López Austin conversation, 29 August 1990).

35. This refers to the two days on which the sun passes through the zenith, something that occurs only in the tropics. It probably occurred close to the summer solstice (Aveni 1980, 65–66).

36. One might imagine this cosmos as being bounded by walls of water. Inside, the sun moved along these watery walls, drying out Earth's Surface during the day; during the night, the sun moved through the moist and rotting underground.

37. This coordinates with the dualistic scheme suggested by López Austin (1988b, 53).

38. Twenty-one varieties of water and fifty-four varieties of earth are listed in the *Florentine*, the vast majority of which are categorized by their usefulness, based on their water properties. Obviously water was a major concern (FC, bk. 11, pt. 12, chap. 12:247–58).

39. Sahagún as quoted in Howard F. Cline (1971, 245) and Klor de Alva (1980, 69).

40. This is roughly comparable to concepts of power or *mana* frequently described in classic literature on comparative religion. See Hvidfeldt's introduction (1958), for a discussion of the issue.

41. The Nahua did not discuss *teotl* by itself, as we are doing here. This was natural, since these powers could not be separated from physical objects. Nahuatl always includes powers in something else by using a prefix form that cannot stand alone (*teo-*). We are the ones who are focusing on these powers as a category that can be distinguished from the physical world. Therefore, I have coined an abstract form of the prefix *teo-* in order to distinguish "powers" (*teoyome*) from "gods" (*teteo*), which did stand alone since gods were considered autonomous beings. By so doing, I underscore the degree to which this project is set firmly in twentieth-century concerns.

I have done this even though Molina gives a word that might be construed as an abstract principle of power (1977, Nahuatl section, 100v). This word *teoyotica* (*spiritualmente*), however, may have been constructed in post-Conquest times by someone like Molina to help with missionizing. Literally translated, *teoyotica* means "with-powerness" (*teo* + *yo* + [abstraction] + *ti* [ligature] + *ca* [postposition, with]). It is followed by a long list of words, all having to do with matters of Catholicism, such as administering the sacraments, excommunion, the clergy, and marriage in the church. Moreover, the word rarely (if ever) appears in Nahuatl texts not concerned with Catholicism. This suggests that it may have been fabricated in order to appropriate for the church's purposes the idea of a cosmos filled with powers.

42. Sam Gill describes a similar kind of masking among the Hopi (1987, 42–44).

43. Although I describe some categories that appear to be indigenous, this is not one of them. Rather, these levels of existence are no more than a heuristic device intended to lend coherency to some complex material.

44. Again, male/female fertility here is indicated as a kind of necessary "twoness."

45. Jade attracts moistness, as do all things of the underworld, and therefore must be open to rottenness (FC, bk. 11, pt. 12, chap. 8:222–23). As Nezahualcoyotl says in his poem about the fleeting moment, it too must "shatter."

46. See n. 2:19 for a discussion of the problems translating *mahceua* and chapter 4 for a discussion of personal merit.

47. See Durán (1971, 281–86) for information on transgressions and their rectification.

48. The Tewa have a similar moist-dry, raw-cooked metaphor (Ortiz 1969, 16–18). Lévi-Strauss would have had fun with this.

6. Burning and Binding Fires

1. Like Tezcatlipoca, iconographically, Huitzilopochtli's left foot is distorted.

2. For an expansion on the lack of divisions between the sacred and profane and the supernatural and natural, see López Austin (1990, 147–69).

3. López Austin 1990, 180–85, 200–204; and conversation, 30 August 1990.

4. Gods ate only things such as the aroma of copal and flowers, tobacco smoke, and blood (conversation, López Austin, 30 August 1990). They didn't eat the earth's corn and therefore were not subject to the same patterns of change that people were. Although nobles ingested some immortality with their special food because it also was godly food, as humans in the Fifth Sun, they still ate corn grown on Tlalticpac. Huitzilopochtli and the tutor, however, were tied to the apparently special corn of Aztlan, where *space-time* did not operate in the same way. Perhaps Coatlicue and her tutor did not want the Mexica's rich gifts because they would have tied them to Tlalticpac. In matters of eating, Aztlan appears as the inversion of earth—that which gives control over life in one place produces death in the other.

5. See also López Austin (1990, 185–86).

6. If history were not eternal, then the only other possibility would be that all would simply end, followed by nothing. One can only speculate on the issue, but it seems to me that this is not a good possibility. No mention of what happens after the Fifth Sun is ever made, except that it is eaten by the forces of night. There may be more than one reason for this. It may have been a moot point to discuss what came after, for no one would survive to experience it. Or more likely, just as everything else is limited in Nahua worldviews, the ending was limited to the Mexica-Tenochca, meaning that someone else's age would follow.

"The Myth of the Four Suns" shows how the numbers were manipulated to create five ages out of four calendrical divisions (myth 1, see also Appendix 2).

This myth is so widespread that it seems likely that many groups manipulated the numbers so that they would be living in the Fifth Sun, for calendrical calculations were manipulated to create new realities. The Mexica-Tenochca, for example, rewrote history in the fifteenth century. The Classic Maya, moreover, kept calendrical track of a city's royal events only if they enjoyed an independent status. As soon as a city was conquered, they stopped recording what their elite did. In a sense, they did not exist, a state of affairs maintained by not recording history. In a way, contemporary histories do something similar when they exclude women and other minorities (Wolf 1982). A similar situation may have existed here. It is not that things ended in nothing; when a group like the Mexica-Tenochca completely failed, they were no longer recorded, for now they were the conquered rather than the conquerors.

7. A number of Nahua poets and philosophers expressed their acceptance of the real constancy of impermanence (Miguel Leon-Portilla 1980, 1992; Bierhorst 1985).

8. The Mayan story tells about a false sun called 7-Macaw that must be deformed before the proper sun and moon take their places (Tedlock 1985, 86–94).

9. The following authors all treat the issue of chaos in a diverse range of cultural settings: Burkhart (1989), Carrasco (1982, 1987b), Eliade (1954, 1969), Norman Giardot (1985, 67–99), Charles H. Long (1963), Wendy Doniger O'Flaherty (1975), Sahlins (1985), Brian K. Smith (1985, 79–96), and Valeri (1985).

10. López Austin, conversation, 30 August 1990. In the rite of Tlacaxipehualiztli, for example, it is said that the captor did not eat his captive because he was considered the "father" of his captive. Hence to eat him would be to "eat my very self" (FC, bk. 2, pt. 3, chap. 21:54).

11. In the *Codex Chimalpopoca*'s version of the Fifth Sun's birth (myth 5; CC 1992a, 147–49; 1992b, fols. 77:27–78:23), Tonatiuh arrives from the same place that new babies come from, Tamoanchan. Hence the sun is not the return of an old sun, but the fiery birth of a new baby sun.

12. For a diverse variety of works on the close link between life and death in sacrificial rituals, see the nonspecialist works of Durkheim (1965), Frazer (1963), Heesterman (1985, 45–58), Hocart (1970), and Robertson Smith (1886). For specialist works see Caso (1953), López Austin (1988b), and Matos Moctezuma (1987).

13. The same is true for adulterers since sexuality, like death, is a form of creativity. In this case, the *tlahtlacotin* were sacrificed by stoning (Durán 1971, 96).

14. Sahagún as quoted in Howard F. Cline (1971, 245) and Klor de Alva (1980, 69).

15. Elsewhere (Read 1994a; 1995b) I have explored these jointly reciprocal and coercive socio-cosmic relations. Because of the extreme complexity of the topic, there is neither time nor space to discuss them here. Although no one

theorist can adequately describe something as intricate as Mexica-Tenochca social relations and concepts of hegemony, the works of a number of authors have proved useful. Besides Michael Walzer (1983), whose work seems especially helpful, I suggest looking at the following: Richard Newbold Adams (1975), Catherine Bell (1981), Diane Z. Chase and Arlen F. Chase (1992), Mary Douglas (1986), Michel Foucault (1980), and Ross Hassig (1992).

16. See Arnold van Gennep (1909), Victor Turner's expansion on van Gennep's model of the rite of passage (1969), and Hubert and Mauss's similar three-stage treatment of sacrificial rituals (1898).

17. While I am not denying the comparative value of a three-stage ritual model, I am attempting to avoid what Stanley Tambiah warned against, a "mechanical" use of one that "masks" the unique richness of any given situation (1979, 140).

18. I borrow the term "ordinarily sacred" from Lynda Sexson's book of the same name (1992). This wonderfully creative and witty book not only proposes that the sacred cannot be separated from the profane in human experience but also demonstrates this with both its manner of writing and a marvelous range of stories, anecdotes, and images to get the reader's own creative juices flowing.

19. Locating patterned order is the very basis for learning and, therefore, existence. According to Ray Birdwhistell, a human being is not simply a "blackbox with one orifice for emitting a chunk of stuff called *communication* and another for receiving it." Rather, people learn because they are able to pattern their experiences. "Being in some measure predictable constitutes the *sine qua non* of sanity and humanity." Indeed, even the insane operate according to patterns; it is just that these patterns are inappropriate to their own societal norms (1970, 3, 14, 24). This means that repetitious experiences are at the very heart of meaningful human existence because they create patterns.

20. Sacrificial warring has an enormously long history in Mesoamerica, stretching back through the Classic and pre-Classic Maya (Read 1995a). The Flowery Wars apparently were both ritualized and actual warfare between Tenochtitlan and six other urban centers to the east of the Valley of Mexico in and around Tlaxcala. Staged at a particular time, their sole purpose was to collect captives for sacrifice in the enemy's city, but apparently they often overstepped these boundaries and easily degenerated into all-out battle with deaths occurring on the field.

21. J. Z. Smith (1982) has noted something similar when he spoke of ritual as offering a chance to "think good" because it allows people to create an ideal situation or, as J. C. Heesterman (1979) has suggested, to "control catastrophes."

22. Buddhism, for example, bases itself on the reality of impermanence.

23. Birdwhistell notes that communication is never "a simple additive process." In fact, "[h]uman culture is possible because we do not have to do it this way—because we learn in a patterned way." Because learning takes place in a societal situation which produces a "natural habitat," it is never the sum of a number of parts but the seeking of shared regularities within a full, social, and,

I might add, physical context (1970, 7, 65–79). In other words, what people learn to be true is never a simple sequential process ensuring that an end event has anything at all to do with its beginning. Learning about one's "natural habitat" is more like a child's game of telephone, which incorporates so many unexpected twists and turns that the results are never totally predictable.

24. See William Bright (1990, 437–52) for further examples of parallelisms used by Nahuatl speakers.

25. A single cache containing forty-two skeletons of children between the ages of two and six has been unearthed at the Templo Mayor. It is arranged in five layers, the top one consisting of eleven jars adorned with Tlaloc's face. Normally two children of about six or seven were sacrificed, one on a mountaintop and one in the basin. See López Luján (1993, 192–205, 356), Johanna Broda (1983, 145–64), and Durán (1971, 154–71).

26. This thirst-stricken world was described as a serpent (FC, bk. 6, pt. 7, chap. 8:37).

27. López Austin notes that not all sacrifices were prepared in this rather extensive manner (conversation, 30 August 1990). Because sacrificial ritual moved a variety of powers for varying purposes, ritual preparations would have to be done in ways appropriate to each ritual purpose and context. Not all things ate the same thing; they needed to be fed differently.

28. Conrad and Demerest noted this paradigm shift as one that was adaptive to drought but maladaptive to political exploitation and expansion. While they are largely correct in noting its importance in the political expansion up to the Conquest, they fail to account for the possibility that more paradigm shifts might be made to deal with the new problems arising from the necessity to control a large domain. If the Mexica adapted once, they could do it again. The real problem here is with the Conquest; we don't know what might have happened if the Spanish hadn't walked in, for, clearly, the Spanish upset the political balances in Mesoamerica significantly.

Interesting possibilities, however, do lie in a Marxist approach to this material for answering questions on how and why elite classes exploit other people, how and why people agree to be exploited, and how and why the elite themselves also are controlled and manipulated by their own systems of exploitation. In other words, that people are exploited is not a particularly interesting question in this case, for exploitation is an obvious possibility when the manipulations of powers are integral to the cosmological system itself. It is also too simple (not to mention a bit grim!) to presume that an inborn greedy and self-centered human nature causes people to seek power over others, for there are too many examples to the contrary. But how and why people (often well intentioned) found themselves in power-fraught social contexts is indeed a very interesting question, for it has application well beyond this situation (Read 1994a).

While Conrad and Demerest began to get at some of these issues, much remains to be explored. The intimate workings of the Mexica systems themselves need to be understood in fuller detail in order to know how thinking human beings manipulated them in the first place. Therefore, these questions need to be considered by means of (a) an in-depth study of how paradigm shifts evolved up to and through the Conquest; and (b) a study that avoids a simplistic understanding of human nature and takes into account some of the operant, cognitive patterns of human adaptation.

29. Ritual participation in sacrifice also may be at least partly understood by some psychological hypotheses. Inga Clendinnen has suggested a few. She describes sacrificial participation as partially due to a balance between physical control involving force and drugs and psychological factors involving rewards, dislocation, and ritual conditioning (1991, 88–98). Certainly war captives and slaves, while doomed because of their own actions, were not always entirely willing participants; escape for them, while possible, was rarely plausible. In some rites, the offering's compliance may have been assisted with drugs (Durán 1971, 132). Others were physically removed from friendly, familiar havens and held under circumstances severe enough to bring on emotional dislocation, a sense of unreality so strong that it could create new realities. Being locked in small cages and tortured would have encouraged such emotional estrangement. Future rewards were offered for sacrificial participation, but as noted above, they must be understood in a communal more than individual sense. Psychological conditioning, however, may be one of the most intriguing and, ultimately, disturbing possibilities, for its power rests in the everyday, that which is least questioned.

Appendix 2

1. Any Mexica ability to count long periods of time with precision should not be confused with the Mayan Long Count. The Mayan Long Count disappeared ca. 900 C.E. along with the demise of the Classic Mayan elite. The count that I believe the Mexica could have used was done for similar purposes (to keep track of royal histories) and was just as precise as the Long Count but done in a different way. If Edmonson is right about the progressive nature of the calendar (1988), then this is entirely possible.

2. The *Codex Fejérváry-Mayer* belongs to the Borgia group of calendrical manuscripts. These manuscripts are pre-Conquest and possibly Mixtec. They may come from Southern Puebla and/or Western Oaxaca, although some think the Gulf also is a possibility (facsimile 1901; Wauchope 1964–76, 14: 99–100, 128; Aveni 1980, 156; Quiñones Keber 1995, 107).

3. Aveni gives a detailed explanation of the iconography of the *Fejérváry-Mayer's* frontispiece and how the Mesoamerican calendrical system in general worked (1980, 156–58). This example from the *Codex Fejérváry-Mayer* is only one of many depicting this graphic shaping of time. Other examples include the *Codex Tudela*, post-Conquest, Valley of Mexico (facsimile 1980); and the *Codex Tro-Cortesianus* (*Codex Madrid*), pre-Conquest, Lowland Maya (facsimile 1967).

4. The post-Conquest *Codex Tudela* (Valley of Mexico) shows some of the same orientations as the *Codex Fejérváry-Mayer*, such as cardinal directionality associated with particular sets of dates and a general counterclockwise motion. The shape of the frontispiece of the *Codex Fejérváry-Mayer* is possibly a symbolic flower, for the equivalent depiction in the earlier Mayan *Codex Tro-Cortesianus (Codex Madrid)* was considered shaped like a flower (López Austin, conversation, 17 August 1988). The importance of cardinal directionality has already been noted at Teotihuacan, although many more Mesoamerican sites also mark the cardinal directions.

5. The present-day Quiché Maya also associated the four cardinal directions of their calendrical system with body parts (B. Tedlock 1982, 141).

6. Peter van der Loo has found this same arrangement in other codices belonging to the Borgia group (1987, 51–57). The five day-glyphs depicted in each corner of the *Fejérváry-Mayer*'s frontispiece are the five glyphs that appear on the right-hand edge of each quarter when the 260 days of the *tonalpohualli* are graphed out into four sectors of sixty-five days each (see figure 18).

7. Like the *Fejérváry-Mayer*, the *Codex Aubin* also belongs to the Borgia group. See appendix 2, n. 2.

8. While people of European heritage tend to orient their maps toward the north, placing it at the top of the page, Mesoamericans orient theirs toward the rising sun in the east.

9. For further information on Mesoamerican calendrics in general, see Aveni (1980, 133–217), Broda (1969, 1983, 1989), Caso (1967, 1971), Closs (1986), Edmonson (1988), Sáenz (1976), Satterthwaite (1965), and Umberger (1981).

10. The Mixtec codices shared a number of things with the post-Conquest calendars of the Mexican Highlands, such as style, day names (which varied regionally throughout Mesoamerica), and the workings of the various calendar rounds. Edmonson (1988) skillfully describes the relationship of many Mesoamerican calendars.

11. Mesoamerican codices are often collections of different manuscripts which may have diverse provenances, gathered together according to the whims of their European collectors.

12. While it is clear that the *xiuhmolpilli* is calculated according to the sun, what the *tonalpohualli* is based on is not clear. Suggestions have included pregnancy (it is very close to a nine-month period) and a lunar count (Aveni 1980, 151). Some feel that it may have originated at the Mayan site of Copán, where the sun's passage across the zenith divides the year into two parts of 105 and 260 days (ibid., 148). While the importance of keeping track of the sun as a temporal marker is obvious in this system, as Edmonson (1988) has shown, that does not preclude the accurate marking of other celestial objects as well. The Mesoamerican calendrical system tracked the paths of Venus and Mars as well (Aveni 1980, 150; D. Tedlock 1985).

13. See Colby and Colby (1981), B. Tedlock (1982), and van der Loo (1981).

14. It is unclear how the twenty-four hours of the day were governed. A day may have been counted from noon to noon, from sunset to sunset, or even midnight to midnight, and seems to have varied throughout Mesoamerica (Broda 1969, 33–34; Caso 1967, 53; Edmonson 1988, 67, 187). Sahagún, however, tells us that a child's birth date was calculated using midnight as the division. If a child was born at that hour, its fortune was determined by the signs of both days (FC, bk. 6, pt. 7, chap. 36:197). This seems to indicate that the Mexica counted a day from midnight to midnight.

15. Although the evidence is not clear yet, it seems likely that the *trecenas* were associated with the powers of the cardinal directions. The goddess Xochiquetzal, for example, appears as the deity governing *trecena* 19, which appears in the western quarter when the *tonapohualli* is graphed into four blocks of sixty-five days each. This goddess also was associated closely with the west. Mayahuel, the patron of *trecena* 8, is the goddess of pulque. Her *trecena* appears in the southern quarter and most gods of pulque are associated with the south.

16. Pulque is an intoxicating, fermented drink made from the maguey.

17. As with everything else involving the count of the months, there is confusion over which month begins the year. Edmonson (1988, 10, 142, 222, 226), assigns Izcalli as the beginning point for the Mexica calendar because that maintains coherency with a unified system based on an unbroken day count. Paso y Troncoso (Caso 1971, 45) suggests that this round of the *Borbonicus* describes the year, 1-Rabbit, as ending with the month, Izcalli, and the following year, 2-Reed, beginning with the next month, Atlcahualo. Broda (1983) also begins the year with Atlcahualo and ends it with Izcalli.

18. Caso noticed the possibility that a year could be named by its last day rather than its first and suggested that the *nemontemi* (the five extra days in each solar year) were said "not to be counted" because they did not have any festival days associated :vith them (1967, 55, 39). Even though they were too dangerous to celebrate, this did not mean that they were not figured into the calendrical calculations. Edmonson, for example, categorizes the Mexica calendar as one which was "terminally" named, and because the *nemontemi* were "not counted," they did not figure into the naming of the year. This meant that the 360th day became the key day for naming. He moreover suggests that this was done so that the calendar could be adjusted to the exact solar year by adding an extra day to the *nemontemi* every 219 years (1988, 10–11, 276–77).

Although evidence is not clear, I am inclined to side with Caso and Edmonson on this matter. To use the 360th day as the key naming day for a year is coherent not only with the terminal naming for the suns in "The Myth of the Four Ages" but also with general attitudes on identification, divination, and the *nemontemi*. Naming constituted an act of existential identification. Recall both the existential power naming had for identification and that the second sun was given a new name after it had been reshaped into the moon in "The Birth of the Fifth

Sun." One would not want to name the year for one of the five dangerous *nemontemi* days because one would create a dangerous year.

19. For her calculations, Broda (1983) used the cycle of the months appearing in Sahagún's *Florentine Codex*.

20. Motolinía (1971, foldout between 54–55), the *Boban Calendar Wheel* (Caso 1967, figs. 22a, 22b), and a small temple at Tlaltelolco show clockwise-oriented calendars. Aveni has investigated archaeological ritual sites ringing Tenochtitlan (all associated with the month of Atlcahualo) which, according to Sahagún, also proceed in a clockwise direction (conversation, 9 September 1993). Pedro Carrasco, however, assigns a counterclockwise motion to the monthly cycle and orients it to the four quarters, the solstices, and equinoxes. In this scheme, Ochpaniztli precedes the fall equinox, Panquetzaliztli precedes the winter solstice, Tlacaxipeualiztli precedes the spring equinox, and Etzalcualiztli precedes the summer solstice (1979, 52–60).

Although (again) the evidence is not at all clear, it is possible that the counterclockwise direction was associated with the structuring of time within a divinatory and broadly cosmological sense, while a clockwise motion was associated with agricultural rituals connected to primarily state and civil concerns. Rudolf van Zantwijk, (1977, 232–34) makes a similar proposal suggesting that the solar calendar operated exactly opposite to the *tonalpohualli*. Given that most examples of clockwise direction apparently are associated with agricultural or monthly calendars, this aspect of solar motion may have been intended to reverse time ritually, in much the same way that the sun reverses its own motion along the horizon.

21. The particular calendrical theories presented in these sections on coordinating the divinatory and solar calendars have been aided and tested by a computer program devised by Edward C. Read.

22. This, of course, assumes that the night-lord sequence continues to repeat itself as do all the other cycles, something suggested by the pattern of particular night lords appearing on these two folios. Since the night-lord cycle does not end evenly at the end of 260 days (it ends one short of a complete rotation of nine) almost all *tonalpohuallies* end on the eighth lord, suggesting that the next *tonalpohualli* round should begin with the ninth. This offsets the whole sequence by one, allowing for a progressive count.

There has been some question about whether the night lords do, in fact, proceed progressively. The only evidence from calendars even remotely associated with the Mexica for this cycle simply stopping when 260 days are completed comes from the *tonalpohualli* in the *Tonalamatl Aubin*. Herein, the last night lord, 8: Tepeyolotl, wears a headdress with the ninth night lord, Tlaloc, on it. This could indicate a doubling of the eighth and ninth lords in order to make the cycle come out even (van der Loo 1987, 61–62, 241).

However, this codex is filled with unusual inconsistencies and mistakes, especially in the Lords-of-the-Night round. There appear to be several different hands at work on the piece, a number of them quite unskilled. The mistakes are often the logical kinds of mistakes a beginner might make, such as mixing up two depictions of deities who share similar iconographic traits. The last two *trecenas* of the calendar are almost totally out of sequence. The provenance of the calendar is not completely known, though it is probably early post-Conquest from Tlaxcala (conversation, Xavier Noguez, 8 August 1988). Its unusual depiction of the *tonalpohualli,* nevertheless, makes it a very questionable source.

On the other hand, the *Codex Borbonicus,* the *Codex Tudela,* and the *Codex Cospi* (calendars which do not contain any obvious mistakes) show no doubling of the night lords anywhere. Instead, each begins with the first night lord in the sequence and counts them in continuously rotating cycles until the last day of the 260-day count. Each ends, as it should, on the eighth lord.

23. Edmonson (1988) sees a tremendous historical continuity (with documentable changes) in the year-bearer count of the *xiuhmolpilli,* which he views as the means by which an extremely accurate marking of the sun's motions (including the solstices and the equinoxes) could be made.

24. It would take nine 52-year rounds (468 solar years) before both the days and the nights were completed at the same time.

25. The *Fejérváry-Mayer* is considered a member of the Borgia group of codices (Wauchope, vol. 1:99, 128).

26. One obvious question, of course, is whether they adjusted for leap year or not. Even Sahagún makes conjectures on this topic, suggesting that an extra day was added to the *nemontemi* every four years (FC, bk. 4, pt.5, app.:144). As with many other things, however, the answer to this question is not clear. Both Broda (1983) and Edmonson (1988, 276–77) believe that such adjustments were used, while Michel Graulich (1981) holds the contrary position. My own position is that they must have been adjusting the calendar in some way. The logic of transformation, the central importance of the specific powers held by each day, and the fact that rituals such as the New Fire rite were coordinated with celestial events would seem to indicate the necessity for such precision. Moreover, the agriculturally coordinated months of the *metztli* cycle would be out of synch with the actual seasons very quickly if they did not. Given that they were trying to manipulate specific powers to make things work efficiently, not adjusting for leap years seems extraordinarily inefficient.

27. The synodic period of Venus takes 584 days and has a long tradition of use in Mesoamerican calendrical calculations (Aveni 1980, 84–86); i.e., (65 × 584 = 37,960) × 26 = 986,960 days or 2704 years.

28. Venus is beginning to emerge as one of the most important celestial objects in Mesoamerican calendrics. For further information on Venus, see Aveni (1988, 1989) and D. Tedlock (1985).

29. 2,704 years = fifty-two *xiuhmolpilli* (52 × 52), 1,690 Venus rounds (1,690 × 584 days), and 3,796 *tonalpohualli* rounds (3,796 × 260). But the Lords of the Night are off by two.

30. The Lords of the Night reflect this order/counterorder pattern in the Bind-ing-of-the-Years count. While their sequence is off by one in the year-binding rite just as it is in the *tonalpohualli* counting forward, counting backward (clock-wise rather than counterclockwise) the lords even out after nine year-binding rites. I suspect patterns of motion/counter motion like this helped structure calendrical and ritual cycles as they may have for the count of the months. Counterclockwise motions allow one to count forward for very long sequences, while clockwise motions keep track of the ending days belonging to various repetitious cycles. Moreover, counter motions are very easy to calculate if one uses the squared-off circle arrangement of the *Fejérváry-Mayer* and the *Borboni-cus*, for one simply needs to count in the opposite direction.

31. In the Mayan myth of the "Popol Vuh," although one of the hero twins becomes the sun and the other becomes the moon, one of those twins is also extremely closely tied to the cycles of Venus (D. Tedlock 1985, 40, 159–60).

BIBLIOGRAPHY

FC: *Florentine Codex* (Sahagún 1953–82).

HI: *Historia de las Indias de Nueva España e islas de la tierra firme* (1984, vol. 2) or *The History of the Indies of New Spain* (1994), by Fray Diego Durán.

CC 1992a: *Codex Chimalpopoca* (1992a), the English translation.

CC 1992b: *Codex Chimalpopoca* (1992b), the Nahuatl transcriptions.

Acosta, Joseph de.
1978   *Vida religiosa y civil de los Indios (Historia natural y moral de las Indias).* Reprint. Mexico City: Universidad Nacional Autónoma de México.

Adams, Richard E. W.
1991   *Prehistoric Mesoamerica.* Revised ed. 1992. Norman: University of Oklahoma Press.

Adams, Richard Newbold.
1975   *Energy and Structure: A Theory of Social Power.* Austin: University of Texas Press.

Alarcón, Hernando Ruiz de.
1984   *Treatise on the Heathen Superstitions that Today Live Among the Indians Native to This New Spain, 1629.* Translated by J. Richard Andrews and Ross Hassig. Norman: University of Oklahoma Press.

Andrews, J. Richard.
1975   *Introduction to Classical Nahuatl.* Austin: University of Texas Press.

Arnheim, Rudolf.
1954   *Art and Visual Perception: A Psychology of the Creative Eye.* Berkeley: University of California Press.

Aveni, Anthony.
1977   *Native American Astronomy.* Austin: University of Texas Press.
1980   *Skywatchers of Ancient Mexico.* Austin: University of Texas Press.
1981   "Tropical Archeoastronomy." *Science* 213, no. 4504 (10 July): 161–71.
1989   *Empires of Time: Calendars, Clocks, and Cultures.* New York: Basic Books.

Aveni, Anthony F., and Sharon L. Gibbs.
1976   "On the Orientation of Precolumbian Buildings in Central Mexico." *American Antiquity* 41, no. 4 (October): 510–17.

Baudet, Henri.
1976   *Paradise on Earth: Some Thoughts on European Images of Non-European Man.* Westport, Conn.: Greenwood Press.

Beardsley, Monroe.
1958   *Aesthetics: Problems in the Philosophy of Criticism.* New York: Harcourt, Brace, and World, Inc.

Bell, Catherine.
1992   *Ritual Theory, Ritual Practice.* Oxford: Oxford University Press.

Benson, Elizabeth P., and Elizabeth H. Boone, eds.
1984   *Ritual Human Sacrifice in Mesoamerica.* Washington D.C.: Dumbarton Oaks Research Library and Collection.

Bierhorst, John, translator.
1985   *Cantares Mexicanos: Songs of the Aztecs.* With commentary by John Bierhorst. 2 vols. Stanford: Stanford University Press.

Birdwhistell, Ray L.
1970   *Kinesics and Context: Essays on Body Motion Communication.* Philadelphia: University of Pennsylvania Press.

Bonifaz Nuño, Rubén.
1981   *The Art of the Great Temple: México-Tenochtitlan.* Mexico City: Instituto Nacional de Antropología e Historia.

Boone, Elizabeth Hill.
1987   "Regional Variations in the Painted Manuscripts of the Aztec Empire." Paper presented at symposium, "Strategies of Aztec Empire Building." Eighty-sixth annual meeting of the American Anthropology Association, Chicago, November. Photocopy.

Bright, William.
1990   "'With One Lip, With Two Lips': Parallelisms in Nahuatl." *Language* 66, no. 3: 437–52.

Broda, Johanna.
1969   *The Mexican Calendar as Compared to Other Mesoamerican Systems.* Edited by Josef Haekel and Engelbert Stiglmayr. Series Americana 4, Acta Ethnologica et Linguistica, nr. 15, Institut für Völkerkunde der Universität Wien. Vienna: Herbert Merta.
1983   "Ciclos agrícolas en el culto: Un problema de la correlación del calendario Mexica." In *Proceedings of Forty-Fourth International Congress of Americanists, Manchester, 1982,* edited by Norman Hammond, n.p. Reprinted in *Calendars in Mesoamerica: Native Computations of Time,* edited by Anthony Aveni and Gordon Brotherston. BAR International Series 174. Oxford, 145–64.
1989   "Astronomy, Cosmovision, and Ideology in Pre-Hispanic Mesoamerica." In *Ethnoastronomy and Archeoastronomy in the American Tropics,* edited by Anthony F. Aveni and Gary Urton. New York: New York Academy of Sciences, 81–123.

Burkhart, Louise.
1989   *The Slippery Earth: Nahua Christian Moral Dialogue in Sixteenth Cen-tury Mexico*. Tucson: University of Arizona Press.

Carochi, Horacio.
1910   *Compendio del arte de la lengua Mexicana*. Mexico City: La Biblioteca Mexicana, 1790. Reprint. Edited by Ignacio de Paredes. Puebla, Mexico: El Escritorio.

Carrasco, Davíd.
1981   "Templo Mayor: The Aztec Vision of Place." *History of Religions* 20, no. 3 (February): 275–97.
1982   *Quetzalcoatl and the Irony of Empire*. Chicago: University of Chicago Press.
1987a   "Mesoamerican Kings." In vol. 8 of the *Encyclopedia of Religion*, ed-ited by Mircea Eliade. 16 vols. New York: Macmillan, 326–28.
1987b   "Star Gatherers and Wobbling Suns: Astral Symbolism in the Aztec World." *History of Religions* 26, no. 3 (February): 279–94.
1991   "The Sacrifice of Tezcatlipoca: To Change Place." In *To Change Place: Aztec Ceremonial Landscapes*, edited by Davíd Carrasco. Boulder: University of Colorado Press, 32–57.
1995   "Cosmic Jaws: We Eat the Gods and the Gods Eat Us." In *Journal of the American Academy of Religion* 63, no. 3 (Fall): 429–63.

Carrasco, Pedro.
1979   "Las fiestas de los meses Mexicanos." In *Homenaje al Doctor Paul Kirchhoff*, edited by Barbro Dahlgren. Mexico City: Instituto Nacional de Antropología e Historia, 52–60.

Caso, Alfonso.
1953   *El pueblo del sol*. Mexico City: Fondo de Cultura Económica.
1967   *Los calendarios prehispánicos*. Mexico City: Universidad Nacional Autónoma de México.
1971   "Calendrical Systems of Central Mexico." In vol. 10, *Handbook of Middle American Indians*, edited by Robert Wauchope. 15 vols. Aus-tin: University of Texas Press, 333–48.

Chase, Diane Z., and Arlen F. Chase, eds.
1992   *Mesoamerican Elite: An Archaeological Assessment*. Norman: Univer-sity of Oklahoma Press.

Clendinnen, Inga.
1991   *Aztecs: An Interpretation*. Cambridge: Cambridge University Press.

Cline, Howard F.
1971   "Missing and Variant Prologues and Dedications in Sahagún's Historia General: Texts and English Translations." In vol. 9 of *Estudios de cultura*

Náhuatl. Mexico City: Universidad Nacional Autónoma de México, 237–52.

Closs, Michael.
1986   *Native American Mathematics.* Austin: University of Texas Press.

Codex Aubin.
1893   As reproduced in *Histoire de la nation mexicaine.* Paris: Ernest Leroux.

Codex Borbonicus.
1974   With commentary by K. A. Nowotny. Facsimile ed. Graz, Austria: Akademische Druck, U. Verlagsanstalt.

Codex Borgia.
1963   With commentary by Eduard Seler. Facsimile ed. Mexico City: Fondo de Cultura Económica.

Codex Boturini.
1831–48   As reproduced in vol. 1 of *Antiquities of Mexico,* edited by Lord Edward King, Viscount Kingsborough. 9 vols. London: Robert Havell.

Codex Chimalpopoca.
1938   As reproduced in *Die Geschichte der Königreiche von Culhuacan und Mexico,* translated by Walter Lehman. Stuttgart and Berlin: W. Kohlhammer, 1938.

Codex Chimalpopoca.
1992a   As reproduced in *History and Mythology of the Aztecs: The Codex Chimalpopoca,* translated by John Bierhorst. 2 vols. Tucson: University of Arizona Press.

Codex Chimalpopoca.
1992b   As reproduced in *The Codex Chimalpopoca: The Text in Nahuatl with Glossary and Grammatical Notes,* edited by John Bierhorst. 2 vols. Tucson: University of Arizona Press.

Codex Cospi.
1968   With commentary by K. A. Nowotny. Facsimile ed. Graz, Austria: Akademische Druck, U. Verlagsanstalt.

Codex en Cruz.
1981   With commentary by Charles Dibble. Facsimile ed. 2 vols. Salt Lake City: University of Utah Press.

Codex Fejérváry-Mayer.
1901   Facsimile ed. Paris: Duc de Loubat.

Codex Mendoza.
1938   Edited by James Cooper Clark. Facsimile ed. London: Waterlow and Sons.

Codex Telleriano Remensis: Manuscrit Mexicain.
1899   Facsimile ed. Introduction by Dr. E. T. Hamy. Paris: Duc de Loubat.

Codex Tro-Cortesianus.
1967   With commentary by Ferdinand Anders. Facsimile ed. Graz, Austria: Akademische Druck, U. Verlagsanstalt.

Códice Aubin.
1980   As reproduced in *Códice Aubin: Manuscrito Azteca de la Biblioteca Royal de Berlin, Anales en Mexicana y geroglíficos desde la salida de las tribus de Aztlan,* edited by Antonio Peñafiel. 1902. Reprint. Mexico City: Editorial Innovación.

Códice Chimalpopoca: Anales de Cuauhtitlán y leyenda de los soles.
1945   Translated by Primo Feliciano Velázquez. Mexico City: Universidad Nacional Autónoma de México, Instituto de Historia.

Códice Garcia Granados.
1979   In *Los códices de México,* edited by Yolanda Mercader Martínez. Cover photo. Mexico City: Instituto Nacional de Antropología e Historia, Secretaría Educación Pública, Museo Nacional de Antropología.

Códice Tudela.
1980   With commentary by José Tudela de la Orden. Facsimile ed. Madrid: Ediciones Cultura Hispánica.

Códice Vaticano Latino 3738.
1964   As reproduced in vol. 2 of *Antiquities of Mexico,* edited by Lord Edward King, Viscount Kingsborough, n.p. 9 vols. London: Robert Havell, 1831–1848. Reprinted in vol. 3 of *Antigüedades de México.* With a prologue by Agustín Yánez and commentary by José Corona Nuñez, n.p. 4 vols. Mexico City: Secretaría de Hacienda y Crédito Público.

Códice Xolotl.
1980   Edited by Charles E. Dibble. Facsimile ed. Mexico City: Universidad Nacional Autónoma de México.

Colby, Benjamin N. and Lore M. Colby.
1981   *The Daykeeper: The Life and Discourse of an Ixil Diviner.* Cambridge: Harvard University Press.

Conrad, Geoffrey, and Arthur Demerest.
1984   *Religion and Empire: The Dynamics of Aztec and Inca Expansionism.* Cambridge: Cambridge University Press.

Daly, Mary.
1973   *Beyond God the Father: Toward a Philosophy of Women's Liberation.* Boston: Beacon Press.

Davies, Nigel.
1973   *The Aztecs: A History*. Norman: University of Oklahoma Press.
1981   *Human Sacrifice: In History and Today*. New York: William Morrow and Co.

Dewey, John.
1934a   *A Common Faith*. New Haven: Yale University Press.
1934b   *Art as Experience*. New York: Perigree Books, 1980.

Douglas, Mary.
1986   *How Institutions Think*. Syracuse, New York: Syracuse University Press.

Durán, Fray Diego.
1971   *Book of the Gods and Rites and the Ancient Calendar*. Translated by Doris Heyden and Fernando Horcasitas. Norman: University of Oklahoma Press. Original manuscripts entitled *Libro de los ritos y ceremonias en las fiestas de los dioses y celebración de ellas*, 1576–79; and *El calendario antiguo*, 1579. National Library, Madrid.
1984   *Historia de las Indias de Nueva España e islas de la tierra firme*, edited by Angel María Garibay K. Reprint. 2 vols. Mexico City: Editorial Porrúa. Original manuscripts entitled *Libro de los ritos y ceremonias en las fiestas de los dioses y celebración de ellas*, 1576–79; *El calendario antiguo*, 1579; and *Historia de las Indias de Nueva España e islas de la tierra firme*, 1580–81. National Library, Madrid.
1994   *The History of the Indies of New Spain*. Translated by Doris Heyden. Norman: University of Oklahoma. Original manuscript entitled *Historia de las Indias de Nueva España e islas de la tierra firme* 1580–81. National Library, Madrid.

Durkheim, Emile.
1965   *The Elementary Forms of the Religious Life*, translated by Joseph Ward Swain. London: George Allen and Unwin, 1915. Reprint, New York: Macmillan Co., Free Press.

Duverger, Christian.
1983   *La flor letal: Economia del sacrificio Azteca*. Mexico City: Fondo de Cultura Económica.

Edmonson, Munro S.
1988   *The Book of the Year: Middle American Calendrical Systems*. Salt Lake City: University of Utah Press.

Eliade, Mircea.
1954   *The Myth of the Eternal Return: Or, Cosmos and History*. Bollingen Series, no. 46. Princeton: Princeton University Press.
1958   *Patterns of Comparative Religion*. Clinton, Mass: New American Library.

1969   *The Quest: History and Meaning in Religion*. Chicago: University of
        Chicago Press.
1985   "The Sacred and the Modern Artist." In *Art, Creativity, and the Sacred*,
        edited by Diane Apostolos-Cappadona. New York: Crossroads Publish-
        ing Co, 179–83.

Fagen, Brian.
1991   *Ancient North America: The Archaeology of a Continent*. 2nd ed. Lon-
        don: Thames and Hudson.

Foucault, Michel.
1980   *Power/Knowledge: Selected Interviews and Other Writings, 1972–1977*,
        edited by Colin Gordon. New York: Pantheon Books.

Fowler, Melvin L.
1989   *The Cahokia Atlas: A Historical Atlas of Cahokia Archaeology*. Studies
        in Illinois Archaeology no.6. Illinois: Illinois Historic Preservation
        Agency.
1991   "Mound 72 and Early Mississippians at Cahokia." In *New Perspectives
        on Cahokia: Views from the Periphery*, edited by James B. Stoltman.
        Monographs in World Archaeology #2. Madison, Wisc.: Prehistory Press,
        1–28.

Frazer, Sir James George.
1963   *The Golden Bough: A Study in Magic and Religion*. Abridged ed. (13
        vols. in 1). New York: Macmillan Co., 1922; Macmillan Paperbacks.

Garibay K., Angel María, editor and translator.
1978   *Llave del Náhuatl*. 4th ed. Mexico City: Editorial Porrúa.

Giardot, Norman.
1985   "Behaving Cosmogonically in Early Taoism." In *Cosmogony and Ethi-
        cal Order: New Studies in Comparative Ethics*, edited by Robin W. Lovin
        and Frank E. Reynolds. Chicago: University of Chicago Press: 67–99.

Gibson, Charles.
1964   *The Aztecs under Spanish Rule: A History of the Indians of the Valley of
        Mexico, 1519–1810*. Stanford, Calif.: Stanford University Press.

Gilkey, Langdon.
1985   "Events, Meanings, and the Current Tasks of Theology." *Journal of the
        American Academy of Religion* 53, no. 3 (Winter): 717–34.

Gill, Sam.
1982a   *Beyond "the Primitive": The Religions of Nonliterate Peoples*. New Jer-
        sey: Prentice Hall.
1982b   *Native American Religions: An Introduction*. Calif.: Wadsworth.
1987   *Native American Religious Action: A Performative Approach to Reli-
        gion*. Columbia: University of South Carolina Press.

Gillespie, Susan D.
1989   *The Aztec Kings: The Construction of Rulership in Mexica History.* Tucson: University of Arizona Press.

Girard, René.
1977   *Violence and the Sacred.* Translated by Patrick Gregory. Baltimore: Johns Hopkins University Press.

Glass, John B.
1964   *Católogo de la colección de códices.* Mexico City: Museo Nacional de Antropología, Instituto Nacional de Antropología e Historia.

Gonzalez Aparicio, Luis.
1980   *Plano reconstuctive de la region de Tenochtitlan.* Mexico City: Instituto Nacional de Antropología e Historia.

Gonzalez Torres, Yolotl.
1985   *El sacrificio humano entre los Mexicas.* Mexico City: Instituto Nacional de Antropología e Historia, Fondo de Cultura Económica.

Gossen, Gary H.
1974   "A Chamula Solar Calendar Board from Chiapas, Mexico." In *Mesoamerican Archaeology: New Approaches,* edited by Norman Hammond Norman. Austin: University of Texas Press, 217–53.

Graulich, Michel.
1981   "The Metaphor of the Day in Ancient Mexican Myth and Ritual." *Current Anthropology* 22, no. 1 (February): 45–59.
1988   "Double Immolations in Ancient Mexican Sacrificial Ritual." *History of Religions* 27, no. 4 (May): 393–404.

Guzmán M., Virginia, and Yolanda Mercader M.
1979   *Bibliografía de códices, mapas, y lienzos del México prehispánico y colonial.* 2 vols. Mexico: Instituto Nacional de Antropología e Historia.

Hall, Robert.
1984   "The Misunderstood Case of the Flayed Princess or The Honor of the Aztecs Restored." Seventh Annual Midwest Mesoamerica Conference, Loyola University, Chicago, March. Photocopy.

Harner, Michael.
1977   "The Ecological Basis for Aztec Sacrifice." *American Ethnologist* 4, no. 1, (February): 117–35.

Harris, Marvin.
1977   *Cannibals and Kings: The Origins of Cultures.* New York: Random House.

Harvey, Herbert R., and Barbara J. Williams.
1986   "Decipherment and Some Implications of Aztec Numerical Glyphs. In

Native American Mathematics, edited by Michael Closs. Austin: University of Texas Press, 237–60.

Hassig, Ross.
1992   *War and Society in Ancient Mesoamerica*. Berkeley: University of California Press.

Heesterman, J. C.
1979   "Veda and Dharma." In *The Concept of Duty in South Asia*, edited by Wendy Doniger O'Flaherty and J. Duncan M. Derrett. Delhi: Vikas Publishing House PVT, 80–95.
1985   "The Case of the Severed Head." In *The Inner Conflict of Traditions: Essays in Indian Ritual, Kingship, and Society*. Chicago: University of Chicago Press, 45–58.

"Historia de los Mexicanos por sus pinturas."
1968   In *Teogonía e historia de los Mexicanos: Tres opúsculos del siglo XVI*, edited and translated by Angel María Garibay K. Mexico City: Editorial Porrúa, 23–68.

Historia Tolteca-Chichicmeca: Anales de Quauhtinchan.
1947   Prologue by Paul Kirchhoff. Mexico City: Antigua Librería Robredo de José Porrúa e Hijos.

"Histoyre du Mechique."
1905   Edited by Edouard de Jonghe. *Journal de la Société des Américanistes de Paris* n.s. 2, 1–41.

Hocart, A. M.
1970   *Kings and Councillors: An Essay in the Comparative Anatomy of Human Society*. Edited and with an introduction by Rodney Needham, with a foreword by E. E. Evans-Pritchard. Originally published Cairo: Printing Office Paul Barbey, 1936. Chicago: University of Chicago Press.

Holly, Michael Ann.
1984   *Panofsky and the Foundations of Art History*. Ithaca: Cornell University Press.

Hubert, Henri, and Marcel Mauss.
1898   *Sacrifice: Its Nature and Function*. Translated by W. D. Halls, with a foreword by E. E. Evans-Pritchard. Chicago: University of Chicago Press, 1964; Midway, 1981. Originally published as "Essai sur la nature et la fonction du sacrifice." In *L'Année sociologique* (Paris), 29–138.

Hvidtfeldt, Arild.
1958   *Teotl and Ixiptlatli: Some Central Conceptions in Ancient Mexican Religion*. Copenhagen: Munksgaard.

Ixtlilxochitl, Don Fernando de Alva.
1985   *Obras históricas*. Edited by Edmundo O'Gorman. 4th ed. 2 vols. Mexico City: Universidad Nacional Autónoma de México.

Jennings, Francis.
1993   *The Founders of America.* New York: Norton.

Johnson, Mark.
1987   *The Body in the Mind: The Bodily Basis of Meaning, Imagination, and Reason.* Chicago: University of Chicago Press.
1993   *Moral Imagination: Implications of Cognitive Science for Ethics.* Chicago: University of Chicago Press.

Jones, Lindsey.
1989   "The Hermeneutics of Sacred Architecture: A Reassessment of the Similitude between Tula, Hidalgo, and Chichén Itzá, Yucatan." Ph.D. diss., University of Chicago.

Karttunen, Frances.
1983   *An Analytical Dictionary of Nahuatl.* Austin: University of Texas Press.
1986   "Indirection and Inversion." Presented at the eighty-fifth annual meeting of the American Anthropology Association, Philadelphia (November). Photocopy.

Katz, Friedrich.
1969   *The Ancient American Civilizations.* New York: Praeger.

Kidwell, Clara Sue.
1992   "Systems of Knowledge." In *America in 1492: The World of the Indian Peoples before the Arrival of Columbus,* edited by Alvin M. Josephy, Jr. New York: Alfred A. Knopf, 369–403.

Kirchhoff, Paul.
1952   "Mesoamerica: Its Geographic Limits, Ethnic Composition and Cultural Characteristics." In *Ancient Mesoamerica,* edited by John A. Graham. Reprint 1966. Calif.: Peek, 1–14.

Klein, Cecelia.
1982   "Woven Heaven, Tangled Earth: A Weaver's Paradigm of the Mesoamerican Cosmos." In *Ethnoastronomy and Archaeoastronomy in the American Tropics,* edited by Anthony F. Aveni and Gary Urton. New York: New York Academy of Sciences, 1–35.

Klor de Alva, Jorge J.
1980   "Spiritual Warfare in Mexico: Christianity and the Aztecs." Ph.D. diss., University of California, Santa Cruz.

Klor de Alva, Jorge, H. B. Nicholson, and Eloise Quiñones Keber, eds.
1988   *The Work of Bernardino de Sahagún: Pioneer Ethnographer of Sixteenth-Century Aztec Mexico.* Austin: University of Texas Press.

Krickeberg, Walter.
1966   *Altmexickanische Kulturen.* Berlin: Safari-Verlag.

Kubler, George.
1967   *The Iconography of the Art of Teotihuacan.* Washington, D.C.: Dumbarton Oaks Research Library and Collection.
1962   *The Shape of Time: Remarks on the History of Things.* New Haven: Yale University Press.

La Faye, Jacques.
1976   *Quetzalcoatl and Guadalupe: The Formation of National Consciousness, 1531–1813.* Chicago: University of Chicago Press.

Lakoff, George.
1987   *Women, Fire, and Dangerous Things: What Categories Reveal about the Mind.* Chicago: University of Chicago Press.

Leach, Edmund.
1976   *Culture and Communication: The Logic by Which Symbols Are Connected.* Cambridge: Cambridge University Press.

Léon-Portilla, Miguel, editor.
1980   *Native Mesoamerican Spirituality: Ancient Myths, Discourses, Stories, Doctrines, Hymns, Poems from the Aztec, Yucatec, Quiche-Maya and Other Sacred Traditions.* New York: Paulist Press.
1992   *Fifteen Poets of the Aztec World.* Norman: University of Oklahoma Press.

Lévi-Strauss, Claude.
1963   "Introduction: History and Anthropology." In *Structural Anthropology.* New York: Basic Books, 1–27.
1966   *The Savage Mind.* Chicago: University of Chicago Press.

Lok, Rossana.
1987   "The House as a Microcosm." In *The Leiden Tradition in Structural Anthropology,* edited by R. De Ridder and J. A. J. Karremans. Leiden: E. J. Brill, 211–23.

Long, Charles H.
1963   *Alpha: The Myths of Creation.* Chico, Calif.: Scholars Press.

López Austin, Alfredo.
1973   *Hombre-Dios: Religión y política en el mundo Náhuatl.* Mexico City: Universidad Nacional Autónoma de México.
1974   "The Research Method of Fray Bernardino de Sahagún: The Questionnaires." In *Sixteenth Century Mexico: The Work of Sahagún,* edited by Munro S. Edmonson. Albuquerque: University of New Mexico Press, 111–50.
1985   "La construcción de la memoria." In *La memoria y el ovido: Segundo simposio de historia de las mentalidades.* Mexico City: Instituto Nacional de Antropología e Historia, Secretaría Educación Pública, 75–79.

1988a *Una vieja historia de la mierda.* Mexico City: Ediciónes Toledo.
1988b *The Human Body and Ideology: Concepts of the Ancient Nahuas.* Translated by Thelma Ortiz de Montellano and Bernard Ortiz de Montellano. 2 vols. Salt Lake City: University of Utah Press.
1990 *Los mitos del tlacuache: Caminos de la mitología mesoamericana.* Mexico City: Alianza Editorial Méxicana.
1993 "El arbol cósmico en la tradición Mesoamericana." In *Iichiko Intercultural* no. 5 (June): 47–66.

López Luján, Leonardo.
1993 *Las offerendas del Templo Mayor de Tenochtitlan.* Mexico: Instituto Nacional de Antropología e Historia.

Matos Moctezuma, Eduardo.
1984 "The Great Temple of Tenochtitlan." *Scientific American* 251, no. 2 (August) 80–88.
1987 "Symbolism of the Templo Mayor" In *The Aztec Templo Mayor,* edited by Elizabeth Hill Boone. Washington, D.C.: Dumbarton Oaks Research Library and Collection, 185–207.

Mauss, Marcel.
1967 *The Gift: Forms and Functions of Exchange in Archaic Societies.* Translated by Ian Cunnison. With an introduction by E. E. Evans-Pritchard. Originally published as "Essai sur le don, forme archaïque de l'échange," 1925. New York: Norton.

Mercader Martínez, Yolanda.
1979 *Los códices de México.* Mexico City: Instituto Nacional de Antropología e Historia, Secretaría Educación Pública, Museo Nacional de Antropología.

Miles, Margaret.
1985 *Image as Insight: Visual Understanding in Western Christianity and Secular Culture.* Boston: Beacon Press.

Molina, Fray Alonso de.
1970 *Vocabulario en lengua Castellana y Mexicana.* Preliminary study by Miguel Leon Portilla. 2nd. facsimile ed. Mexico City: Editorial Porrrúa.

Moreno de los Arcos, Roberto.
1967 "Los cinco soles cosmogónicos." In vol. 7 of *Estudios de cultura Náhuatl.* Mexico City: Universidad Nacional Autónoma de México, 183–210.

Motolinía, Fray Toribio de Benevente o.
1971 *Memoriales o libro de las cosas de la Nueva España y de los naturales de ella.* Edited and with notes and analytical study by Edmundo O'Gorman. 2d ed. Mexico City: Universidad Nacional Autónoma de México.

1984   *Historia de los Indios de la Nueva España*. With critical study, appendices, notes, and indices by Edmundo O'Gorman. 4th ed. Mexico City: Editorial Porrúa.

Nicholson, H. B.
1966   "The Significance of the 'Looped Cord' Year Symbol in Pre-Hispanic Mexico." In vol. 6 of *Estudios de cultura Náhuatl*. Mexico City: Universidad Nacional Autónoma de México, 135–48.
1973   "Phoneticism in the Late Pre-Hispanic Central Mexican Writing System." In *Mesoamerican Writing Systems*, edited by Elizabeth P. Benson. Washington D.C.: Dumbarton Oaks Research Library and Collection, 1–46.

O'Flaherty, Wendy Doniger.
1975   *Hindu Myths: A Sourcebook Translated from the Sanscrit*. Harmondsworth, U.K.: Penguin Books.

Ortiz, Alfonso.
1969   *The Tewa World: Space, Time, Being, and Becoming in a Pueblo Society*. Chicago: University of Chicago Press.

Ortiz de Montellano, Bernard R.
1990   *Aztec Medicine, Health, and Nutrition*. New Brunswick: Rutgers University Press.
1978   "Aztec Cannibalism: An Ecological Necessity?" *Science* 200 (May): 611–17.

Otto, Rudolf.
1979   *The Idea of the Holy: An Inquiry into the Non-rational Factor in the Idea of the Divine and Its Relation to the Individual*. 1923. Reprint. Oxford: Oxford University Press.

Panofsky, Erwin.
1955   "Iconography and Iconology: An Introduction to the Study of Renaissance Art." In *Meaning and the Visual Arts*. Garden City, N.Y.: Doubleday and Co., 26–54.

Pasztory, Esther.
1976   *The Murals of Tepantitla, Teotihuacan*. New York: Garland Publishers.
1983   *Aztec Art*. New York: Harry N. Abrams.

Payne, Stanley E., and Michael P. Closs.
1986   "A Survey of Aztec Numbers and Their Uses." In *Native American Mathematics*, edited by Michael P. Closs. Austin: University of Texas Press, 213–36.

Peirce, Charles Sanders.
1932   *Collected Papers of Charles Sanders Peirce: Elements of Logic*. Vol. 2. Edited by Charles Hartshorne and Paul Weiss. 2 vols. Cambridge: Harvard University Press.

1957   *Charles S. Peirce: Essays in the Philcsophy of Science.* Edited by Vincent Tomas. New York: Liberal Arts Press.

Phelan, John.
1970   *The Millennial Kingdom of the Franciscans in the New World.* Berkeley and Los Angeles: University of California Press.

Quiñones Keber, Eloise.
1995   *Codex Telleriano-Remensis: Ritual, Divination, and History in a Pictorial Aztec Manuscript.* Austin: University of Texas Press.

Radin, Paul.
1920   "Sources and Authenticity of History of Ancient Mexicans." In *University of California Publications in American Archaeology and Ethnology* 17, no. 1 (June): 1–150.

Read, Kay A.
1986   "The Fleeting Moment: Cosmogony, Eschatology, and Ethics in Aztec Religion and Society." *Journal of Religious Ethics* 14, no. 1 (Spring): 113–38.

1987a   "Negotiating the Familiar and the Strange in Aztec Ethics." *Journal of Religious Ethics* 15, no. 1 (Spring): 2–13.

1987b   "Human Sacrifice." In *Death, Afterlife, and the Soul,* edited by Lawrence E. Sullivan. New York: Macmillan Co., 1989, 16–20. Originally published as "Human Sacrifice: An Overview." In vol. 6 of *Encyclopedia of Religion,* edited by Mircea Eliade. 16 vols. New York: Macmillan, 515–18.

1991a   "Buddhism." Introduction and ed. In *Religious Worlds: Primary Readings in Comparative Perspective,* edited by John Dominic Crossan. Dubuque, Iowa: Kendall Hunt, 69–139.

1991b   "Binding Reeds and Burning Hearts: Mexica-Tenochca Concepts of Time and Sacrifice." Ph.D. diss., University of Chicago.

1994a   "Sacred Commoners: The Motion of Cosmic Powers in Mexica Rulership." In *History of Religions Journal* 34, no. 1 (August): 39–69.

1994b   "Asteroids and Reeds: Mexica Challenges to Issues of Ethical Diversity." Unpublished manuscript (1994).

1994c   "His Breath and Word, His Face and Teeth: Verbal Images of Rulership in the *Florentine Codex.*" Presented at II Simposio de Códices y Documentos Sobre México, Siglos XII–XVII (June, Taxco, Mexico). Photocopy.

1995a   "Sun and Earth Rulers: What the Eyes Cannot See in Mesoamerica." *History of Religions Journal* 34, no. 4 (May): 351–84.

1995b   "Huitzilopochtli and Quetzalcoatl: Ethical Images of Rulership at Tenochtitlan and Teotihuacan." Presented at the International History of Religions Conference (August, Mexico City). Photocopy.

forthcoming   "Sex, War, and Mexica Rulers: Mexica Royal Images of Boundary Breaking and Making." In *Homenaje a la Dra. Doris Heyden,* edited by Maria J. Rodriguez-Shadow. Instituto Nacional de Antropolía e Historia. Mexico City.

Read, Kay, and Jane Rosenthal.
1986   "Xochiquetzal and the Virgin of Ocotlan." Paper presented at the fifth annual meeting of the American Anthropology Association, Philadelphia, November. Revised 1988. Photocopy.

Recinos, Adrián, translator.
1950   *Popol Vuh: The Sacred Book of the Ancient Quiché Maya.* English version prepared by Delia Goetz and Sylvanus Morley. Norman: University of Oklahoma Press.

"Relación de Tequizistlan y su partido."
1986   In vol. 7 of *Relaciones geográficas del siglo XVI: México,* edited by René Acuña. 10 vols. Mexico City: Universidad Nacional Autónoma de México, 213–54.

Ricard, Robert.
1966   *The Spiritual Conquest of Mexico.* Translated by Lesley Byrd Simpson. Berkeley: University of California Press.

Ricoeur, Paul.
1960   "The Symbol . . . Food for Thought." *Philosophy Today* 4 (Fall): 196–207.
1976   *Interpretation Theory: Discourse and the Surplus of Meaning.* Fort Worth: Texas Christian University Press.
1985   "The History of Religions and the Phenomenology of Time Consciousness." In *The History of Religions: Retrospect and Prospect,* edited by Joseph M. Kitagawa. New York: Macmillan, 13–30.

Robertson, Donald.
1959   *Mexican Manuscript Painting of the Early Colonial Period: The Metropolitan Schools.* New Haven: Yale University Press.

Robertson Smith, William.
1886   "Sacrifice." *Encyclopaedia Britannica,* 9th ed. Boston.

Sáenz, César A.
1976   *El fuego nuevo.* Serie Historia 18. Mexico City: Instituto Nacional de Antropología e Historia.

Sahagún, Fray Bernardino de.
1953–82   *The Florentine Codex: A General History of the Things of New Spain.* Translated by Arthur J. O. Anderson and Charles E. Dibble. Monographs of the School of American Research, no. 14. 12 bks., 13 pts. Santa Fe, N.M.: School of American Research; and Salt Lake City: University of Utah.

1978   "MS Palatino de Madrid, ff. 161 vt. ss." In *Llave del Náhuatl*, edited and translated by Angel María Garibay K. 4th ed. Mexico City: Editorial Porrúa, 131–35.
1979   *Códice Florentino*. El manuscrito 218–220 de la colección Palatina de la Biblioteca Medicea Laurenziana. Facsimile ed. no. 4. 3 vols. Mexico City: Archivo General de la Nación.
1982   *Historia general de las coses de Nueva España*. With annotations and appendices by Angel María Garibay K. 5th ed. Mexico City: Editorial Porrúa.

Sahlins, Marshall.
1985   *Islands of History*. Chicago: University of Chicago Press.

Sanday, Peggy Reeves.
1986   *Divine Hunger: Cannibalism as a Cultural System*. Cambridge: Cambridge University Press.

Santamaria, Francisco J.
1983   *Diccionario de mejicanismos*. 4th ed. Mexico City: Editorial Porrúa.

Satterthwaite, Linton.
1965   "Calendrics of the Lowland Maya." In vol. 3, *Handbook of Middle American Indians*, edited by Robert Wauchope. 15 vols. Austin: University of Texas Press, 603–31.

Schaffer, Lynda Norene.
1992   *Native Americans before 1492: The Moundbuilding Centers of the Eastern Woodlands*. New York: M. E. Sharpe.

Schele, Linda, and David Freidel.
1990   *A Forest of Kings: The Untold Story of the Ancient Maya*. New York: William Morrow.

Sexson, Lynda.
1992   *Ordinarily Sacred*. First published 1982. Charlottesville: University of Virginia Press.

Shweder, Richard A., and Edmund J. Bourne.
1984   "Does the Concept of the Person Vary Cross-Culturally?" In *Culture Theory: Essays on Mind, Self, and Emotion*, edited by Richard A. Shweder and Robert A. LeVine. Cambridge: Cambridge University Press, 190–91.

Silverberg, Robert.
1968   *Mound Builders of Ancient America: The Archaeology of a Myth*. Athens, Ohio: Ohio University Press.

Siméon, Rémi.
1981   *Diccionario de la lengua Náhuatl o Mexicana*. 2d ed. Mexico City: Siglo Veintiuno Editores, 1981.

Smith, Brian K.
1985   "Sacrifice and Being: Prajapati's Cosmic Emission." *Numen* 32, no. 1 (Summer): 79–96.

Smith, Jonathan Z.
1978   *Map Is Not a Territory: Studies in the History of Religions.* Leiden: E. J. Brill.
1982   *Imagining Religion: From Babylon to Jonestown.* Chicago: University of Chicago Press.

Sullivan, E. Lawrence.
1988   *Icanchu's Drum: An Orientation to Meaning in South American Religions.* New York: Macmillan.

Sullivan, Thelma D.
1983   *Compendio de la gramática Náhuatl.* Mexico City: Universidad Nacional Autónoma de México, 1983.
1988   *Compendium of Nahuatl Grammar.* Edited by Wick Miller and Karen Dakin. Translated by Thelma D. Sullivan and Neville Stiles. Salt Lake City: University of Utah Press, 1988. Originally published as *Compendio de la gramática Náhuatl.* Mexico City: Universidad Nacional Autónoma de México.

Taggert, James M.
1983   *Nahuat Myth and Social Structure.* Austin: University of Texas Press.

Tambiah, Stanley.
1979   *A Performance Approach to Ritual.* Proceedings of the British Academy, London. Vol. 65. Oxford: Oxford University Press.

Tax, Sol, editor and translator.
forthcoming   *The World of the Panajachel: As Told by Its Maya People in 1936 and 1937.* Chicago: Native American Educational Services.

Tedlock, Barbara.
1982   *Time and the Highland Maya.* Albuquerque: University of New Mexico Press.

Tedlock, Dennis.
1985   *Popul Vuh: The Definitive Edition of the Mayan Book of the Dawn of Life and the Glories of Gods and Kings.* New York: Simon and Schuster, Touchstone.

Tonalamatl de Aubin.
1981   With commentary by Carmen Aguilera. With diagrams by Eduard Seler. Facsimile ed. Tlaxcala, Mexico: Gobierno del Estado de Tlaxcala.

Torquemada, Fray Juan de.
1975–83   *Monarquía indiana: De los veinte y un libros rituales y monarquía indiana, con el origen y guerras de los indios occidentales, de sus pobla-*

zones, descubrimiento, conquista, conversión y otras cosas maravillosas de la mesma tierra. 7 vols. Mexico City: Universidad Nacional Autónoma de México.

Townsend, Richard F.
1979   *State and Cosmos in the Art of Tenochtitlan.* Washington, D.C.: Dumbarton Oaks Research Library and Collection.
1987   "Coronation at Tenoctitlan." In *The Aztec Templo Mayor,* edited by Elizabeth Hill Boone. Washington, D.C.: Dumbarton Oaks Research Library and Collection, 371–409.
1992   *The Aztecs.* London: Thames and Hudson.

Tracy, David.
1981   *The Analogical Imagination: Christian Theology and the Culture of Pluralism.* New York: Crossroads.

Turner, Victor.
1969   *The Ritual Process: Structure and Antistructure.* Ithaca: Cornell University Press.

Tylor, Edward Burnett.
1970   *Religion in Primitive Culture.* With an introduction by Paul Radin. Originally published as chapters 11–14 of *Primitive Culture,* London: John Murray, 1871, 1874. New York: Harper and Row, 1958; Gloucester, Mass: Peter Smith.

Umberger, Emily.
1981   "Aztec Sculptures, Hieroglyphics, and History." Ph.D. diss., Columbia University.
1987a   "Antiques, Revivals, and References to the Past in Aztec Art." *RES* no.13 (Spring): 63–105.

Vaillent, George C.
1944   *Aztecs of Mexico: Origin, Rise, and Fall of the Aztec Nation.* Harmondsworth: Penguin Books; reprint, Garden City, N.Y.: Doubleday and Co., 1966.

Valeri, Valerio.
1985   *Kingship and Sacrifice: Ritual and Society in Ancient Hawaii.* Translated by Paula Wissing. Chicago: University of Chicago Press.

van der Leeuw, Gerardus.
1967   *Religion in Essence and Manifestation.* Originally published as *Phänomenologie de Religion.* Tübingen, 1933. Translated by J. E. Turner. 2 vols. Gloucester, Mass: Peter Smith.

van der Loo, Peter.
1981   "Rituales con manojos contados en el grupo Borgia y entre los Tlapanecos de hoy dia." In *Los indígenas de México en la época prehispánica*

y en la actualidad, edited by Janren and Leyenaar. Leiden: E. J. Brill, 232–43.

1987   *Códices, costumbres, continuidad: Un estudio de la religión Mesoamerica.* Indiaanse Studies 2. Leiden: Archeologisch Centrum R.U.

van Gennep, Arnold.
1909   *The Rites of Passage.* Translated by Monika B. Vizedom and Gabrielle L. Caffee. London: Routledge and Kegan Paul.

van Zantwijk, Rudolf.
1977   *The Aztec Arrangement: The Social History of Pre-Spanish Mexico.* Norman: University of Oklahoma Press.

Vivó Escoto, Jorge A.
1964   "Weather and Climate of Mexico and Central America." In vol. 1 of *Handbook of Middle American Indians,* edited by Robert Wauchope. 15 vols. Austin: University of Texas Press, 187–215.

Walzer, Michael.
1983   *Spheres of Justice: A Defense of Pluralism and Equality.* New York: Basic Books.

Wauchope, Robert, editor.
1964–76   *Handbook of Middle American Indians.* 15 vols. Austin: University of Texas Press.

Wolf, Eric R.
1959   *Sons of the Shaking Earth.* Chicago: University of Chicago Press.
1982   *Europe and the People without History.* Berkeley and Los Angeles: University of California Press.

INDEX

Agriculture, 6, 7, 100, 224, 239n.9. *See also* Corn

Alva Ixtlilxochitl, Fernando de, 13

Anales tradition, 105–106, 226, 263–64nn. 30–31

Analogy and analogical thinking: in contemporary scholarship, 29–30; sacred and profane dichotomy and, 32–35, 37–39. *See also* Metaphor and metaphorical thinking

Ancestors: and Huitzilopochtli, 9; and "First Couple," 70–71; and transformation, 77; bones of, 111–12; and children, 115, 180; and powers of rulers, 148–49, 160; and marriage, 156; and Chichimeca, 184–85; and gender, 257n.121. *See also* Aztlan

Anderson, Arthur, 241n.33

Animistic entities: concepts of *teyolia, tonalli,* and *ihiyotl,* 111–12, 265n.5; food and powers of, 159–61; and reciprocity, 169; and death, 264n.2

Astronomy: and Pleiades, 63, 103, 124; and equinoxes, 63, 251n.66; and horizon-line alignments, 63–64, 252n.70; and calendar, 101, 211, 224, 234, 261–62n.17, 277n.12; and solstices, 143, 211, 216; and dark objects, 234. *See also* Moon; Sun; Venus

Aveni, Anthony, 63, 276n.3, 279n.20

Aztec: use of name, xxiii, 4, 203, 237n.1, 238n.4

Aztlan, 78–83, 88, 111, 199

Bierhorst, John, 252n.72, 265n.7

Binding-of-the-Years. *See* New Fire Ceremony

Biological and historical models of transformation, 35–37, 65–67, 74, 82

Birdwhistell, Ray, 178, 274n.19, 274–75n.23

Birth: of Huitzilopochtli, 76; and transformation, 84, 115; death of women in and underworld, 111, 133, 257n.121; and naming ceremony, 179; and sacrifice, 187. *See also* Children; Fifth Sun

Bloodletting: and New Fire ceremony, 126, 128–29

Bones: and creation myth, 63, 71–73, 85, 111; of ancestors, 111–12

Boone, Elizabeth, 106, 263–64n.31

Bourne, Edmund, 186

Broda, Johanna, 103–104, 106, 143, 223–24, 252n.68, 278n.17, 279n.19, 280n.26

Cahokia (Illinois), xviii, 238n.5

Calendar, Mexica: and spiral, xviii; and cosmology, 9–11, 260n.9; and solar years, 25–27, 92, 278–79n.18; system of calculations, 94; and shaping of time, 95; and spinning of time, 99–108; patterns and characteristics of, 211–14; and *Codex Fejérvary-Mayer,* 214–16; and *Codex Borbonicus,* 216–27; and "The Myth of the Four Suns," 233–34, 272–73n.6. *See also* Days; *Tonalpohualli* (divinatory calendar); *Xiuhmolpilli*

Calpulli (social group), 8, 9, 148, 200

Camaxtli (god of hunting), 144

Carrasco, Davíd, 34, 161, 165, 181, 240n.21, 243n.45, 251n.63, 261n.15, 268n.14

Carrasco, Pedro, 279n.20

Caso, Alfonso, 278n.18

Chalchiuhtlicue (goddess), 141

Chalchiuitl (greenstone), 62–63, 200

Change. *See* Transformation

Chaos, 163–64, 198

Chichimeca hunter-gatherers, 184–85, 200

Chicomoztoc (Place of Seven Caves), 6, 76, 200

Children and babies: and corn, 111, 177, 264–65nn.3–4; naming rituals, 114–16, 118, 133, 179–80, 187, 266n.11; and New Fire ceremony, 125, 126; and hunting, 133–34; and excretion, 135; sacrifice of, 143, 177–78, 180, 183, 187, 275n.25

Chinampa system (irrigation), 7, 200, 239n.9

Cihuacoatl (Snake woman), 85, 87, 200

Cinteotl (day god), 115

Clendinnen, Inga, 243n.47, 276n.29

Coatlicue (goddess), 76, 200–201, 256n.108, 272n.4

Codex Aubin, 21, 22, 26, 93, 216, 219, 224, 227, 277n.7

Codex Borbonicus, 21, 102, 213, 216–27, 231, 241n.26, 255n.99, 280n.22

Codex Chimalpopoca, 13, 252n.72, 253n.79, 270n.31, 273n.11

Codex Fejérvary-Mayer, 212, 213, 214–16, 219, 224, 227, 229, 269n.24, 27, 270n. 32, 276nn.2–3, 277n.4, 6, 280n.25, 281n.30

Codex Mendoza, 21–22, 23, 26, 187

Codex Telleriano Remensis, 10, 14

Codex Vaticano Latino, 14, 138, 161, 269n.26

Commoners. *See* Macehualtin

Community: and death, 181–83; and reciprocity of rulership, 195–96. *See also* Social organization

Completion: and destruction, 84; as eternal,

86–87; and re-presentation, 88; and sacrifice, 120, 167, 172, 194–98; and cosmic house, 137; and process of transformation, 163, 164, 234, 263n.28; success and failure, 174
Conrad, Geoffrey, 275–76n.28
Conversation: as approach to interpretation, 3, 16–29
Cooking: and cosmic house, 137–38. *See also* Eating
Copil (nephew of Huitzilopochtli), 76–78, 201
Corn: and diet of Mexica-Tenochca, 7, 255n.105; and Nanhuatzin, 67, 85, 172, 248n.36; and binding of people to earth, 110; and hunting metaphors, 130, 133–34; and seasons, 144; and sacrifice, 164, 176; and children, 177, 264–65nn.3–4; development of, 237n.3; and sun, 248n. 36; and divination, 255n.99
Cosmic house, 137–44, 157
Cosmic meal, 144–55
Cosmology: topography of, 8–9, 138–39, 270n.28; and calendar, 9–11, 260n.9; and sacred versus profane, 35; spatio-temporal reality and inversions, 88; and cardinal directions, 92, 250–51n.58, 277nn.4–5,8; and calendar, 100–101; and cosmic house, 137–44; and transformation, 198
Coyolxauhqui (sister of Huitzilopochtli), 76, 201, 257n.121
Creativity: and metaphor of sacrifice, 41; and transformation, 59–60, 60–61; and concept of *poliui*, 86; and history, 120. *See also* Destruction
Creator couple (Tonacateuctli and Tonacacihuatl), 147
Culhuacan (Place of the Grandparents), 96, 260n.12

Daly, Mary, 242–43n.43
Days: names of, 92; cycles of, 99, 208; and food as metaphor, 253n.77. *See also* Nemontemi
Dead. *See* Death; Mictlan (land of dead)
Death: and transformative change, 36–37, 39, 59; and sacrifice, 77, 178; in "Return to Aztlan," 82; and completion, 87; timing of destruction, disappearance, and, 110–14; and eating, 130–37; and divination, 151; and morality of destruction, 165–68, 174–75; and moral community, 181–83; and animistic entities, 264n.2
Demerest, Arthur, 275–76n.28
Destruction: and transformative change, 36–37, 59–60, 74–75, 84–88; in "Four Suns," 69–70; in "Return to Aztlan," 82; of gods, 83; of Fifth Sun, 83–84; timing of death, disappearance, and, 110–14; and *poliui*,

119; death and morality of, 165–68, 174–75; and reciprocity, 198
Dibble, Charles, 241n.33
Diet: of Mexica-Tenochca, 7, 239n.11, 255n. 105, 268n.12. *See also* Corn; Eating
Directions. *See* Cosmology
Disappearance: timing of destruction, death, and, 110–14; and cosmic house, 137; and transformation, 149; and sacrifice, 180
Divination: and powers of cosmos, 150–51; and corn, 255n.99
Divinatory Calendar. *See* Tonalpohualli
Drought: in Mexican Highlands in mid-1400s, 132, 177, 180, 275n.28
Durán, Fray Diego, 67, 76, 78, 185, 238–39n. 4, 257n.119, 258n.127, 266n.3, 267n.4, 6
Durkheim, Emile, 33, 35

Eagle, 58, 86, 87, 166, 172, 173, 201
Earth Monster, 129, 140, 141, 142, 270n.29
Earth's surface. *See* Tlalticpac
Eating: cosmos and sacrificial rituals, xix, 29, 124, 191; and transformative change, 36, 59, 73, 162; and first couple, 71; and gods, 74, 272n.4; and destruction, 85; and death, 111, 130–37, 181–83; and powers of animistic entitites, 159–61. *See also* Cooking; Diet
Edmonson, Munro S., 211, 261n.16, 262nn. 19–20, 276n.1, 277n.10, 12, 278nn.17–18, 280nn.23,26
Ehecatl (wind being), 15, 171, 250nn.54,57
Eliade, Mircea, 33–34, 40, 103, 116, 119, 120, 161, 165, 173, 243n.45, 261n.15
Equinoxes, 63, 251n.66
Eschatology: death and process of continuing, 113, 119; use of term, 252n.71
Eternity: and historical change, 161–65, 193, 272n.6. *See also* Transformation
Ethics: and good versus evil, 39, 168; of human sacrifice, 242n.42. *See also* Values
Excretion and excrement: and hunting, 132; and sacrificial feeding exchange, 135–36; and *tlacotli*, 153; earth and underworld, 172

Face (*Ixtli*), 86, 95, 109, 110, 129–30, 147, 202, 264n.2
Feeding. *See* Eating
Fertility: transformative change and agricultural, 74, 224; and destruction, 85; and New Fire ceremony, 126; and sacrificial feeding exchange, 135. *See also* Sexuality
Fifth Sun or Age: birth of, 26, 48–60, 74–75; and New Fire ceremonies, 47; and transformation, 65; destruction of, 83–84, 201; count of, 233. *See also* Four-Movement
Fifty-two year round. *See* Xiuhmolpilli

Fire: and first couple, 71; Xiuhtecutli and, 141; and logic of sacrifice, 157–69. *See also* New Fire ceremony

Fire drill, xix, 26, 27, 28, 47, 123, 156, 226, 238n.6, 241n.32

First couple, 67, 70–71, 86, 87, 113, 148, 153, 205

"Fleeting Moment, The," 113–14

Florentine codex, 13, 14–15, 48, 75, 76, 139, 143, 240n.20, 241n.33, 263n.26, 266n.14, 269n.28

Flowery Wars, 125, 132–33, 177–78, 180, 183, 201, 274n.20

Fortunes. *See* Divination

Four-Movement (4–Ollin), 8, 11, 37, 65, 85, 201. *See also* Fifth Sun

Four Suns, 67–70, 202, 233–34

Fourth Age, 94–95

Four Year-Bearers, 201–202

Frazer, James George, 258n.123

Freidel, David, 256n.116

Gamio, Manuel, 240n.17

Gender: of earth monster, 141; and ancestors, 257n.121; of earth and sky deities, 270n.31

Genetics: as biological analogy, 35–36, 41, 85–86; and powers of ancestors, 157

Gillespie, Susan, 261n.15

Graulich, Michel, 268n.10, 280n.26

Hearts: and New Fire ceremony, 126; eating and hunting, 133; of *tlacotli,* 153

Heesterman, J. C., 274n.21

Hegemony: sacrifice and rise of Mexica-Tenochca, 181, 183

Hierophanies: concept of continuing, 119, 170

Historia de las Indias de Nueva España e islas de la tierra firme, 13

History: and calendrical system, 11; sixteenth-century Spanish works as references on pre-Conquest, 13; and biological models of transformation, 35–37, 82; and mytho-ritual use of Teotihuacan, 61–63; and space-time, 87; chronological concept of, 105; shaping of, 110; and emergence from Aztlan, 111; transformative moments in, 116–18; and creativity, 120; and transformative role of sacrifices, 161–65, 170–74; and transformative repetitions, 179–81; as sacred, 198. *See also* Eternity

Huitzilopochtli (patron deity of Mexica-Tenochca), 9, 11, 26, 75–76, 83, 87, 88, 133, 143, 148, 202, 256n.112, 257n.121, 272n.4

Hunn, E., 239n.10

Hunting: eating and death as transformative

change, 130, 132; and seasons, 144; sacrifice and ritualized, 180; and Mexica diet, 268n.12

Hyidfeldt, Arild, 145

Iconography: and conversational approach to interpretation, 24–27

Iconology: and conversational approach to interpretation, 27–29; use of term, 240–41n.39

Ihiyotl (animistic entity), 111–12, 115, 159, 202

Ilhuicatl (Sky-Water), 71, 100, 120, 136, 138, 139, 141, 202

Indigenous peoples, contemporary: groups with pre-Conquest ties, 15–16; and calendrical systems, 99–108; stories of, 134; images of sky, earth, and underworld, 142, 143. *See also* Panajachel Maya; Quiché Maya

Inversions: rhythmic pairings of, 165; and dualistic oppositions, 167; eagle and jaguar, 173; success and failure, 173–74. *See also* Cosmology; Death; Eating; Transformation

Irrigation system, 7, 200, 239n.9

Ixtli. See Face

Jaguar, 58, 86, 87, 156, 172, 173, 201

Johnson, Mark, 40

Karttunen, Frances, 262n.20

Kidwell, Clara Sue, 146, 259n.133

Kirchhoff, Paul, xvii, 237n.3

Klor de Alva, Jorge, 145

Krickeberg, Walter, 145

Languages: diversity and range of Native American, 4. *See also* Nahuatl

Leach, Edmund, 268n.9

"Legend of the Sun," 13, 48–60, 66–67, 135

León-Portilla, Miguel, 241n.31

Logic: of destructive transformation, 84–88; of sacrifice, 157–69

Lok, Rossana, 15

López Austin, Alfredo, 110, 111, 119, 120, 135, 148–49, 158, 244n.2, 264n.2, 266n.13, 270n.31, 271n.37, 275n.27

Macehualtin (commoners), 83, 110, 150, 159, 185, 203

Magicians. *See* Shamans

Mahceua (merit), 114–16, 117–18, 151, 185, 192, 203, 246–47n.19, 264n.1

Malinalxochitl (sister of Huitzilopochtli), 203

Mana (Mani), 145, 203, 246n.11, 271n.40

Maya, 5, 99, 203, 224, 239n.9, 253n.77, 268n.12, 273nn.6,8, 274n.20, 276n.1,

277n.12, 279n.33. *See also* Panajachel Maya; Quiché Maya
Mayahuel (goddess of pulque), 220–21, 278n.15
Merit. *See Mahceua*
Mesoamerica: boundaries of, xvii–xviii, 17, 237n.3, 238n.3
Metaphor and metaphorical thinking: in contemporary scholarship, 29; and process of transformation, 84–85, 253n.77, 254n.94; and Nahuatl language, 183, 249nn.41,45–47, 250nn.49–50, 251n.59. *See also* Analogy and analogical thinking
Mexican Highlands: and history of Mexica-Tenochca, 6; environment and geography of, 6–7, 203
Mexica-Tenochca: use of name, xvii, xxiii, 4, 203, 238–39n.4; history of, 5–6
Mexica Zócalo, 6
Micteca (people of the Land of the Dead), 9, 203
Mictlan (land of the dead), 8–9, 16, 63, 71, 101, 111, 112, 120, 136, 139, 142, 149, 203
Mictlancihuatl (Lady of death), 9, 71, 186, 203, 225, 226
Mictlantecuhtli (Lord of death), 9, 61, 71, 73, 136, 203, 221, 223
Miles, Margaret, 17
Mississippian cultures: Mesoamerican influence on, xviii, 237–38n.5
Molina, Fray Alonso de, 144, 271n.41
Moon, 60, 76, 101, 223. *See also* Tecuiçiztecatl
Motecuhzuma the Elder (Motecuhzuma I), 5, 27, 38, 67, 149, 160, 204
Motecuhzuma II, 61
Myth: and New Fire ceremony, 170–74
"Myth of the Four Suns, The," 233–34, 272–73n.6

Nagao, Deborah, 241n.34
Nahua: use of name, 4, 204; oratory and narrative skills, 48
Nahualli (alter ego), 204, 254n.93
Nahuatl language: contemporary use of, 4, 204; and "Legend of the Suns," 13; parallelism in, 179, 182; and translation, 244–45nn.2–8, 265n.7, 270n.29; and *mahceua*, 246–47n.19
Naming: and transformative process, 109–10, 115; children and rituals of, 118, 187, 266n.11
Nanahuatzin or Nanahuatl, 58, 59, 60, 66, 74, 85, 87, 134, 171, 172, 204, 248n.35
Native Americans: diversity and range of languages, 4; sacrifice and stereotypes of, 237n.2; vision questing of shamans,

256n.116. *See also* Cahokia; Indigenous peoples; Spiro
Nature: and deformative transformation, 85; god, man, and, 159
Nemontemi (days), 106–107, 204, 223, 234, 279n.18, 280n.26
Nene. *See* First couple
New Fire Ceremony or Binding-of-the-Years: and temporal transformation, xviii, 28, 45; and sacrificial transformation, xix, 103, 124–27, 164, 170–75; and calendar, 11, 26, 27, 89, 101, 102, 105, 223, 231; and fire drill, 47, 123; and nowness, 118; and inversions, 166, 281n.30; description of, 199
Nezahualcoyotl (poet-ruler), 113, 162, 204, 265n.7, 272n.45
Night: Lords of, 101, 106, 107, 123, 153, 202, 219, 223, 224, 225, 226, 234, 279–80n.22, 280n.30; mythical female creatures of, 125; *tlahtlacotin* and forces of, 172. *See also Tlahtlacolli*
Nobles (*Pipiltin*), 148–49, 159, 185, 205

Olmec, 5, 61, 204, 211, 251n.62
Ometeule (Lord of Twoness), 14
"Once Again It Will Be," 104
Oral tradition: and sixteenth-century Mexica story-telling, 47; and Nahua oratory and narrative skills, 48; in contemporary Mesoamerica, 244n.1
Ortiz de Montellano, Bernard, 7, 239n.11
Otto, Rudolf, 33, 161
Oxomoco, 205, 258n.99

Panajachel Maya, 138, 142
Panofsky, Erwin, 241–42n.39
Panquetzaliztli (month), 103, 124, 223, 279n.20
Performance: and Nahuatl oral tradition, 48, 245nn.3–4
Plato and Platonic visions, 33, 138, 161
Pleiades (constellation), 63, 103, 124
Poliui: and progressive acts of destructive creation, 86, 88, 110, 119, 205, 253n.78
Ponce de León, Pedro, 240n.18
Popol Vuh, 244n.1, 252n.73, 253n.77, 255n.106, 260n.9, 281n.31
Power: of the sacred, 33, 38, 254–55n.97; and sacrifice, 39–43, 154, 187–88, 191; and concept of *teotl*, 145–46, 271n.41; of celestial beings, 146, 147; and divination, 150–51; *mahceua* and systematic interchange of, 151; and ancestors, 157; of rulers, 159, 160; of the mundane, 175–88; contemporary rethinking of, 194–95; and contemporary ethical issues, 196–98; and Teotihuacan, 246n.11

Primeros Memoriales, 136
Primordium. *See* Eliade, Mircea
Profane. *See* Sacred and profane

Quetzalcoatl: in *Florentine Codex,* 15, 139; and birth of the Fifth Sun, 58; and creation of humans, 63, 71–73, 85, 111, 134, 136, 151; and Cihuacoatl, 85, 87; and New Fire ceremony, 126; and transformation, 147–48; guises of, 205
Quiché Maya, 143, 234, 244n.1, 252n.73, 255n.106, 258n.123, 277n.5

1–Rabbit (year), 92, 199, 225, 226, 229, 230, 231, 278n.17
Read, Edward C., 279n.21
Reciprocality: and sacrificial rituals, 154; limitations of, 169, 175; communal ties and sacrificial duties, 183–87; and sacrificially ethical process, 197–98; and socio-cosmic relations, 273–74n.15
2–Reed (year), 11, 199, 231, 232, 278n.17
Re-presentation: and expressive imagery, 20; and completion, 88; and solar years, 92; and shape of time, 95, 96, 98, 190–94; and transformation, 116, 261n.15; and contemporary stories, 134; and cosmic house, 137; and ancestors, 157; and sacrifice, 192–94
Ricoeur, Paul, 34, 40, 96, 98, 99, 116, 238n.2, 261n.15
Ríos, Pedro de los, 14
Rituals: calendar system and state, 101, 223; and myth, 170–74; cosmological and social structures and authority of, 177; of sacrificial transformation, 187–88. *See also* New Fire ceremony; Sacrifice
Rope. *See* Spinning; Spirals and spiraling
Rosenthal, Jane, 244n.2
Rulers and rulership: limits to powers of, 38; ancestors and powers of, 148–49, 159, 254n.86; and reciprocity, 169, 185; and community, 195–96; and agricultural fertility, 224; and gender, 257n.121; and time, 260n.8

Sacred and profane: contemporary scholarship on, 32–35, 37–39, 243n.47, 274n.18; sacrifice and power of the ordinary, 39–43, 176–78; and logic of sacrifice, 157–61, 170; and history as eternal, 193
Sacrifice: cosmos and act of feeding, xix, 120, 144–55; and transformation, 28–29, 129–55, 161–65, 170–74, 187–88, 190–92; human, 31–32, 143, 177–78, 183, 237n.2, 242n.42, 275n.25, 276n.29; and power of the ordinary, 39–43, 176–78; of Copil, 76–78; and New Fire ceremony, 103; re-

alities of, 123–29; theorizing about, 127–29; and reciprocality, 154, 183–87; definition of from religious perspective, 154–55; logic of, 157–69; re-presentations of, 192–94; and stereotypes of Native Americans, 237n.2. *See also* Children
Sahagún, Fray Bernardino, 14–15, 48, 75, 92, 96, 97, 104, 124–25, 136, 185, 226, 240n. 20, 241n.33, 251n.65, 267n.6, 278n.14, 280n.26
Schele, Linda, 256n.116
Seasons: division of into dry and wet, 143–44
Seler, Eduard, 269n.19
Seven Caves, Place of. *See* Chicomoztoc
Sexson, Lynda, 40, 243n.46, 274n.18
Sexuality: and transformative change, 36–37, 39, 74, 135, 273n.13; and Nanahuatzin, 85; and bond of people with earth, 110. *See also* Venereal disease
Shamans: and divination, 150; and *nahualli,* 254n.93; dreaming and vision questing, 256n.116; and priests, 258nn.123,129
Shweder, Richard, 186
Sky-Water. *See* Ilhuicatl
Smith, Jonathan Z., 30–31, 274n.21
Social organization: concrete-relational style of, 186; and reciprocity, 273–74n.15. *See also Calpulli;* Community; Rulers and rulership
Solstices, 143, 211, 216
Souls. *See* Animistic Entities
Space. *See* Time and space
Spanish (sixteenth-century), 3, 12–15, 17, 24, 29, 31, 127, 138, 211, 241n.27, 246n.19
Spinning: and shape of time, 98–99; and calendrical system, 99–108; and sacrificial completions, 194–98
Spirals and spiraling: and nature of time, xviii, 95–99, 116–17, 260–61n.14; and fifty-two-year cycle, 11; and calendrical system, 213
Spiro (Oklahoma), xviii, 238n.5
Sullivan, Lawrence, 243n.44
Sun (Tonatiuh): and fifty-two year cycle, 37, 208; Pyramid of, 60, 61; and calendar, 101; death in war and Sky of, 111; eternity and transformation of, 162, 273n.11; and Venus, 234
Sun Stone, 130, 131, 259n.135

Taggert, James, 134
Tambiah, Stanley, 274n.17
Tamoanchan (place of the western tree), 61, 62, 74, 85, 205, 254n.97, 273n.11
Tata. *See* First couple
Tecuiçiztecatl (moon), 58, 60, 66, 85, 87, 153, 163, 171, 172, 205

Tecuitlatl (*Spirulina geitlerii*), 7, 239n.11
Tedlock, Barbara, 258n.123
Tedlock, Dennis, 244n.1, 260n.9
Templo Mayor (Great Temple), 2, 5, 6, 9, 10, 11–12, 13, 14, 28, 29, 61, 181, 205–206, 252n.68
Tenochtitlan, 4, 5–12, 47, 60, 76, 82, 88, 190–91, 206, 251n.62, 256n.114, 279n.20
Teoatl (godly water), 138
Teotihuacan (urban center), 5, 6, 47, 60–65, 85, 86, 206, 246n.11
Teotl (power or god), 145–46, 206, 271n.41
Teoyome (cosmic powers), 150, 160, 190, 206
Texcoco, Lake, 5, 6, 206, 257n.120
Teyolia: death and animistic entities, 111, 112, 115, 159, 206; and hunting, 133
Tezcatlipoca (god), 26–27, 136, 139, 147–48, 156, 207, 254n.85
Time: spiral of, xviii, 95–99, 116–17, 260–61n.14; and transformative change, 39; limits of time spans, 83, 114–16; and inevitability of change, 84; naming of, 89–95; shaping of, 95–99, 261n.15; and spinning, 99–108; and nowness, 108, 116; destruction, death, and disappearance, 110–14; double nature of, 119–20. *See also* Calendar; Time and space
Time and space: unity of, 11–12, 28, 263n.29; and transformative process, 47, 63–64; and Birth of the Fifth Sun, 59, 66; and spatio-temporal equations, 60, 84, 94; and horizon-line astronomy, 63–64; shaping of, 86; and completion, 87, 88, 163; and calendrical calculations, 94; doubling back and piling up of, 190–94. *See also* Time
Tlacaellel (Mexica statesman), 132–33, 149, 181, 207
Tlacaxipehauliztli (festival month), 63, 279n. 20
Tlahtlacolli (Messed up ones), 107, 119, 123, 124, 152, 166, 168, 172, 175, 207, 234, 267n.5, 273n.13
Tlaloc (god of rain), 9, 11, 12, 61, 87, 111, 126, 134, 162, 207, 279n.22
Tlaloques (rain deities), 139, 141, 177–78
Tlalteuctli (Earth Lord), 71
Tlalticpac (earth's surface), 63, 101, 107, 120, 132, 136, 137, 139, 141, 207
Tlatelolco (town), 7–8, 11
Tlazolteotl (goddess of filth), 152, 221
Toltecs, 62, 88, 207
Tonacatecuhtli (Lord of Produce), 61, 74, 207–208
Tonalço (dry season), 143, 208
Tonalli (animistic entity), 111–12, 114–15, 159, 208, 259n.4

Tonalpohualli (divinatory calendar), 106, 115, 117, 120, 150–51, 208, 214, 216, 219–23, 224–33, 261–62n.17, 262n.21, 277n. 12, 278n.15, 279n.22, 281n.30
Tonatiuh. *See* Sun
Townsend, Richard, 146
Tracy, David, 238n.2
Transformation: temporal and calendrical, xviii, 28, 45; and sacrifice, xix, 28–29, 129–55, 161–65, 187–88; and eternal change, 35; biological and historical models of, 35–37, 65–67, 74, 82; serial, 58, 70; destruction and creation, 58–60, 69–70, 84–88; and eating, 73; and chronological concept of history, 105, 106, 108; process of deformative, 109; moments of in history, 116–18; and disappearance, 149; and New Fire ritual, 170–75; history and repetitions of, 179–81; and cosmic order, 198
Trecenas (weeks), 115, 219–23, 227, 229, 231, 278n.15, 280n.22
Tula (urban center), 62, 63, 86, 88, 156, 207, 251n.63
Tzitzimime (creatures of night), 125

Uixachtlan (hill), 103, 125, 147
Underworld. *See* Mictlan

Values: biological models and interdependent ecology of, 182–83. *See also* Ethics
Van der Leeuw, Gerardus, 33
Van der Loo, Peter, 277n.6
Van Zantwijk, Rudolf, 279n.20
Venereal disease, 59, 74, 247n.25, 266n.12
Venus (planet), 101, 234, 277n.12, 280n.27–28

Walzer, Michael, 196–97
Wars: and calendars, 100; death in and underworld, 111. *See also* Flowery Wars

Xiuhmolpilli (solar round), 101, 106, 120, 208, 214, 216, 219, 224–33, 262n.20, 277n.12, 280n.23
Xiuhtecutli (Old Fire God), 141, 209
Xochicalco (archaeological site), 26, 63
Xochiquetzal (goddess of weaving and sexuality), 115, 266n.12, 278n.15
Xolotl (god), 58, 85, 132, 171, 209
Xopan (green time-place), 143, 209

Yaonáhuac, 134
Years: calendrical signs and solar, 25–26, 101, 103, 224–27, 262n.24; and cardinal directions, 92; and *nemontemi*, 106–107. *See also* Calendar; 1-Rabbit; 2-Reed

KAY ALMERE READ
is an associate professor of comparative
religions in the Religious Studies Department at
DePaul University. She is the author of a number of
articles on pre-Conquest religious traditions and is
currently working on both a book on Mexica
rulership and ethics and an encyclopedia of
Mesoamerican mythology.

www.ingramcontent.com/pod-product-compliance
Lightning Source LLC
Chambersburg PA
CBHW070449100426
42812CB00004B/1244